IN SEARCH *of a* BEAUTIFUL FREEDOM

also by FARAH JASMINE GRIFFIN

Read Until You Understand:
The Profound Wisdom of Black Life and Literature

"Who Set You Flowin'?":
The African-American Migration Narrative

Beloved Sisters and Loving Friends:
Letters from Rebecca Primus of Royal Oak, Maryland,
and Addie Brown of Hartford, Connecticut, 1854–1868

If You Can't Be Free, Be a Mystery:
In Search of Billie Holiday

Clawing at the Limits of Cool:
Miles Davis, John Coltrane, and the Greatest Jazz Collaboration
Ever (coauthored with Salim Washington)

Harlem Nocturne:
Women Artists and Progressive Politics During World War II

IN SEARCH *of a*
BEAUTIFUL
FREEDOM

NEW AND SELECTED ESSAYS

FARAH JASMINE GRIFFIN

W. W. NORTON & COMPANY
Celebrating a Century of Independent Publishing

For information about permission to reproduce selections from this book, write to
Permissions, W. W. Norton & Company, Inc., 500 Fifth Avenue, New York, NY 10110

For information about special discounts for bulk purchases, please contact
W. W. Norton Special Sales at specialsales@wwnorton.com or 800-233-4830

Manufacturing by Lakeside Book Company
Book design by Marysarah Quinn
Production manager: Lauren Abbate

ISBN 978-0-393-35577-2 (pbk)

W. W. Norton & Company, Inc., 500 Fifth Avenue, New York, N.Y. 10110
www.wwnorton.com

W. W. Norton & Company Ltd., 15 Carlisle Street, London W1D 3BS

1 2 3 4 5 6 7 8 9 0

FOR MY SISTER, MYRA

CONTENTS

INTRODUCTION   XI

I. LEARNING HOW TO LISTEN   1

Ladies Sing Miles   3

When Malindy Sings: *A Meditation on
Black Women's Vocality*   13

Returning to Lady Day: *A Reflection on Two Decades
"In Search of Billie Holiday"*   41

Songs of Experience: *Odetta*   44

Quiet, Stillness, and Longing to Be Free:
*The Ethereal Soul of Syreeta Wright, Minnie Riperton,
and Deniece Williams*   49

Following Geri's Lead   67

II. LOOK WHERE YOUR HANDS ARE NOW   81

Wrestling till Dawn: *On Becoming an Intellectual
in the Age of Toni Morrison*   83

Albert Raboteau: An Appreciation
*(Drawn from Remarks on the Occasion of His Retirement
from Princeton University, April 26, 2013)*   98

Minnie's Sacrifice: Frances Ellen Watkins Harper's Narrative of Citizenship 108

Zora Neale Hurston's Radical Individualism 122

Hunting Communists and Negroes in Ann Petry's *The Narrows* 143

"It Takes Two People to Confirm the Truth": *The Jazz Fiction of Sherley Anne Williams and Toni Cade Bambara* 159

Learning How to Listen: *Ntozake Shange's Work as Aesthetic Primer* 173

Remaking the Everyday: *The Interior Worlds of Kathleen Collins's Fiction and Film* 183

A Place of Freedom: *Gayl Jones's Brazilian Epic* 190

III. TREATING THE SERPENT'S STING 197

Textual Healing: *Claiming Black Women's Bodies, the Erotic, and Resistance in Contemporary Novels of Slavery* 199

"Ironies of the Saint": *Malcolm X, Black Women, and the Price of Protection* 223

Conflict and Chorus: *Reconsidering Toni Cade's The Black Woman: An Anthology* 239

That the Mothers May Soar and the Daughters May Know Their Names: *A Retrospective of Black Feminist Literary Criticism* 258

At Last . . . ?: *Michelle Obama, Beyoncé, Race, and History* 282

IV. ON CRISIS AND POSSIBILITY 299

On the Fourth Anniversary of September 11   301

Human Rights and the Katrina Evacuees   303

DNC Day 2: *Will America Accept First Lady Michelle?*   305

Loving Billie Holiday Doesn't Mean Black Girls
Aren't Suffering: *A Response to Joshua DuBois
and My Brother's Keeper*   308

Teaching African American Literature During
COVID-19   312

Banning Toni Morrison's Books Doesn't Protect Kids.
It Just Sanitizes Racism.   316

Ancient Histories and New Worlds: *Allison Janae
Hamilton*   320

ACKNOWLEDGMENTS   323

NOTES   325

CREDITS   351

INDEX   357

INTRODUCTION

THE SELECTION OF ESSAYS gathered here, spanning over three decades, tells a story of a people, an art, and a writer in search of beauty and freedom. The collection's title alludes to Alice Walker's classic volume, *In Search of Our Mothers' Gardens: Womanist Prose* (1983). That book helped to shape many of us formed as intellectuals and writers in its wake. It also identified a specifically womanist (defined as Black feminist) aesthetic, mapped the direction of Black feminist literary and cultural criticism, and proved the essay to be a powerful form for the articulation of creative, critical, and innovative thought. Walker identified the necessity of recovering Black women artists like Zora Neale Hurston, established the importance of providing a critical vocabulary for the discussion and exploration of Black women's creativity, and offered a model of reading and analyzing literary texts and intellectual thought by figures who were neither women nor Black from the critical perspective that took into consideration the concerns of Black women as critical readers. I first encountered *In Search of Our Mothers' Gardens* as a college student and aspiring writer and it helped me to identify my intellectual calling. The essays in my own collection are part of a body of work that has emerged from that vocation.

The second half of the title alludes to both the historic quest of Black people for political freedom and what literary critic (and my dear friend) the late Cheryl Wall, has identified as an idea—freedom—that has most engaged African American essayists for at least four centuries. In *On Freedom and the Will to Adorn: The Art of the African American Essay* (2018), Wall asserts the essay has allowed Black writers to explore concepts of freedom while the very genre itself has provided writers with artistic freedom. Furthermore, she notes that the essay opens a "window into the writer's mind."

I have always felt most at home in the essay form. Over the years it has provided me the opportunity to explore ideas, posit theoretical interventions, offer observations, and develop my voice. Central to the pleasure I take in both reading and writing essays is my experience of them as an invitation to think along with the writer or reader, an invitation to watch an idea unfold. Whether strictly critical or academic, or more introspective and personal, I find the essay to be the most intimate of nonfiction forms. The most important African American thinkers, from W. E. B. Du Bois, Langston Hughes, and Zora Neale Hurston to Richard Wright, Ralph Ellison, and James Baldwin, to Amiri Baraka, June Jordan, Audre Lorde, and Toni Morrison, have all used the essay to advance a project of critical thought that provides insightful observations about race, class, gender, culture, and politics. The essay is a capacious form that can be mobilized to help inform political action, critical thinking, or personal reflection. In this collection, one finds pieces that seek to accomplish all of these.

While literary essayists are among my earliest influences, I entered the academy during a period when Black feminist literary historians, critics, and theorists produced an exciting body of innovative work. Their discoveries, discussions, and debates took place and shape in a series of now-classic essays. Even as the profession insisted upon the production of academic monographs for career advancement, some of the most important ideas found expression in essays by thinkers as diverse as Barbara Christian, Thadious Davis, Mae Gwendolyn Henderson, Deborah McDowell, Hortense Spillers, Cheryl Wall, Sylvia Wynter, and others. Furthermore, anthologies and essay collections like Toni Cade's *The Black Woman*, Gloria T. Hull and Patricia Bell-Scott's *All the Women Are White, All the Blacks are Men, but Some of Us Are Brave: Black Women's Studies*, Cheryl Wall's *Changing Our Own Words: Essays on Criticism, Theory, and Writing by Black Women*, and Patricia Williams's *Alchemy of Race and Rights: Diary of a Law Professor,* set the foundation and advanced the intellectual project of an entirely new field of study. Because of the centrality of the essay to both the literary tradition and the academic fields to which I hoped to contribute, it has been the form that has provided me the space to explore a range of ideas and kinds of writing, from academic to impressionistic to journalistic.

While I am best known as a critic of literature and music, this collection also demonstrates my interest in other art forms, including visual art, film, and my engagement with contemporary political and social issues. It contains essays that speak to diverse audiences both within and outside the classroom. There are essays that are motivated by my teaching and those that are motivated by a sense of political urgency. As do my full-length books, (perhaps even more so), this volume represents the depth, breadth, and expanse of my thinking and writing.

Because this selection of essays, drawn from almost three times as many pieces, maps the arc of my work and career, it also documents a period of great change and transformation in multiple intersecting fields of inquiry, including but not limited to Black studies, feminist studies, cultural history, the study of Black intellectuals, and jazz studies. It is my hope that these essays will continue to inspire deeper conversation and thinking among scholars, students, and readers who are interested in race, gender, history, and culture. Most importantly, I hope all those who spend time reading them will find pleasure, insight, and inspiration in doing so.

LEARNING HOW
TO LISTEN

This section takes its title from the incomparable Abbey
Lincoln's composition. The essays gathered here map
my attempts to write about the meaning and context of
African American music-making. Though I am neither
musician nor musicologist, I have learned much from both.
Here I write as a critic, cultural historian, and personal
essayist interested in all aspects of African American
expressive culture. These pieces, which grow from my
curiosity and concern, range from an effort to theorize
the cultural meanings attributed to Black women's singing
in the United States, to reflections on individual artists
whose music both teaches and inspires me, none more so
than my dear, brilliant, and virtuosic friend and collaborator, the late Geri Allen.

LADIES SING MILES

There's something in his [Miles's] sound that is so strong,
so masculine. But at the same time, there's another thing
so intimate it seems almost feminine. He covers everything.
His music speaks to all of us on a very real level. His artistry
is something we should all value. I know I do.

—CASSANDRA WILSON

I also remember how the music used to sound down there
in Arkansas, when I was visiting my grandfather, especially
at the Saturday night church. Man that shit was a mother-
fucker. I guess I was about six or seven. We'd be walking
on these dark country roads at night and all of a sudden
this music would seem to come out of nowhere, out of them
spooky looking trees that everybody said ghosts lived in. . . .
I remember a man and a woman singing and talking about
getting down. Shit, that music was something, especially
that woman singing.

—MILES DAVIS[1]

W HILE WALKING ALONG a country road, a boy named Miles
was moved by a Black woman's singing. Her voice, an indelible part of the Southern night, floating like ghosts through the trees,
would haunt his own playing throughout his life. Like Jean Toomer
before him, Miles Davis recalled the impact of that voice on his own
artistic sensibility. While Toomer tried to render it in writing, Davis
carried her melody in his horn. Davis's biographer Quincy Troupe
writes that Davis heard that "voice of an old Black churchwoman

singing plaintively" and, knowing it was special, filed it away and returned to it in his own "lonely trumpet sound."[2] Perhaps this is what women, particularly Black American women, especially creative Black American women, hear in Davis's horn. Perhaps we hear something akin to our own voices.

For some, Miles Davis's music seems to provide a safe aural space where we can be emotionally vulnerable. His horn is seductive not because it is harshly masculine but because it is not. In the sounds that emanate from Miles there is space for a woman's tears, vulnerability, anger, love, sexuality, creativity: a space simply to be. Perhaps this is why many felt so betrayed by his admission of emotional, verbal, and physical violence against women. His music seemed to provide such a safe space, a space that allowed for personal, creative, and spiritual growth, that we experienced these admissions as brutal slaps to our collective brown faces.

How do we come to terms with the violation? Writers and critics Pearl Cleage and Hazel Carby have devoted their efforts to eloquent and sophisticated critiques of him. Cleage sounds the much-needed alarm, calling our attention to the horror hidden beneath that beautiful sound. Carby theorizes the disjuncture between his behavior toward women and the possibilities for more progressive gender relations found in his music. Musician vocalists Shirley Horn and Cassandra Wilson have devoted entire albums in seeming defense of him. Horn and Wilson call us to remember the beauty with which he left us, to recall why we fell in love with him in the first place. Horn gives us a Miles she knew: a man who was different from the abuser of women who emerges from his autobiography or the pens of Cleage and Carby. Wilson manages both to celebrate and criticize him. In so doing she transports Miles to a place where she can express her own creative ambition through, over, and at times, against him.

In her now classic essay "Mad at Miles" Pearl Cleage writes that Miles Davis served as an escort to a deeper dimension of womanhood. "I spent the night curled up . . . listening to Miles Davis play me into the next phase of my life . . . The Bohemian Woman Phase . . . now I'm thirty phase . . . The need of a current vision of who and what and why I am phase. The cool me out quick cause I'm hanging by a thread phase."

This is a testimony to the spiritual power Cleage grants Davis's music. Here is an intimacy beyond that of the seduction ritual she describes later on and for which Miles provides the soundtrack. This relationship between listener and musician allows her to become the woman she wants to be, the woman who by playing Miles will "give the gentleman caller an immediate understanding" that she was "a woman with the possibility of an interesting past, and the probability of an interesting future."

What is it about Davis's music that grants him such entry into a woman's life? I think his music promises a feather bed upon which to fall while taking the risks required of a multidimensional womanhood. That sometimes lonely, always lyrical horn seems to promise, "Go on, I will bear you aloft, allow you to fly, and I will provide a soundscape for your landing." Who wouldn't fall in love with such a man? We forget that the music, not the man, made this promise. Is it possible to separate the two? Cleage poses this question when she asks, "Can we continue to celebrate the genius in the face of the monster?" Later she asks, "How can they hit us and still be our heroes? How can they hit us and still be our leaders? Our husbands? Our geniuses? Our friends?" Then she answers her own question: "They can't. Can they?"[3]

I want to suggest that these men should not be our heroes and they ought not to be our leaders. We need to reserve these roles for those who provide protection for our needs, interests, and physical selves. But unfortunately, the men in the first group are often our friends, brothers, fathers, and yes, they are our geniuses. Because genius is quirky like that—it can appear in the oddest places.

If we lend Charles Mingus's autobiography the credence we lend Davis's, then certainly he was as misogynist and abusive. Davis's bandmate Coltrane seems to have been far more progressive in his relations with women than either Miles or Mingus. He suffered harsh criticism for putting his gifted second wife, Alice, in his band, not as vocalist but as pianist, replacing the revered McCoy Tyner.

He believed her capable of providing the sound he needed for the music he wanted to create. Coltrane scholar Salim Washington notes, "Classic recordings of this band [including Alice Coltrane], such as *Live in Japan* or *Live at the Village Vanguard*, are evidence that . . . Alice found a way to support his direction with a piano style that was devoid of bebop clichés or conventions."[4]

Nonetheless, Mingus doesn't receive our scorn in the way that Miles does, and while we love him, sisters don't seem to be invested in Coltrane in the same kind of way (though perhaps we should be). Again, I think it is because of the promise of safety and understanding offered by Davis's horn—the safety of the Black woman's voice within a Black man who, for all we knew, appeared to like Black women.

His symbolic gestures serve as an example of this sensibility. While he was personally involved with women across the color line, during much of his career, Davis refused to allow record labels to put white women on his album covers. Instead, he often insisted that his ladies of the moment, his Black ladies, serve as cover models. His wife Frances appears on more than one cover, as do his two later wives, Cicely Tyson and Betty Mabry. On one hand, someone could interpret this as one-dimensional objectification of women; on the other hand, in the context of white supremacist standards of beauty and what some Black women view as a fetish for white women on the part of some Black jazz musicians, it is in no way insignificant that Davis insisted Black women grace his album covers.

Suppose we think of Davis as some think of Thomas Jefferson. Architect and theorist of democracy, Jefferson was a slaveholder, and if we believe *Notes on the State of Virginia*, also a white supremacist. We must be harshly critical of his white supremacy and challenge those who offer excuses for it. Yet, we also must recognize the value of his contributions that allow us as a people and as a nation to move beyond his own limitations. From the beginning, struggles for Black American freedom have been built upon the tenets of freedom and equality for all espoused in Jefferson's Declaration of Independence. Much of that struggle has focused on pointing out the failure of the nation to live up to its promise of democracy, insisting upon the hypocrisy of a government that claims to be founded upon such principles and yet denies them to a significant portion of its population. The contradictions of the nation are the flaws at the core of its being; bringing attention to these flaws and working to address them makes for a better nation in the long run.

I think a similar reading of Miles does the same thing for his music and for jazz, as well. This reading comes to terms with the human capacity for contradiction, an understanding that recognizes Davis as both Prince of Darkness and Bearer of Light.

Hazel Carby's controversial rendering of Miles Davis in her book on Black masculinity, *Race Men*, attempts to do just this. Carby is critical of the sexist man, makes the connection between the sexism in the life and its embodiment in a misogynistic, socially homogenous musical arena, and argues nonetheless that the music offers new possibilities for gender relations.

Carby writes, "I think it's very important to challenge the apparent distance between Davis's violence against women and the genius of his music as if they were enacted on different planes of existence." According to Carby, Davis's disdain for women resulted in his need to create a distance between them and a homogenous realm of male creativity where his music was born. The absence of women from this space grows from a contempt for them, a sense that their presence is antithetical to the atmosphere where the music can happen. She argues this is a false division because in many instances the world of women's labor enables the conditions that create this male creative realm. Significantly, Carby finds that a male-only environment offers alternative, nonhierarchical versions of masculinity even as it banishes women. She turns to *Kind of Blue* to reveal a level of "intimacy and interdependence" between musicians that creates "an unconventional, gendered vulnerability."

For Carby, Miles's legendary distance from the audience allowed him to protect his world from the "world of women perceived as the threatening realm of bitches."[5] I have learned a great deal from Carby's eloquent and sophisticated analysis of Davis's music. However, I differ with her on this point. It was not necessarily the world of women that Davis feared in guarding his creative space. The audience comprises men and women. Perhaps a division emerges between those part of the music-making and those not. What happens when women are part of the creative space as creative contributors to it? Before moving on, let me say that I am not defending Davis or providing an excuse for his abhorrent abuse of woman. However, I am curious about the women in his musical space—his interaction with them and the possibilities offered by his music for female artists.

Miles Davis, as discussed, often physically and emotionally abused the women in his life. According to some reports, so did Billie Holiday, who, although beaten by men, reportedly beat women as well. She certainly referred to them as "bitches" on occasion. Incidentally, Holiday is one woman whom Davis respected a great deal professionally. He even cites her influence on his own playing. Furthermore, as a young musician he worked with her. In his autobiography he notes, "I loved playing with Coleman Hawkins and behind Billie when I got a chance. They were both great musicians, really creative and shit." Later he notes, "Whenever I'd go to see her, I always asked Billie to sing 'I Loves You, Porgy,' because when she sang 'don't let him touch me with his hot hands,' you could almost feel that shit she was feeling. It was beautiful and sad the way she sang that. Everybody loved Billie."[6]

He later recorded his own version of the song. If Davis looked up to Holiday, he served as a mentor to another female vocalist, Shirley Horn.

The phrase, "Honey from a horn so sweet," sung at the end of her version of "Blue in Green," characterizes Shirley Horn's depiction of her friend and mentor. Horn, already an accomplished pianist, came to Davis's attention following her first recording, *Ashes and Embers*. After hearing the album, he invited her to come to New York so that he could hear her play in person. Shortly thereafter, Davis insisted that the young pianist and vocalist open for him at the Village Vanguard. As a result, Horn got greater exposure and went on to sign a Mercury Records recording contract with Quincy Jones.

Even before meeting Miles Davis, Horn had been identified as a

gifted artist. She started playing the piano at four; she began studying composition at twelve and has always led her own trio. Davis was
familial: "He was like an uncle to me." While at the Vanguard, she
often sat in with Davis, though she didn't record with him until 1991
on her album *You Won't Forget Me*; he is guest soloist on the title
tune. In 1998, she recorded her tribute to him, *I Remember Miles*. In
addition to her performance, Horn also arranged all the songs and
coproduced the album.

I Remember Miles is a memorial, testimony, and a celebration. A
reproduction of a Miles Davis sketch graces the cover of the album.
A gift from Davis to Horn, the sketch depicts a man and a woman
wrapped in an embrace; they appear to be kissing, though it is
unclear whether they kiss as lovers or as friends. It is signed with *x*'s
(kisses) and "Miles." The ambivalence of the cover sketch characterizes the entire album—both the images and the music. A sepia photo
on the inside cover shows a young Horn dressed elegantly in an off-
the-shoulder cocktail dress, holding a martini and looking off into
the room.

Davis sits next to her, looking in her direction, pensively listening.
He may be looking at her chest; he may be looking beyond her. Again,
the viewer is not certain. Clearly, the two people are very close, yet the
nature of their relationship remains unknown. In the accompanying
booklet appears a photo of an older Davis and Horn taken in 1990 at
the recording session for *You Won't Forget Me*. The photo reveals a
couple that shares a deep affection. They look at each other, he listening attentively and lovingly, like an older brother or a man still in love.

With the exception of one tune, all of the songs on *I Remember
Miles* are associated with early Miles (1956–1963). Most of them are
ballads; Horn recalls, "He liked for me to sing ballads." He renders
each song with such care, tenderness, and beauty that it rises above
the trite sentimentality often associated with love songs. Horn's
musicianship, her singing, piano-playing, and arranging create an
intimate space where the work remembered happens with dignity
and grace.

Horn's spare, haunting way with lyrics, the space where a note lingers, and the way she drives a dramatic tension between voice and piano all help us hear Miles Davis's horn as a female voice. On the one hand, his influence on her seems clear; on the other hand, perhaps he heard his voice in the way she handled a lyric and in her phrasing. After all, Davis recorded three of the songs here, "Baby Won't You Please Come Home," "I Fall in Love Too Easily," and "Basin Street Blues," on *Seven Steps to Heaven*, *after* hearing Horn do them at the Vanguard.

On *I Remember Miles*, the brilliant Roy Hargrove often accompanies Horn. Their encounter on "I Got Plenty of Nothing" recalls that between Sarah Vaughn and Clifford Brown on "September Song." Behind her, Hargrove is playful, flirtatious, now urging, now echoing. In his solos he takes off on exuberant flights. Horn is the grounded one, her voice swinging him back to earth. "My Man's Gone Now" is an extended drama, not unlike Davis's recording of it on his *Porgy and Bess* album. But it is on the final song, an instrumental version of "Blue and Green," that one hears the impact of her loss. Her piano, so much like the spare, space-filled playing that Davis liked in his own pianists, seems to leave open space for him to enter. Yet, no friend responds to her call; no one fills the void. Instead comes Horn's voice, "Honey from a horn so sweet." While she is talking about the lost voice of Miles, the listener hears that honey in this Horn.

In 1997, Cassandra Wilson became one of the few women to receive a commission by Jazz at Lincoln Center. She used the opportunity to explore the work of Miles Davis. Wynton Marsalis, director of Jazz at Lincoln Center, had been one of the most vocal critics of Davis's experimentation with hip-hop, rock, fusion, and smooth jazz; Wilson chose to present Davis's music in the house that Wynton built. Although Miles was renowned for his sexism, Wilson featured female musicians such as Regina Carter and Quartette Indigo, as well as her regular male band. Her album *Traveling Miles* grew out of that commission and allowed her to combine a devotion to the jazz tradition with the desire to open out into different musical arenas.

The inside cover of the album portrays Wilson sitting, apparently in a recording studio. Surrounded by music stands, she sits casually, dressed in a sweater, khakis, and loafers. The portrait echoes a photograph of Davis during the recording of *Kind of Blue*. She even wears an ascot as he did in the earlier photographs. Advertisements for the album show Wilson, dressed in a white petticoat and brown leather jacket, walking along the railroad like legendary bluesmen. Within the lyrics and the music Wilson conjures Miles the ancestor, who is not unlike those legendary bluesmen. He travels from country roads to Seventh Avenue, from Manhattan to the mythical land of the Yoruba deities—Ile Ife, from this world to the world beyond. His horn, like the voice of the old Black woman, floats from the landscape and through the heavens. Though the music, lyrics, and stories they tell evoke Davis, Wilson is the teller of this tale, the conjurer of this set. Davis paved the road she travels to this space—a space she creates by producing, writing lyrics, composing music, and singing. She is in full control of the narrative.

The very first song on the album is Miles's "Run the VooDoo Down," for which she provides lyrics: the musician, conjurer of these lyrics, is a female, "she'll run the voodoo down." It closes with a reprise of the song, and this time she is accompanied by West African vocalist Angélique Kidjo. The duet is among the most complicated music on the album. Wilson recalled, "It was tough, singing that section, but I love that weird intervallic stuff." The song's lyrics, sung in English and Yoruba, make connections between Africa and the Americas. Eventually, the women's voices overlap, and it becomes impossible to distinguish Kidjo's call from Wilson's response. The song closes with Wilson answering in the first-person blues narrative that opens the album.

On at least three other songs, "Seven Steps to Heaven," "Someday My Prince Will Come," and "Never Broken (ESP)," Wilson features another female artist, the violinist Regina Carter. On "Seven Steps to Heaven," where we have come to expect a dialogue of horns, two "feminine" instruments, the woman's voice and the violin, are featured. At first, Lonnie Plaxico's bass lays the ground, and Stefon Harris's vibraphone and Eric Lewis's piano create a sphere where a humming Wilson and Carter begin to talk to each other. Wilson pulls from her lowest register, her voice becoming androgynous and only reaching into its upper limits to plead, "Help me climb that road." Regina Carter does just that with a quick-paced, ebullient climb.

Wilson feels a particular affinity for Davis: "Miles was the man who introduced me to the depth and breadth of jazz: he allowed me to understand how far it could be stretched. Like Jimi Hendrix, he could open windows, break the rules and get away with it."[7] This is the path that Davis forged for Wilson. She uses the Miles album as an opportunity to combine the interests and emphases that she has found compelling her throughout her career. In addition to writing the lyrics to five Davis classics, she also composes four of her own, and she produced the album as well. For fans of easy listening, she offers one of Miles' more controversial choices, Cyndi Lauper's "Time After Time." On *Traveling Miles*, Wilson is composer, lyricist, producer, and leader.

While Horn focused on an earlier Miles, Wilson is most interested in the post–*Bitches Brew* works. These fit within her own emerging musical philosophy, which entailed refusal to be contained by categories and tradition. Miles Davis's legacy is not one that binds, but one that allows Shirley Horn and Cassandra Wilson to explore their own individuality. In June of 1999, the two women played on a double bill at Carnegie Hall. Both performed from their Miles tributes. The presentations and styles could not have been more different. Horn, with Charles Ables on bass and Steve Williams on drums, sang to an almost silent house, the audience hanging on her every word, sitting on edge, anticipating each note. Wilson had them dancing in their seats with her funk-inflected set. Drummer Marcus Baylor, percussionist Jeffrey Haynes, and bassist Lonnie Plaxico were joined by Carter and Harris, creating a mix of genres where the spirit of Miles playfully hovered above. One gets the sense that he would have felt at home in either set. Miles Davis's music gives Cassandra Wilson and Shirley Horn space to explore their own creative visions. Their voices render the exquisite feminine quality at the core of his own distinct sound.

WHEN MALINDY SINGS

A Meditation on Black Women's Vocality

PICTURE THE FOLLOWING:

1. Marian Anderson singing at the Lincoln Memorial in 1939.
2. Whitney Houston singing "The Star-Spangled Banner" at the Super Bowl in 1992, during the Gulf War.
3. Aretha Franklin singing "The Star-Spangled Banner" at the 1992 Democratic National Convention.
4. Santita Jackson singing "The Star-Spangled Banner" at inaugural events for William Jefferson Clinton, January 20, 1997.
5. The anonymous Black woman who sang at the first public memorial for the victims of the Oklahoma bombing.
6. Jessye Norman singing at an event at New York University Law School's Tishman Auditorium in support of Clinton before his impeachment, December 14, 1998. (Toni Morrison speaking at the same event.)
7. The anonymous Black woman singing "Amazing Grace" immediately following the Littleton, Colorado, shootings or the Texas church shootings.
8. Chaka Khan singing at the close of the Republican National Convention in Philadelphia, August 2000.
9. Related but distinct: Mahalia Jackson at the 1963 March on Washington.
10. Related but distinct: Fannie Lou Hamer at the 1964 Democratic National Convention in Atlantic City.

I say "picture" because these images and our memories of them are as much about the spectacle as the sound. The recognizably Black woman—singing rather than speaking—is a familiar sight for American audiences. While each instance, each woman, each voice is unique—these women do not "sound" alike—the physicality is familiar. The woman stands before a crowd in front of a microphone, mouth open, positioned to sing.

The patriotism of the first eight moments is striking. Each occurs when the nation is trying to present an image of itself to itself and to the world. On at least three of these occasions, the Black woman's voice is the clarion call following heinous displays of American racism and its ugly relatives. The last two scenes are also created in response to American racism, but they signal a challenge to, a critique of the United States.

Marian Anderson sings at the Lincoln Memorial because the Daughters of the American Revolution refuse to allow her to sing at Convention Hall. The Oklahoma federal building was bombed by avowed white supremacists. The shooters in the Littleton, Colorado, tragedy espoused racist beliefs. The other instances are not quite as explicit, but just as ironic. Whitney Houston rallies the nation behind a war that has nothing to do with democracy, behind an army made up of the poor, disproportionately poor Blacks, whites, and Latinos who turn to the military because the nation denies them employment and educational opportunities. Jessye Norman serenades a president who, though more comfortable in the presence of Black people than his predecessors, ended "welfare as we knew it," and in so doing sank thousands of poor women and children into greater poverty; a president who, as a candidate, left the campaign trail so that he could execute an intellectually disabled Black man; a president responsible for silencing the voices of two Black women—Lani Guinier and Jocelyn Elders. Nonetheless, he is a president with unprecedented popularity among a large number of African Americans. He has even been called (not without controversy) "the first Black president."

Only Mahalia Jackson's and Fannie Lou Hamer's voices were used to rally the troops for social struggle. Because the vision proposed by

Marian Anderson on the steps of the Lincoln Memorial had not been born by the 1960s, Jackson's was a voice insisting on a hearing, standing between the Washington Monument and the Lincoln Memorial as the illegitimate daughter of the American Revolution, demanding a seat at the table. Fannie Lou Hamer's voice helped folks to withstand the police batons and fire hoses of the segregationist South. Hers was also the voice raised as witness to the hypocrisy of the 1964 Democratic Convention in Atlantic City. Bernice Johnson Reagon picked up where Mrs. Hamer left off when she sang with the SNCC Freedom Singers and has continued to do so as the founding member of Sweet Honey in the Rock. In the 1960s Abbey Lincoln's articulate screams on Max Roach's *Freedom Now Suite*, and Nina Simone's defiant "Mississippi Goddam" joined Aretha's call for "Respect," to provide not just the soundtrack but the announcement of a new militancy. Unlike Mahalia at the March on Washington, these women made demands, not requests. Black audiences endowed them with the responsibility of communicating Black frustration, anger, aspiration, and hope.

Approximately two decades following Mahalia Jackson's appearance at the March on Washington, in 1997 Santita Jackson sang at the inauguration of Bill Clinton and implied that the demand was heard; that we are now one big, unified, biracial family. The younger Jackson sang for a party for which her father is a powerful operative and in which her brother would become an elected official. Perhaps the most cynical of these images (for I do not believe they are all cynical) is Chaka Khan appearing as part of a parade of colored faces performing multiculturalism at a convention for a party whose delegates were overwhelmingly white and whose platform offered little to the majority of Black Americans. (Ironically, it did produce a powerful, speaking Black woman cabinet member in Condoleezza Rice.)

These various images demonstrate the way the Black woman's voice can be called upon to heal a crisis in national unity as well as provoke one. As scholars such as Benedict Anderson have noted, the nation is a fictive construct of community. The image of the "mother of the nation" is one that allows this construct to figure itself as reproduced. But the spectacle of the singing Black woman at times of national crisis does not represent the "mother of the nation"; instead, that spectacle sometimes invokes a figure that can make no claims on the family unit, though she is "just like one of the family." A figure that serves the unit, who heals and nurtures it but has no rights or privileges within it—more mammy than mother. Here, I am not suggesting that the individual women themselves chose to serve as mammies but instead that this figure of the singing Black woman is often similar to the uses of Black women's bodies as nurturing, healing, life- and love-giving for the majority culture. This representation of the voice is in stark contrast to representations of that voice in the service of disenfranchised Black people, as a voice that poses a challenge to the United States, revealing its democratic pretense as a lie. And yet, this image contains both these possibilities.

Certainly, racism is as American as the African American women's vocal tradition. Perhaps more so, in fact, because it is central to the founding of the nation; whereas the voice, that peculiar Black voice, is in it but not of it at the nation's beginning. Since Marian Anderson, the voice and the spectacle of the singing Black woman often has been used to suggest a peacefully interracial version of America. In the majority of these spectacles there is the suggestion that the Black woman singer pulls together and helps to heal national rifts. This singing spectacle offers an alternative vision of a more inclusive America. It may not be representative of the United States as it is, but it projects an image of what participants long for it to become. On the other hand, the Black woman's singing voice can signal a crisis in the spectacle of national unity; it can even invoke such a crisis by mobilizing dissent and forging a space of resistance. Representations of the voice suggest that it is like a hinge, a place where things can both come together and break apart.[1]

What other American voice resonates in this way, mobilizes in this way, evokes a picture of national unity at times of crisis and yet is also capable of invoking a crisis in a tenuous national unity as well? How does a vocal tradition that first emerged in the creation and service of an oppressed people end up in service to a nation that has been hostile to the aspirations of Black people? Of course, "the voice" is not stable and unchanging. It varies in tone, timbre, and meaning; it changes according to artist, time, and context.

What follows is more meditation than theory, more questions than conclusions on the meanings of Black women's singing. Here, I am focusing on representations of Black women singers across genres, including gospel, jazz, opera, and rhythm and blues, over a period of one hundred years. First, I will review the language early white observers and later Black writers have used to define the sound and the power of Black American singing voices in order to situate the voice historically and to demonstrate its place in narratives of nation. In so doing I will try to tease out the meanings with which this voice has been invested. I will then explore an alternative myth of a Black woman's singing—a myth of origin for other forms of Black expressivity, especially jazz. These myths are also myths of origin for a Black nation, where the originary voice is rendered as female but represented by males. My project shares much with and has benefited a great deal from the brilliant work of Lindon Barrett in *Blackness and Value: Seeing Double*. We are both concerned with the Black singing voice as "a site of the active production of meaning."[2]

How Shall We Sing the Lord's Song in a Strange Land?

> By the rivers of Babylon,
> There we sat down,
> Yea, we wept, when we remembered Zion.
> We hanged our harps upon the willows
> In the midst thereof.
> For there they that carried us away captive
> Required of us a song:
> And they that wasted us required of us mirth,
> Saying,
> Sing us one of the songs of Zion.
> How shall we sing the Lord's song
> In a strange land?

—PSALM 137

Black Americans have long seen parallels between our own situation and that of the Old Testament Jews, captives exiled in Babylon. "How can we sing the Lord's song in a strange land?" But sing they did and in so doing created one of the richest vocal traditions the world has known. Black women's voices are central to that tradition.

Before I am accused of essentialism, let me clarify what I mean by "the Black woman's voice." First, I am here most interested in the way that voice has been described. I am as concerned with the image as I am with the sound. Second, I do not mean the voice that comes out every time any Black woman anywhere opens her mouth to sing. Nor do I want to imply that there is something in the structure of the Black diaphragm, neck, throat, and tongue, teeth, or mouth that contributes to a certain vocalization. No, I don't mean a Black voice as markedly different as skin color or texture of hair. Instead, I am talking of a cultural style. A particularly New World style with roots in West Africa. (The centrality of the singing voice is something shared with many West African societies from which the enslaved were taken.)[3] In the United States it is a style transformed, nurtured, and developed in the tradition of the spirituals, field hollers, and work songs, and sustained in Black Church and/or blues and jazz venues.[4]

One finds the most in-depth discussions about the existence and origins of "the Black voice" in opera. (For some time, Black singers were considered interlopers in the field, prompting one critic, the German Dr. Geerd Heinsen, to claim that the Black voice was "too Negroid for the French vocal line."[5]) Here we find adjectives used to describe singing voices: *rich, dark, heavy, throaty.* These are adjectives borrowed from colors and textures—things that appeal to senses other than sound—a practice Roland Barthes found particularly irritating.[6] Students of Black music such as Zora Neale Hurston, Christopher Smalls, Amiri Baraka, Nathaniel Mackey, Brent Edwards, and Robert O'Meally encourage us to think less in terms of adjectives and more in terms of verbs when describing Black cultural practices, including singing. These writers stress functions, effects, and processes in their descriptions of Black music. They use words like stretching, reaching, conversing, sliding, imitating, swinging, rocking.[7]

According to Eileen Southern, during the early days of the nation, Black singing was described as "distinctive for its high intensity and use of such special effects as falsetto, shouts, groans and guttural tones. A strong, clear voice was favored, but Europeans generally described the sounds of the African voice as 'a rud noyse,' 'a strong nasal sound,' or 'very loud and shrill'" (14). These descriptions assert the unfamiliarity of the voice, the "otherness" of it. In these descriptions Black voices are *other* as in *foreign*. The Black voice is part of the Black body; the Black body was deemed the very antithesis of all that was white and therefore human.

Many white American observers writing during the Civil War contributed to this discourse on the Black voice. They stressed the impossibility of notating Black American singing on the Western scale. Lucy McKim Garrison, coeditor of *Slave Songs in the United States*, observed:

> It is difficult to express the entire character of these Negro ballads by mere musical notes and signs. The odd turns made in the throat and the curious rhythmic effect produced by single voices chiming in at different irregular intervals, seem almost as impossible to place on the scale as the singing of birds or the tones of an Aeolian Harp.[8]

Her coeditor, William Allen, lamented:

> What makes it all the harder to unravel a thread of melody out of this strange network is that, like birds, they seem not infrequently to strike sounds that cannot be precisely represented by the gamut and abound in "slides from one note to the another and in turns and cadences not in articulated notes."[9]

Numerous others cautioned about the impossibility of "writing out" or finding "musical characters to represent" Black singing. In both instances we get Black singing compared to the singing of birds.

Birds are part of the natural world; for many whites, Black people were thought to be closer to the natural world. Bird's songs are beautiful, mysterious, and functional. Furthermore, they are not thought to be the products of intellect, though recognized as a complex form of communication.

Interestingly, from the anonymous composers of the spirituals and folk tales to later poets such as Paul Laurence Dunbar and Abbey Lincoln, Black people have likened themselves to birds: birds in flight, birds incapable of flight, caged birds, free birds, but most especially singing birds. For the white observer, Black singing is birdlike because it escapes categorization. It does not attend to the rules of Western literacy or notation. Nathaniel Mackey refers to this as the "fugitive spirit" of Black music in its refusal to "be mapped, captured, notated."[10] Perhaps this is why the Black singing voice not only struck an unfamiliar chord but at times a threatening one, as well. Lindon Barrett writes:

> Notations of the disturbing acoustic qualities of the diaspora singing voice often accompany the misrecognition of its cultural significance and its dismissal as a meaningful artefact. . . . In New World slave societies affront to Western aesthetic sensibilities one often finds a further corollary in fears concerning the potential threat posed by the singing voice to Western sociality or polity. . . . The singing voice proves a disturbing announcement of the vacuity of African and African diasporic cultures, but nevertheless, also an announcement of a threat to Western societies and psyches. (63)

(A brief aside: Not all Black observers were as distinct from whites that heard the voices for the first time. Rebecca Primus, a freeborn Northern Black woman who established a school for the freedmen on the Eastern Shore of Maryland, was one Black listener who found Black Southern singing strange and unfamiliar.)

In addition to the distinctive, different sound of Black singing, observers also noted the strange effect that sound had on listeners. Eileen Southern writes, "American literature contains numerous references to female slaves of colonial times who kept young audiences spellbound, and adults too with their ancient tales." In all these cases the voice is unfamiliar, uncanny, almost otherworldly. (Years later this would hold true for jazz vocalists such as Billie Holiday, Shirley Horne, Carmen McRae, and Cassandra Wilson, all of whom possess the power of holding audiences spellbound with their "stories.") It is a voice capable of casting spells. It is certainly a voice concerned with its connection to the world of the spirit, its ability to invoke the presence of the divine. So the sound heard as "other," as in "foreign," is also a sound that is "other" like the mystery that is God.[11]

In the instances cited by Southern, it is not just a matter of the voice but the way it tells the tale; the form in which it relays the message. The tone of the voice, its inflections, its register, the cadence, the pauses and silences—these are all as important and in some instances more important than the words themselves. Patti LaBelle's version of "Isn't It a Shame" is an example of a vocalist's ability to render meaning without words. In the midst of a song that mourns the end of a relationship, LaBelle stops singing lyrics altogether and begins to moan. The pain about which she sings is beyond conventional speech. She moans a melody that tells a familiar tale of loss and desperate loneliness. It starts with a simple phrase, climaxes in a moan that is almost a holler before resolving to a whimper. At this point the voices of the other two singers, Nona Hendryx and Sarah Dash, come in to help lift her back up, providing aural support so that she can stand and reenter the realm of language and lyrics.

Now of course I don't want to suggest that Patti LaBelle and those unnamed Black women cited by Southern represent one invariable, unchanging style, but rather that there is a tradition that values experimentation and risk taking in form as well as content. It is a tradition that seeks to, in fact needs to, communicate beyond words when they are no longer capable of rendering meaning. I imagine this was especially important for persons who were forced to speak in a tongue that was not their native one.

Interestingly, in other cultures, "Blackness" has been used as a descriptor of certain voices and not of the singers. This quality of "vocal darkness" usually comes from cultures where the pitch of the speaking voice is lower.[12] However, in an essay titled "Cante Moro," the Spanish poet García Lorca offered a meditation on the "dark sounds" of the music of the Romany people, another dark-skinned oppressed people, known as "gypsies." Both Ralph Ellison and Nathaniel Mackey have drawn links between these dark or Moorish sounds, flamenco, and Black American blues. In the United States "vocal darkness" is associated with an oppressed minority, identifiable by their skin color; we hear a whole range of meaning in the voices of Black singers. For instance, anyone familiar with the racial history of the United States will probably hear irony as well as patriotism when Ray Charles sings "America"; it is not a matter of his individual politics but the vocal tradition out of which he sings, the voice. This is a voice that resounds with echoes of the cotton and tobacco fields, chain gangs and railroad, juke joints and storefront church.

The Black Church has been the primary site for the development of a distinctive Black singing style and tradition. Ralph Ellison describes that style and tradition in his essay "As the Spirit Moves Mahalia," noting that Mahalia Jackson's voice is part of an art form that "depends upon the employment of the full expressive resources of the human voice."[13] Gospel music seems to contain most of the elements identified with Black singing. The gospel quality has come to characterize other types of singing associated with Black people, most especially rhythm and blues and soul as well as jazz. Portia Maultsby notes that across genre Black vocalists

> bring intensity to their performances by alternating lyrical, percussive, and raspy timbres; juxtaposing vocal and instrumental textures; changing pitch and dynamic levels; alternating straight with vibrato tones and weaving moans, shouts, grunts, hollers, and screams into the melody.[14]

To experience the growl, falsetto, humming, and moaning in one song, listen to Andy Bey sing "You'd Be So Nice to Come Home To," Nina Simone sing "Be My Husband," Sweet Honey in the Rock or Shirley Caesar sing anything. "Be My Husband" is based on a traditional African American work song. It provides an excellent example because the lack of elaborate instrumentation allows us to hear the dips, curves, bends, and flights of Simone's voice. At one point her voice shifts focus from melody to rhythm—keeping time like a hammer or hoe might have. Here she demands, there she pleads: She is both strength and vulnerability. When not singing we can hear an audible breathiness reminding us that the voice is situated in the body. At times she will substitute her voice with clapping hands, again embodying the song. Instead of hiding the breathing, denying the body of the singer in an effort to mimic an out-of-body spiritual transcendence, here we have a reminder of the relationship between body, breath, and spirit; a reminder that transcendence is acquired through the manipulation of bodily functions (chanting, singing, breathing, shouting, dancing).

While the Black Church is the training ground for many of our most well-known singers, from Miss Anderson to Dinah Washington, Sarah Vaughan, Aretha and Whitney, it is not the sole repository of this sound. One can hear many of these qualities in the voice of Billie Holiday, a Catholic girl who didn't have the huge voice of her sisters but did have a certain way of approaching a note that is also born of this tradition. Billie Holiday, whether singing "Strange Fruit" or "Lover Man," exposed our national and personal frailties, obsessions and secrets. In her voice, first and foremost, we hear an almost brutal honesty.

Descriptions of Black singing, particularly Black women's singing, have been especially important to Black writers. Frederick Douglass's classic description articulates a theory of the relationship between Black singing and the social and political condition of Black people's lives:

> They would make the dense old woods, for miles around,
> reverberate with their wild songs, revealing at once the

highest joy and the deepest sadness. They would compose
and sing as they went along consulting neither time nor
tune. The thought that came up, came out—if not in the
word, in the sound;—and as frequently in the one as in
the other. They would sometimes sing the most pathetic
sentiment in the most rapturous tone, and the most rapturous sentiment in the most pathetic tone . . . . They
would sing, as a chorus, to words which to many would
seem unmeaning jargon, but which, nevertheless, were
full of meaning to themselves. I have sometimes thought
that the mere hearing of those songs would do more to
impress some minds with the horrible character of slavery than the reading of whole volumes of philosophy on
the subject would do . . . . They were tones loud, long, and
deep . . . . Every tone was a testimony against slavery, and
a prayer to God for deliverance from chains . . . to those
songs I trace my first glimmering conception of the dehu-
manizing character of slavery.

Douglass sets the tone that future Black writers would employ in
their own attempts to represent and interpret Black singing. There
is the secretive and communal nature of the performance, in the
woods (in contrast to the public entertaining function of singing the
songs for an audience of whites). There is the emphasis on the meaning conveyed in the sound and on the sound as more representative
of the people's condition than words in a book. And yet the only
access we have to the sound is his written effort to describe it. The
most elaborate articulation of this aesthetic comes nearly a century
later in the work of LeRoi Jones, especially his important *Blues People* (1963).

Toward the end of Toni Morrison's novel *Beloved*, an army of
Black women march to 124—the house where former slave Sethe,
her daughter Denver, and the ghost of slavery, Beloved, reside. Once
there, their voices rise in a wall of sound that exorcises the ghost.

Where the yard met the road, [Sethe and Beloved] saw
the rapt faces of thirty neighborhood women. Some
had their eyes closed; others looked at the hot, cloud-
less sky. Sethe opened the door and reached for Beloved's
hand. Together they stood in the doorway. . . . Women
searched for the right combination, the key, the code, the
sound that broke the back of words. Building voice upon
voice until they found it and when they did it was a wave
of sound wide enough to sound deep water and knock
the pods off Chestnut trees. It broke over Sethe and she
trembled like the baptized in its wash. (261)

The ocean of sound, a virtual force of nature, that which continues
to communicate when language breaks down, baptizes Sethe. Black
women singing in unison confront the evil legacy of white supremacy
and the slave trade, fight it and, in this instance, win. In a text so
obsessed with dismembered and abused Black bodies and psyches,
the voice emerges as that part of the body and psyche best suited for
creating and healing community. In this text, the physical violence of
slavery and its aftermath dismembers Black bodies, but the discourse
of slavery that deconstructs and categorizes Black people as inhuman is as substantial and even longer lasting than physical violence
("list her animal characteristics on one side her human on the other,"
Schoolteacher instructs his "pupils"). Slavery and white supremacy
enact physical and discursive dismemberment; the voices of singing
Black women dismember the ghost of slavery and break the back of
words both in order to communicate beyond them and to destroy
their power over Black bodies. And it is this dual action—the breaking of physical and discursive bonds—that precipitates the healing.
(*Beloved* the novel might be likened to a song that attempts to do the
same thing.)

There are numerous literary and historical examples of how Black
women's voices or representations of Black women's voices not only
soothed white children with lullabies but also healed, nurtured, sus-

tained Black people. Importantly, all these discussions of Black wom-
en's singing focus as much on the listener as they do on the singer. In
other words, voices create an aural space where listeners can momentarily experience themselves as outside of themselves, as "home" or
as "free." This space can be simultaneously political, spiritual, and
sensual.[15] It is the context of the listening or the hearing that embodies the voice with meaning.

Black singing helped Black people gather the strength to fight
when they had no weapons; it invited and prepared the way for visitations from ancestors and the Holy Ghost. It saved the souls of sinners
and made the saved backslide. It laid the foundation for diverse artistic visions. It expressed their longing for safety, for shelter, for love,
for divine retribution, and for freedom.

It is this understanding of the meaning and function of Black
women's singing that informs a century-old myth that situates a
Black woman's voice as the origin of Black male literary and musical
productivity and as the originary, founding sound of the New World
Black Nation.

When Malindy Sings: A Myth of Origin

> G'way an' quit dat noise, Miss Lucy—
> Put dat music book away;
> What's de use to keep on tryin'?
> Ef you practise twell you're gray,
> You cain't sta't no notes a-flyin'
> Lak de ones dat rants and rings
> F'om de kitchen to de big woods
> When Malindy sings.
> You ain't got de nachel o'gans
> Fu' to make de soun come right,
> You ain't got de tu'ns an' twistin's
> Fu' to make it sweet an' light.
> Tell you one thing now, Miss Lucy,
> An' I'm tellin' you fu' true,
> When hit comes to raal right singin',

'T'ain no easy thing to do . . .
Y' ought to hyeah dat gal a-wa'blin;
Robins, la'ks an' all dem things.
Heish dey moufs an' hides dey faces
When Malindy sings.
She jus spreads huh mouf and hollahs,
Come to Jesus, twell you hyeah
Sinnahs' tremblin' steps and voices,
Timid-lak a-drawin' neah;
Den she tu'ns to "Rock of Ages"
Simply to de cross she clings,
An' you fin' yo' teah's a-drappin;
When Malindy sings
Who dat say dat humble praises
Wif de Master nevah counts?
Heish you mouf, I heyea dat music,
Ez hit rises up an' mounts
Floatin by de hills an' valleys
Way above dis buryin' sod,
Ez hit makes its way in glory
To de very gates of God!
Oh, hit's sweetah dan de music
Of an edicated band;
An' hit's dearah dan de battle's
Song o' triumph in de lan'
It seems holier dan evenin'
When de solemn chu'ch bell rings,
Ez I sit an' ca'mly listen
While Malindy sings . . .

    —PAUL LAURENCE DUNBAR, "When Malindy Sings," 1895

"In the beginning there were no words. In the beginning was the sound, and they all knew what that sound sounded like." This statement comes from one of our greatest wordsmiths—Toni Morrison. Not light at the beginning, but a universe of sound: birds, wind, water, and the human voice, a woman's voice, and, depending on the teller of the tale, a Black woman's voice. A number of writers and musicians identify a moment of hearing that voice as an epiphany: a moment that leads suddenly to insight, understanding, and a hearing of the potential of one's own artistic voice (if not at the moment of hearing, then later, upon reflection, certainly at a signal point in the text). This sound, which is not captured, is represented by the artist in poetry, prose, and music. While it is often the singing of men and women that constitutes the moment of epiphany, it seems most often to be the woman's voice that structures the myth.

Let us now turn to four such instances: W. E. B. Du Bois in *The Souls of Black Folk*, Jean Toomer in *Cane*, and Miles Davis/Quincy Troupe in *Miles: The Autobiography* (later elaborated in Troupe's *(Miles and Me)*. We will close with Cassandra Wilson's contribution to or revision of this myth. There are numerous other examples that will not be examined here, but two of the most significant are worth noting before we move on. James Baldwin famously attributes Bessie Smith's recordings with helping him to access the language and tone of his first novel, *Go Tell It on the Mountain*. August Wilson asserts hearing Smith's recordings of "Nobody in Town Can Bake a Sweet Jellyroll Like Mine"

> was a birth, a baptism, a resurrection and a redemption all rolled up in one. It was the beginning of my consciousness that I was a representative of a culture and the carrier of some very valuable antecedents. With my discovery of Bessie Smith and the blues I had been given a world that contained my image, a world at once rich and varied, marked and marking, brutal and beautiful and at crucial odds with the larger world that contained it and preyed and pressed it from every conceivable angle.[16]

But here, we shall focus on three sons of the North or Midwest who encounter the sound of Black singing in the South and in whom it strikes some ancient cultural memory. (Du Bois hears concertized spirituals at Fisk, Toomer hears the singing in rural Sparta, Georgia, where he has gone to work in a school, and Davis in rural Arkansas where he visits his grandfather's farm. Wilson is a daughter of the South who hears her own voice in Miles's horn.) Consequently, one mythical source of Black modernity is the haunting voice of a Black woman.[17] By calling these encounters mythical I am by no means suggesting they did not happen, that they are not situated in history; in fact, it is possible that they happened so much, that the tale is told so often it is recognizable, familiar, and therefore easy to invoke. But I am most interested in the rendering of the tale and in the cultural work of the telling.

Scholars Leslie C. Dunn and Nancy A. Jones identify "myths of vocal gender" throughout Western culture. The sirens who lure men to death are but one of the many archetypal figures that "anchor the female voice in the female body" and confer upon it "conventional associations of femininity with nature and matter, with emotion and irrationality." Dunn and Jones write that from classical myth to nineteenth-century opera, we find a fantasy of origins "that serves to explain and justify the placing, or rather displacing, of the female voice in a patriarchal culture through its alignment with the material, the irrational, the pre-cultural, and the musical." This voice is then contained "within a textuality identified as masculine, thus opposing her literal, embodied vocality to his metaphorical, disembodied 'voice'" (7). To this list I would like to add the singing New World Black woman whose voice, linked to nature, inspires cultural memory in the hearer and sets him on his own path of creative discovery.

The title of this section (and of this essay) is taken from Paul Laurence Dunbar's classic dialect poem, "When Malindy Sings," first published in 1895, later set to music by Oscar Brown Jr. and performed and recorded by the extraordinary Abbey Lincoln. The poem sets up many of the tropes of the myth of origin that appear in the later works I mention above. (Of course, Douglass's description precedes even this, as does Lucy McKim Garrison's.) First, we read of someone trying to describe Malindy's voice—we never hear that voice, neither speaking nor singing. The poet's persona relays it to us, and we know this witness is Black because of the use of dialect. So Malindy's voice, which sends notes a-flying, the voice that rings from the kitchen to the woods, a voice based in her so-called natural organs, is set in opposition to written Western music—the lines and dots. When Malindy sings, musicians with instruments stop playing and even the mockingbird is intimidated. Her voice goes "to de very gates of God!" Dunbar formalizes the description of a Black woman's voice as of nature and of the divine, as racially essential based in bio-logical difference, as incapable of capture in notation. He is not the first to give these kinds of descriptions, but he sets them in poetry in a way that has implications for our myth of origin. We, as readers, as hearers far away from the plantation, have access to this voice only through the words of the learned male poet who represents it to us in the voice of someone who has heard it. So, we are twice removed from Malindy's song, which has become the basis and inspiration for the poem.

In 1903 W. E. B. Du Bois closes his classic *Souls of Black Folk* with a meditation on the meaning of Black music: "The Sorrow Songs." Of the spirituals he writes:

> The songs are indeed the siftings of centuries; the music is far more ancient than the words, and in it we can trace here and there signs of development. My grandfather's grandmother was seized by an evil Dutch trader two centuries ago; and coming to the valleys of the Hudson and Housatonic, Black, little, and lithe, she shivered and shrank in the harsh north winds, looked longing at the hills, and often crooned a heathen melody to the child between her knees. . . . The child sang it to his children and they to their children's children, and so two hundred years it has traveled down to us and we sing it to our chil-dren, knowing as little as our fathers what its words may mean, but knowing well the meaning of its music. This was primitive African music; . . . the voice of exile.

Du Bois gives the songs a lineage that is almost Biblical in nature. It is ancient in origin and historically situated in the terror of the slave trade. Here we see the careful construction of the myth. His grandfather's grandmother is African. She is Black, little, and lithe. The landscape of New England is utterly foreign to her, and, out of a longing for home, she looks to the hills and sings in an unknown tongue. This moment of passing the tradition on to the child between her knee initiates a familial and racial tradition. Malindy's forebear is here not just a Black woman who can sing but an African woman who is most importantly a mother: Mother of a New World race. Du Bois adds another dimension to the tale—we know little of what the words mean, but that doesn't matter, because the meaning is in the sound and only the initiated can hear. The lyrics he reproduces are:

> *Do bana coba gene me, gene me!*
> *Do bana coba, gene me, gene me!*
> *Bend' nuli, nuli, nuli, nuli, bend'le.*

As Du Bois renders these lyrics and transcribes the melody on the pages of *Souls*, they appear as a modified blues form, with the repetition of the first two lines before the resolution of the third. Furthermore, he transcribes the song in the complex, dark key of D-flat, one of the keys favored by African American improvisers. In *Souls*, Du Bois claims his grandmother was Bantu. However, scholars and linguists have not been able to locate these lyrics within a Bantu language group. Du Bois's biographer David Levering Lewis notes that the closest translation seems to have come from a Wolof song from Senegambia—a song about confinement and captivity: "gene me, gene me, [gene ma, gene ma,]" "Get me out, get me out, get me out." Significantly, a large number of the enslaved Africans brought to the Americas came from the Senegambia region. Some scholars have drawn a connection between the musics of this region and the blues forms that developed in the United States (especially in the Mississippi Delta).[18] While here Du Bois's grandmother is a "little Black

Bantu" living in New England, in other versions of the tale told in *Dusk of Dawn* and elsewhere, Du Bois attributes the song to his great grandfather's wife or to another ancestor named Violet. In all cases, the song is transmitted by a Black woman.

Twenty years after Du Bois, Jean Toomer draws from his experience in Sparta, Georgia, to render the Black woman's singing voice as an indelible part of a changing landscape and a dying era. In his autobiographical writings, Tommer recalled hearing the voices in Georgia:

> A family of back-country Negroes had only recently moved into a shack not too far away. They sang. And this was the first time I'd ever heard the folk-songs and spirituals. They were rich and sad and joyous and beautiful. . . . I realized with deep regret, that the spirituals, meeting ridicule, would be certain to die out.

Here Toomer recalls the voices of a family, not of a woman or of women. He also notes that the spirituals represented a dying tradition: one that he sought to preserve in *Cane*, which he called a swan song. These voices float above and through the narratives and poems of *Cane*. In "Blood Burning Moon," the story that closes the first Southern section of the book, Louisa, a young woman torn between two lovers, one Black and one white, begins to sing as she goes to meet the Black Tom. Her song is a foreboding and a foreshadowing of Tom's murder of her white lover and his own eventual lynching by a white vigilante mob.

> The slow rhythm of her song grew agitant and restless. Rusty black and tan spotted hounds, lying in the dark corners of the porches or prowling around back yards, put their noses in the air and caught its tremor. They began plaintively to yelp and howl. Chickens woke up and cackled. Intermittently, all over the countryside dogs barked and roosters crowed as if heeding a weird dawn or some ungodly awakening. The women sang lustily.

Here again the voice is otherworldly not because it is from another planet but because it is part of an unseen world that parallels our own rational one. It is both spiritual and material, both mystical and natural. As with Dunbar before him, Toomer represents the voice carried by the breeze, held by the trees, creating a mystical landscape and leading directly to the ears of God. It is a prophetic voice, yet it is one that we cannot hear, that is only brought to us in the work of the literate male poet. It is his source and his inspiration, contained and refined for our consumption.

By the time Miles Davis and Quincy Troupe construct Davis's life story, they are able to contribute to this myth of origin by situating Miles as the hearer of her song, and in so doing they help to construct him as a mythic figure. The mythical voice comes at the end of a chapter where Davis and Troupe chronicle Davis's musical origins. The chapter has situated him as a child of Black privilege: professional, college educated parents, his mother the musician who played violin and piano, his grandmother an organ teacher. So, his musical lineage is maternal before he meets the great musical fathers who will shape him. "I got my looks from my mother and also my love of clothes and sense of style. I guess you could say I got whatever artistic talent I have from her also" (14). It is a world that witnesses the 1917 race riot, to which he attributes some of his distrust of some white people (although his neighborhood was integrated). At the close of the chapter, he highlights two formative experiences: listening to a radio show called *Harlem Rhythms* (it was around this time he started taking music lessons) and hearing a Black church-woman sing.

At the end of the first chapter of *Miles: The Autobiography* we are told:

> But before the lessons, I also remember how the music used to sound down there in Arkansas, when I was vis-iting my grandfather, especially at the Saturday night church. Man that shit was a motherfucker. I guess I was about six or seven. We'd be walking on these dark country

roads at night and all of a sudden this music would seem
to come out of nowhere, out of them spooky-looking trees
that everybody said ghosts lived in. . . . I remember a man
and a woman singing. . . . Shit, that music was something
especially that woman singing. But I think that kind of
sound in music, that blues, church, back-road funk kind
of thing, that southern, mid-western, rural sound and
rhythm. I think it started getting into my blood on them
spook-filled Arkansas back-roads after dark when the
owls came out hooting. So when I started taking music
lessons I might have already had some idea of what I
wanted my music to sound like.

Music is a funny thing when you really come to think
about it. Because it's hard to pinpoint where it all began
for me. But I think some of it had to have started on that
Arkansas road. (29)

Ending the first chapter this way is as much a political and aesthetic
choice as it is a genealogical one. The paragraph starts emphatically
with "But before the lessons" (a preliterate state). And then we get a
description that elaborates upon that of Toomer and Du Bois. From a
country road, a country church, the woman isn't described nor is her
voice, really, but its eerie, haunting sound and its connection with
nature again seem to act as a conduit between different realities. So
Davis situates this supernatural, Southern, Black female sound as the
source of his own. Music lessons will help to structure and distill that
voice, and once again the male artist will become our only access to
that earlier, more "primitive sound."

Here are three different renderings of the myth of origin for a
written and musical art form. The myth then becomes structured in
history and helps to create a myth about the hearer. In *Miles and Me*,
Quincy Troupe returns to this story and elaborates upon it in a way
that only a poet familiar with the tropes of the tradition might do.
The quotation is lengthy by necessity. Troupe writes:

The lonely voice of an old Black church woman singing plaintively in the dusky glow of a backwater country evening, somewhere few come to, save mosquitoes or rats or evil white men dressed in bed sheets, carrying guns and flaming crosses.

In the midnight air the trains never seem to stop whistling past their wheels humming. The roads are unpaved, empty, and eerie in the twilight just before the hants come out to enter everybody's imagination and shut down those dusty roads. The voice of the old black woman floats above the shadows and trees, disembodied yet whole. It rides up there and cruises alongside the night birds circling above some unseen church or log cabin, in some out-of-the-way location back in the bushes, hidden. The voice also circles. Plaintive. Haunting. Achingly real.

And if you had the privilege of hearing that voice, perhaps you wouldn't file it away as anything special, something to imitate and relate to for the rest of your life—a reference point for your own life's experiences, making you sensitive, alert, cognizant of other beautiful, necessary things. But that's the way Miles heard it.

Perhaps the voice would remind you of a lonely trumpet sound. But maybe you wouldn't know that what you heard was special because you couldn't see that old Black woman's face. And, if you could have met her, you might have been too busy watching her chew on some snuff to see the wisdom in her old eyes. But Miles did see that face, saw it when he heard her voice. He saw the whole scene, took it all in. Knew that it was real and special and filed it away for later use. (2–3)

This rendering situates the young boy Miles in the midst of a Toomeresque landscape. The mythic tropes are catalogued: an old Black churchwoman's voice, ghosts, nightriders, and trains. This is the landscape that produced the blues. It is an age-old myth with historically specific resonance. The voice again floats above the trees—"disembodied"—removed from its source. It is "plaintive" "haunting," "achingly real." The authenticity ("real") is guaranteed by its proximity to violence and terror ("achingly"). And the young boy Miles is special from the very beginning because in hearing the voice, he can see the face. And, as if seeing the face of God, he is forever changed, is himself touched with a bit of divinity and chosen to pass it along through his horn. To hear the voice is to witness the history. To embody the voice, to play it, to represent it, is to bear witness to that history. The Miles of these passages situates the origin of one of the most original, recognizable, and innovative sounds in the music within a matrilineal lineage that is Black and Southern.

Long before his death, Miles Davis was a mythic figure. This mythology provides a way of dealing with the complexities of the historical, the human Miles. By situating his musical origins in this particular cultural narrative, he becomes as inaccessible as that old Black woman's voice, or accessible primarily as inspiration, as mythical ancestral figure who himself floats above as the source of others' creativity. Nowhere is this more evident than in Cassandra Wilson's song "Traveling Miles," which ironically returns the sound to the mythical source—the voice of a Southern Black woman.

Now, of course this particular Southern Black woman is herself an accomplished musician who had to master the complexity of Miles's music before lending her interpretation to his myth as well as her own emerging one. In one moment Wilson's Miles, he sits at the crossroads like Esu, the next he is born of lightning and thunder like Shango. His horn, like the voice of the old Black woman, emanates from the landscape and through the heavens. Though the music and lyrics and the stories they tell invoke Davis, Wilson is the teller of this tale, the conjurer of this set. Davis paved the road she travels to this space: a space she creates by producing, writing lyrics, composing music, and singing. She is in full control of the narrative.

The very first song on the CD is Miles's "Run the VooDoo Down," for which she provides lyrics. The CD closes with a "Voodoo Reprise," and this time Wilson is accompanied by West African vocalist Angélique Kidjo, who is from Benin. So not only do we have the voice of the Black Southern woman, but she is in dialogue, conversation with a voice that represents Du Bois's African forebear. The duet between the two women dominates: sung in English and in Yoruba, the song returns the sound to the "source": the Black woman's voice. And yet these are thoroughly contemporary voices whose meeting is made possible by the circulation of global musical culture. The song, like the spiritual tradition it invokes, makes connections between Africa and the Americas and provides a context for contemporary Africans and African Americans (broadly defined) to forge a common cultural identity. In other words, it isn't about sources and origins at all. Kidjo calls in Yoruba; Wilson responds in Yoruba. Eventually the women's voices overlap, and it becomes impossible to distinguish the call from the response. Finally, Wilson answers in the first-person blues narrative with which she opens the CD.

Through her rendering of Davis's music, which he claims has its origin in the absent Black woman's voice, Wilson reclaims the authority of the female voice, locating it not only as a mythical point of origin but as an ongoing participant in the construction of the music we call jazz. (An earlier and quite extraordinary attempt to render the Black female voice as central to the making of improvisatory music while also acknowledging important connections between Africa and the Americas is Amina Claudine Myers's masterpiece, "African Blues" [*Amina Claudine Myers Salutes Bessie Smith*, 1980]).

BLUE NOTES AND BUTTERFLIES

Significantly, in both instances, the Black woman's voice that calls into being a version of the United States as it wishes itself to be and the Black woman's voice as the source of Black artistic creativity, the voice expresses a quality of longing: longing for home, for love, for connection with God, for heaven, for freedom. It also seems to be a conduit between what and where we are and what and where we want to be.

Perhaps it makes perfect sense that this Black voice in the United States has become a quintessential American voice. It parallels the development of the nation. It is one of its founding sounds, and the singing Black woman one of its founding spectacles. But because it develops alongside and not fully within the nation, it maintains a space for critique and protest. Here, I am reminded of Jacques Attali, who writes that the "appropriation and control" of music "is a reflection of its power. . . . With music is born power and its opposite: subversion." He asserts, "Music, the quintessential mass activity, like the crowd, is simultaneously a threat and a necessary source of legitimacy: trying to channel it is a risk that every system of power must run."[19] The spectacle of the singing Black woman at times of crisis as well as the myth of the Black woman's voice as the source of and represented by Black male creativity are both evidence of this attempt to channel the power and subversive potential of music.

If we consider the ways that the American State Department selected jazz to represent national culture abroad during the Cold War, even as the government continued to deny Black Americans full citizenship at home, or the contemporary global circulation of contemporary hip-hop culture, then the Black woman's voice as representative American voice doesn't seem so ironic after all. When we consider the United States' uncanny ability to co-opt and commodify voices of dissent, it doesn't appear so contradictory.

However, contemporary use of Black women vocalists at times of national crisis is not always an act of cynical co-optation. (Nonetheless, because there is more than cynical co-optation does not mean that vigilance vis-à-vis this possibility can let up in moments of profound healing.) If this voice soothed white children in the early days of the nation, then later it nurtured whites in the same way those Black women nannies and mammies did, and thereby became a mark of white identity, as well, even as those so nurtured deny this mark or view it with condescension. For Black Americans, Black women's singing has articulated our most heartfelt political, social, spiritual, and romantic longings and in so doing has given us a sense of ourselves as a people beyond the confines of our oppression.[20] Furthermore, because of its ability to express human longing for love, freedom, and spiritual meaning, this voice is representative of much of the human condition, whether it be a people's longing for home or freedom or a nation's longing for an idealized vision of itself.

This was especially evident in a memorial service following the events of September 11, 2001. As part of a number of ecumenical services that took place around the city of New York, Riverside Church hosted an afternoon of dance, music, and prayer on September 16, 2001. Lillias White, an extraordinary African American vocalist who has appeared on Broadway, sang Duke Ellington's "Come Sunday." Throughout his career, Ellington and his collaborator Billy Strayhorn often used singers for wordless vocals in their extended compositions. Singers such as Adelaide Hall and Kay Davis were used like instruments in these works and produced exciting and unique performances. Ellington was steeped in the classic studies of Black life and culture (at his death he is said to have had a library of eight hundred volumes on African American history), so it is not surprising that in his own epic work inspired by that history, *Black, Brown, and Beige*, the Black female voice would come to occupy a central place. In the first section of the extended work, Black, Ellington offered "Come Sunday," a spiritual. At its initial performance, Johnny Hodges provided the exquisite saxophone solo, but subsequently Ellington added words and invited Mahalia Jackson to sing them. Her rendition was recorded in 1958. Ellington later wrote, "This encounter with Mahalia Jackson had a strong influence on me and my sacred music, and also made me a much handsomer kind in the right light" (Ellington. *Music Is My Mistress*). "Come Sunday" returns in his later sacred concerts; he even recorded an especially beautiful version with the white Swedish vocalist Alice Babs.

Listening to versions of "Come Sunday," reading accounts of Ellington's writing and presenting it make it clear that *Black, Brown, and Beige* was not only an effort to "create a tone parallel to the history of the American Negro," as Ellington has said, but that it was also a gift to the world. As an astute student of African American history and a major contributor to its culture, Ellington knew that history and the cultural traditions it has produced can be healing balms during times of uncertainty. This is one of the reasons why we so often turn to Black musical traditions during times of national crisis. When Lillias White made her offering of Ellington's "Come Sunday," she helped to articulate national pain and confusion, and one had the sense that, like Malindy, her voice took those concerns to the very ears of God. The "my people" of "Come Sunday" was initially meant to be the descendants of US-born slaves, an oppressed minority. However, in this instance, it not only articulated the confusion and pain of the diverse peoples of the United States but also of "God's People"—at any given moment the inhabitants of the United States, Jews, Black Americans, Palestinians, Iraqis, or Afro-Colombians— any people suffering the consequences of violence and oppression.

The moment White's voice joined the air, like the blue notes it rendered, it was a voice that brought with it a specific, collective blue-Black history, capable of expressing human desire. As with butterflies (whose beauty is born of fierce, difficult, and dangerous struggle),[21] that voice and those of us transported inside its sound are *momentarily* transcendent, ephemeral, beautiful, and, for a time, free before returning to a reality that might still be filled with danger and struggle.

RETURNING TO LADY DAY

A Reflection on Two Decades "In Search of Billie Holiday"

IN ALL HONESTY, when, as a child, I discovered Billie Holiday, I was looking for my father. After his death, I sought him in all the things I knew he loved, especially books and music. I listened. I read. In Lady's voice I heard something beyond what I sought of him: I heard the seeking itself. In her voice there was the longing, the yearning that I felt but had not the words to express. To long for something you will never have, to aspire for a destination you will never reach—that is what I heard in Billie Holiday's voice. In her sound there is a quiet depth, an interiority that is nonetheless reaching, aspiring. Where will she land? It is always someplace unexpected, perhaps not where she was headed, but, oh the journey there, and the place itself is beautiful; not because it satiates, but precisely because it doesn't.

When, as an adult, I wrote about her in *If You Can't Be Free, Be a Mystery*, she was the object of my desire and longing. I wanted desperately to treat her well, to refuse previous portrayals that lingered too long on the tragedy and too little on the genius. I turned away from the torch songs, the ones that are quite literally about longing, to the hip, sassy, flirtatious ones: the buoyant "No Regrets" and "Them There Eyes" of her youth; the grown woman versions of "Billie's Blues," "Fine and Mellow," or the defiant, "Strange Fruit." Listen closely to the version of "No Regrets" recorded in 1936 and you hear a woman who hasn't lived long enough to have regrets anyway. In these songs there is a biography, one that acknowledges the struggle that was her life, but that reminds us of the many ways she fought, defiantly, and at times with militancy: "Before I be your dog / I'll see you in your grave." She did not shout or yell; she didn't need to. The clarity, the full-on stare of those statements, and those to whom they are directed know better than to cross her.

But to attend to Lady closely is to be haunted by her voice, to always return to it. Listen and you will hear her everywhere: in restaurants, bars, soundtracks, and in the voices of emerging jazz and pop artists. And, that haunting suggests, you haven't finished, you need to listen more: Did you hear what you thought you heard? Listen again: Seek out later versions and contexts of the tune you thought you knew. Joni Mitchell, who claims Billie Holiday as one of her most formative influences, shares this insight about Lady Day: "Billie Holiday makes you hear the content and intent of every word she sings—even at the expense of her pitch or tone. Billie is the one that touches me deepest." Like Morrison's *Beloved*, she touches us deep "on the inside." Her voice is an invitation to listen to your own interior voices as well.

In the years following the publication of my book about her, I returned to Lady only sporadically. I had ingested so much of her, I felt I needed to breathe, I needed to exhale her. When I did return, it was to "You're My Thrill." Mitchell recorded this one in tribute to Billie on her own album of standards. There is a raw eroticism to 1949's "You're My Thrill," a wanting and desire so intense as to frighten. Is this all-encompassing desire only for a lover? Might it also be for the momentary bliss, the all-too-brief, ever-evasive peace brought on by heroin? ("Where's my will, why this strange desire?") I want here to at least acknowledge that possibility.

In truth, I initially turned to Billie Holiday, and continued to turn to her, because of what I heard in her but also because I had questions about addiction. I knew and loved people who struggled with various forms of substance abuse. It was the mid-'70s and heroin was back with a vengeance in my working-class Black community; it would soon be supplanted by crack. I had family members who fell prey to both. In the days before Narcan and safe spaces to shoot up and calls for the humane care of addicts; in the days before the face of opioid addiction was white, addicts were hunted, arrested, stigmatized and treated like shit. And in our family, in our community, their struggles were known but whispered about. No one wanted to bring attention to them, least of all the addicts themselves. This was especially the case with heroin addiction. We neither named nor talked about it. It was a loud secret. There it was, out there, waiting. Was it waiting for me?

In the loud silence, in the quest and questioning, Lady provides answers. Later, because I did not want to join the chorus of those who seemed overly consumed with Lady the junkie, I focused my attention on how poorly she was treated by the authorities and the tabloids. Indeed she had suffered the same fate of other poor Black addicts, perhaps more so because of her fame. She was arrested on her death bed for possession and use. Her secret was open.

Billie Holiday neither denied nor evaded the fact of her addiction. In all of her adult life, there are two constants: her music and her habit. And she spoke openly of each. She spoke about the difficult dance of kicking the habit, only to pick it up again. But she did more than that. In a first-person piece, attributed to her but said to have been written by William Dufty (who also wrote *Lady Sings the Blues*), she talks matter-of-factly about her addiction, without shame. "MAYBE I NEEDED HEROIN TO LIVE" she exclaims in the tabloid piece, recently republished in the very valuable *Billie Holiday: The Last Interview and Other Conversations*. I didn't deal with this version of Holiday in my own book. I don't recall consciously choosing not to, but this Holiday is a Holiday of refusal, refusing even my own attempts to present an alternative version of her life. This one isn't the kick-ass, genius woman instead of the tragic addict. This one is the kick-ass, genius, Black woman who makes no excuses for her addiction. Who explains the logic and the why of it. Who is neither apologetic nor ashamed. She notes her parents, neither of whom ever indulged in drug use, died at a much younger age than she: "Heroin not only kept me alive—maybe it also kept me from killing." Who am I to say this isn't true? Holiday closes the interview with, "I hold no regrets and I carry no shame." I didn't read this when I was first searching for answers in her life and her voice. I wish I had. There is a finality here. This is a destination, an unexpected landing: to come to the end with neither regret nor shame.

SONGS OF EXPERIENCE

Odetta

S OME ARTISTS CREATE visions of the future. Others illustrate
how to get there by showing us where we have been. In doing so,
they lay out what we are up against and remind us of our strength,
fortitude, and resilience. Their work accompanies us on the journey,
joins us in struggle, points out the way, and carries us when necessary.
Odetta, who passed away in December 2008, at age seventy-seven,
was of this latter group. She was singular, awe inspiring, and real.

With a voice that was recognizable from the first note, Odetta, a
woman known by one name, was a historian and an activist, a culture
bearer and a freedom fighter. Like Joseph's coat, her voice had many
colors. It could be soft and gentle, as in "When I Was a Young Girl"
and "All the Pretty Little Horses," or a rhythmic and hard-driving
force of nature, as in "If I Had a Hammer." She was most often
described as a contralto, but her range knew no limits or boundaries.
Singing high falsetto one minute, digging deep and guttural the next,
she was equally at home with the blues, spirituals, and work songs
of African Americans as with Anglo-American and Irish folk songs.
And yet, whatever form Odetta chose, she was first and foremost a
spellbinding storyteller. In light of this power, it is not surprising
that she became one of the major voices of the civil rights movement.
When she sang "Joshua Fit the Battle of Jericho," whether in a concert
hall or in an intimate club, she became a prophet herself—not in the
sense of foretelling the future, but in speaking truth to power. The
walls would literally shake with the final notes and the word *down*. In
the words of fellow activist and singer Bernice Johnson Reagon, "She

sang all the way in over and through." To hear Odetta live was also an embodied experience: The sound would reverberate through her listeners' bodies. And even as she narrated an ancient battle, one as old as humankind, she made it resonate with contemporary struggles against white supremacy, war, and economic exploitation, imbuing her audience with a sense of power and possibility. The walls came tumbling down in Jericho, she seemed to be saying, and they will come down again.

Although Odetta of course credited Martin Luther King Jr. with leading and directing the civil rights movement, she understood the real force of that engagement to be in hundreds of anonymous communities nationwide. In interviews, she often talked about community activists such as Rosa Parks and other people deeply engaged in social struggles in their own neighborhoods even before King arrived. For Odetta, such ordinary people laid the ground-work and prepared for when King came into leadership. Like Ella Baker, Odetta understood that social movements were built from the ground up, and she likewise saw her own role as that of servant to the cause. In 1963, she performed at the March on Washington, singing "We Shall Overcome" and something that she had recorded as the "Freedom Trilogy": a medley featuring "O Freedom," "Come and Go with Me to That Land," and "I'm On My Way." And when the marchers finally made it to Montgomery, Alabama, in 1965, Odetta sang for them upon their arrival. But she had been singing music that offered a testament to both suffering and resistance well before civil rights organizers discovered her and asked her to use her voice to help feed and sustain the movement's participants. As she recalled,

> People heard of what I was doing, our intellectuals and our politicians, and what I was doing—the folk music—fit into what their work was, so they called me in. And I was really the shy kid sitting on the side waiting for them to tell me, or someone to tell me, that it was time to go and do the song.

She also said: "The music put me in a position where those who were actually working on the problems could come and I could be of service."

Born in Birmingham, Alabama, in 1930, Odetta had experienced Jim Crow segregation firsthand before moving to Los Angeles with her family when she was six years old. It was on the train to California that she recalled the "first big wound" inflicted on her by institutionalized racism. The Black passengers were removed from the car where they had been seated, and Odetta never forgot the humiliation and pain of that experience. She attributed another wound to an educational system that taught about happy, singing slaves.

Ironically, that same educational system would lead to Odetta's musical career. A teacher in Los Angeles recognized her talent and encouraged her to take formal music training. She was being groomed as the next Marian Anderson. Throughout Odetta's teenage years she studied opera and Western classical music. But while she loved Anderson and the Western classical tradition, she knew it wasn't a good fit. She was performing in a production of *Finian's Rainbow* when she discovered both folk music and the Bay Area's bohemian scene. There, she began her reeducation. She learned to play guitar and immersed herself in the history of the blues, work songs, and spirituals. She listened to the Smithsonian Folkways recordings and read interviews with musicians by collectors such as Alan Lomax. She made trips to the Library of Congress and began buying records. The enslaved sang, it was true, but they were far from happy: They sang in order to protest and transcend their condition, and they and their progeny left Odetta a treasure trove of songs, textures, and rhythms that she made her own. Finding a history that had been absent in her schoolbooks, Odetta said the music "straightened my back and kinked my hair." (In fact, although Abbey Lincoln is perhaps more famous for being the first female Black performer to wear her hair natural, she credits Odetta with having inspired her to do so. Odetta later recalled, "What is called an Afro or natural used to be called an Odetta.")

In the mid-1960s, Odetta, Lincoln, Nina Simone, and Miriam

Makeba signaled a shift in the iconography of Black women singers. They were not gospel divas, blues queens, or sassy R & B performers. They were not supper club chanteuses or ladies of jazz. Or, to put it differently, they were not only these things. They were politically outspoken, Pan-African in their sensibilities, diverse in their repertoires, uncontrolled by record-industry categorization, and defiantly Black in their aesthetic. Yet even among this group of extraordinary women, Odetta was unique. Unlike the others, she did not become politicized after gaining fame. She already possessed a passionate anger at injustice when the folk-music scene, a politically progressive space, provided her with a vehicle through which to channel that anger. The songs, she said, healed her. She was always explicitly political, most obviously singing against racial injustice and economic exploitation. She challenged gender norms as well—not only did she perform songs associated with men, especially with Lead Belly, but when she sang blues and work songs, she would inhabit the persona of the prisoner on a chain gang. It was in this genre that her voice was most powerful, itself becoming like a percussion instrument. A shy young woman, Odetta would completely give herself over to the songs.

It wasn't until later in her life that she recorded music made famous by the blues queens, to whom she paid tribute on the 1999 album *Blues Everywhere I Go*. Here we get the socially conscious "Unemployment Blues," "Homeless Blues," and the "W.P.A. Blues," but also "Oh, Papa" and a beautiful version of W. C. Handy's "St. Louis Blues." Odetta told interviewer LaShonda Barnett: "When my generation really started to listen to the women blues singers of the twenties, thirties, and forties, we heard and felt energy. So, in response to that energy, the way we approached those songs was to holler! . . . We thought that energy came from hollering. Ms. [Alberta] Hunter would just lean back and throw it out at you. She left you alone to take it wherever you felt you were big enough and bad enough to take it."[1] But Odetta doesn't holler on *Blues Everywhere I Go*. She plays with her upper range, and then she almost sing-talks the lyrics—listen to the second verse of "Please Send Me Someone to Love." It is understated and subtle, playful yet sincere. Significantly, Odetta did not accompany herself on guitar on this album; instead, she worked with a band that included a guitarist, pianist, bass player, and drummer. As a result, like the blues queens of old, she could concentrate wholly on the lyrics.

If she attributed much of what she learned about singing to Hunter and other famous and nonfamous singers of Black folk music, she was herself the inspiration for numerous other artists. Bob Dylan famously described Odetta as "the first thing that turned me on to folk singing." Similarly, Joan Baez noted: "She was my goddess. I learned everything she sang." Odetta would never acquire the fame of Dylan or Baez, but her legacy has even further reach than theirs. As a young Spelman College student, Bernice Johnson Reagon was taken by Howard Zinn, her history professor, to hear both Baez and Odetta. Experiencing Odetta proved life-changing for the young activist singer, who began performing with the SNCC Freedom Singers around the same time and would later go on to found the all-woman a cappella group Sweet Honey in the Rock. According to Reagon, "Odetta reached back a path to me and others looking for ways to find our own way of creating." Further, Reagon has said, "She was just . . . what I needed to begin my life as a freedom fighter and a freedom singer."

Both a freedom fighter and a freedom singer, Odetta left us a body of work that has yet to be fully explored. Just as you think you know her, listen again to the beautiful, haunting 1957 record *At the Gate of Horn*. To listen closely to this album is to hear anew, to know that there is still work to be done, and that, nevertheless, there is great beauty in the struggle.

QUIET, STILLNESS, AND LONGING TO BE FREE

The Ethereal Soul of Syreeta Wright,
Minnie Riperton, and Deniece Williams

OUR STORY BEGINS, not with a woman, but with a man. He doesn't steal the show. Instead, he provides the occasion for bringing together three singers—Syreeta Wright, Minnie Riperton and Deniece Williams, and he is, in part, responsible for our having their voices on record. In 1974, Stevie Wonder produced both Syreeta Wright's *Stevie Wonder Presents: Syreeta* and Minnie Riperton's *Perfect Angel*. That same year he released his own *Fulfillingness' First Finale*, an album on which Wright, Riperton, and Williams sang background vocals as members of the group Wonderlove. Within two years, Williams released her own debut album, *This Is Niecy*, produced by Earth, Wind & Fire cofounder, the late Maurice White. The collaboration between Wonder and Wright, Wonder and Riperton, and White and Williams challenges understandings of the relationship between Black men and women during the Black power era—an era often understood as a period when Black masculinity and sexism dominated Black public culture, a period that consequently witnessed the emergence of Black women, especially writers, who worked in opposition to this masculinist domination. In light of this, I am especially interested in the contribution of these singers' voices to Wonder's unique sound and the aesthetics of the individual albums. How does each woman communicate a break with traditional notions of Black women's big-voiced vocality in American popular music? What aesthetic pathways do they forge? None of them represent figures defiantly breaking away from male mentors, lovers, and friends, nor are they instruments or victims of Black male genius. There is no Ike and Tina here. For that matter, there is no Phil and Ronnie Spector either. In these instances, the relationship between the Black male producer/artist and the woman artist reveals men who are engaged in a collaborative process as fellow vocalists and songwriters.

STEVIE'S SEVENTIES

By the time he released *Fulfillingness' First Finale* in 1974, Stevie Wonder was a major Motown talent. Between 1968 and 1971, Wonder had a number of successive hits on the R&B charts including "I Was Made to Love Her," "My Cherie Amour," "For Once in My Life," and "Signed, Sealed, Delivered I'm Yours." The latter song was cowritten with twenty-four-year-old Syreeta Wright, a Motown secretary/ singer, who became Wonder's first wife in 1970. A year later, when he turned twenty-one, Wonder's contract with Motown expired and the young couple left Detroit for New York. He returned to Motown on the condition that he get absolute creative control over his music and that he could establish his own production company. He called it Black Bull Music and used it to produce other artists' music. Along with Marvin Gaye, the newly independent Wonder ushered Motown into the '70s with a new sound: more mature, politically and socially conscious, overtly sensual, but also spiritual. Sometimes the music is haunting; at other times it is ethereal. As music scholar Guthrie Ramsey notes, "Stevie Wonder announced in the 1970s that African Americans were no longer interested in "baby, baby songs. . . . His pronouncement sought to capture the political urgency of that moment."[1] (Ramsey 217) From 1972 until 1976, Wonder released a spate of Grammy-winning albums that dominated the charts. These included *Music of My Mind*, (1972), *Talking Book* (1972), *Innervisions* (1973), *Fulfillingness' First Finale* (1974), and the double-album masterpiece, *Songs in the Key of Life* (1976). These albums yielded now-classic tunes such as "You are the Sunshine of My Life," "Superstition,"

"Living for the City," "Higher Ground," "Golden Lady," "All in Love Is Fair," and "Boogie on Reggae Woman," among others. In an interview with NPR's A Martínez, poet and critic Hanif Abdurraqib notes that this "classic period" of Wonder's career, "is fascinating not only because of the quality of the work or the fact that . . . the albums get progressively better . . . but the small window of time in which these projects were released. From *Music of My Mind* to *Songs in the Key of Life*, from '72 to '76, the corners that he was able to turn as an artist are pretty fascinating to look back on."[2]

Introspective, soulful, sensual, and political, *Fulfillingness' First Finale* was Wonder's first album to top *Billboard*'s pop charts. Background vocals were supplied by Paul Anka, the Jackson Five, the Persuasions, and Wonder's regular backup singers, Wonderlove, which at various times included Deniece Williams, Lani Groves, Shirley Brewer, Minnie Riperton, Yvonne Wright, and Syreeta Wright (no relation). By this time, Wright was divorced from Wonder, but the two continued to collaborate for the next twenty years. On *Fulfillingness*, Wonderlove is as important as the synthesizer and the clavinet in establishing Wonder's unique sound.[3] Their beautiful soprano voices bring a feminine sensuality that lifts Wonder's own vocals. Reflecting on the importance of background singers for the documentary *20 Feet from Stardom* (2013), Wonder confirms that he and other innovative artists of the 1960s and '70s broke from the past in that they, "want[ed] background singers that were free enough to put feeling in what they were singing." Wonder is speaking of popular music, because gospel (and later soul) had long offered women the space to free themselves musically. In the '70s, pop and rock opened up this space for background vocalists whom the genre had restrained in the past.[4] The word *free* stands out in Wonder's quotation. It suggests his respect for his background vocalists as artists who have something of their own to contribute to the sound they are making.

On the haunting "Creepin'", one of *Fulfillingness*' most well-known tunes, Riperton is as much a partner in a duo as she is a backup singer. This is a technique pioneered by Wonder and Wright in earlier songs such as "Signed, Sealed, Delivered I'm Yours" (1970), the first song Wonder produced on his own and the first to feature Wonderlove, consisting of Lynda Tucker Laurence, Syreeta Wright and Venetta Field, and "If You Really Love Me" (1971). In the latter tune, which Wright cowrote, she partners with him, her vocal moving into the foreground. The song appears on his album *Where I'm Coming From* (1971), which also introduces his use of the synthesizer, an instrument that became an integral part of his sound.

Wright lifts the tune, rhythmically and melodically, insistently pushing Wonder forward. The sound embodies the role she played in their relationship: She introduced him to East Asian spiritual practices, meditation, and the sitar. In turn, he encouraged her to write songs. They shared songwriting credit on a number of his hits. Theirs appears to have been a reciprocal creative relationship. Wonder also provided ample space for soprano voices in his music and featured them in the songs and albums he produced for other artists. During this period, he wrote and produced "It's a Shame," which was cowritten with Wright, for the Spinners and "Tell Me Something Good" for Chaka Khan and Rufus. Incidentally, Aretha Franklin's recording of Wonder's "Until You Come Back to Me" was one of her biggest hits, as well.

SYREETA WRIGHT

Born in 1946 in Pittsburgh, Rita Wright was the eldest of the three sopranos. When she was a teenager, her family settled in Detroit, where she eventually found work at Motown as a receptionist. While there, she sang background for a number of Motown groups, cut several demos, especially for Diana Ross, and was renamed Syreeta Wright by Motown producers. Berry Gordy and others felt Wright's voice was similar to Ross's, so much so that by 1969, she was considered for the Supremes as Ross embarked on a solo career. (To my hearing, Wright's voice is much fuller and more soulful than Ross's.) Jean Terrell ultimately replaced Ross.

Wright's collaboration with Stevie Wonder began shortly before their brief marriage in 1970 and continued for decades. She is the

prominent female vocalist on his late-'60s hits and the female soloist
on the surrealistic *Journey into the Secret Life of Plants* (1979). Wonder
produced her fist solo album, *Syreeta*, for the label MoWest in 1972.
Called "breathtaking and vastly overlooked" by music critic Mark
Anthony Neal, *Syreeta* is a beautiful and original album that contained Smokey Robinson's "What Love Has Brought Together," her
cover of John Lennon and Paul McCartney's "She's Leaving Home,"
and the Wonder original "Black Maybe."[5] Her voice is soft, but also
rich. It contains depth and fullness. On the Lennon-McCartney
tune, she brings feeling and a sound that is reminiscent of Aretha
Franklin—to a musical setting that is at times both baroque (with
instrumentation reminiscent of the harpsichord) and psychedelic.
Wright is the single songwriter on "Happiness," an expressive and
aspirational tune heralding the will to be happy as a spiritual way of
being in the world. In spite of its originality and beauty, the album
was not a commercial success, though it has become a source of inspiration for other artists, from Erykah Badu and Common to Solange.

In 1974, Wonder produced Wright's second solo album for
Motown, *Stevie Wonder Presents: Syreeta*. The album reached #116
on the US pop chart and #53 on the R & B chart. (I cite these chart
positions only as a way of indicating how the album fared commercially.) It is a beautiful work showcasing Wright's versality in genres
as diverse as soul, R & B, funk, and reggae. The most autobiographical
tune, "Cause We've Ended as Lovers," chronicles the Wright/Wonder
relationship and finds her at the top of her range. Written by Wonder
and later recorded as a dazzling instrumental by guitarist Jeff Beck,
"Lovers" is a poignant, slow ballad, filled with delicate imagery of the
early romance, and questions the possibility of an enduring friendship. The song opens with the sound of a quiet summer rain and
ethereal vocalizations of backup singers who seem to carry the tune
on angels' wings. Syreeta enters on high notes accompanied by two
guitarists, Michael Sembello and Marlo Henderson, with Wonder on
piano. The song is plaintive, introspective, quiet. It communicates
from a space of interiority, and thus offers a sense of vulnerability. It
is not an anthem to independence or anger, but an offer of compro-

mise, of negotiation, a request to have a long-term relationship shift registers, to not throw away all that has been invested in the sharing of their lives. The song asks if there is a different way of imagining the future; it asks if the former lovers can imagine something different. As the lyrics say: "Cause we've ended now as lovers, does our love for one another have to end?" This question is repeated several times, and by the final chorus, it is preceded by a melancholy hum/moan that suggests both deep pain and hope. The question leaves an opening, an invitation to a dialogue, to imagine a different future, different from what we know, different from what might be expected, different from the way it's always been done.

"Lovers" begins a suite of six songs that blend together to tell the story of a relationship and its demise. The suite's fifth song, "I Wanna Be by Your Side," with former Spinners lead vocalist G.C. Cameron, ought to be a classic R & B duet. He and Wright would record a duet album, *Rich Love, Poor Love*, in 1977. (In fact, the song seems to anticipate that Wright would find her greatest commercial success with a duet she recorded with Billy Preston, "With You I'm Born Again" (1979)).

The Cameron/Wright song builds from a sensual flirtation between the two singers to a full-scale interaction of their two voices, pulling, pushing, challenging, and fully enjoying each other. The musicality of Wright's soprano is most evident in the wordless vocalizations that embody nearly a third of the singing. The song itself does not end but the melody and chords merge directly into "Universal Sound of the World," whose lyrics offer a prayer of gratitude to God for the gift of music. Although the album closes with a playful reprise of "Sweetest Kisses" with Wonder, because it is the only real duet, the dominant male voice at album's end is Cameron's, suggesting a successful relationship with another man and with the ending expression of gratitude. The song's persona insists that the most important relationship is the one she has with God. As such, though it chronicles the demise of a love affair, the album is hopeful and thrusts toward the future. It seeks to reimagine possibility, to see new beginnings in endings. The ease with which the music moves from "I

Wanna Be by Your Side" into "Universal Sound of the World," asserts there is no secular/sacred divide. In fact, the consensual erotic relationship here is a vehicle to approach the Divine.

Though some Black stations, like Philadelphia's WDAS FM, played selections from the album regularly, it was not a commercial success. As noted above, Syreeta would finally reach a larger audience with the release of "With You I'm Born Again" (1979). She would die in 2004 at the age of fifty-eight from congestive heart failure.

MINNIE RIPERTON

Chicago-born, virtuosic, and classically trained vocalist Minnie Riperton first signed with legendary Chess Records when she was fifteen years old. There she recorded with the girl group the Gems and provided background vocals for Chess stars like Fontella Bass (Riperton can be heard on Bass's 1965 hit "Rescue Me."), Etta James, Ramsey Lewis, and Bo Didley. At Chess she was part of a dynamic music community that included studio musician Maurice White, producer Charles Stepney, and guitarist-songwriter Richard Rudolph, who would become Riperton's collaborator, soulmate, and husband. Riperton eventually joined the funk rock group Rotary Connection, with whom she recorded five albums before releasing her fist solo effort, *Come to My Garden*, in 1970. Rotary Connection was a highly regarded, musically experimental, racially integrated band. By the band's second and third albums, *Aladdin* and *Peace*, Riperton emerged from the background to lead vocalist. The psychedelic rock of Rotary Connection ushered in opportunities for them to open for major rock stars such as the Rolling Stones, Led Zeppelin, and Janis Joplin. Although the group acquired a loyal following, Chess, a blues label, didn't know how to successfully market them.

Produced and arranged by Charles Stepney, Riperton's *Come to My Garden* is a lovely gem of an album that introduces Riperton as a solo artist. To listen closely to it is to be transported to a quietly magical place of flowers, fireflies, full moons, and a "baby's dream." The first song, written by Rudolph and sung from the perspective of a flower, "Les Fleurs" is unique and exquisite, a masterpiece that should have helped to make her a star. Throughout the album, Riperton's voice is a vehicle that carries her listeners on a gentle ride. A combination of pop, opera, soul, rock, and what Stepney termed "chamber soul," this haunting album is difficult to categorize according to available marketing genres, and consequently received little radio play.

Though it was not a commercial success, *Come to My Garden* continues to be recognized as an important offering, and found immediate appreciation among other musicians, including Stevie Wonder. Wonder and Riperton met in 1971 at the Chicago Black Expo, a Black business and cultural trade exposition with daily workshops and nightly concerts. Within a year, Riperton had joined Wonderlove and can be heard on *Fulfillingness' First Finale*, especially on the now-classic song "Creepin'." As noted above, at one point in the song, Riperton briefly sings alongside Wonder rather than in the background.

By 1973, Riperton and Rudolph moved to Gainesville, Florida, to raise their two children, Marc and Maya. The couple joked that, frustrated with the whims of the music industry, they were in semiretirement. Nonetheless, they continued to make music. According to an oft-repeated story, Steve Slutzah, a college intern for Epic Records, heard Riperton with Rotary Connection, sought her out, and convinced her to return to recording. She did so with the agreement that Stevie Wonder would serve as co-producer, with Rudolph, of the album. The result was *Perfect Angel*. Wonder was under contract with Motown, so he appears on the Epic release as "El Toro Negro" and is listed as playing drums, bass drum, piano, electric piano. cymbals, and providing vocals. He, Riperton, and Rudolph wrote all of the album's songs. Of Slutzah, she later said: "I would like to give special thanks to Don Ellis and Steve Slutzah who drove through the swamp to find me and ate dinner with alligators."[6] Of her experience working on the album she recalled, "It was one of the most beautiful experiences I've had in the studio."[7]

Background vocals on *Perfect Angel* were provided by members of Wonderlove, including Deniece Williams. The album contains a number of exquisite performances, including "Reasons" (not to be confused with the Earth, Wind & Fire hit tune of the same name), which opens the record with a ripping guitar solo, followed by Riperton's proclamation about the reasons for her life, which include "the sweet delight to sing with all my might, to spark the inner light of wonder burning bright." By song's end, we hear the delight, the wonder, and the inner light as her five-octave voice lifts to the whistle register, leaves birdsong and borders on a technical sound. Her vocalizations invoke nature and technology. Instead of pitting the two sounds against each other, they exist together—a merging that refrains from being antagonistic. At Riperton's command, the one is an extension of the other. Her voice contains absolute possibility. The rest of the album is an invitation to join her in promise of the delight with which "Reasons" opens.

"Loving You" was the album's surprise hit when, at the urging of Riperton and Rudolph, it was finally released as a single. After recording the album's eight songs, Wonder had suggested Rudolph and Riperton add another in order to make the work reach the industry's standard length. They decided to contribute a lullaby they'd written for their daughter Maya. Wonder plays piano and synthesizer, and Rudolph found recordings of a mockingbird to mimic the original in their first home recording, which inadvertently captured birds singing in the background. There is no percussion, so Riperton's voice floats throughout the melody, free and soaring, giving way to the birds.

The album was released in June 1974. It presented a marketing dilemma for Epic, who found Riperton's style uncategorizable. Label executives didn't know if she was an R & B, soul, pop, or rock artist. These generic categories are confining, enclosing efforts to stifle the freedom that Riperton's music embodies. Her music resists such enclosure. The songs on the album represented her eclectic musical interest and taste. Given her experience and upbringing as a classically trained singer who was part of Chicago's vibrant music scene, one that included rock, classical, avant-garde jazz, as well as blues and rhythm and blues, Riperton resented having to be pigeonholed into categories that were considered "Black." Rock stations picked up the first single, "Reasons," but R & B stations did not. A few middle-of-the road stations began playing "Loving You," after which Epic decided to release it as a single in January 1975. After appearances on *Soul Train* and *American Bandstand* helped the song reach a broad audience, it reached #3 on the R & B charts and #1 on the pop charts. On these broadcasts, Riperton, dressed in flowing white cotton peasant gowns, her Afro adorned with baby's breath, appeared as a flower child communing with birds, a sensual earth mother, a beautiful, playful woman whose openness and free sexuality were not condemned. She represented a new version of Black bohemian femininity. The enormity of her gift, the discipline of her musical training, her pop/rock sensibilities, and her grounding in Black music traditions from jazz to R & B all lent to a hybrid, emergent aesthetic sensibility. On the cover of *Perfect Angel*, her Afro sits halo-like over a face that appears natural, adorned only with a mischievous smile. She wears no jewelry. She's dressed in overalls, without a shirt and holding a melting ice-cream cone. Though her complexion and Afro may suggest Kathleen Cleaver or Angela Davis, she is more hippie than revolutionary. Her interracial marriage and the rock influence of some of her music furthered this image. Her genre-blending music and that voice, seemingly effortless, rises above both generic and racial boundaries.

In 2017, Capitol Records released a remastered *Perfect Angel (Deluxe Edition)*, which includes the original nine songs and an additional ten extended or alternate band takes of each tune. The bonus tracks include longer jams, some songs where Wonder joins her as duet partner, and conversation, discussion, and banter between the two of them. The latter lends a real sense of the broader creative energy, collaboration, comradery, and joy that went into the making of the album.

Riperton would follow *Perfect Angel* with three other solo releases, *Adventures in Paradise* (1975), *Stay in Love* (1977), and *Minnie* (1979), which yielded the hit "Memory Lane" before she succumbed to breast cancer in July 1979. She was thirty-one years old.

DENIECE WILLIAMS

On one song on Riperton's *Perfect Angel,* "Every Time He Comes Around," Deniece Williams provides background vocals reminiscent of Cissy Houston's on the Aretha Franklin classic, "Ain't No Way." As with Houston, here, Williams leaves words behind and as such transports the song. Her voice counters the heavy rock-funk of the guitars, bass, and electric piano. The sexual promise of Riperton's lyrics along with Williams' astral sonic projections assure the encounter that follows will be both funky and transcendent! At song's end it is Williams we hear, not Riperton. Williams takes us up and out, joining the chirping bird who leads to the introduction of the next track, "Loving You."

Within two years of Riperton's critical and commercial success, Deniece Williams released her debut effort, *This is Niecy,* on Columbia Records in 1976. Wonder hoped to produce Williams as well, but after spending five years touring as part of Wonderlove, Williams, disillusioned with life on the road and hoping to save her marriage, decided to leave show business. She took a job as an operator for the telephone company, but continued to write songs, several of which she sent to Earth Wind & Fire's offices, thinking they'd be perfect for Philip Bailey's falsetto. Maurice White, cocreator and leader of Earth Wind & Fire, and his coproducer, Charles Stepney, liked the material but wanted to produce an album for Williams. By 1976, Maurice White, singer, songwriter, musician, arranger, bandleader, and producer, was one of the most widely respected figures in popular music. He contributed the sound of the African thumb piano, the kalimba, and dynamic horn arrangements to the sound of Earth Wind & Fire. The band had two number-one albums, *That's the Way of the World* (1975) and *Gratitude* (1975). A third album, *Spirit* (1976), peaked at number two. White heard Williams with Wonder and, seeking a female voice for his new label, Kalimba, approached her about recording her own songs.

Born in Gary, Indiana, in 1950, June Deniece Chandler grew up in the Pentecostal Church and planned to become a registered nurse like her mother. She dropped out of Morgan State after two years; she wasn't a very good student, but she did love to sing. Shortly thereafter, she moved to Chicago, sang in a local club and recorded a few songs for the Toddlin' Town label. Williams' cousin, John Harris, who worked for Stevie Wonder, encouraged the star to listen to her sing, and Wonder immediately invited her to join Wonderlove. By then, Williams was the married mother of two boys. Although she eventually left Wonderlove and returned home, her marriage did not last and she soon found herself a single mother lacking the support of her church community, which abandoned her because she chose to sing secular music. Nonetheless, the moral and ethical sensibilities of her Pentecostal upbringing never left her. She later recalled her own discomfort in having been separated from the Church and affirmed her feeling that music is her God-given gift and ultimately her mission and ministry. For Williams, while the music is her spiritual calling, the stage and the road are labor: necessary but not necessarily sites of joy or fulfillment.

Reminiscing about working with Wonder and White, Williams notes the difference between the two men, while recalling each experience with fondness and respect:

> "I loved working with Maurice White. He was very different from Stevie. With Stevie we'd get on stage and we'd have fun. He'd get up there and start writing new music, and we'd be singing and acting like we have rehearsed it all the time. We were very loosey-goosey, but incredibly creative. Maurice was very precise. He was putting on one of the most incredible shows in show business at that time. He taught me the business of music, and planning and executing a plan and executing a show."[8]

This is Niecy is essentially an extension of Earth, Wind & Fire's characteristic sound, with Williams on lead vocals instead of Bailey. Earth, Wind & Fire members play on the album: Verdine White is on bass, Maurice White on drums, and Sidney Barnes and the White brothers sing background vocals. Though the two share an uncommonly broad vocal range, unlike Riperton, Williams's voice contains the musical traditions of the Black Pentecostal Church. Where Riperton's high notes are light and fluttering, Williams's seem rounder and fuller.

The album is a showcase for Williams' song-writing skills, her distinct sound and vocal and emotional range. The songs are upbeat and fast paced, both lyrical and funky. Some of them, like "It's Important to Me," sound like quintessential Earth, Wind & Fire tunes. "How'd I Know that Love Would Slip Away" (which was later recorded by the group, the Emotions, who were also produced by White) is a classic White arrangement: lush and airy horns and falsetto harmonies. But it is "Free" that is the album's breakout hit. During live performances, Wonder would give the band ten minutes to perform before he joined them on stage. "Free," which Williams wrote, was one of the numbers they performed. Williams recalled, "One night I would perform 'Free' and Earth, Wind & Fire was in the audience. After the concert Maurice White's attorney came up to me and said 'boy we really love the way you sing and we really love that song you sing. Who wrote that song?' I said 'well, I did with some of the [band] members. He asked 'do you have more songs' and I said 'yes. I'm writing. I have a lot of songs."

Opening with bells, triangles, cascading trills, Williams enters with the lyric intro "Whispering in his ear / My magic potion for love," suggesting we are going to get a recipe for seduction, but when the electric guitar and drums guide her into the song's chorus, we realize it is an anthem of her independence, "And I just got to be me, free, free." Her singing is softly feminine—yes, she encourages and supports her man, "But I want to be free, and I just got to be me." The lyrics alternate between what she does to sustain a romantic relationship and her insistence that she maintain her own position, independence, and uniqueness. It's an interplay of balance between a relationship and her individuality. Starting out slow, the initial verses are almost conversational, but soon the song soars to anthem-like heights, driven by the rhythm, a slow groove. The most dramatic musical element—Williams's high notes—resound on those parts of the lyrics that emphasize the latter. The words *free* and *me* find Williams's voice at its most agile and mobile, dancing at the top of her range. "Free" is an anthem of the desire to honor conventional romantic love but to assert the necessity of honoring one's own path as well. But who can listen to this song—its heights and flights—and not also hear an anthem of Black aspiration? Soaring up there like Abbey Lincoln's "Bird Alone," a sight (and sound) of glory?

On the charts, it reached #2 on Black singles, #25 on US pop singles, and #1 on UK pop singles. Though "Free" is the breakout hit of her debut, the album's most introspective work comes at the end. Nearly eight minutes long, "If You Don't Believe" was written by Williams and songwriting team Clarence McDonald and Fritz Baskett. The horns join the background voices, and Oscar Brashear's trumpet both solos and duets with Williams to provide one of the prettiest songs of the era. A slow ballad, the song is an expression of extensive longing. There are long instrumental stretches in between Williams' vocals. Williams finds her own whistle range before taking the song into a gospel flourish crescendo with her voice riding atop acoustic and electric pianos, tambourine, and bass. The song ends not with Deniece's voice but with the trombone solo, leaving us wanting more of her voice.

The album cover for Williams's debut anticipates the visual art of Mickalene Thomas. Emerging from a background of '70s floral print, bedecked in a black-and-yellow gown, yellow feather boa, and big straw hat, Williams is bohemian flower child meets Jimi Hendrix rock royalty and Pentecostal hat-wearing church lady—hers is a merging of eclectic style sources. She appears fun-loving, inviting, and Free.

Williams has outlived both Wright and Riperton, and followed the success of "Free" with a number of hits, especially the duet, "Too Much, Too Little, Too Late" (1978), she recorded with pop star Johnny Mathis and the single pop tune "Let's Hear It for the Boy" (1984), which became her second number-one hit. She has continued to record and perform and has released several gospel songs, which have earned her four Grammy Awards. Additionally, she has had a successful career as a songwriter; her songs have been recorded by artists as diverse as Merry Clayton, the Whispers, Billy Preston, the Emotions, and Frankie Valli.

MEANING IN THE SOUND

In opera, the coloratura soprano[9] is reserved for girlish, flirtatious roles, the ingénues whose vocal agility delights the audience. In the recordings of the mid-'70s discussed in this essay, the soprano voice does not connote that innocence of the ingénue, nor is it cute. It is a sound that I call "ethereal soul:"[10] While feminine and flirtatious, it is also aspirational, sensual, spiritual, and at times otherworldly. It reaches and transports; it lifts as it climbs. Its delicacy signifies a freedom beyond the earthly realm and yet, in the case of Williams and Wright especially, it never loses connection with earthly struggles and desires. It is both embodied and transcendent.

These voices cleared a pathway for singers like Mariah Carey and most importantly for the neo-soul artists Erykah Badu and Jill Scott. While Carey and Scott possess the technical virtuosity of Riperton and Williams, Badu seems the heir to Wright's legacy. Although Common sampled "Black Maybe," on his own "U, Black Maybe," it seems the perfect song for Badu both lyrically and musically. In addition to establishing a place for the higher range in a tradition dominated by big-voiced belters and gospel and blues shouters, Wright, Riperton, and Williams also pioneered images that challenged the slick glamour of the R & B queen, by suggesting an alternative playful, soft, natural, and sensual femininity. More recently, Washington, DC–based singer-songwriter Cecily carries both their sound and their visual aesthetic forward for a new generation.

Historically, the 1970s are a moment of political possibility and disappointment. It is the era of Richard Nixon, who was elected in 1972, as the "law-and-order" president. (Shirley Chisholm ran as an independent in the race.) In March of 1972, the National Black Political Assembly met in Gary, Indiana. Attended by over eight thousand people, the convention popularized the slogan "It's Nation Time." This is an era of postindustrial cities, urban renewal, and the federal government's decimation of the most radical parts of the Black power movement. It signals a move from Black radical grassroots politics into aspirational electoral politics.

The late literary critic Barbara Christian, writing about African American literature in the 1970s, notes that the period is character- ized by a driving question: "What, in fact, does 'Blackness' mean?" Answers to this question varied, but all pointed toward the truth that "the concept of Blackness was neither simple nor fixed."[11] One answer came from a bevy of talented Black women writers: Toni Cade Bambara, Toni Morrison, Ntozake Shange, and Alice Walker. I like to think of Wright, Riperton, and Williams as counterparts, peers, and sisters in this project of redefining Blackness to include a more diverse representation of Black women. But they were not only engaged in a process of redefining Black womanhood. They were also of a time that produced the better-known and more commercially successful singer-songwriters such as Carole King, Joni Mitchell, and Carly Simon, who were also rewriting the script of American wom- anhood for a new generation.

Why does this particular moment produce these more ethereal, introspective, angelic voices? Is there a longing for something con- tained in the promise of their song? If "the blues" is formulated to mean melancholia, blues music sought to confront and transcend that melancholia. The women discussed here produce a music within that aesthetic that is also calming and peaceful, at times transcendent. They are not singing the formal blues, but Wright and Williams, in particular, are still within a blues aesthetic. Among those high notes are some bent ones, as well. Wright, Riperton, and Williams finger the edges of R & B, and they still retain its soulfulness.

Theorist Kevin Quashie argues that Blackness is commonly under- stood as "expressive, dramatic, and loud." According to Quashie, "These qualities . . . reflect the equivalence between resistance and Blackness. Resistance is, in fact, the dominant expectation we have of Black culture."[12] He offers "quiet" as an alternative metaphor for the full range of one's inner life. Wright, Riperton, and Williams engage in this aesthetic of quiet. If the blues are a music that confronts life's pain, misery, and difficulty, and by calling it out, by naming it and engaging it, offer a means to transcend it, then these three ladies do that and more. Their quiet aesthetic expresses and inspires a sense of interiority, while at the same time reaching out and pointing up toward a sense of possibility and futurity.

In this way, quiet is not opposed to resistance but a necessary component of it. The reflection, the introspection are required to sustain us for the long fight. It is a space to hear the inner voice that guides the outward action, a sound that reminds us of our humanity and that to which we aspire, a space to return to in the midst of the onslaught.

The music of Wright, Riperton, and Williams was certainly not the only music of the time. It is not the only music that came across the airwaves, but it is the sound that holds something I want to capture about the era: A sound that says, "This is also who we are, this is who we can be." It is a sound created in collaboration with men like Wonder and Maurice White, a music open to possibility and to change. It is a pre-disco, pre-hip-hop, pre-crack-epidemic sound: A sound in flight. In an essay commemorating the legacy of Maurice White, music writer Jason King describes what I hear in Wright, Riperton, and Williams: They "concocted music that meant to shield us from a world constantly threatening to harden us and turn our hearts cold."[13] They communicated a longing for freedom, and with each climbing note allowed us to experience it, however momentarily.

On a personal note, it is this element of the sonic world they created that helped me to recreate the world of my childhood and early teen years as I wrote *Read Until You Understand: The Profound Wisdom of Black Life and Literature* (2021). Their voices (along with Diana Ross's "Touch Me in the Morning" and "Theme from Mahogany" and Aretha Franklin's "Daydreaming") helped unlock the sound and feel of my household during a period I write about as both scholar and memorialist. Those voices were an archive of sound to which I returned and to which later generations of artists have turned as well. During a time when we were bombarded with images of violence against Black people, Solange Knowles's *Seat at the Table* (2016) embraced a similar sound to assert Black people have interior selves that need to be tended to. Significantly, on her Instagram, she also covered "Black Maybe" as a response to the killings of Alton Sterling and Philando Castile. She wrote: "Been singing Syreeta's 'Black Maybe' over and over again trying to comfort my weary heart . . . But what is comfort when the images of slain Black bodies left to bleed, is sketched into your being . . . over and over again." So she returned, yet again, to the quietude of this music, with its sense of healing and possibility, with its promise that another world is not only necessary, but possible.

FOLLOWING GERI'S LEAD

FOLLOWED Geri Allen's career for almost twenty years before I met her, going to hear her at clubs, festivals, and concert halls; purchasing records and then CDs; and reading any interview I could find. Surprisingly, our first meeting as friends, colleagues, and collaborators happened on the campuses of some of our nation's greatest institutions of higher learning. Geri was both an artistic and intellectual leader whose life-long project was to ensure the ongoing relevance of the music to which she'd devoted herself. She especially wanted it to be relevant to African American audiences. This informed her reading, her performance, and her pedagogical practices.

Geri's relationship to institutions of higher learning was not only as a performer, but also as a teacher, administrator, and someone deeply engaged with ideas. She served on the faculties of the University of Michigan and the University of Pittsburgh. Our mutual friend the historian Robin Kelley and I were immediately struck by her brilliance and depth of knowledge when she visited the jazz study group at Columbia University. She would go on to collaborate with that group for the next decade. However, it was an encounter with her at Emory University in March 2005 that would profoundly influence the direction of my own work. Musician, composer, and minister Dwight Andrews had organized a three-day series of panels and concerts celebrating the life and music of composer and music educator William Dawson. The conference "explore[d] the role of race and ethnicity in the creation of music and other art forms; the intersection between concert and vernacular traditions; the cross-fertilization of artistic genres; and the impact of new modes of music creation and dissemination."[1]

In many ways, this description fits the multidimensional nature of Geri's work. Always interested in the role of race and ethnicity, she became even more interested in gender. She worked closely with artists across form and genre, continued to create new music, and sought new modes of dissemination. On the second day of the Dawson conference, before my presentation, I walked into the hall and saw Geri sitting there by herself. I had a brief fangirl moment: I didn't want to disturb her, but I did want to say hello. As I walked tentatively to her, she looked up, smiled, and said, "Oh my goodness, you're the lady who wrote that book," and reached into her bag and pulled out my book on Billie Holiday. We hugged each other; I sat down, and there began one of the most important friendships and collaborations of my life. It was a transformative moment. I had been a bit of an interloper into the field of music with that book. I had not been trained as a musicologist or ethnomusicologist; I was not a musician, though I read and listened widely. Encouraged by my beloved community in the jazz study group at Columbia University, I took a chance and started writing. Although I hoped my colleagues in the academy would read the book, my ideal readers were lovers of the music both within and outside the profession. I dedicated *If You Can't Be Free, Be a Mystery* to my parents and to "Black artists everywhere."[2] And here was one of the most important artists, an ideal reader, affirming it and me. Recently, musicologist Guthrie Ramsey reminded me of the complicated reception of the book, and I told him quite honestly that I don't recall being aware of that. I explained that once Geri responded in the way she did and because of the long conversations with her that followed, I felt that the work had been received in the way that I wanted it to, and that I wanted it to be part of a larger body of writing, some but not all of which would be academic. Geri helped make that possible, not only through literal opportunities, but also because she, along with Robin, Guthrie, and musician Salim Washington became my major interlocutors. I realize now that in many ways, I was following Geri's lead. For an all-too-brief moment in time, we accompanied each other as we attempted to experience a deeper intellectual, political, aesthetic, and spiritual relationship to and through the music we loved. In the pages that follow, I will not argue that Geri Allen was a genius. I take that for granted. She was. Instead, I hope to share the multitude of ways that genius manifested itself, especially in her quiet, steady leadership.

"Following Geri's Lead" takes on multiple meanings:

First, if we follow the shape and arc of her career, what does it tell us about the history and cultures of jazz? How will it reshape the histories we write? Here, I mean not only what we write about women and jazz, but also about the broad and deep narratives we write about the music itself and her place in it.

Second, she is both collaborator and leader in many capacities. As a bandleader, she was an innovator and a visionary who created opportunities for others through her inclusive and broad outlook. As a leader in the field of jazz education, she had distinct ideas about jazz pedagogy, and with the assistance of her brother Mount, she pioneered the use of technology in presenting the music and making possible performance collaborations not bound by shared location. For instance, as part of our tribute to Mary Lou Williams in March 2013, Geri helped to organize a cyber-symposium with Internet2 technology to engage musicians and scholars in five venues simultaneously.

Finally, we might think about what it means to follow her lead as ancestor-guide, inspiration, and example.

What follows is a set of deeply personal, preliminary thoughts on Geri as leader and on the implications of her life's work for our study, playing, and understanding of the music.

Geri's 2006 Telarc release *Timeless Portraits and Dreams* opens with the spiritual "Oh Freedom," melding almost seamlessly into the Antoine Roney original "Melchizedek," which includes ample quotation of Geri's own "Angels." This purposeful opening with "Oh Freedom" serves as an invocation: "the act or process of petitioning for help or support"; specifically, "a prayer of entreaty." A lesser-known definition of invocation is "a formula for conjuring," an incantation.[3]

Geri's choice to open with "Oh Freedom" is a gesture toward all of these meanings. It is indeed an invocation, a recognition, and an invitation to the ancestors and the Holy Spirit to guide and bless the endeavor, but also a way of honoring and walking in the Black freedom struggle:

> Oh freedom, Oh freedom, Oh freedom
> over me,
> And before I'd be a slave I'd be buried in my
> grave,
> And go on home to my Lord and be free.[4]

Geri includes the lyrics in the liner notes. This is no "by and by in the afterlife" song. It is a song of resistance sung by generations of freedom fighters. With this opening, she is making an offering to the tradition and a promise to the future. The spiritual flows into "Melchizedek," which Geri says is written for the King of Peace. But the name means the "king of righteousness" and it appears in the fourteenth chapter of the Book of Genesis.[5] He is both king and priest. In bringing the two songs together, she reveals her understanding that there is no separation between the spirituals and jazz. For Geri, they are produced of the same culture, they are both sacred music, they both bear witness to a people's ongoing struggle to be free. This album includes a wide variety of Black music: jazz standards, spirituals, and jazz originals. It features Carmen Lundy, Jimmy Cobb, Ron Carter, George Shirley, Wallace Roney, Donald Walden, and the Atlanta Jazz Chorus under the direction of Dwight Andrews. There are standards like Gershwin's "Embraceable You," Charlie Parker's "Ah-Leu-Cha," and lesser-known jazz works, such as "Just for a Thrill" by Lil Hardin Armstrong. On this recording, Geri once again uplifts the work of Black women composers and includes works by Hardin, Mary Lou Williams, and her own beautiful blues "Our Lady," written not for Mary, Mother of Christ, but for our Lady Day.

This recording gives a strong sense of Geri's own sense of history. Jazz situated in, in conversation with, stretching, and at times led by other forms of Black music culture. For Geri, jazz as a form was open to a vast array of influences but deeply grounded in African American history and culture. Here we have a celebration of the music in that context.

If the invocation is "Oh Freedom," the benediction is "Lift Every Voice and Sing," otherwise known as the Negro national anthem, with which Geri closes the recording. In her most recent book, *May We Forever Stand: A History of the Black National Anthem*, the brilliant Imani Perry writes of the song:

> It tells the singer to see herself or himself as emerging magnificently through struggle. It nurtures an identity rooted in community. It is a song that moves regionally and internationally, yet holds fast to a sense of particular belonging. It has had a remarkable longevity due to both its beauty and its vision.[6]

Certainly the same might be said of *Timeless Portraits and Dreams*, but most important, of Geri's own sense of the history of Black music and especially the history of jazz, which also moves regionally and internationally yet holds fast to a particular "belonging."

I think of this album as a guide through Geri's own understanding and conception of the music she played and the way she believed it should be taught and passed on. First, jazz is not separate from other forms of Black music. It is born of those forms that precede it and helps to shape those that follow. It is always in conversation with these other forms, as well as music born of different cultures. This understanding informed her pedagogy. She believed the student of jazz needs to know the history and context of its birth and its development. She was a voracious reader and one of the most intellectually curious people I knew. She kept up with the latest jazz studies scholarship, not only to be informed by it but also to judge the degree to which it respected the context, the history, and the political and cultural import of the music. In one of the best interviews I've read, conducted by Angélika Beener, Geri asserts:

It's OK for people to have opinions, that's fine . . . and it's OK to publish opinions, and that's fine. I feel strongly that there is a renaissance of amazing scholars in this area of African American music and culture. I'm looking at the writers, people like Farah Jasmine Griffin, people like Robin D. G. Kelley, and George Lewis . . . people of that ilk, who really are establishing a level of responsibility for how we will write about the music and how we talk about the music. And I just feel that these are the ways to look, [instead of] getting so upset about some of these other things that are not really dealing with the real core of what is happening in the culture. Like the book that Kelley did on Monk . . . that sets the bar of what the expectation of jazz scholarship should be . . . real, substantive research on the music, based on a respect for the cultural criteria accepted by the field . . . [and] the folk. The music truly deserves this level of care. Ten years, you know, Kelley did that research. That kind of time and that kind of love and appreciation for the subject matter, is where I want to go personally to find out, what the facts were, on a much deeper level. These discussions about our innovators' contributions are thrilling. And I think we're going to see more of this.[7]

"A level of responsibility"—it resonates. Her sense of responsibility to the music, to its past and its future, to her peers and her students, a sense of responsibility that required a profound discipline, was daunting. In emphasizing the importance jazz history and tradition held for Geri, I by no means want to suggest an aesthetic conservatism on her part. This was not the case. For Geri, jazz was innovation. Among her earlier recordings were Afrofuturistic ventures. She is one of the few pianists to play with Ornette Coleman. She worked with Betty Carter, and Cecil Taylor was a major inspiration to her. So Geri was no traditionalist in the vein of Wynton Marsalis. She saw the music on a continuum. I think her emphasis on history and tradition stemmed from two things: (1) what she feared was an effort to de-emphasize jazz as an African American form, a living tradition whose practitioners need to know, acknowledge, and honor it as a product of Black culture; and (2) her desire to influence and inform the way that history was represented so that women and avant-garde artists were not marginalized or ignored.

A Conversation with Mary Lou was a theatrical piece born of the collaboration between Geri, actress S. Epatha Merkerson, and me. And although I will gesture toward the making of our shared projects, I want to talk about them in the broader sense of the kinds of conversations and collaborations Geri initiated and sustained with the other artists and with the tradition itself.

Conversation and dialogue are the words that most often come to mind when I think of Geri as leader. On the bandstand, even when she is the leader, she is in conversation. She may set the tone, suggest a direction, but always she seems to say, "What do you think?" "Let me hear what you have to say." She is creating space for your response, your questioning, and your questing. Sometimes she is goading you: "Go on . . . Go on . . . Keep going . . . Jump! . . . OK, now come back . . . I got you." Even Geri the soloist is in conversation, with those who inspire her, with the various emotions within her, with God, with herself, and with the future. Collaboration is a form of conversation as well. The source of my greatest joy, and not a little bit of frustration, were the collaborations I embarked upon with Geri and Epatha.

It all started with a conversation. A phone call and a series of discussions about her idea to do a show at the Apollo that would honor the great jazz women who performed there. She asked me to be the historian on the project, and I agreed. And later, she set up a meeting between herself, me, and Epatha, who had also agreed to work on the project.

It's an afternoon, possibly January, during the week, a Tuesday or a Wednesday, because I run from a seminar I conduct at the Schomburg to Epatha's Harlem abode. She greets me with a warm smile and down-to-earth spirit. She, Geri, and I sit at a large round table . . .

eating, drinking ... was it tea? Wine? I don't remember. I just know we are immediately comfortable. Three sisters who love this music and love Black people, and we are laughing and singing, and Epatha is pulling up the music, and I am recalling obscure tracks and anecdotes, and before you know it, we are mapping this thing out. Geri is happy, quietly encouraging, laughing. Soon it becomes clear, when we start talking about our Queens, that we are also talking about folk not conventionally recognized as jazz artists. Our discussions reach the blues, gospel, and soul royalty, and pretty soon we get to Bessie, Mahalia, and Clara Ward, and I'm coming up with anecdotes about when this one performed and when that one performed, and at some point, someone asks, "How can we organize this?" And one of us comes up with a conceit and a narrative about the Apollo as a sacred space, as hallowed ground. And at some point, I don't remember when, Geri says, "I'm going to need somebody to write the script. Farah, you can do that." "No, I cannot." "Yes, you can, you just did. Epatha, you direct."

And before either of us can object, Epatha is directing and I am writing the script, and our debut show will be at the Apollo with Dianne Reeves, Lizz Wright, Tia Fuller, Terri Lyne Carrington, and Geri's trio with Kenny Davis and Kassa Overall. Eventually, what feels like a million more people join, including the Howard University a cappella choir, Afro Blue, the DJ Val Jeanty, two hoofers, and Maurice Chestnut. Because I add a bit about Pearl Bailey and Moms Mabley, the oh-so-talented comedic actress Karen Malina White is on board. At the last minute, perhaps two days before our first performance, Geri would add an organ. But that was all to come. On that Tuesday or Wednesday in Harlem, I left Epatha's apartment elated and scared to death. *What have I gotten myself into? She needs a playwright, not a historian.*

Together, the three of us embarked on a roller-coaster ride that started with a conversation, and that included many more between us, the tradition we honored, Geri's vision and genius, and all the other artists on that stage, and the brilliant, sophisticated, all-knowing Apollo audience who spoke to us during the show, during intermission, and afterward. "I love it, but how could you have Sarah Vaughan singing 'I'm Glad There is You?' when that was Gloria Lynne's song first and she sang it here at the Apollo and she was from Harlem. I know, 'cause I was here." I look at Epatha with a look that says "I told you so." And she breaks out laughing and we hug each other because we got through it and were the better for it. Now she was a director and I was a scriptwriter, something we both aspired to be but had not articulated to Geri. She just knew and she presented the opportunity and said, "Do it." And we had to rise to the occasion because you have to bring your best when you are writing for and directing Dianne Reeves, Lizz Wright, and Terri Lyne Carrington. That demands a certain level of responsibility and discipline.

I don't know about others, but for Epatha and me, collaborating with Geri went something like this:

> GERI: "Hello, ladies, would you like to take a ride on a carousel with me?"
> FARAII: "Why yes, I love carousels. They are pretty."
> EPATHA: "They are boring, but I like the company, so let's go."

And then as we approach it, I ask, "Where are the horses?" And Geri says, "Oh, there are no horses." So, we get on and we strap ourselves in, and before long, we realize there are no horses because it's not a carousel, it's a roller coaster. And we realize it's not just any roller coaster, but a super-duper, triple-loop cyclone or something. And Epatha and I are holding each other screaming. But not Geri; she's just smiling because she can see the whole thing and while we are freaking out about being upside-down, she already sees the end and knows we will survive. We get off, exasperated, and declare: "That's it. Can't do it. My nerves can't take it." Geri is gracious and thankful, and bearing gifts. The evening ends and we are giddy; days later, we have the postperformance meeting to evaluate what worked and what didn't. Geri sweetly says, "Would you ladies like to go on another ride with me?" And we both say, "Yes, can't wait."

Collaborating with Geri was exhilarating and exhausting, and you are a better thinker and artist for it. You have grown creatively and spiritually, and you have been so steeped in love that you can't wait to return. Like the improvising artist, you bring all that you have to the moment, and then you step out on faith.

We learned to trust the process, to trust the vision, even as the nuts and bolts of making it happen seemed impossible. We went from the Apollo to three nights at Harlem Stage, where we debuted *A Conversation with Mary Lou* featuring the remarkable Carmen Lundy, thanks to the tireless Ora Harris and the Kennedy Center. And the process was a true collaboration. I wrote, they read, I rewrote. Epatha saw the stage and might tell us that what we thought we could do, we couldn't do, but we could do this instead. Epatha and I created ways to highlight Geri; we let her genius guide us, and the music guided all of us. We did it all in service to the music, and for Epatha and me, out of love for Geri. And in return, we got each other and these creative projects that were bigger than any one of us together.

From her reading of my book on Billie Holiday, Geri heard something in the sound of my writing, in the sound of my voice, spoken and written. "Your writing is very musical," she would say. And she would try to get me to write a spoken word piece to be on one of her albums. "I'm a bad poet," I'd say. But she would push back: "Would you write the liner notes?" "I'd be honored." Geri had a sense of your capacity and your gift. She'd insist that you live up to it, that you step outside of your comfort zone. At first, she would feel out what felt safe and lay the foundation for you to perform. "Read from the Billie Holiday book while I play 'Our Lady.'" "Write the liner notes." And then, certain that you could do something different, something more, certain of her vision and the broader picture, she would "encourage" you to take bigger risks by placing you in situations where you had to leap out on faith, and her belief in you.

An exploration of Geri's collaborations reveals her insight as a thinker and a visionary. Her gift for seeing the whole picture, hearing its sound, was extraordinary. I think one course of study about Geri would be an exploration of her collaborations: with her own band, with Terri Lyne and Esperanza, and with Terri Lyne and David Murray. It might venture out to a consideration of her interest in technology and explore the collaboration with her brother in introducing innovative technology into performance and the classroom.

As an aside, I want to say something brief about Geri's commitment to ensuring that the music reached audiences, especially Black audiences that might not otherwise hear it. This was yet another way she sought to keep the music relevant. I helped her organize a series of residencies. She did them at Harvard, Princeton, and the University of Pennsylvania. Whenever possible, she held master classes for the students, performed with the jazz band, and gave a concert with her own band. But she also requested that we set up performance presentations at local high schools. In New York, we did it at the Thurgood Marshall High School, and Geri knew that Kassa Overall and Maurice Chestnut could attract the students' attention with hip-hop rhythms. She wanted the young people to know that all jazz was their music, that they could bring themselves and the sounds of their generation to it. She seemed to say "Come on in. Join the conversation." As a professor of music and later as a director at the University of Pittsburgh, she sought out the best high school–aged musicians and built relationships with high school music teachers and church directors of music in search of musically talented young people. At the Apollo, our extravaganza was part of the Harlem Jazz Shrines Festival, a series that takes place every spring in different Harlem venues, theaters, churches, restaurants, and bars. A ticket to each performance cost $10. Our Great Jazz Women of the Apollo was held on Mother's Day weekend, and one of the stagehands (someone needs to write a book about the Apollo's stagehands; I actually wrote them into the script, and they were among the first to take a bow) thanked us for having the show during Harlem Jazz Shrines because he bought tickets for ladies from the senior center/nursing home and also for a group of mothers from a nearby shelter for mothers and children. Beautiful things happen in Geri's wake. She set things in motion, and there is a shimmering ripple effect, much like her shimmering playing on the piano. Where Geri led, love and beauty followed.

Geri found inspiration and influence far and wide. She was not bound by the tradition she held in such reverence. She was freed by it. As much as she was grounded in a sense of community, it was the basis from which she soared. When we think of her, we should also think of her as a cosmopolitan artist who traveled widely in her music, her ideas, and her person.

That's one of the reasons I so love her recording *Flying Toward the Sound*; it encompasses her journey in this life and beyond. The recording, though solo piano, provided yet another opportunity for collaboration. Carrie Mae Weems provided the photograph, cover concept, and art films. I wrote the liner notes. While I often visited Geri in the recording studio, it was a special treat to spend time on the set when Weems was making the films. In my liner notes for that recording, I wrote:

> She hails from a culture that celebrates flight as a metaphor for freedom. From the folk tales of the enslaved Africans who abandon the fields and fly back to Africa to the fugitive slave narratives of the 19th century; from Paul Laurence Dunbar's exquisite poem of 1899, "Sympathy," with its singing caged bird [the inspiration for Maya Angelou's "I Know Why the Caged Bird Sings" (1970)] to Abbey Lincoln's "Bird Alone" (1991), African American culture is dominated by images and sounds of movement, mobility, fugitivity, and flight. Geri Allen is nothing if not deeply rooted in the cultures of Africans in America. She is also a highly accomplished, cosmopolitan, world-class artist. As such, like the music she plays she is always open to new influences.[8]

Upon hearing Native American legends, especially "Legend of the Flute," that resonated with her own people's love of music and near-mystical celebration of flight, she found inspiration as well. *Flying Toward the Sound* is a musician's journey. She conceived of the project in relation to three modern jazz pianists in whom she found inspiration and in whose lineage she falls: Cecil Taylor, McCoy Tyner, and Herbie Hancock. She does not play their music, instead she plays toward it, around it, through it, to her own voicing. The suite is titled "Refractions." Like light entering through a prism, Geri envisioned the project as the music of Taylor, Tyner, and Hancock, entering the prism that is herself, only to be bent, reshaped, and colored anew, resulting in a flight of light and sound.

Until the recording of *A Child Is Born* in 2011, I would say *Flying Toward the Sound* was her most introspective and spiritual work. Here, she is an artist looking deep within and making connections between what she finds through this practice of interiority and that of the larger world. In nine original compositions, composed during her Guggenheim Fellowship, she engages the music of her guides to meditate on the meaning of family, particularly motherhood and creativity: "Faith Carriers of Life" and "Your Pure Self (Mother to Son)." But it is "God's Ancient Sky" that is the project's spiritual centerpiece. It flies to places of great spiritual power—the Western Wall of Jerusalem, St. Mary's of Zion in Axum, Ethiopia—and then over the great natural cathedrals—the ocean, the desert, the forest, and the mountains. The repetition played with her left hand gives us drama and a sense of permanence, it moves us along, while the melody played by the right is broad, spacious, and panoramic—it flies. At times, we are given roots, complex and twisted, but roots nonetheless, while the right hand takes ever more risks. It glides, sails, dips, and soars. In its entirety, the song is almost sixteen minutes long, embodying both the groundedness of a daily spiritual and artistic practice that allows for flights of creativity and improvisation in life and in music; parental love that provides a safety net for children to soar; and the jazz tradition that does the same for innovators such as Taylor, Tyner, Hancock, and Allen.

All the pieces that precede "God's Ancient Sky" lead to it as light going through a prism. The first three are devoted to Tyner, Taylor, and Hancock. She introduces themes associated with each artist and then integrates them throughout. "Flying Toward the Sound" is for Tyner. "Dancing Mystic Poets at Twilight" is a highly percussive, polyrhythmic piece not unlike the compositions of Taylor, who inspired it. "Red Velvet in Winter," for Herbie Hancock, is orchestral, making use of the full range of the piano, a kaleidoscopic world in itself. Here, Geri leads and we gladly follow to a sonic universe of her making.

Let us imagine a study of jazz and a construction of jazz history in which she is not an addendum—"a woman in jazz"—but where she is a central component in any narrative we write, where it is impossible to think about the trajectory of the music without thinking about her. Where we place her in a lineage of those who influenced her and those whom she influenced, perhaps especially pianists, but not only pianists. Vocalists, percussionists, bassists, horn players, and those of us who are not musicians but actors, dancers, writers, photographers, painters, as well. She hailed from a culture that celebrates flight as a metaphor for freedom, and through her music and her grace, she touched that longing, that struggle, and that capacity for freedom in all of us.

II.

LOOK WHERE YOUR HANDS ARE NOW

At the end of Toni Morrison's *Jazz*, the narrator speaks directly to the reader:

> I can't tell anyone that I have been waiting for this all my life and that being chosen to wait is the reason I can. If I were able I'd say it. Say make me, remake me. You are free to do it and I am free to let you because look, look. Look where your hands are. Now.

With this evocative paragraph, which I have always heard as a seductive whisper, the narrator is revealed as the book itself. Morrison establishes the relationship between book and reader as an intimate one; she insists that the act of reading is an act of making and remaking both the book and the reader. The essays of this section offer critical readings of a number of books or describe my ongoing relationship with the work of single authors. All of these pieces seek to model reading as a process of intimate intellectual engagement. Because many derive from my teaching, which is an invitation to my students to join me on a journey of discovery, it is my hope that the essays will invite and assist other readers to enter, explore and further appreciate the books and writers considered here.

WRESTLING TILL DAWN

On Becoming an Intellectual
in the Age of Toni Morrison

Now I discover that in your company it is myself I know.
That is the astonishing gift of your art. . . .
You gave us ourselves to think about, to cherish.
　　　　　—Toni Morrison, "James Baldwin: His Voice
　　　　　Remembered; Life in His Language" (1987)

I.

Summer brought Bomb Pops, endless games of Double Dutch, *Wild-flower* by New Birth, and *Sula.* In those days, everything was measured "before Daddy died" and "after Daddy died." That summer was certainly after Daddy died, but not too long after, because I was still a girl, not yet a teen, still jumping rope, still missing my daddy. And into that big, empty space came books and music and daydreams of endless summers. There was never any shortage of books, music, and daydreams. And yet, somehow, there was never enough.

The boys in South Philly wore their hair cut close, Black Muslim-style, and girls not much older than me were starting to get pregnant. My Pierce Street friends and I passed around paperback books after dog-earing the sex parts. There was *Howard Street, Daddy Was a Number Runner, Black Boy,* and there was *Sula.* Some of these books had the stamp from the Point Breeze branch of the Philadelphia Public Library, others belonged to the Philadelphia school system, and still others had been previously owned by some unknown somebody.

No one really understood Sula, but some of the older girls did say that she "slept with" her best friend's husband: "How could she!!!" (I don't think I knew what "slept with" meant.) Mostly, I remember the sound of the words and that some of the people seemed familiar. I *knew* people who used drugs like Plum did. I *knew* Plum—so sweet, so high. I knew madmen like Shadrack who had gone to Vietnam or "the white people's college" or on a bad drug trip only to return home "not right in the head." And Sula herself reminded me of my aunt Eunice, who always said had she been a boy she would have run away forever, but she was a woman, so she always ended up back home. Like Aunt Eunice, but more like Sula, I wanted nothing more than to leave and come back after a long mysterious trip somewhere out there. And I had a friend like Sula's best friend Nel, only her name was Sandra and I loved her.

The cover of the book had a thin brown woman kneeling down, face surrounded by a halo of an Afro. And there was a yellow rose, like the ones my aunt Eartha grew. This was a time when Black women graced the covers of books: Angela Davis on her autobiography and the beautiful model on Toni Cade's *The Black Woman*. (At the time, I did not know Morrison edited both women's books.) But this one was different; it was a painting, not a photograph.

Sula contained a world not unlike my own: a world where magic occurred, except we didn't think of it as magic. I wanted to live in those pages where ordinary life took on a deeper dimension because of the sound and order of the words used to describe it. I wanted to hear those words, to be as beautiful as they were, to stay forever enveloped in their embrace. The very fact of this book, with the soft brown woman on the cover, said I could and should read and dared to suggest that maybe, just maybe, one day I could write, as well. In *Sula*, I found music in words.

II.

At the Baldwin School for Girls in Bryn Mawr, Pennsylvania, we didn't read any books by Black authors. There was an essay by James

Baldwin in eleventh grade English; he and Richard Wright joined Truman Capote and pages of others on the summer reading list. As a scholarship student at this elite school, I had been given detailed instructions by my mother: You are not there to make friends; you are there to get As. Your identity as a Black girl is not to be found there. It probably won't even be affirmed. That is why you come home. That is why you "remember where you come from." I did make friends there. And I learned to read critically and to write. We read Chaucer in Middle English, the Metaphysical poets, *Hamlet*, *Wuthering Heights*, *Crime and Punishment*, *Portrait of the Artist as a Young Man*, *The Love Song of J. Alfred Prufrock*, *Long Day's Journey into Night*. The Baldwin School nurtured what had been a longstanding passion for literature. In learning *how* to read, this I knew for sure: Toni Morrison could hold her own in this company. Her prose could withstand the most rigorous of readings. And, just as she seemed to know the world from which I came, she also seemed to know this one. I could connect her to these writers. She seemed to speak this tradition at the same time that she spoke to me. At this time, she led the pack of my growing collection of Black women writers: Gwendolyn Brooks, Toni Cade Bambara, Maya Angelou, and Ntozake Shange. I read these writers on my own: outside of school but away from my friends on Pierce Street.

Along with these new authors, I'd acquired another group of friends, girls from my old magnet middle school, especially Vanessa Garrett, and a small group of girls who also attended Baldwin, many of whom shared my secret passion for the emerging group of Black women writers. These writers were my spirit guides and my word warriors. These women were a bridge between the world of South Philly and the world of the Baldwin School and beyond. I met Pecola Breedlove and wept. To have limned the depths of that tragedy made Morrison a witness. She *saw* Pecola's reality and told her story to a world that had refused to listen to a Black girl's cry. To bear witness: *This is what white folk do to us and this, in turn, is what we do to each other*. I was a dark-skinned girl who had been called *BLACK* with the venom that only ghetto children can hurl the word. And yet, I came from a fiercely protective family, so my experience was more that of Claudia and Frieda than Pecola. At times, within my family, I was as precious and adored as Maureen Peal! They tried fiercely to protect me from the color prejudice of my own people and the tactics of older men who often preyed upon girls that, like Toomer's Karintha, ripened too soon. (There was a copy of *Cane* in Baldwin's library.) Karintha, whose "skin is like dusk on the eastern horizon . . . [w]hen the sun goes down."[1] But it was to Sula I returned again and again, because even in death she was less defeated than either Karintha or Pecola. At this stage, I turned to Morrison not only to find a reflection and affirmation of a world that was familiar to me. This was the beginning of my development as a literary critic. I didn't know that then; I wanted to be a creative writer. I began to read her not only for the stories she told but for the way she told them.

When allowed to pick my own texts for one of my final papers, I chose *Sula* and *for colored girls who have considered suicide*. I focused on the tree imagery with which both books end. One describing a transcendent death: "'Sula?' she whispered, gazing at the tops of trees. 'Sula?' Leaves stirred; mud shifted; there was the smell of overripe green things. A soft ball of fur broke and scattered like dandelion spores in the breeze."[2] The other describes a recommitment to a transcendent life where the persona is taken up by the tree, caressed in its branches, kissed by the wind, and transformed into morning dew.[3]

In both instances, the trees are associated with, embody, and nurture the spirits of these complicated, tortured women. In both instances, the trees contain a life force that ensures a kind of immortality and that acknowledges the sacred in the individual.

During the spring of 1981, Diane Jarvis Hunter, one of the best English teachers the world has produced, gave me the *Newsweek* with "Toni Morrison: Novelist" on the cover. Fellow members of our Black student union, which I led, gave me a hardback copy of *Song of Solomon* as a going away gift. I read *Tar Baby* that summer.

Toni Morrison: Novelist. What did she have to know to write like this? What did she read? Did she write at dawn? At midnight? Where and how far did her imagination roam?

III.

At Harvard, I lost—then found—my way. I still loved to write, but I realized I wasn't a very good poet. (That was obvious once I read my classmate Fred Moten's work.) I wrote for *The Crimson* but soon learned I didn't want to be a journalist. I fell for a dark chocolate boy whom I loved almost as much as I loved books. During one of our multiple dramatic, tumultuous breakups, he gave me a gift: two books he'd seen in one of Harvard Square's multiple bookstores, Gloria Naylor's *The Women of Brewster Place* and Mary Helen Washington's *Midnight Birds*. He knew my mind and my heart's true longing. As a student, I met Maya Angelou, Paule Marshall, Toni Morrison, and Alice Walker, all of whom came to read and give talks. My professors, Nathan Huggins and Werner Sollors, made sure I got to meet each of them. Marshall and Morrison were the kindest. Once again, outside of class, I began to read those pamphlets published by Kitchen Table Press; I discovered the Combahee River Collective, the essays and poetry of Audre Lorde. I discovered Adrienne Kennedy and Frances Harper and Zora Neale Hurston. (I also started to read Edith Wharton—who blew, blew, blew my mind.) Harper would be the subject of my senior thesis, but it was Alice Walker who dominated my literary psyche. Mostly because she published *In Search of Our Mothers' Gardens* and helped me to really, really appreciate the essay as a literary form. Yes, *The Color Purple* came out then, and I admired it almost as much as *Meridian*. But it was those essays, those critical, literary, personal, and political essays that set the stage for the future I saw unfolding before me. The essays on Hurston were influential, yes, but she also wrote about Flannery O'Conner *and* Frances Ellen Watkins Harper. Because of Walker, I began to settle into, became comfortable with, a form that would claim me: the nonfiction essay. And I learned that criticism could indeed be poetic.

As for my relationship with Ms. Morrison—I began to distrust her seduction of me. And I grew angry because of all the damaged and dead women in her corpus. I wanted answers, and she left me with too many questions. Truth be told, I was not yet ready for her, not for what she still had to offer me. There were others who gave voice to my pain and my longings, others who affirmed the space from which I had come, others who wrote bold and beautiful language, others who said this is what it might mean to be a Black woman in a white man's world. Morrison seemed to say that and something more, something deeper. And she questioned that framing: that we were living in a white man's world. In fact, she seemed to think it was her world, to be made and remade according to her liking. She seemed to be saying something big and expansive, and I did not yet have the intellectual tools to wrap my brain around it. This was the moment—a moment, one of many—when I became aware of my own intellectual and imaginative limitations. I understood the story, but I needed to know more. She eluded even as she continued to beckon.

IV.

And then came *Beloved*. I started it three times. During the spring semester of my first year in graduate school, I came home to Pierce Street. I sat on my mother's couch after she had gone to bed, and I opened the book again. As I had done with Cornel West's *Prophesy Deliverance!* only months before in that same spot, I opened the book and did not close it until well after dawn. I read it all night long. I read parts of it aloud. I scribbled notes and expletives in the margins. I cried at its pain and at its beauty. I thought "Aw, Toni . . . " and "Damn, Toni!" I heard the poetry and I saw the colors. By daybreak I was spent. She had whipped my ass and blessed me at the same time. I sat in a state of awe at the accomplishment and at the witness. I had come face to face with her genius. My head buzzed like a madwoman. *Could she have? Did she really?* I read *Beloved* in the midst of other reading. I was also encountering Lukács, Adorno and Benjamin, Foucault and Gramsci, Fanon, Spivak and Said, the Western Marxists and the French feminists. Cornel West, John Blassingame, Robert Stepto, Hazel Carby, Michael Denning, Jean Agnew, and Margaret Homans were among my teachers. Saidiya Hartman, Errol Louis,

Tera Hunter, and Lisa Sullivan were my classmates, teachers, and intellectual compatriots. At every encounter, my intellectual equilibrium was shattered and rebuilt.

In this context, Toni Morrison was not only Novelist. The implications of her fiction on thought were becoming clearer. She was engaging, informing, and shaping my understanding of history, narrative, power, domination, and language. Her prose started to shape and define my sense of the relationship between space and time. She taught me about form and content. In Morrison there was no ahistorical celebration of fragmentation; fragmentation was not only psychic—it was real; it was literal. She understood that premodern, modern, and postmodern forms of power operated on Black bodies simultaneously. She knew that Black diasporic peoples were the first modern, indeed the first postmodern, subjects. Herein lie the answers. And, she did all of this in absolutely breathtaking prose. No ugly language here. Her words opened doors, welcomed you in, insisted you become involved with them. After reading *Beloved*, I knew I could write about my people and call them my people and do so with a sense of awe, wonder, and a critical sensibility. I also knew that "my people" contained multitudes.

Cornel West invited Saidiya and me to come to Princeton because Ms. Morrison would be giving an inaugural lecture. "I will introduce you to her." It was February. It was freezing cold. We left New Haven at daybreak, took Metro-North to Grand Central, the subway to Penn Station, New Jersey Transit to Princeton Junction, the Dinky to Princeton, and then we walked up. It was a pilgrimage. In those days, we traveled near and far to see and hear Toni Morrison and Hortense Spillers. Morrison gave a talk that shared much with her essay "Unspeakable Things Unspoken," and she read from what would become the final pages of *Jazz*. That talk and reading changed the course of my intellectual life. Until that moment, I had been wavering between a dissertation on Black women writers and the legacy of slavery and one focusing on Black artists and the African American migration experience. I was leaning heavily toward the latter, but the former seemed hipper, trendier. It would allow me to

demonstrate my ability to engage some of the theorists I'd been reading who made connections between the body and writing, especially
Luce Irigaray, Hélène Cixous, and Jacques Lacan. However, I left
Princeton knowing that I would write about migration and that to do
so would broaden my intellectual contribution to a body of knowledge about Black peoples. I also left Princeton committed to writing
about literature and the arts with clarity and the conviction of my
own voice.

Later, while constructing a framework informed by Antonio
Gramsci, Michel Foucault, Georg Simmel, and Richard Wright, I
realized that my most important theorist would be Toni Morrison.
Through her criticism and her fiction, she gave me critical categories
like the ancestor, and she suggested a literal and narrative space that I
would theorize as "safe space" or "the South in the city"; she helped to
identify the literary history I sought to document and was situated at
the center of the shift in dominant portrayals of migration that would
take place after the civil rights movement. Prior to that movement,
Richard Wright's representation of the South and the migrants' experience of urbanization dominated (in spite of Hurston's presence).
In this view, the South was the site of the crime: our enslavement,
brutalization, and exploitation. The city enacted a more sophisticated
form of power, one that constructed us as urban subjects. It kept us
confined and contained in ghettos and limited our social mobility
even as it created our desire for a life denied us. With *Song of Solomon*
Morrison reconsidered the South. Yes, it was the site of the crime
against our humanity, the site of our suffering. But it also housed the
bodies and spirits of our ancestors, whose blood nourished the soil
and established our birthright. Furthermore, unlike Albert Murray's
South to a Very Old Place, Morrison's South was very African.

That talk at Princeton and a rereading of her oeuvre also affirmed
what my reading and experience taught me: that mobility and migration were the dominant tropes of Black life in the modern world;
"Move. Walk. Run."[4] While *Jazz* did not appear in the dissertation, it
would become the subject of the final chapter of the book.

V.

Toni Morrison's criticism was important, yes. "Unspeakable Things Unspoken," "The Ancestor as Foundation," and eventually *Playing in the Dark*. But the fiction, especially *Song of Solomon* and *Beloved*, also had tremendous theoretical and philosophical implications. In her corpus she put forth an intellectual agenda just as powerful as that of Eliot or Joyce or Wright or Ellison. She had their intellectual ambition, yet she wasn't as beholden to the Western Literary Tradition. She certainly wasn't dismissive of it; in fact, she was as grounded in it as were they. But it did not seem to mystify or mesmerize her. Nor did she find the nationalist implications of the Black struggle stifling. She seemed genuinely fond of Black people, certainly more so than did Wright and even Ellison; she was not afraid of painting them in a critical light. Yet, unlike James Baldwin, she did not seek the role of spokesperson. In the pages of *Paradise,* she gives us dark-skinned town founders, so imprisoned by memories of their own victimization by lighter-skinned Blacks that they become the victimizers. (I finished *Paradise* on a plane from Illinois, and upon landing went directly to a phone booth and called my friend, the poet, Harryette Mullen: "What does this ending mean?")

I also read *The Iliad, The Odyssey,* and *Medea* because of Morrison. I came to Faulkner through her, and not vice versa. (An aside: I came to a deeper understanding of him through Thadious Davis, whose brilliant work on the Mississippian anticipates Morrison's insights in *Playing in the Dark*. But that is for another essay.)

I find that Morrison informs the large as well as the small, the sweeping epic and the specific gesture. Her words enter your imagination and provide a way of knowing and seeing the world we inhabit. For example, let us return, yet again, to *Sula*:

> In that place, where they tore the nightshade and black-berry patches from their root to make room for the Medallion City Golf Course, there was once a neighborhood.[5]

In this opening sentence, we have the disruption, the displacement, the dispossession: this could be the rupture of the slave trade,
Black farmers' land loss at the hands of racial terrorists, the towns
bombed and burned, urban renewal, or gentrification. The organic
landscape destroyed to make way for a site of elite leisure, the
pesticide-ridden, manicured greens of a golf course. While the black-
berry patches and nightshade are a metaphor for the neighborhood's
Black inhabitants, later Morrison gets more specific, naming a space
so that it becomes place:

> They are going to raze the Time and a Half Pool Hall,
> where feet in long tan shoes once pointed down from
> chair rungs. A steel ball will knock to dust Irene's Palace
> of Cosmetology, where women used to lean their heads
> back on sink trays and doze while Irene lathered Nu Nile
> into their hair. Men in khaki work clothes will pry loose
> the slats of Reba's Grill, where the owner cooked in her
> hat because she couldn't remember the ingredients with-
> out it.[6]

A community is violently torn from its roots, resulting in what
Mindy Fullilove brilliantly calls "root shock." For Fullilove, root
shock describes the consequences of such dispossession, particularly the loss of income, social organization, and ability to adequately
organize a political response, as well as the resulting psychological
trauma of communities that experience urban renewal. Through the
use of metaphor and metonymy, Morrison's prose provides vivid,
concrete imagery to explain complex social and historical phenom-
ena. In other instances, she provides explanation for something
familiar, naming a feeling or an action that we have long experienced
or witnessed, but for which we have no name or working definition.
Consider this moment, when the fair-skinned Helene encounters the
devaluing gaze of the white conductor on the Jim Crow car. She is
struck by "[a]n eagerness to please and an apology for living."[7] From
the moment you read this, whenever encountered with that sensibil-

ity in yourself or another, you will be taken back to this explanation: it describes a price paid by some oppressed people in a context that offers them nothing but disdain. As with Richard Wright's Bigger Thomas, who never feels Blacker than when he is under the insistent and defining white gaze, Helene, a woman separated from him by class and skin tone, possesses a different impulse but a similar sense of self-hatred.

In most of Morrison's novels, she will step away from a central character, away from the plot's action, to give us a meditation on the group. In so doing, she identifies a sensibility, a worldview, a history. In an oft-quoted passage from *The Bluest Eye*, she introduces us to a group of Black migrant middle-class women:

> They come from Mobile. Aiken. From Newport News. From Marietta. From Meridian. And the sound of these places in their mouths make you think of love.

IIIIIIIIIII

> You don't know what these towns are like, but you love what happens to the air when they open their lips and let the names ease out. . . .
> [T]hese girls soak up the juice of their home towns, and it never leaves them. They are thin brown girls who have looked long at hollyhocks in the backyards of Meridian, Mobile, Aiken, and Baton Rouge. . . . Their roots are deep, their stalks are firm, and only the top blossom nods in the wind. They have the eyes of people who can tell what time it is by the color of the sky. Such girls live in quiet Black neighborhoods where everybody is gainfully employed. . . .
> They go to land-grant colleges, normal schools, and learn how to do the white man's work with refinement. . . . Here they learn the rest of the lesson begun in those soft houses with porch swings: . . . . how to behave. The care-

ful development of thrift, patience, high morals, and good
manners. In short, how to get rid of the funkiness. The
dreadful funkiness of passion, the funkiness of nature,
the funkiness of the wide range of human emotions.[8]

For pages, Morrison gives us a detailed, poetic portrait of this
particular group of migrant women. In so doing, she distinguishes
them from other migrants. She tells us what they've kept and what
they've given up in their steady climb toward respectability, toward
representativeness. She at once creates a category and uses it to show
that Black people are not homogenous. In these moments, Morrison
steps back, takes in the entire history and psychology of a people or
a group or a nation—and provides a portrait grounded in the complex humanity of those she describes, whether it be the free men and
women of *Beloved* or the Black Southern men of *Song of Solomon*. She
gives us what the historians cannot give us, what the anthropologists
reach for: "a knowing so deep." In so doing, she articulates a particular philosophy of history. One that turns to the scrap in the archive,
to those who live on the edges of town, the ones who sit just outside of
history's conventional narrative. She calls our attention to that which
moves at the margin.

Until *Beloved*, those marginal ones, ignored by historians, invisible to urban planners and mapmakers, were living individuals
and their communities. With the publication of *Beloved*, Morrison
includes those who were even more marginal: "the sixty million and
more," those with the unmarked graves. As early as *Sula*, she had
suggested that the dead dwell among us. Recall Nel's encounter with
Sula's spirit in the windblown tree. Morrison's notion of history is not
straightforward, linear, or necessarily progressive. History is always
there, right next to the present. Left unattended, it haunts, makes a
mess of things. With attention, it may give of itself, may inform, and,
sometimes, it may provide a map. And yet, one must not become its
prisoner. With *Beloved*, she seemed to give me a sense of direction
for my own work. What she says of Sixo and the Thirty-Mile Woman
describes not only a beautiful romance but also the task of those of

us who would write about the forgotten ones: "She is a friend of my mind. She gather me, man. The pieces I am, she gather them and give them back to me in all the right order. It's good, you know, when you got a woman who is a friend of your mind."⁹ Who doesn't want a lover like that? But here we also have a metaphor for the task of the engaged intellectual, those of us who would be scholars or artists: to gather the pieces, the scraps, to give them shape, form, narrative, meaning, to put them together in the right order and to give them back, an offering, a gift. Also, to the young feminist that I was then, Paul D's desire to put "his story next to" Sethe's had a particular resonance. It challenged me to write not the story of men as if it were the story of all Black people; nor to write only the story of Black women. Instead, I should write a narrative where the stories of men and women were next to each other, side by side.

VI.

In that 1981 *Newsweek* article, Morrison describes herself as "a middle-aged colored lady." I now occupy that stage in life, except after a lifetime of reading Morrison, I am not sure I can lay claim to colored ladyhood. I am still reading, wrestling with, and learning from her, the towering intellectual figure of our time. (Unfortunately for me, her publication record still defines the number of books that constitute a "body of work." It's a horribly abusive game that I play with myself. To have a body of work, I must publish the number of books she has published. It was simply aspirational in 1987; now it feels impossible!)

For those of us who read her consistently, closely, attentively, Morrison continues to inform our way of seeing and knowing the world around us. (Her phrases are as close to my tongue as Biblical verses are to those raised in the church.) As she said about James Baldwin, we can say of her that she has given us a "language to dwell in." Many of us have become comfortable with what we think we know about Morrison. We come to her work seeking what we are already sure we will find there. We look for the clever new way she may tell us something she has told us many times before. But she refuses. She is too busy thinking, imagining, standing at the edge of the unknown and daring to go there.

With *A Mercy*, Morrison goes back before the beginning. She reminds us that there is always a "before" that makes our "beginnings" possible. She looks at this place in North America before it becomes the United States of America: a place with limitless obstacles and limitless possibility. She is *the* premier US writer, and this is her meta-statement. In *A Mercy*, she presents a world, as yet untamed, with pliable boundaries. A world filled with birds, bugs, natural beauty, disease, passion, pestilence, and utter chaos. As in the past, with Hagar, Reba, and Pilate or Sula, Hannah, and Eva, she gives us a household of three "unmastered" women, but this time they are the white Rebekka, the Native American Lina, and Sorrow, who is of mixed heritage. And there is Florens, the young slave girl "with the hands of a slave and the feet of a Portuguese lady."[10] After the death of Jacob, Rebekka's husband, the women become a family of orphans, left to fend for themselves. This is a new American narrative. The moment of what might have been ... the moment when those who would possess power turned away from one set of possibilities: a family of orphans, needing and clinging to each other in spite of emerging hatreds.

At this time, race is moored in myth and mystery, but does not yet define one's status as slave or free. White supremacy is not yet the dominant governing ideology, and thus, white characters are not flattened by it. Instead, they are as interesting and complicated as the Africans and Native Americas, and all are shaped by the others.

Significantly, the landscape may be the novel's most animated character. The topos Morrison describes is so distant from our own that it appears magical and magnificent without needing to be described in surrealistic terms. Morrison reveals the magical in the ordinary: "Sudden[ly] a sheet of sparrows fall from the sky and settle on the trees. So many the trees seem to sprout birds, not leaves at all."[11]

Here we get a land more ancient than Eden. The land (not Founding Fathers, sacred documents, religious exiles, or settler colonists) sits at the beginning of this history. And to that land came the dangerous, superstitious theologies of the Baptists, Anabaptists, and the Catholics. The so-called pagan beliefs of the Native American Lina honor the sacredness of the landscape far better than the newcomer Christians.

A Mercy is an exploration of the meaning of freedom at a time when it could have been much more expansive, a time when our national identity was beginning, to be but not yet entirely constructed at the expense of its Black and Indigenous peoples. It is not insignificant that the book was published just a week after the United States elected its first non-white president. A perfect time to reconsider our beginnings, to explore our origins, and to question our received myths and meanings.

In our own time, Morrison, our spellbinding storyteller, continues to teach, to instruct, to question. She brings heartbreaking pain, breathtaking beauty, and awe-inspiring mystery to the stories we tell about ourselves. To wrestle with her on the page is still a struggle and a blessing—one that awakens a yearning for more from her and most importantly, more (and better) from ourselves.

ALBERT RABOTEAU: AN APPRECIATION

(Drawn from Remarks on the Occasion of His Retirement from Princeton University, April 26, 2013)

I WAS NEVER Professor Raboteau's student in the conventional sense: I did not take classes with him, nor did he serve on my dissertation committee. In fact, we never worked at the same institution, or served as co-panelists at a conference. Consequently, this is not a testament to a personal relationship. Instead, I offer an appreciation for a man and for a body of work that has helped to define the field of African American studies and that has shaped my own intellectual project.

I, like many others, met, engaged, and developed a relationship with Albert Raboteau on the page, through readings and rereadings of his writings on African Americans and religion. I first read *Slave Religion* in John Blassingame's graduate seminar in the fall of 1986. I was a new graduate student in the American studies PhD program, torn, as I have always been, between my love of history and my love of literature. Literary studies underwent profound changes during that time, and with those changes I felt as if I were standing on constantly shifting sand. History was also undergoing significant changes, but it seemed more grounded and grounding to me. Unlike the new developments in literary studies, which was awash with the insights of poststructuralist theory, in history, people still mattered, narrative still had a place, and the archive, while the subject of critique, might yet yield something of significance.

Yale was a heady place in those days. Cornel West was there, as were bell hooks, Adolph Reed, Sylvia Ardyn Boone, and Robert Stepto. The American studies program was home to Michael Denning, Jean-Christophe Agnew, and Hazel Carby was on her way from Wesleyan. My graduate student community included Tera Hunter and Saidiya Hartman, both of whom would become major scholars and thinkers. I was introduced to new ideas, to new ways of thinking, at lightning speed, and encountering poststructuralist thought, French feminism, Western Marxism, postcolonial and critical race theory for the first time.

This is the context in which I met Albert Raboteau on the pages of that beautiful book, *Slave Religion*. It became a space, like the Clearing, in Toni Morrison's *Beloved*. It was where I went to hear the voices of the dead, the ancestors, to see them presented with care and attention, taken seriously, listened to, analyzed with rigor. Because I read it for Blassingame's seminar, we focused on it as a work of history: its use of sources, especially the WPA narratives; it's interventions in the field of history and in historiography. But *Slave Religion* had implications far beyond the history of religion. Religion was its subject, but its theoretical and methodological interventions were far-reaching. It was a model for a way of doing African American studies. Here is only some of what I think that text offered those of us who worked within African American historical, cultural, and literary studies.

IIIIIIIII

SLAVE RELIGION offered what I came to think of as a third way, a way out of a Manichean bind that insisted on a world of contrasts and black and white. While Raboteau deconstructed binary oppositions, he did not invert them, did not seek to show how they were simply inversions of each other. This is to say he did not perform cleverness by demonstrating his ability to play intellectual games. There was simply too much at stake. Instead, he said it isn't Herskovits *or* Frazier, it isn't rebellion *or* docility. For him, there were strengths and weaknesses in both sides of the debate about African continuities versus the complete rupture of all ties to the continent. He posited a both/and, AND he asserted there is a third way of understanding the experience of the enslaved: a way that requires greater specificity and subtly, a way that encompasses far more people than either of the extremes.

For instance, Raboteau's starting point was the diaspora, the dispersal of Africans, through the slave trade, to various points in the Americas and the relationship between the religious practices of those enslaved in Latin America, the Caribbean, and the United States. As such, he established the similarities and the differences between them. His assertion about spirit possession provides an example that proves fruitful for the examination of cultural forms. Raboteau writes that the "theological interpretation and meaning of African spirit possession" differs from the shouting experience of "American evangelicalism," but suggests that "patterns of motor behavior" may be an African continuity. In this gesture, he acknowledges both continuity and rupture, and rupture leaves a space for the creation of something else. The same movement, pattern, rhythm, timbre, may not in fact have the same meaning in the North American context. The pattern may have persisted, though its meaning may have been lost or transformed. On the other side of the rupture, Raboteau does not present us with a rootless or damaged people, but instead his conclusions call our attention to the resilience, creativity, and tremendous capacity of the enslaved to affirm their humanity. He writes:

> Even as the Gods of Africa gave way to the Gods of Christianity, the African heritage of singing, dancing, spirit possession and magic continued to influence Afro-American spirituals, ring shouts, and folk beliefs. That this was so is evidence of the slaves' ability not only to adapt to new contexts, but to do so creatively.

Similarly, Raboteau resists the dichotomy that sees Christianity as fostering either rebellion or docility. Instead, he posits religious mutuality, not as an alternative, but as *a third way* (emphasis mine) that is supported by evangelical Christianity. The complexity of peoples and cultures coming into contact with each other yields all three: rebellion, docility and mutuality. This lends to a more subtle analysis. It does not try to create a romantic sense of mutuality, it does not in any way deny the brutality of slavery, but instead he uses the witness of both the enslaved, their masters, and observers to demonstrate the power and impact of Black spiritual expression to influence whites, while remaining open to influences from white religious practices. (I am still struck by images of white women getting the Holy Ghost during sermons of Black preachers or while observing the enslaved as they worshiped.) Raboteau uses the voices of the enslaved to demonstrate the way they creatively engaged and transformed Christianity. Furthermore, he demonstrates how their interpretation of the religion emphasized and gave voice to its most prophetic dimensions. In a particularly beautiful sentence, he writes:

> At the core of the slave's religion was a private place, represented by a cabin room, the overturned pot, the praying ground, and the hush harbor.

I find this sentence breathtaking. Here, the historian takes evidence from slave testimony about their religious life, and then as poet, culls through that testimony to give it to us as a distillation, a set of images, a spiritual and material geography. These are simple images, not grand cathedrals, but a cabin room, a pot, the very earth itself, the hush harbor. Here he reveals the interiority of the enslaved: That space denied by the master's representation of them, and too often denied by those of us who focus too exclusively on acts of overt resistance. Here, Raboteau anticipates a turn that takes place in African American studies decades after the publication of *Slave Religion*. This turn is most evident in Kevin Quashie's *The Sovereignty of Quiet: Beyond Resistance in Black Culture* (2012). While writers like Morrison imagined the interior lives of the enslaved, I can think of few if any other scholars who explored this space.

||||||||||

IN A FORM LIKE the spirituals, Raboteau finds a place that allows for "an intensely personal and vivid communal experience in which an individual received consolation for sorrow and gained a heightened sense of joy because his experience was shared." This sentence resonates with my own efforts to understand so much of Black American life. For instance, I knew the jam session and the blues performance exhibited this tendency toward personal expression and shared experience. Though jazz scholars have resisted the spiritual dimension of jazz and focused instead on individual expressions of genius and virtuosity, in my own work I have insisted upon the attention to the spiritual basis and nature of much so-called Black secular expression. My book on Billie Holiday ends with a communal jam session that calls upon ancestors and honors elders, a session set in a ring shout–inspired circle that allows for individual flight and risk-taking in a shared moment of joy, appreciation, transcendence, and love. Certainly, other Black thinkers have presented the jazz performance in this way. Recall the end of Baldwin's *Sonny's Blues*, set in the Village jazz club, where Sonny's solo allows him to articulate his blues, to order his chaos, to create beauty and issue it as an offering to those gathered, those who affirm and love him and are in turn fed and nurtured by his sharing. Think of Trane, practicing incessantly, not only to perfect his craft, but as a spiritual practice: those repetitive long tones, an exercise in breath, a meditation, a prayer, played even before scales . . . the performances on stage with his fellow band members and an audience . . . an expression of sorrow, longing, joy, transcendence, and a glimpse of the divine. To acknowledge the interiority of a practice is not to relegate it to an expression of docility or to deny its capacity to foster rebellion, but more importantly, to acknowledge that any act that affirms the humanity of the enslaved may be seen as a form of resistance to constant efforts to deny and destroy it. Raboteau writes:

Slave rebelliousness should not be thought of exclusively

in terms of acts such as revolt for religion itself, in a very
real sense, could be an act of rebelliousness, an assertion
of slave independence, which sometimes required out-
right defiance.

Later he writes: "Religion was for slaves a place of meaning, freedom
and transcendence." This sentence continues to resonate with me,
even more than it did when I first read it. My entire career has been
devoted to identifying and exploring those spaces where, in the midst
of the onslaught, in the belly of the beast, Black people have sought
meaning, freedom, and transcendence. Herein is a refusal to give way
to despair.

Throughout his oeuvre, but especially in *Slave Religion* and *A Fire
in the Bones* (1995), Professor Raboteau listens to the voices of the
dead and bears witness to what they share with him. He insists that
we as intellectuals also refuse the temptation of despair. He reminds
us that we owe it to the ancestors AND to the generations of tomorrow to refuse despair. His is a call to scholars of the Black experience
to view their work as part of the prophetic tradition of Black witness.
Entering into the burgeoning field of African American history and
African American studies, Raboteau identified for himself the "goal
of re-writing American history" as one of both "personal significance
and political impetus" that confronted a myth of the "American
past . . . that denied Black people any past or agency of significance."
In so doing, it denied all Americans the difficult, complex, and rich
truth of their own national identity. So, it is not surprising that when
reading Raboteau, one meets a man on a mission, a man with a sense
of purpose and justice. As African American studies sought academic
legitimacy, as it became more institutionalized, it has sometimes lost
this sense of purpose.

In the essays of *A Fire in the Bones*, in the pages on conjure in
Slave Religion and *Canaan Land*, and those devoted to Noble Drew
Ali and the Moorish Science Temple and the Nation of Islam, Raboteau reveals those expressions of Black religious life that do not fall
within Protestant Christianity even as they engage it. Here we find

gems that are richly suggestive and provocative enough to give birth to new work. These pages offer an invitation for further exploration: an invitation taken up by a number of his own students who have produced a body of work that fleshes out the political and cultural diversity of Black religion in the United States: from Yvonne Chireau's pathbreaking work on conjure, *Black Magic: Religion and the African American Conjuring Tradition* to Judith Weisenfeld's original engagement of religion and film, *Hollywood Be Thy Name: African American Religion in American Film, 1929–1949*, to Eddie Glaude's *Exodus!: Religion, Race, and Nation in Early Nineteenth-Century Black America*, which as Eddie notes, "found its beginnings in Al's work," to Richard Turner's *Islam in the African-American Experience*, and numerous others. Through his writing and his teaching, Albert Raboteau has helped to solidify the study of Black American religion, and in so doing has helped to transform the study of American religion and American history, as well. (As an aside, there are a few other subjects that Raboteau mentions that, for selfish reasons, I long to see further explored by future scholars. In *Slave Religion*, he asserts, "Not all slaves took solace in religion. Some slaves would not accept belief in a supposedly just God who could will or permit slavery. If God was all-just and all-powerful, why did the innocent suffer and injustice reign? was a question which devastated faith in the minds of some slaves." He continues: "There is no way of knowing how many slaves were doubters, agnostics, or atheists, but it is clear that some saw Christianity as meaningless, a sham, a white man's religion—a fact which should temper generalizations about the piety of all slaves." (314) I can only imagine the difficulty of researching this aspect of Black Americans' relationship to religion, but I long for it, if only because it provides a historical basis for an orientation held by my own father, a self-avowed agnostic, who had flirted with the Nation of Islam, before returning to agnosticism.

IIIIIIIIIII

I HAVE all too briefly outlined what I've gleaned intellectually from meeting Al Raboteau through his writing and the implications of his work for the study of Black American history and culture. There are some other dimensions, beyond the scholarly realm, that I have always felt in the work. In addition to the intellectual rigor and insight, I have always experienced Professor Raboteau's writing as a work of Beauty, Humility and Love. These are terms that sometimes make academics uncomfortable, I know, but I will try to explain and provide evidence of each:

Beauty: There are many dimensions of beauty in Raboteau's work. There is the effort with which he constructs a sentence, the pull to provide us not only with information but also with imagery. There is the way the writing sings. There is the beauty of the stories he tells: Beauty not prettiness; the epic encounter of Africans with the West and the syncretic cultures that are born from the violence of that encounter is anything but pretty. But it has borne its own kind of beauty. Raboteau's writings are full of beautifully structured sentences that contain entire histories. Listen to him here at the end of *Slave Religion*:

> People who had been through the fire and refined like gold reveal the capability of the human spirit not only to endure bitter suffering but also to resist and even transcend the persistent attempt of evil to strike it down.

Again, note the use of figurative and allusive language, here referencing Zechariah 13:9:

> And I will bring the third part through the fire, and will refine them as silver is refined, and will try them as gold is tried. They shall call on my name, and I will hear them; I will say It is my people and they shall say, The Lord is my God. (KJV)

This is a favorite passage of Black Christians. I think here of the

Clark Sisters' song that references the same passage. Like the spirituals, the sentence links Black people with the Old Testament Hebrews as a chosen people, whose suffering leads to their transformation. Furthermore, the sentence then raises the suffering of this specific group to the universal. Here, they represent the capacity of humankind to resist and transcend evil. (Here, I think he fulfills Said's call that intellectuals who hail from oppressed groups not only represent their people's suffering, but situate their story alongside those of others who have suffered similar fates, to acknowledge both the specificity and the universal dimensions of their struggle.) Raboteau creates a profound and powerful statement, with beautiful imagery that encompasses the history of Black people.

Humility: When reading Raboteau, one senses a man who is humble in the face of the project before him. Humble in the face of something greater than himself. The profundity of the story that he tells might be overwhelming or could lend to a sense of arrogance in his ability to do so. One never senses that in this work. It never screams, "Look at me!" or "Listen to me!" Instead, it offers a gift: herein lie the voices of the dead, who have something to teach us if only we are willing to listen. "As I became fascinated by the voices of former slaves preserved in narrative accounts of their lives under slavery, not just as historical evidence but as voices that seemed to be speaking directly to me . . . I tried to capture the tenor of these voices, their rhythms, and especially the wisdom they conveyed." His is the humility of the hearer, the witness, the historian, and the poet who listens and imbues his own voice with the sound of theirs and "passes it on." There are few artists and intellectuals who are capable of doing this; they become vessels for bearing the tradition in ways that allow them to posit their own original offering and interpretation. Those of us who read their work, who witness their performance are fed and moved by having done so. It's like the experience of watching Savion Glover dance, seeing and hearing the masters of the form in him, and witnessing him take that tradition and create a rich, new complex tale of his own. That is also the experience of reading Albert Raboteau . . . a humility that allows him to be open. An openness that allows him to receive the stories of those who preceded him.

Love: Here is not only the care with which he presents the enslaved or the ancestors, but also a vision of humanity that suffuses the work. His people are not good or evil but persons capable of doing good and evil. They are people who adapt to change or are transformed by contact with others. The very ability to identify points of mutuality without denying the brutality of the Black/white encounter, suggests a capacity for love: Love as a process that is difficult and messy, but absolutely necessary for our survival. But the love is most evident in the way that he uncovers hidden histories, whether they be the religious life of the enslaved or the difficult and beautiful history of Black American Catholics. In all instances, the discovery, the excavation, the bringing to light is done with such tenderness and respect that it can only be likened to an act of love. One senses here a thinker who is open to growth and change, willing to say I didn't get it right the first time (about African religions, for instance). His capacity for growth and change emerges out of a sense that it is through this radical openness that we reach our highest selves as individuals, as communities, as a nation, and as human beings. Thank you, Professor Raboteau, for the gift of your work, your model, and your witness.

MINNIE'S SACRIFICE

Frances Ellen Watkins Harper's Narrative of Citizenship

BORN TO FREE PARENTS in Maryland in 1825, Frances Ellen Watkins Harper was one of the most well-known women of her day. During her life, she was a poet, activist, novelist, and orator. After teaching at Union Seminary in Ohio (later named Wilberforce University), Harper was unable to return to home, because Maryland prohibited the entrance of free Blacks. Instead, in 1853, she went to Philadelphia—the Black cultural and political capital of the nineteenth century. There, she lived in an underground railroad station, a home where fugitive slaves were hidden and where she listened to the tales of runaways. These tales, coupled with her exile from the state of her birth, influenced her decision to become an abolitionist. Because of her education and self-presentation, she became a major orator, giving speeches and reading her poems around the country. During this period, she published her first collection of poetry, *Poems on Miscellaneous Subjects* (1854).

Throughout her career, Harper published essays, short stories, and serial novels in Black publications, such as the *Christian Recorder* and the *Weekly Anglo-African*. From 1865 to 1875—the period roughly coinciding with Reconstruction (the period following the Civil War)—she traveled extensively throughout the South, lecturing to Black and white audiences. She also lived with the freedmen and recorded her observations in a series of letters published in Black and abolitionist newspapers. According to Harper scholar Frances Smith Foster: "Harper had a particular gift for combining social issues, Afro-Protestant theology and literary innovations."[1]

Following Reconstruction, she continued to write and was one of the founders of the burgeoning Black women's club movement. Harper died on February 20, 1911.

Two of Harper's novels, *Minnie's Sacrifice* (1869) and *Iola Leroy* (1892), reflect her experiences in the Reconstruction South. *Minnie's Sacrifice* is the story of Minnie and Louis Le Croix, both mixed race, who are raised to believe they are white until early adulthood, and who, like Iola Leroy, choose to cast their lots with the newly freed slaves of the South. They dedicate themselves to the moral, economic, and political uplift of the freedmen. The marriage of these two educated, fair-skinned mulattos assures their role as part of a leadership elite who will help to guide the emerging Black nation made up of newly freed slaves and an educated, propertied, mixed-race middle class. *Iola Leroy*, Harper's most well-known work, though set in the Reconstruction South, expresses the concerns of the 1890s, a period known as the nadir of African American history.

The plot of *Iola Leroy* is similar to that of *Minnie's Sacrifice*, but it focuses more on an individual character, the biracial Iola Leroy. As with Minnie and Louis, Iola believed herself to be white until the death of her white father. Sold into slavery, Iola witnesses firsthand the horrors of the institution. Following its abolition, she joins a community of educated free Blacks, comprising professionals and intellectuals and including her new husband. The novel is longer and wider ranging than *Minnie's Sacrifice*. Harper uses it as an opportunity to explore issues as diverse as women's suffrage, Black civil rights, and temperance. Furthermore, she articulates a theory of Black intellectuals that greatly resembles and precedes W. E. B. Du Bois's Talented Tenth—the educated elite who would provide leadership for the Black masses.

Though very similar, the two novels are products of their times. During Reconstruction (1865–77) African Americans made major advances following the end of slavery. The period saw the establishment of refugee centers, hospitals, and schools for free Blacks and poor whites. In 1867, Congress passed the Reconstruction Act and established the Freedman's Bureau to protect Black lives and rights.

By 1868, over 4,000 schools were founded, including Morehouse, Fisk, Hampton, Howard, and Atlanta. The period also witnessed the passage of three major constitutional amendments: the Thirteenth Amendment, outlawing slavery; the Fourteenth Amendment, making the freed persons citizens; and the Fifteenth Amendment, granting Black men the right to vote. During the decade following the Civil War, the newly enfranchised Blacks helped to elect a Black governor of Louisiana, sent sixteen Black congressmen to Washington, DC, and changed the complexion of state legislatures throughout the South.

The end of Reconstruction is marked by the withdrawal of federal troops from the South in 1877. At this time, the Democrats returned to power and the Ku Klux Klan, founded in 1866, stepped up its campaign of racial harassment and terrorism. The 1890s witnessed major setbacks for Black Americans. In 1895, Frederick Douglass died and Booker T. Washington delivered his accommodationist Atlanta Exposition address. The Atlanta Exposition gave Washington the opportunity to address Southern white leaders about the South's race problem. In 1896, the Supreme Court decision in *Plessy v. Ferguson* made Jim Crow—the doctrine of so-called "separate but equal"—the law of the land. Finally, during this period, the number of lynchings increased dramatically. Over 90 percent of these were the result of white mob violence on Black men.

While Harper had published poems prior to the Civil War, it was during Reconstruction that she began to publish longer fiction. An early Black feminist, Harper focused much of her attention on the women of the South, and they would emerge as the most significant characters in her creative writing as well. Although Black women were not granted many of the privileges of citizenship, including the right to vote, Harper saw them as central to the development of a New South. Minnie of *Minnie's Sacrifice*, Iola of *Iola Leroy*, and Aunt Chloe of *Sketches of Southern Life* are feminists and express their anger and protest over the fact that Black women are not enfranchised at the same time as Black men.

Harper's Reconstruction writings differ from those that follow.

In her important study of post-Reconstruction writings by Black women, *Domestic Allegories of Political Desire: The Black Heroine's Text at the Turn of the Century,* Claudia Tate argues that following the failure of Reconstruction, Black women's "novels of 'genteel domestic feminism'... reflect the viewpoint widely held among turn-of-the-century African Americans that the acquisition of their full citizenship would result as much or more from demonstrating their adoption of the 'genteel standard of Victorian sexual conduct' as from protesting racial injustice." According to Tate, these novels allowed Black Americans to define themselves politically during a time when hard-won civil rights gains were under assault.[2] This was certainly the context in which *Iola Leroy* was published.

The writings of Reconstruction differ from *Iola Leroy* in several important ways. Among these, the most significant is Harper's articulation of her notion of Black citizenship. These works—letters, three volumes of poetry, and the serialized novel, *Minnie's Sacrifice*— suggest that during Reconstruction, Harper moved from the integrationist vision of her abolitionist days and toward an emergent Black nationalism.

In the context of the time, Black nationalism would have been a radical political stance that differed from much of the abolitionist movement in its consistent challenge of the fundamental tenets of white supremacy as well as calling for the eradication of slavery. Elizabeth J. West writes: "Although its meaning has not remained unchanged, Black nationalism in its broadest sense means the collective effort of Blacks to secure social, political, and economic group interest."[3] Martin R. Delany, Alexander Crummell, and Henry Highland Garnet are widely recognized as the major proponents of Black nationalism in the nineteenth century. I have never seen Harper listed among them. In its insistence on Black landownership, what I am referring to as Black nationalism preceded the social vision of Booker T. Washington. However, its proponents never advocated a capitulation to white supremacy as did Washington.

Harper's Reconstruction writings all directly engage the issues that consumed the nation during this critical period of American history. These texts offer a direct commentary on urgent political debates. Furthermore, as critics like Hazel Carby, Claudia Tate, Carla Peterson, and Frances Foster have argued about *Iola Leroy,* all of Harper's Reconstruction writings served a pedagogical function. They were written and published as Harper's contribution to the public debate about Black citizenship, and they sought to teach, inform, and shape the opinions of her Black audiences. They were also written during a time when Harper became aware of the increasing class divisions within the Black community that emerged following emancipation. Finally, Harper's Reconstruction writings were also more experimental and more democratic than novels or slave narratives in their content but especially in their form and reach. As objects, books assume a certain kind of audience: a literate one with the leisure time to read. Because Harper's Reconstruction writings included open letters from the road and the text from her speeches, both of which were published in newspapers, she reached a broader audience than she would have had she only published books. In addition, she read her poems aloud at public gatherings, and audiences eagerly awaited her recitation of them.

Minnie's Sacrifice was published in installments in the Black publication the *Christian Recorder,* a publication of the AME Church. As such, it is meant to be read in quick snatches of time, to be read aloud. Finally, *Minnie's Sacrifice* is of special significance in the African American literary tradition, in that it is one of the very first novels by an African American to portray Black women as victims of lynching as well as rape. Frances Foster's discovery of this novel significantly alters our reading of the early African American literary tradition.

I want to suggest that Harper's articulation of a more radical notion of Black citizenship is more explicit during this period than later, because Reconstruction provided more room for a greater range of discussion and debate about Black participation in American social, civic, and economic life. This was certainly not the case during the 1890s—a period that witnessed the systematic dismantling of the minimal progress made during Reconstruction. By "radical notion of Black citizenship," I mean Harper's insistence that, in order for the newly freed Blacks to participate fully as citizens of the American democracy, they not only needed the franchise, but also should: (1) be granted access to quality education; (2) benefit from the redistribution of land; and (3) be granted protection from racial violence. In fact, for Harper, these three things were even more important than the franchise, for she believed that without the acquisition of education, land, and protection, the freedmen would be incapable of exercising their right to vote in an informed and responsible manner. Melba Joyce Boyd, Harper's biographer, notes that Harper's vision for the freedmen included a program of "Literacy, Land, and Liberation."

Harper's growing Black nationalism is most evident in her advocating of cross-class alliances between Blacks and free people of color, rather than a coalition between poor whites and the freed people. She addressed her writings to free Blacks and free people of color in an effort to convince them of their shared fate with the former slaves. However, unlike President Johnson, who warned poor whites against aligning themselves with former slaves because the freedmen were their competitors, Harper questioned the viability of such an alliance because she recognized poor whites' investment in whiteness. This investment allowed them to support racist agendas that were not in their best interest.

In a letter dated July 26, 1867, which was later published as "Affairs in South Carolina" in the *National Anti-Slavery Standard* (August 1867), Harper writes:

> Freedom comes to the colored man with new hopes, advantages and opportunities. He stands on the threshold of a new era, with the tides of new dispensation coursing through his veins; but this poor "cracker class," what is there for them? They were the dregs of society before the war, and their status is unchanged. I have seen them in my travels, and I do not remember ever to have noticed a face among a certain class of them that seemed lighted up with any ambition, hope or lofty aspirations. The victims and partisans of slavery, they have stood by and seen

their brother outraged and wronged; have consented to
the crime and have received the curse into their souls. . . .
I think the former ruling class in the South have proved
that they are not fit to be trusted with the welfare of the
whites nor the liberty of the Blacks.[4]

In this letter, Harper understands the plight of poor whites to be
that of a people who have been exploited by an elite class but whose
capitulation to that elite contributes to their own oppression. She
identifies white supremacy as the ideology that facilitates this capitulation. Over a century later, this would become the central argument
of Edmund Morgan's classic *American Slavery, American Freedom*.
In contrast, Johnson misinformed poor whites that Black enfran-
chisement would lead to an "alliance of Blacks and planters" and as
such would restore the prewar slavocracy, of which, in his view, poor
whites were true victims.

By 1865, Johnson's policies and the newly elected representatives
drawn from the prewar slave-owning class created an atmosphere
that led one visitor to the South to note that "Murder is considered
one of (southern whites) inalienable state rights." In Texas alone,
while five hundred white men were indicted for the murders of Blacks
between 1865 and 1866, not one was convicted.[5] Harper documents
state-sanctioned terrorism against the freedmen in her letters. Later,
this becomes central to her Reconstruction fiction as well. Such acts
of violence are not as explicit in *Iola Leroy*.

In a letter from Eufaula, Alabama, dated December 9, 1870, and
published in William Still's *The Underground Railroad*, Harper notes:
"A number of cases have occurred of murders, for which the punishment has been very lax, or not at all, and it may be will never be."
She recounts the murder of a Black man who had married a white
woman, and the beating of a Black woman by a group of white men
who forced themselves into her cabin. These acts of violence against
the freedmen as well as other acts of political and economic disenfranchisement are central to Harper's creative writing.

Harper published three volumes of Reconstruction poetry, *Moses:*

A Story of the Nile (1869), *Poems* (1871), and *Sketches of Southern Life* (1872). The last of these, *Sketches of Southern Life*, draws most extensively on her experiences in the South, and it begins to map out the terrain of Harper's political vision for the newly emancipated Blacks. It is also pioneering in its introduction of the persona Aunt Chloe, who is of the newly emancipated folk but who is not pushed to the margins of the poem's narrative as such characters are in the novel *Iola Leroy*. While the protagonist of *Iola Leroy* is a member of an educated mulatto elite who cast their lot with the poor freedmen, Aunt Chloe is a former slave who speaks in dialect. However, unlike the folk characters of *Iola Leroy*, Aunt Chloe learns to read, is articulate, literate, political, and comes to own property.

Carla Peterson notes that the Aunt Chloe poems are significant in that they "are no longer grounded in sentimental culture." According to Peterson, these poems posit a notion of home that is no longer "the sentimental site" of those victimized by the slave system. Instead, it is a "political locus in which the socially active and empowered work collectively to implement Black political Reconstruction."[6] This theme of the home as a site of activism and empowerment becomes one of Harper's major concerns throughout Reconstruction. Furthermore, Aunt Chloe is one of the first nonelite Black characters in Black writing. She is juxtaposed against the stereotypes of loyal, loving Black "aunts" of southern lore. The Aunt Chloe poems present Harper's vision for the newly freed Blacks, especially for the women, in whom she held such faith.

Louis Le Croix, of *Minnie's Sacrifice*, articulates Harper's political opinions and vision. Throughout the narrative, Louis's perspective on the possibilities for Black participation in American democracy shifts significantly. At first, upon arrival in the South, Louis notes:

> We are going to open a school, and devote our lives to the up building of the future race. I intend entering into some plan to facilitate the freedmen in obtaining homes of their own. I want to see this newly enfranchised race adding its quota to the civilization of the land. . . . We

demand no social equality, no supremacy of power. All we ask is that the American people will take their Christless, Godless prejudices out of the way, and give us a chance to grow, an opportunity to accept life, not merely as a matter of ease and indulgence, but of struggle, conquest, and achievement.

In asking not for social equality, but for access to literacy, the removal of social and political barriers, and the chance for the freedmen to prove themselves, Louis prefigures Booker T. Washington. Furthermore, his notion of Black citizenship is even less radical than that of the early proponents of Reconstruction Radicalism. Eric Foner notes that "Reconstruction Radicalism was first and foremost a civic ideology, grounded in a definition of American citizenship. On the economic issues of the day no distinctive or unified Radical position existed."[7] The Radicals advocated equal opportunity regardless of race. Like Louis, the Radicals felt that the national government had to guarantee "equal political standing and equal opportunity in a free-labor economy."[8] Neither the Radical Republicans nor the earlier Louis call for federal protection of Southern Blacks or for the redistribution of land. Note the "us" and "them" sensibility of this passage. There is the "we" of the mulatto class who help the "freedmen." And the "we" of the leadership class and the freedmen who are not included under the rubric of "the American people."

As the narrative develops and as Louis becomes more aware of the constant threats of violence under which Southern Blacks live, he becomes an advocate not only of Black suffrage, but of Black self-defense as well. Speaking to the freedmen, he says, "Defend your firesides if they are invaded, live as peaceably as you can, spare no pains to educate your children, be saving and industrious, try to get land under your feet and homes over your heads."[9] In their insistence on Black self-defense, Ida B. Wells and Malcolm X echo Louis's words. Wells admonished Black readers and audiences to take up arms in self-defense against the terrorism of lynch mobs. Malcolm X criticized the turn-the-other-cheek doctrine of Martin Luther King

and encouraged Black Americans to defend themselves against racists and bigots. Through Louis, Harper articulates her theme of literacy, land, and liberation, as well as a critique of a federal government
that refuses to protect its very own citizens.

Louis also blames the federal government for providing an atmosphere that would allow for the emergence of the Ku Klux Klan in
1866: "If Johnson was clasping hands with rebels and traitors was
there no power in Congress to give, at least, security to life? Must
they wait till murder was organized into an institution, and life and
property were at the mercy of the mob? And, if so, would not such a
government be a farce, and such a civilization a failure?"[10] In calling
into question the federal government's ability and willingness to protect the freedmen, Louis might be commenting on Johnson's veto of
the Civil Rights Act of 1866. The bill sought to assert "national power
to protect Blacks' civil rights." It was a radical act which "defined all
persons born in the United States (except Indians) as national citizens
and spelled out rights they were to enjoy equally without regard to
race—making contracts, bringing lawsuits and enjoying the benefit
of 'all laws and proceedings for the security of person and property.'
No state law or custom could deprive any citizen these rights."[11]

As radical as the bill was, it did not create a federal force to protect
the rights of citizens. This was left to the states. The federal courts
were expected to enforce the bill. The primary focus of the bill was
on eradicating discriminatory state laws and not on protecting the
freedmen from violence. Johnson claimed that guaranteeing Blacks
full citizenship would discriminate against white people. In spite of
the flood of reports coming in from the Freedman's Bureau documenting numerous acts of violence against Blacks who sought to
exercise their rights, Johnson asserted: "The distinction of race and
color is by the bill made to operate in favor of the colored against the
white race."[12] In an effort to counter Johnson's veto, the Republicans
introduced the Fourteenth Amendment, which declared all persons
born or naturalized in the US national and state citizens with all the
rights and privileges thereof.

Louis grows more and more convinced of the need for Radical

Reconstruction as he confronts and tries to counter the continuing violence and violation of citizens' rights in the South. Although Blacks remained committed to the Republicans, Harper, through Louis, was critical of the party. "My faith is very strong in political parties," he says. However, the narrator notes: "Yet there were times when his words seemed to him almost like bitter mockery. Here was outrage upon outrage committed upon these people, and to tell them to hope and wait for better times but seemed like speaking hollow words."[13] Furthermore, Louis, like Harper, differs from even the most radical Republicans in that he knows that political rights mean little without economic independence for the freedmen. Eventually, Harper joined the freedmen in their plea for redistribution of land. For most freedmen, landownership was an integral part of their definition of freedom. In calling for land for the freedmen, Harper and Louis depart from Southern mixed-race landowners.

One consequence of Louis's outspokenness is the danger it brings to him and his family. The violence that Harper reports in her letters provides her with material that drives her narrative in that she incorporates specific instances of violence into the novel. For instance, in a letter from Darlington, South Carolina, dated May 13, 1867, Harper relays the true story of a lynching of a young Black woman:

> About two years ago, a girl was hung for making a childish and indiscreet speech. Victory was perched on our banners. Our army had been through, and this poor, ill-fated girl, almost a child in years, about seventeen years of age rejoicing over the event, and said that she was going to marry a Yankee and set up housekeeping. She was reported as having made an incendiary speech and arrested, cruelly scourged, and then brutally hung. Poor child! she had been a faithful servant—her master tried to save her, but the tide of fury swept away his efforts.[14]

Harper's letter refers to the murder of a young Black woman, Amy Spain, who was lynched in Darlington in 1865. She is reported to have shouted "Bless the Lord the Yankees have come." The story of her lynching appeared in *Harper's Weekly*, September 30, 1865. This episode also finds its way onto the pages of *Minnie's Sacrifice*. A recently freed slave woman tells Louis:

> Well, you see it was jist dis way. My darter Amy was a mighty nice chile, and Massa could truss her wid any ting. So when de Linkum Sogers had gone through dis place, Massa got her to move some of his tings over to another place. Now when Amy seed de sojers had cum'd through she was might glad, and she said in a kine of childish way, 'I'se so glad, I'm gwine to marry a Linkum soger, and set up house-keeping for myself.' I don't spect she wer in arnest 'bout marrying de sojer, but she did want her freedom. Well, no body couldn't blame her for dat, for freedom's a mighty good thing . . . Well, when she said dat, dat miserable old Heston—Well, he had my poor girl tuokened up, and poor chile, she was beat shameful, and den dey had her up before der sogers and had her tried for saying 'cendiary words, and den dey had my poor girl hung'd.[15]

Harper's audiences would have been used to stories of Black women's experiences of sexual harassment and abuse. Writers such as Douglass and Harriet Jacobs had provided scintillating suggestions of the sexual exploitation of Black women. However, these audiences probably were not as used to the Black woman being the object of lynching and other forms of murder. *Minnie's Sacrifice* adds Black female martyrs to the pantheon of murdered Black men that fill Black political and literary history. Furthermore, the story of the young girl's death is recounted at the funeral of the novel's heroine, Minnie. That the story of the lynched girl is narrated at the funeral of the more privileged lady links the two women and suggests that despite differences of class and color, their fates are inextricably bound. Unfortunately, the installment that narrates the circumstances of Minnie's death has not been found; however, earlier chapters suggest that her death might have resulted from the political work in which she and her husband are engaged.

Finally, while Harper relays the historical account of this story in her own voice and language in her letter, in the novel she allows the young woman's mother to tell the story in dialect. Harper gives voice to the less educated freedwoman, and in so doing allows her to draw the link between her own child and the fair, lovely, educated Minnie. The mother and her daughter come from the class of Blacks most vulnerable to white Southern violence, and Harper reminds her reader of this by focusing on the violence done to the child and not that done to Minnie or one of her class. As such, she seems to be saying to her reader, "You must have sympathy for all victims of such violence, not simply those with whom you identify."

The concluding installment of the series is Harper's direct address to her readers about the pedagogical and political intent of the story. It reads like the traditional "Dear Reader" of abolitionist literature, except the intended reader is not from a Northern middle-class white audience, but from a Northern middle-class Black one. "May I not modestly ask that the lesson of Minnie shall have its place among the educational ideas for the advancement of our race?"[16] Harper's plea is to the newly educated Black elite: "It is braver to suffer with one's own branch of the human race . . . for the sake of helping them, than to attempt to creep out of all identity with them in their feebleness, for the sake of mere personal advantages."[17]

Some might argue that this plea is a classic example of the doctrines of racial uplift—doctrines that recent scholars identify as elitist. Racial uplift was the name given to the belief that the Black elite could "uplift" the masses of poor Black people by being moral exemplars and acting as spokespersons for and representatives of "the race." I read Harper's plea as a call to those who might have greater access to opportunity because of the brief but significant gains of Reconstruction. Harper warns them not to abandon those Blacks who are incapable of taking advantage of such opportunities because of continued violence and other forms of opposition from the Southern states. By aligning Minnie's death with that of Amy, Harper is also telling her readers that their fates are aligned with those of the most oppressed freedmen. In fact, their position was indeed quite tenuous. The Black upper class was quite small, and their economic security was always in jeopardy. In spite of this, Carla Peterson notes, "The post-bellum period witnessed the slow emergence of a new class structure and sensibility that separated the mass of common laborers from a growing Black professional and business class. This class was not always able to comprehend the labor issues facing Black workers and felt at times that the political and social interests of the two groups no longer necessarily coincided."[18] Harper's plea was not only to this growing Black professional and business class of the South, but also to Black Northerners, who she feared would lessen their vigilance once the cause of abolition was won.

In closing, the final call of the novella is a call for action as well as a warning to her readers not to be fooled by the appearance of progress. The novella serves as a warning about the very tenuous nature of Black citizenship and the necessity of remaining vigilant against the forces that would seek to deny it. Finally, it also illustrates Harper's belief in the power of fiction to engage political issues and to shape public opinion. By ending her narrative with the death of the major character and not with a scene of familial bliss or racial progress, Harper asserts that in the midst of great progress and social change, the status of Black people remains precarious. By the time Harper again turned to fictionalize her Reconstruction experiences in 1892, those hard-won elements of Black citizenship were already being dismantled. A consideration of her Reconstruction writings sheds new light on her better-known later efforts and suggests the way that the political climate influences the form and content of creative efforts.

ZORA NEALE HURSTON'S RADICAL INDIVIDUALISM

ZORA NEALE HURSTON befuddles. Though she is widely recognized as a brilliant novelist and as an anthropologist who pioneered an ethnographic methodology, her politics have evoked a more ambivalent response. Critics portray her as reactionary and imperialist; defenders focus on her literary genius, her intellectual originality, and her nuanced attention to Black folk cultures. She has been claimed by feminists, Black conservatives, Black nationalists, and libertarians. As a novelist, playwright, aesthetic theorist, and ethnographer, she took Black humanity and complexity seriously. The innovative nature of her work, her refusal of respectability politics, her insistence on women's sexual, political, and intellectual freedom all seem in conflict with what we have come to think of as Black conservatism.

However, her nearly uncritical celebration of the United States, her lack of attention to racial hostilities, and her fervent anticommunism all align her with the political Right. Elements of her conservatism are evident throughout her career. Her admiration for Booker T. Washington and her ongoing and needling critiques of W. E. B. Du Bois contain seeds that blossomed into a more full-fledged conservative political stance during the last decade of her life. Interestingly, she nonetheless was a staunch anticolonialist.

Throughout her life Hurston was disdainful of those who insist upon Black pathology, instead choosing to focus her own work on Black possibility, creativity, and resilience. She often does so to such an extreme that she seems blind to Black suffering and structural inequality beyond that which is imposed by de facto Jim Crow. Although she claims no interest in history, on the occasions when she does turn to history as a source of explanation, she may be accused of profound historical misinterpretations. This is most evident in her understanding of Reconstruction. For Hurston, it was an era of widespread political fraud and corruption on the part of outsiders from the North and Blacks who were not yet ready for the full responsibilities of citizenship.

This essay seeks to situate Hurston within a broader context of African American political thought and in so doing demonstrate the way she occupies a unique position that eschews social conservatism while embracing political conservatism, even as she advances a protofeminist and anticolonial politics. For my purposes, social conservatism is an ideology that seeks to preserve traditional beliefs about religion, sexuality, and marriage. Political conservatism distinguishes itself from any form of collectivism, insists on the rights of individuals, and emphasizes freedom of choice. For political conservatives, government should empower individuals rather than solve social problems. Interestingly, Hurston supported the US occupation of Haiti but later launched profound anticolonial critiques of the United States and Europe.

Although she is an unconventional woman, a feminist who focuses her attention on the working class, working poor, and migrant workers, she is in no way a part of the Black radical tradition. Instead, she most often espouses a kind of liberal individualism, which at its extreme may turn into libertarianism. For Hurston, government intrusion into or interference with individual interests is the greatest threat to democracy. Significantly, when writing about the Black expressive culture, she highlights the achievements of the collective; in her more political writing, she emphasizes the individual.

Much has been written about the civic and institutional contexts that may have influenced Hurston's worldview: her hometown, Eatonville, Florida, a Black town a few miles east of Orlando, and Black educational institutions. As a child she attended the Robert Normal and Industrial School, founded by Russell and Mary Calhoun, graduates of Booker T. Washington's Tuskegee Institute. In fact, one of the school's first buildings was named Booker T. Washington Hall, and Washington was an early patron of the institution.[1] Hurston later attended college preparatory classes at Morgan Academy in Baltimore. The academy was the high school of Morgan College, another Black institution of higher education. From Morgan, she went on to the most prestigious of the Black universities, Howard. For most of her life Hurston lived and was educated in primarily Black contexts; consequently, she was surrounded by Black excellence and heterogeneity. Unlike W. E. B. Du Bois and Jean Toomer, she did not have to travel south as a young adult to familiarize herself with Southern life. She was reared in the thick of it.

With this foundation, in 1925 she moved to New York, where she lived at times in Harlem, and where she eventually attended Barnard College and Columbia University. At these two institutions she was introduced to the study of anthropology, a discipline that she credits with giving her the critical tools and distance she needed to research the cultures that produced her. The type of anthropology she encountered at Columbia under the tutelage of teachers like Franz Boas also helped to legitimate her sense of the richness of Black vernacular cultures, their inherent Africanness, and the relationship between the folk practices of the Black South and those of the African Diaspora in the Americas. All of these settings no doubt helped inform Hurston's politics. However, for our purposes, her writing—both her fiction and her nonfiction—offers the best articulation of her political thought over time.

Hurston's aesthetic theories as expressed in a series of essays emphasize Black cultural genius and originality. Of the novels, *Their Eyes Were Watching God* (1937) and *Moses, Man of the Mountain* (1939) are of special interest. The former presents the heroic individual as feminist heroine, and the latter attends to questions of power, governance, leadership, and nation building under the leadership of the charismatic Moses. Hurston's ethnographic writings, particularly *Tell My Horse* (1938), share a concern with possibilities of Black self-governance.

In *Tell My Horse*, her ethnography of Jamaica and Haiti, Hurston both humanizes Voodoo, treating it is an important world religion, while at the same time endorsing the US occupation as what John Carlos Rowe calls "a sort of benevolent political and economic intervention, which should be accompanied by qualified efforts to 'win the hearts and minds' of the Haitian elite to democratic ideals and institutions."[2]

Hurston's most sustained aesthetic statement, "Characteristics of Negro Expression" (1934), synthesizes dominant elements of Black expressive culture. For Hurston, aesthetic excellence signifies the health and wholeness of the people. Consequently, in this view, slavery did not leave Black people damaged. The depth of their culture provides proof of their endurance, strength, and creativity. It is possible that aesthetic achievement informs her sense that Blacks need few social or political remedies save the removal of barriers to their achievement. Originality is a hallmark of genius. Hurston locates Black genius not in exceptional individuals but in the masses of unknown, unnamed Black people who have produced a distinct aesthetic sensibility. For Hurston, Black aesthetics are distinct from, and in many ways completely opposite of, Western aesthetics. She writes: "The Negro is a very original being. While he lives and moves in the midst of white civilization, everything he touches is reinterpreted for his own use. He has modified the language, mode of food preparation, practice of medicine, and most certainly the religion of his new country."[3] In America, Black and Western aesthetics have encountered each other, and while both have been affected, the sheer power of Black expressive culture has all but transformed whites who come into contact with it. Black expression is Black power.

The essay "Spirituals and Neo-Spirituals," published in Nancy Cunard's *Negro: An Anthology* of 1934, extends concepts of "characteristics" by narrowing on one form: the spirituals. Here Hurston takes one of her first published jabs at Du Bois. Though she never names him, she asserts, "The idea that the whole body of spirituals are 'sorrow songs' is ridiculous. They cover a whole wide range of subjects from peeves or gossip to Death and Judgment." Du Bois famously closed his *Souls of Black Folk* with a chapter titled "The Sorrow Songs," an eloquent description, analysis, and theorizing of the meaning of Black religious songs. Hurston not only challenges his description but also questions his sources. Du Bois draws upon concertized spirituals made famous by groups like the Fisk Jubilee Singers. Hurston writes: "There never has been a presentation of genuine Negro Spirituals to any audience anywhere. What is being sung by the concert artists and the glee clubs are the works of Negro composers or adaptors based on the spirituals."[4] Implicit in her critique of Du Bois is the assertion that his interpretation is elitist and values European aesthetic norms. Hurston draws a metaphorical line in the sand here. The venerable Dr. Du Bois is wrong, far removed from the folk culture he seeks to explain.

Their Eyes Were Watching God is celebrated as a feminist classic, a tale of a woman's coming to self-actualization, sexual fulfillment, and spiritual maturity. It embodies the characteristics of Black expression that Hurston identifies: storytelling, spirituality, drama, poetic language, and humor. The novel is all of this and more. It also contains Hurston's understanding of the complex relationship between her insights into Black culture and the ways this understanding informs her political stances. The novel is unconcerned with overt acts of racial injustice, though the legacy of slavery haunts. White people do not occupy center stage, nor are they villains when they do appear. Black people are not concerned with what whites think or do. The novel presents the poetics of Black language in the context of autonomous Black spaces. The removal of whites from the novel's center allows for an exploration of the full range of Black humanity: Black joy, laughter, heterogeneity, gender conflict, love, passion, betrayal, and class and color politics. Although it need not be the case, Hurston's choice to remove whites from the narrative's center at times eschews the reality of racist oppression.[5] There are at least two instances where the absence of white racial oppression seem implausible: (1) the enduring legacy of slavery exists only in Nanny's efforts to police Janie's sexuality, and (2) though the novel highlights the diverse cultures of Blacks in southern Florida, it does not acknowledge their economic exploitation. A largely autonomous Black world allows Hurston to attend to the particularities and specificities of Black Southern life while at the same time touching upon themes that concern all beyond the boundaries of race, region, and nation.

In *Their Eyes* that Black world is inhabited by a diversity of Black people. Janie's color, beauty, and economic security allow her to travel her route to self-discovery. For our purposes, the most relevant part of *Their Eyes* is the conversation Janie has with the elitist, color-struck, class-conscious Mrs. Turner. An unattractive woman, Mrs. Turner nonetheless takes great pride in her features: "Her nose was slightly pointed and she was proud. Her thin lips were ever a delight to her eyes. Even her buttocks in bas-relief were a source of pride. To her way of thinking all these things set her aside from other Negroes."[6] Turner is attracted to Janie's "coffee-and-cream complexion and her luxurious hair" but is unforgiving about her choice to marry Tea Cake, a dark-skinned man. She refers to other Blacks as "common niggers." While Janie (and Hurston) revel in the diversity of Black folk in Black spaces, Mrs. Turner "never dreamt so many different kins ub Black folks could colleck in one place. . . . Ah ain't uster 'ssociatiin' wid Black folks."[7]

Mrs. Turner is the embodiment of a light-skinned elite that hold darker, poorer Blacks in contemptuous disdain. "We ought to lighten up the race," she tells Janie. Of poor Blacks she says, "Ah don't blame the white folks for haten em cause Ah can't stand 'em mah self." She is portrayed in ways that make the reader hold her at a critical distance. The novel depicts her as a hateful and ridiculous figure.

Janie counters her with a more capacious understanding of Black identity: "We uh mingled people and all of us got Black kinfolks as well as yaller kinfolks. How come you so against Black?"[8] Turner despises all the things Hurston holds dear: Black laughter, Black performativity, Black language, play, and humor. She won't even patronize Black professionals.

Turner tries to lure Janie away from Tea Cake and introduce her to her brother, who recently delivered a paper on Booker T. Washington and "tore him tuh pieces!" Turner offers her own critique of Washington: "All he ever done was cut de monkey for white folks. So dey pomped him up. But you know whut dey folks say 'de higher de monkey climbs de mo' he shows folks his behind' so dats de way it wuz wid Booker T. Mah brother hit him every time dey give him chance to speak." Janie replies, "Ah was raised on de notion dat he wuz uh great big man." Then, Hurston writes, "According to all Janie had been taught this was sacrilege, so she sat without speaking at all." If Janie remains silent, the narrator does not; she defines Mrs. Turner as someone who worships whiteness and "built an altar to the unattainable—Caucasian characteristics for all. Her god would smite her, would hurl her from pinnacles and lose her in deserts but she would not forsake his altars."[9]

In a book that makes no reference to any historic or living figure, it is quite telling that Hurston chooses to have Janie admire Booker T. Washington, and that she places the critique of Washington in the mouth of a figure like Mrs. Turner, who represents what Hurston most disdained about the Black elite. Here, she is taking sides in the Washington-DuBois debates, and while Janie is rendered mute in the face of the Du Boisian position, Hurston is not. Hurston is critical of the anti-Washington Harlem-based Black elite, the Du Boisian Black elite, who hold Black Southerners and dark-skinned poor Blacks in utter contempt, who have "classed off" to themselves, yet whose livelihoods and social position depend upon those they disdain. She frequently said that Booker T. Washington was the last great Black leader, a son of the South, an institution builder, a strategist who worked within the confines of Jim Crow and white supremacy to build a Black educational institution and a highly effective political machine. As such, he is not unlike the founders of Black towns such as Eatonville. Most significantly, Hurston believes Washington remained true to Black people. In contrast to Marcus Garvey, whom Hurston claimed took his followers' money and kept it for his own use, she insists, "Booker T. Washington had achieved some local notice for collecting monies and spending it on a Negro school. It had never occurred to him to keep it."[10]

Her admiration for Washington is expressed in her nonfiction writing as well. Hurston was invited to write an entry for the Encyclopedia Americana in 1947. Her entry replaced Du Bois's essay on the "Negro in America," which had appeared in various editions of the encyclopedia since 1904. Hurston's essay praises Washington for "making a place for 'Negro untouchables,' and for never uttering a 'public word or [writing] a line concerning what came to be known as the controversy between himself and Dr. DuBois," whereas Du Bois, she insinuated, did nothing for "the man farthest down' and used his writing to attack Washington unfairly." [11]

Furthermore, Hurston's essay differs from Du Bois's in its assessment of Reconstruction. Whereas Du Bois challenged received notions of the failures of Reconstruction, Hurston writes, "What should have come to the Negro after a period of preparation, was thrust upon him while still in a state of unreadiness, leaving him not only maladjusted to his surroundings, but retarded in progress for generations."[12] This is one of her first discussions of Reconstruction, one upon which she would elaborate in later writings. Her view of the period is a conservative one, which aligns with the Dunning School's interpretation (one which was challenged by Du Bois's *Black Reconstruction in America* of 1935 but nonetheless continued to hold sway for decades). Historians of the Dunning School, named for Columbia University professor William Archibald Dunning, argued that the freedmen were incapable of self-governance, and this made their segregation and disenfranchisement necessary. Eric Foner, also a professor of history at Columbia, writes that the Dunning School "was not only an interpretation of history. It was part of the edifice of the Jim Crow System."[13]

Hurston paints the freedmen of Reconstruction much in the same way she portrays the Hebrews following their escape from Egypt in the novel *Moses, Man of the Mountain*. Moses is a visionary and a nation builder "wishing for a country he had never seen. He was seeing visions of a nation he had never heard of where there would be more equality of opportunity and less difference between top and bottom." He dreams of an egalitarian society, and while the people he leads long for a strongman, a king, he wants only to bring laws so that they may govern themselves.

In Moses's mouth, Hurston puts forth a vision of a free people and their responsibilities to themselves and others: " 'This freedom is a funny thing,' he told them. 'It ain't something permanent like rocks and hills. It's like manna; you just got to keep gathering it fresh every day. If you don't one day you're going to find you ain't got any no more. . . . You done got free of Pharaoh and Egyptian oppressors, be careful you don't rise up none among yourselves.' "[14]

Here, freedom is a process requiring constant vigilance. It is precarious and can easily give way to oppression, which is always waiting to emerge. Furthermore, movements against oppression have the potential to become sources of oppression once they are in the position to govern. There is the suggestion that people are ultimately more committed to maintaining their positions of power and superiority than they are to equality. Freedom requires us to resist this temptation.

Finally, freedom is something the individual must acquire and maintain for herself. Toward the novel's end, Moses reflects:

> He had meant to make a perfect people, free and just, noble and strong, that should be a light for all the world and for time and eternity. And he wasn't sure he had succeeded. He had found out that no man may make another free. Freedom was something internal. The outside signs were just signs and symbols of the man inside. All you could do was to give the opportunity for freedom and the man himself must make his own emancipation. He remembered how often he had had to fight Israel to halt a return to Egypt and slavery. Responsibility had seemed too awful to them time and time again.[15]

While generations of Black Americans found inspiration in the tales of the Hebrews' exodus from Egypt, Hurston returns to that oft-told tale to highlight the struggles of freedom. Moses is liberator of a people, but only the individual can truly free herself.

In Hurston's oeuvre, nowhere is the threat to freedom more evident than in the Caribbean, especially Haiti. She travels to Jamaica and Haiti as a student of anthropology, convinced of the value of Black culture, seeking commonality and continuity between the Black cultures of the Southern United States and those of these two Black island states. Although she does identify both similarities and differences in religion and song, the Hurston of this text emerges as distinctly American.

In an insightful essay titled "Zora's Politics: A Brief Introduction," the most thorough analysis of Hurston's political thought to date, Ernest Julius Mitchell II explains that "the unifying thread across Hurston's various political writings is a staunch anticolonial position. . . . Her support for America's ideals did not blind her to its many political problems. However, the fact that the United States had no colonies when Europe was rocked by waves of decolonization made Hurston's critique of America milder than one might expect."[16] Recounting visits to Jamaica and Haiti in *Tell My Horse*, Hurston is uncritical of the United States. In fact, at times she is celebratory to the extent of exaggerating the freedoms enjoyed by American citizens. For instance, the controversial chapter "Women in the Caribbean" juxtaposes the near gender equality of the US to oppressive and retrograde gender conditions in Jamaica. The United States that Hurston describes is so supportive of women's rights as to be unrecognizable. According to Hurston, in the United States:

> The majority of men in all the states are pretty much agreed that just for being born a girl-baby you ought to have laws and privileges and pay and perquisites. And so far as being allowed to voice opinions is concerned, why they consider that you are born with the law in your

mouth, and that is not a bad arrangement, either. The majority of the solid citizens strain their ears trying to find out what it is that their womenfolk want so they can strain around and try to get it for them, and that is a very good idea and the right way to look at things.[17]

At the time of the book's publication, large swaths of African American women were disenfranchised and barred from various forms of employment and even from attending certain educational institutions. Hurston's is a romanticized view of her country; America serves as an idealized model. Earlier in the text, she distinguishes between the Jamaicans, who are British subjects, and American Negroes, who are citizens of the United States. She writes:

So in Jamaica it is the aim of everybody to talk English, act English and look English. And that last specification is where the greatest difficulties arise. It is not so difficult to put a coat of European culture over African culture, but it is next to impossible to lay a European face over an African face in the same generation. . . . The color line in Jamaica between the white Englishman and the Blacks is not as sharply drawn as between the mulattoes and the Blacks. . . . There is a frantic stampede white-ward to escape from Jamaica's Black mass.[18]

She notes that although some Black Americans, including Frederick Douglass, believed that the Negro must be absorbed by whites, in contrast, the "American Negro" has instead attempted "to achieve a position equal to the white population in every way but each race to maintain its separate identity."[19] For Hurston, Jamaican mulattoes constitute a class of Mrs. Turners who, because they are outnumbered by the Blacks, are destined to fail unless they convince the Blacks "to cease reproduction."[20] But Hurston sees "a new day in sight for Jamaica as Blacks begin to respect themselves and cherish their folk culture."

If embracing Black culture brings a new day to Jamaica by elevating the cultural contributions of the Black masses, in Haiti a perceived valorization of Blacks and the ongoing divide between them and the mulattoes is often exploited by those in political power. As the text turns to Haiti, it describes the brutal massacre leading to ouster of President Jean Vilbrun Guillaume Sam, the culmination of over four hundred years of violence in this, the first Black republic in the Western Hemisphere.

The brutality of slavery is replaced by the brutality of Black and mulatto regimes. Peace and stability come only with the arrival of the USS *Washington*, whose smoke "was a black plume with a white hope," bringing "the end of the revolution and the beginning of peace."[21] In subsequent chapters Hurston defends the occupation, identifying it as a period of peace and prosperity, with no mention of the atrocities that occurred under the Americans, who occupied the nation and controlled its military and economy from 1915 to 1934.[22] Hurston portrays Haiti as a nation rich in culture and spirituality yet incapable of self-governance and unable to escape violence and exploitation at the hands of internal and external actors.

For Hurston, Jamaica and Haiti are spaces populated by Black majorities but divided by class and color within and subjected to European and American powers from without. Under such conditions political freedom is impossible. The position of the American Negro under the US rule of law is represented as virtually ideal.

In order to do this, Hurston must all but ignore the obstacles Black Americans face to achieving full citizenship within the borders of a nation that needs but all too often despises them.

Hurston's most explicit political statements began to appear during the postwar years. From 1943 to 1954, Hurston wrote a series of nonfiction essays, articles, and chapters which grew increasingly right wing. These pieces—"Crazy for This Democracy," "I Saw Negro Votes Peddled," "Why the Negro Won't Buy Communism," "Court Order Can't Make Races Mix"—demonstrate the growth of her own particular brand of conservatism and yield a series of repeated images, tropes, and metaphors that give life to her political understanding of race, state power, and history.

The most comprehensive statement of Hurston's politics did not appear in print during her lifetime. The original manuscript of her autobiography, *Dust Tracks on a Road* (1942), contained a chapter titled "Seeing the World as I See It."[23] Here Hurston articulates her commitment to individualism, her critique of race leadership, and her opposition to American and European imperialism. It was excised at the insistence of the publisher, J. P. Lippincott. (Similarly, Richard Wright's publishers had him excise the final chapters of his own autobiography, *Black Boy*. The removed part was later published as *American Hunger*.) The chapter contains echoes of an earlier essay, "How It Feels to Be Colored Me" (1928), but goes into much greater depth about the ideas that shape her worldview. In the opening paragraphs, Hurston asserts, "I found that I had no need of either class or race prejudice, those scourges of humanity. The solace of easy generalization was taken from me, but I received the richer gift of individualism."[24] In light of this, she rejects constructs such as "Race Problem, Race Pride, Race Man or Woman, Race Solidarity, Race Consciousness and Race Leader."[25] She sees no need for race pride for Blacks or whites because "what seems race achievement is the work of individuals."[26] Race pride and race consciousness have been deadly, according to Hurston, holding humanity back rather than advancing it. Race pride and race consciousness "is the root of misunderstanding and hence misery and injustice. I cannot, with logic cry against it in others and wallow in it myself."[27] This is not the stance of a Black nationalist. Instead, Hurston argues for a radical individualism.

She eschews any notion of race solidarity and insists: "Negroes are just like anybody else. Some soar. Some plod ahead. Some just make a mess and step back in it—like the rest of America and the world."[28] Later on she writes, "Let him who can, go up, and him who cannot stay there, mount down to the level his capabilities rate."[29] Thus she is against Jim Crow because it is an artificial barrier, but beyond its removal, she sees no reason for radical societal transformation.

> It seems to me if I say a whole system must be upset for me to win I am saying that I cannot sit in the game, and that

safer rules must be made to give me a chance. I repudiate
that. If others are in there, deal a hand and let me see what
I can make of it, even though I know some in there are
dealing from the bottom and cheating like hell in other
ways. If I can win anything in a game like that, I know
I'll end up with the pot if the sharks can be eliminated.[30]

Thus Hurston has no place for a structural critique and sees little
impediment to the mobility of exceptional Blacks in a world where
they are allowed to soar. She acknowledges race prejudice but dismisses it as "the last refuge of the weak." Hurston sees individuals as
the crux of democracy.

History does not fare well in this chapter. "Since I wash myself
of race pride and repudiate race solidarity, by the same token I turn
my back upon the past. I see no reason to keep my eyes fixed on the
dark years of slavery and the Reconstruction, I am three generations
removed from it, and therefore have no experience of the thing."[31]
Here, she is Janie, leaving Nanny to history while her eyes are turned
to the horizon. In dismissing history, she also dismisses its legacies and refuses to see the way it informs and shapes the world she
inhabits.

Hurston devotes a significant portion of the essay to the great
distance between theories of democracy and its failed practice. Here
we see the seeds of the essay that would become "Crazy about This
Democracy." For Hurston, the exercise of imperialism and colonialism by Western democracies is hypocritical. She sarcastically writes:

But must a nation suffer from lack of prosperity and
expansion by lofty concepts? Not at all! If a ruler can find
a place way off where the people do not look like him,
kill enough of them to convince the rest that they ought
to support him with their lives and labor, that ruler is
hailed as a great conqueror, and people build monuments
to him. The very weapons he used are also honored. They
picture him in unforgetting stone with the sacred tool of

his conquest in his hand. Democracy like religion never
was designed to make our profits less.[32]

America is no better than Britain in this regard: "We, too, have our
Marines in China. We, too, consider machine gun bullets good laxa-
tives for heathens who get constipated with toxic ideas about a country of their own."[33]

After a lengthy and profound critique of America's imperialism,
Hurston concludes, "I do not brood, however, over the wide gaps
between ideals and practices. The world is too full of inconsistencies
for that."[34] In fact, she asserts a refusal to join the party of protest.
She sees no use in protesting for better conditions for workers. "I will
join no protests for the boss to put a little more stuffing in my bunk.
I don't even want the bunk. I want the bosses' bed."[35] She believes the
United States to be a place where social and economic mobility is possible, so there is no need for organized protest. She will later elaborate upon this in her most right-wing article, "Why the Negro Won't
Buy Communism" (1951), which goes beyond the anticommunism
of mainstream Black political figures and organizations to castigate
by name former friends, acquaintances, and colleagues including
Langston Hughes, Paul Robeson, and W. E. B. Du Bois.[36]

Aspirational and forward looking, Hurston fails to heed Black
suffering, fails to acknowledge the violence Black people, particularly Black Southerners, encountered daily, in large part because
these realities existed alongside the abundance of creativity, joy, and
human complexity that she elsewhere celebrates.

When Hurston is critical of the United States, it is for its foreign
more than its domestic policies. In these contexts, she expresses her
strong anticolonialism. "Crazy for This Democracy," published in the
Negro Digest in December 1945, [37] chastises the US for interfering in
European wars in Asia and for excluding Asia and Africa from the
Atlantic Charter. She humorously notes that the US is not the "Arse-
nal of Democracy" that it has claimed to be; instead it is the "arse-
and-all. . . . The Ass-and-All of Democracy, [which] has shouldered
the load of subjugating the dark world completely."[38]

It is through the critique of her nation's activities in Africa and Asia that Hurston identifies limitations on the practice of democracy within that nation's borders. Noting her love and longing for democracy, she writes, "The only thing that keeps me from pitching headlong into the thing is the presence of numerous Jim Crow laws on the statute books of the nation. I am crazy about the idea of this Democracy. I want to see how it feels. Therefore, I am for the repeal of every Jim Crow law in the nation here and now."[39]

But instead of meeting its demise, Jim Crow was spreading like a cancer, north to Canada and across the Atlantic to South Africa. According to Hurston, the purpose of racial segregation is to instill in the mind of white children the conviction of their superiority and in the minds of dark children their own inferiority. But, she asserts, protest addresses the symptom and not the disease; it may dismantle one law but not the system of laws. Hurston calls for the repeal of all Jim Crow laws once and for all, for both "the benefit of this nation and as a precedent to the world." She calls on the United States to demonstrate leadership in this regard for the health of democracy at home and abroad. Importantly, in this essay Franklin Delano Roosevelt is the political figure for whom Hurston reserves her harshest critique: his foreign policy supports colonizing nations, and his domestic policy addresses racial segregation in a piecemeal fashion, if at all. But Hurston's critique of the US is as a devoted citizen who wishes her nation to be a good actor in the world, an example of the ideals of democracy. Her stance is never anti-American, nor does she call for political or economic revolution. The United States as a constitutional democracy can repeal unjust laws and remove itself from efforts to sustain colonialism.

While some of Hurston's contemporaries turned to communism, and still more worked within mainstream civil rights organizations to challenge and address the nation's shortcomings, Hurston did neither. In fact, she instead turned further to the right, as is evident in two essays, "I Saw Negro Votes Peddled" (1950) and "Why the Negro Won't Buy Communism" (1951), both of which were published in the *American Legion* magazine.

During a period when Black Southerners and their allies would begin the struggle against their disenfranchisement, Hurston claims to have witnessed Florida Blacks who had the vote and sold it. Her evidence is that they voted a straight ticket, and her historical grounding is based on a misreading of Reconstruction, when, she claims, the Negro vote was herded by "greedy Carpet-baggers and their allies, the opportunist-minded southerner who came to be known as the Scalawag."[40] Again, here she adheres to the Dunning School.

In Florida, Hurston witnessed the CIO's effort to organize and register Black voters and "heard about the payment of a dollar to each prospective voter." While she interviews a Black schoolteacher who affirms that a Northern organization has helped to register voters, Hurston asserts, without providing evidence, that the organization pays voters as well. This effort, according to Hurston, resulted in "the long-delayed capture of the South by the left-wing."[41] Those voters who could not be bought with cash, Hurston claims, were convinced by promises of what the FEPC would do for them. (The Fair Employment Practice Committee was created in 1941 by President Roosevelt to implement Executive Order 8802, which banned discrimination in the war industry.) Finally, a class of impoverished voters was given groceries and "free things." Hurston portrays Black voters as wanting something for nothing, as selling their birthright for a mess of pottage, yet she has no evidence other than people voting for those who sought their vote and who made campaign promises that might alleviate some of their suffering and eliminate the barriers to their progress. For Hurston, "the exercise of the franchise, the most potent, the most sacred thing that man had conceived and strived for since humans began to live in communities, was counted as practically nothing."[42]

Blacks ought to hold the right to vote in higher regard than other citizens do, because of the difficulties they encountered in acquiring it. But Black voters, conditioned by Reconstruction politics to be led by exploitive "friends of the Negro," do not carefully consider the issues and vote accordingly; instead they sell their votes for empty promises or $2. Hurston's article fed into the notion that Black Floridians were not prepared for the responsibility of the vote and therefore not prepared for full citizenship rights. Misled by "race leaders" and "friends of the Negro," they voted against their own interests and the interests of the nation.

In June 1951, almost a year into Senator McCarthy's Red Scare, Hurston published "Why the Negro Won't Buy Communism." The article's pull quote reads, "Despite the high-pressure selling of the Paul Robesons, the Benjamin Davis's and the Howard Fasts, the American Negro is too smart to fall for Joe Stalin's brand of up-to-date slavery."[43] Although the article proposes to be about why Blacks reject organized communism, it is also a public rebuke of Black figures most closely aligned with left-wing causes. The article is accompanied by a drawing of an interracial protest with signs "Sign Up for Peace!" "No U.S. Imperialism," "Get Out of Korea!" The article insists upon the exceptionalism of the American Negro, who will refuse the Communist Party's efforts to "lump the American Negro in with all the other colored people of the world so that we will feel that if we fight against the North Koreans, or Mao's hordes, we will be acting against our own best interest."[44] Hurston names Black artists and activists whom she believed had been seduced by communism twenty-five years earlier during a trip to Russia. Many of these people were former friends and acquaintances, including Louise Thompson and Langston Hughes. The article is accompanied by a box with photos of Paul Robeson, Benjamin Davis, Du Bois, Howard Fast, and Langston Hughes, all former colleagues, friends, and acquaintances. Hurston insists that her resistance to Soviet communism is because of USSR's imperialists aim to "be masters of Asia."

Its interest in the American Negro is to use him as a pawn, propaganda, and ultimately soldier for these larger imperialist projects. For this reason, Hurston believes communists "looked down upon us and despised us. They discounted our abilities and integrity infinitely more than those southerners from who they were pretending to defend us."[45] Communism won't work in America, according to Hurston, because there is no grinding poverty; poor and working-class people have access to economic mobility, and there is no "permanent bottom class." Even the Negro "is the most class-conscious individual in the United States."[46] He, like all Americans, would say, "Why kill the boss? He might be the big boss himself next year." If members of the Democratic Party bribed Black voters with promises of "free things," then, according to Hurston, the Communist Party tried to bribe them with sexual access to white women. Both are the proverbial "white mares" said to distract and lure "Black mules."

But Hurston, elsewhere the antiracist and anticolonialist, here asserts the impossibility of an Afro-Asiatic coalition if it is to depend upon the participation of American Negroes. American Blacks feel no bond with Koreans and Chinese: "When numerous Negro homes are mourning the death of their sons, husbands and brothers, and boiling over with rage at the knowledge of butchery and inhuman torture of their loved ones at the hands of these same yellow skins, to now be exhorted to treasure them and take their sides with them is too much to expect of us, even though we are supposed not to be able to remember nor feel resentment at a thing like that."[47] Interestingly, Hurston never acknowledges that Black Americans might mourn deaths lost at the hands of lynch mobs or brutalities at the end of police batons. According to Hurston, the party "has been led astray by the illusion of color. It has been tested and proved that we feel closer to the American white man than to any foreign Negro. The differences between us and foreigners are deep and fundamental."[48] Negroes are Americans first, foremost, and always.

Even if Hurston is correct in her insistence that American Blacks are first and foremost American and also anticommunist, which is likely, her insistence on castigating former colleagues and friends is quite troubling. There is nothing in her assertion of her political beliefs that requires such a public dismissal and critique of Du Bois, Robeson, and Hughes. In fact, the most consistent element of Hurston's political thought appears to be her anti–Du Bois stances on understandings of culture, politics, and history. Her discussion of Negro spirituals in "Characteristics of Negro Expression" does not cite Du Bois by name, but she is clearly critical of the influential chapter "The

Sorrow Songs" with which he closes *The Souls of Black Folk*. Carla Kaplan, editor of the indispensable *Zora Neale Hurston: A Life in Letters*, gives the most succinct description of Hurston's ongoing critique of Du Bois: She battled constantly with W. E. B. Du Bois, for example, and called him Dr. "Dubious": "a propagandist" and "utterly detestable . . . [a] goateed, egotistic, wishy-washy . . . haughty aristocrat." She considered him a mere dabbler in the arts, locked horns with him over the "Florida Negro" project of the Federal Writers' Project, was happy to replace his encyclopedia entry on Negroes because she felt he was "the most pleadingest of all the special pleaders . . . [a] man . . . so subjective that he cannot utter a straight sentence," and was enraged when she was misquoted as saying that "DuBois was the greatest or I do not think so."[49]

The final essay of interest to an understanding of Hurston's political thought is her well-known rejection of the *Brown v. Board of Education* decision, "Court Order Can't Make Races Mix," published in the *Orlando Sentinel* in 1955. While most readers note Hurston's rejection of the decision because of its claim that Black schools are inherently inferior and that allowing proximity to whites is an act of justice, Hurston finds the claim insulting. "I regard the ruling of the U.S. Supreme Court as insulting rather than honoring my race. Since the days of the never-to-be-sufficiently-deplored Reconstruction, there has been current the belief that there is no greater delight to Negroes than the physical association with whites. The doctrine of the white mare."[50]

However, few have noted a second major concern of the essay. According to Hurston the court's action constitutes government "by fiat," "by Decree":

> But the South had better beware in another direction. While it is being frantic over the segregation ruling, it had better keep its eyes open for more important things. One instance of Govt by fiat has been rammed down its throat. It is possible that the end of segregation is not here

and never meant to be here at present, but the attention
of the South directed on what was calculated to keep us
busy while more ominous things were brought to pass.[51]

She warns, "What if it is contemplated to do away with the two-
party system and arrive at Govt by administrative decree? No questions allowed and no information given out from the administrative
department? We could get more rulings on the same subject and
more far-reaching any day." For Hurston, the real threat of the *Brown*
decision isn't the blow it strikes to racial pride but the threat of government overreach. "Govt by fiat can replace the Constitution." For
Hurston, the New Deal was only the most recent example of government overreach: "The stubborn South and the Midwest kept this
nation from being dragged farther to the left than it was during the
New Deal."[52] This is an odd statement from a Black American intellectual for a number of reasons, not the least of which is the South's
overwhelming support for New Deal programs once Black workers
were denied access to some of them. Her distaste for the *Brown* decision is only partially because of her belief in Black excellence. More
importantly, it is based in a right-wing call for the removal of government from what is viewed as social engineering. This is the Hurston
that contemporary libertarians find appealing.

Hurston's politics requires she disregard the suffering of Black
people, that she fundamentally ignore the anti-Black racism that sits
at the core of the nation, and that she ignore the entrenched nature
of white supremacy. Unlike some contemporary Black conservatives,
Hurston is never anti-Black. She celebrates the complexity, sophistication, and beauty of Black aesthetics and the extraordinary wit,
style, and grace with which ordinary Black people conduct their
daily lives. In Hurston's view, slavery and racial oppression have not
thwarted Black people's aspiration toward the full achievement of
their potential. However, her belief in Black resilience and excellence
often blinds her to the more ingrained elements of white supremacy
and their efficacy at halting Black social and political progress.

HUNTING COMMUNISTS AND NEGROES IN ANN PETRY'S *THE NARROWS*

EFORE THE BOTTOM, before Brewster Place, there was the Narrows (also called Eye of the Needle, the Bottom, Little Harlem, Dark Town, Niggertown). Before China, one of the whores in Toni Morrison's *The Bluest Eye,* there was China the whore who lived in the Narrows. Before Alice Walker's sexy blues singer Sugg Avery, there was Mamie Powther the busty, sensual, blues-singing woman desired by all the men of the Narrows and beyond. And, before Milkman Dead, the middle class protagonist of Morrison's *Song of Solomon,* there was Link Williams, the Robesonesque lead character of Ann Petry's third and final novel, *The Narrows.* Although each of the later works are better known than Petry's, her book anticipates many of their major themes. In fact, *The Narrows* foreshadows much of what would follow in all of African American literature; if for this reason only, the book deserves far more critical attention than it has thus far received.

Published in 1953, *The Narrows*—Ann Petry's most ambitious novel—is her masterwork. In spite of this, for the most part, contemporary reviewers found it to be less successful than her first novel, *The Street.* Later critics have also ignored it in favor of the better-known first work. There are a number of reasons for this: Petry's novel was published in a cultural context that also produced Ralph Ellison's *Invisible Man* (1952) and James Baldwin's *Go Tell It on the Mountain*

(1953) as well as the lesser-known small gem *Maud Martha* by Gwendolyn Brooks (1953). Although Brooks received the Pulitzer for her collection of poems, *Annie Allen*, her first and only novel made less of a splash. Following the publication of their first novels, Baldwin and Ellison emerged as leading new literary voices; both produced works focusing on the development of young Black men, and each novel was less overtly political and more experimental than the earlier work of Richard Wright, the dominant figure of African American letters. The form and content of their novels announced a shift from the social realism and naturalism of the '30s and '40s and proved to be more in line with the conservative political climate of the times. This is especially true of Ellison's *Invisible Man*, which was explicitly anticommunist.

Following the emergence of Black feminist literary criticism in the 1970s and '80s, Petry's work began to receive a modicum of attention. With its focus on a working-class Black woman, Lutie Johnson, *The Street* became a vehicle for exploring the intersections of race, class, and gender in Black women's lives. Nonetheless, Petry's other two novels and her short stories have yet to receive the kind of attention devoted to *The Street*.[1] And *The Street* has not yet gained the stature of Zora Neale Hurston's *Their Eyes Were Watching God*.[2] Although Gloria Naylor became an outspoken advocate of Petry's novel, she did not have the same impact as did Alice Walker in her advocacy of Hurston's work. It is possible that later Black feminist critics may have been less interested in *The Narrows* because it does not center around a self-actualized Black female character. Pioneering Black feminist critic Nellie McKay did write an insightful introduction to an edition of *The Narrows*; her essay focuses on the unconventional representations of Black women in the novel.

When other critics have turned their attention to *The Narrows*, they have focused on the volatile interracial relationship at its center. Rarely do they take note of the novel's politics. Vernon E. Lattin, in his essay "Ann Petry and the American Dream" (1978), is one of the few critics to take focus on Petry's political critique of McCarthyism.

It is possible that both contemporary reviewers and literary critics who followed them have been put off by the novel's anti-McCarthy stance and its attention to class. Or perhaps the sensationalism of the interracial romance overshadowed these other elements of the novel. In an important essay on Alice Childress, Lorraine Hansberry, and Claudia Jones, Mary Helen Washington argues for the existence of a radical tradition of Black women writers whose "largely unrecorded history" has fallen victim to "the Cold Warriors [who] tried to wipe the country clean of left-wing ideas."[3] According to Washington, these efforts have been exacerbated by the failure of scholars of the American Left who have produced narratives devoid of African American women and especially by:

> African American canonization practices [that] have always followed the lead of the Cold Warriors, excising the Black Left [so that] we know African American literature of the 1950s through writers like Richard Wright (he tried to be a Communist but publicly renounced the party in 1944), or more typically through Ralph Ellison's conservative, and anticommunist, high modernist *Invisible Man*.[4]

During her time in Harlem, Ann Petry traveled in circles of left intellectuals, artists, and activists. She was the woman's editor of the radical newspaper the *People's Voice*, and she participated in the early stagings of the radical American Negro Theatre alongside Ruby Dee, Ossie Davis, Harry Belafonte, Sidney Poitier, and Alice Childress. This essay seeks to redress the absence of critical writing on the politics of this important novel. For Petry, the responsibility of the artist is to reveal injustice without sacrificing craft.

The Narrows, which is set in a small New England town, Monmouth, Connecticut, is ostensibly the story of the tragic love affair between the married Camilo Sheffield, a white socialite and heiress, daughter of the town's wealthiest family and heir to the Treadway Munitions fortune, and Link Williams, a Black scholar/athlete, son of the town's Black community, the Narrows. When Link tries to end their relationship, Camilo falsely accuses him of rape. He is arrested and released on bail only to be kidnapped and murdered by Camilo's husband and mother. Here I note that Link is the son of the community because he is an orphan who was raised both by the upstanding model of respectability, Abbie Crunch, and the town's powerful, influential, and at times dangerous Bill Hod, "a gambler, operator of houses of ill fame, a numbers king . . . [and] racketeer."⁵ Abbie's well-kept brownstone sits opposite Hod's bar, the Last Chance. Abbie's best friend, the undertaker, Miss Frances K. Jackson (called F. K. Jackson) and Weak Knees, the Last Chance's gifted chef, join Abbie and Bill respectively in rearing the magnificent Link. While the love affair forwards much of the narrative's action, the novel uses the relationship as a vehicle with which Petry forces a confrontation between opposing elements within the narrative: that between Black and white, yes, but perhaps even more important, that between different classes of people. For while the novel offers an important critique of racism, it also offers a stinging critique of class, especially the devastating impact of a market-driven society on the press, the police, and an individual's conception of his or her self. In short, *The Narrows* (as with *The Street* before it) is an eloquent statement of Petry's anticapitalist, antiracist politics.

Furthermore, while the interracial relationship at the novel's center is indeed an exploration of taboo sexuality, *The Narrows* also presents us with other considerations of sexuality, as well. Through the introduction of an explicitly homosexual character, Howard Thomas, as well as the sensual, sex-loving Mamie Powther and her white counterpart, Lola, the redheaded wife of the town's editor (both of whom use their sexual prowess to control their husbands), Petry explores a multidimensional sense of sexuality. Furthermore, by having Link reared by Abbie Crunch and F. K. Jackson on the one hand and Bill Hod and his cook Weak Knees on the other, Petry provides examples of alternative family formations, as well. In fact, after the death of Abbie's husband, the Major, the masculine Jackson steps in as provider and protector. Of F. K. Jackson, Link thinks: "Impossible to think of [F. K. Jackson] hunting a mate, handsome or otherwise.

She was too brusque, too self-sufficient. Perhaps she, in her own person, was the dark handsome lover, and to her Abbie had been [the woman] that the male hunts for and rarely ever finds."[6] It is quite possible that Petry's attention to sex and sexuality as well as the interracial romance landed *The Narrows* on the list of books banned by the National Organization for Decent Literature (NODL). In 1956, the American Civil Liberties Union's *Statement on Censorship Activity by Private Organizations and the National Organization for Decent Literature* notes that NODL was the most prominent, influential, and successful of a number of organizations engaged in censorship activity. Over 160 prominent writers, including Ann Petry, signed the statement.

Before further discussion of the novel, it is important to situate it in the repressive and highly conservative climate of the early 1950s and to provide a discussion of Petry's essay, "The Novel as Social Criticism," which lends insight into the aesthetic and political sensibility that produced the novel.

As noted above, Ann Petry spent much of the 1940s in Harlem, where she worked as a journalist and editor while honing her craft. She was also an active participant in several activist and cultural organizations that were overtly political. As a number of scholars have noted, for Black intellectuals and activists, the Popular Front continued well into the middle of the 1940s.[7] This sensibility informed Petry throughout her life and is most explicitly stated in her essay "The Novel as Social Criticism."

Published four years after *The Street* and three before *The Narrows*, "The Novel as Social Criticism" (1950) (which appeared in *The Writers Book*) is Ann Petry's most sustained aesthetic statement. That it appears alongside essays by W. H. Auden, Pearls S. Buck, Lionel Trilling, and Petry's mentor, Mabel Louise Robinson, its publication also suggests Petry's stature among other writers. In the essay, Petry defends the "sociological novel," which had come under great scrutiny and critique during the years following World War II. Just one year before "The Novel as Social Criticism," in 1949, a young James Baldwin published his scathing critique of Harriet Beecher Stowe's

Uncle Tom's Cabin and his mentor Richard Wright's *Native Son*. Petry addresses these kinds of critiques head on:

> Being a product of the twentieth century (Hitler, atomic energy, Hiroshima, Buchenwald, Mussolini, USSR) I find it difficult to subscribe to the idea that art exists for art's sake. It seems to me that all truly great art is propaganda, whether it be Sistine Chapel, or La Gioconda, *Madame Bovary* or *War and Peace*.[8]

Echoing W. E. B. Du Bois's famous essay "Art as Propaganda," Petry argues for the continuing significance of sociological fiction, identifies its deep roots in Western culture, and distances it from charges of Marxist propaganda without denying the significance of Marxism:

> Not all of the concern about the shortcomings of society originated with Marx. Many a socially conscious novelist is merely a man or a woman with a conscience. Though part of the cultural heritage of all of us derives from Marx, whether we subscribe to Marxist theory or not, a larger portion of it stems from the Bible.[9]

Petry situates Marx in the context of Western thought; his thought has influenced Western society in much the way Freud has—one need not have read either to have experienced their influence. The same might be said of the Bible, although most Westerners are more familiar with the stories of the Bible, especially those that are meant to inform our behavior and our morality. And certainly, especially during the Cold War, even the most right-wing of readers would not argue with the importance of Biblical injunctions.

From here, Petry accomplishes the task of arguing for the importance of sociological fiction in a number of ways: First, she grounds the tradition in the Bible, particularly the Old Testament story of Cain and Abel whereby Cain asks God, "Am I my brother's keeper?" Petry writes:

In one way or another, the novelist who criticizes some
undesirable phase of the status quo is saying that man is
his brother's keeper and that unless a social evil (war or
racial prejudice or anti-Semitism or political corruption)
is destroyed man cannot survive but will become what
Cain feared he would become—a wander and a vagabond
on the face of the earth.[10]

Petry also argues against art for art's sake while insisting upon the
importance of craft, especially in the development of full, complex
characters. "When society is given the role of fate, made the evil in
the age-old battle between good and evil, the burden of responsibility for their actions is shifted away from the characters."[11] According
to Petry, that which distinguishes successful novels from their more
didactic cousins is craftsmanship and the author's development of
characterization and theme: "Once the novelist begins to manipulate
his characters to serve the interests of his theme they lose whatever
vitality they had when their creator first thought about them."[12]

The Narrows is Petry's novelistic example of the theories she
espouses in this little-known essay. Together, the essay and novel
serve as a critical intervention in the midst of an era of censorship
and witch-hunting. In the same year that Petry's essay was published,
Joseph McCarthy gave his first public speech against communists,
alleging, "I have in my hand a list of 205 cases of individuals who
appear to be either card-carrying members or certainly loyal to the
Communist Party." Later that year, the McCarran Act, or the Internal
Security Act of 1950, passed in spite of a veto by President Truman.
Among other things, the act required members of the US Communist Party to register with the attorney general, and communist organizations to provide lists of their members. The act also established
the Subversive Activities Control Board to select individuals and
organizations that had to comply with its regulations.

In 1951, under the leadership of Senator McCarthy, the second
set of House Un-American Activities Committee hearings became
his stage for accusing American citizens of betraying their country.

Having been members in communist organizations or having had friends and associates who were members was evidence enough for McCarthy.

Among the many artists and intellectuals whose lives and careers McCarthyism threatened were a number of African Americans. Mary Helen Washington notes: "Whether on the Left or the Right, African Americas were, by virtue of their Blackness, subversives in the Cold War."[13] The two most famous, Paul Robeson and W. E. B. Du Bois, are especially significant for our purposes, for just as both were undergoing assault, Ann Petry chose to create a DuBoisian, Robeson-esque character in Link Williams. Interestingly, in 1946, Petry wrote to Shirley Graham upon the publication of her book about Paul Robeson that the book was "wonderful! . . . I must confess to feeling very smug because I am able to say that I know you."[14] In 1951, Graham would marry W. E. B. Du Bois; in that same year, he was indicted for failing to register as a foreign agent (the charges would later be dropped) and he ran for the United States Senate on the American Labor Party ticket. The FBI, under J. Edgar Hoover, began their surveillance of Robeson in 1941. In 1952 the HUAC sought to cite him for his refusal to sign the noncommunist declaration, and the State Department denied him his passport.

As with Du Bois, Link Williams is a New England born, Ivy League–educated (Dartmouth) intellectual. As with Du Bois, he writes a thesis about slavery and he aspires to become a scholar of Black history. However, unlike the young Du Bois, Williams is no elitist. In fact, he finds the DuBoisan elitism of Abbie and the Black bourgeoisie repressive and stifling, preferring the more egalitarian environs of the Last Chance, the Dock, Dumble Street. The struggle between Abbie Crunch's racial politics and those of Bill Hod represent the distinction between an uplift ideology of respectability and one that found value in Black vernacular culture. Link recalls Abbie's assertions about his responsibility to "The Race":

> She said colored people (sometimes she just said The Race) had to be cleaner, smarter, thriftier, more ambi-

tious than white people, so that white people would like colored people. The way she explained it made him feel as though he were carrying The Race around with him all the time.[15]

Bill Hod and Weak Knees "re-educated him on the subject of race."[16] Through conversations about contemporary events and Black history Link loses his fear of laughing at white people and learns to appreciate the color Black: "After a month of living with Bill and Weak Knees he felt fine. He felt safe. He was no longer ashamed of the color of his skin."[17]

Link's connection to Robeson is a bit more explicit. In fact, Robeson is the object of conversation between Link and Weak Knees, who articulates a signifying defense of Robeson and critique of the United States. Weak Knees explains to Link:

You know, Sonny, I get sick of all these wha folks askin' me first thing, first drop of a hat, what do I think about Paul Robeson. The meat man he come in here this mornin; a brokedown dogass white man if I ever see one, all bandy legged from carryin' carcasses, and he come in here with my order, and before he gets the meat put down on the table good he wants to know what do I think about Paul Robeson. So I made him happy, I said I thought he oughtta hightail it back to Russia where he come from, and that softened him up, and I waited awhile and I give him a cup of coffee, and then I says, The reason he oughtta have stayed in Russia, mister, is because over there if he went around talkin' about the changes he wanted made, why'd he get hisself shot full of holes, but nobody over there would be goin' around about to piss in their pants because he was a Black man talkin' the wrong kind of politics. ... And if his boy went and married hisself a little white chickadee over there in Russia, the whafolks woudn't wasted their time runnin' to tell all the colored folks they see askin' 'em what they thought about it. I says over there they wouldn't give a damn mister, and I don't give a damn over here. Any country where the folks can't marry each other when they got a heat on for each other why.[18]

Significantly, Weak Knees doesn't claim to share Robeson's politics; in fact, he seems to disagree with him. Nonetheless, he defends Robeson's right to freely express his political opinions, and Weak Knees offers a critique of the United States for its obsession with miscegenation and laws against interracial marriage. Consequently, here we have an argument against the racial politics of the United States as well as a defense of civil liberties, but no explicit statement about capitalism. Furthermore, Weak Knees foreshadows the exact taboo over which Link will lose his life—the fact that he and a white woman fall passionately in love with each other. Petry reserves expressions of critiques of capitalism for the photographer Jubine.

As with Robeson, Link Williams is a charismatic scholar-athlete whose voice is "a deep resonant musical voice. A perfect speaking voice." His Aunt Abbie looked at "the line of his throat, at the slight thrust of his chin, at the smoothness of his skin, the perfection of his nose and mouth, the straightness of his hair and thought 'Sometimes, just sometimes, I wish he weren't so very good looking." Indeed, it is his dignity, his nobility, and his beauty that help incite the fury of racists, the envy of most men and the lust of women Black and white. Following Camilo's accusation of rape and her car accident where she runs down a poor child of the Narrows, the photographer, Jubine, himself a communist, who has "the unkempt look of a Bolshevist" sells a photograph of Link to a New York tabloid. The photograph is an effort to counter any possible attempts to portray him as a dangerous animalistic rapist. The editor of the Monmouth newspaper, Bullock, who has refused Jubine's photograph and chosen not to run a story critical of Camilo under threat of losing her family's advertising money, looks at the photograph and thinks:

So here was this Negro standing on the dock, lordlylook-
ing bastard, leaning against the railing, head slightly
turned, profile like Barrymore's, sunlight concentrated
on his left side, so that the head, the shoulders, the whole
length of him had the solidity of sculpture, the picture
damn near had the three-dimensional quality of fine
sculpture. There was an easy carelessness about the leaning position of his body, controlled carelessness, and
the striped T-shirt, the slacks; the moccasins on the feet
suited his posture.

Every woman who saw this nigger's picture would cut
it out, clip it out, tear it out, and drool over it. Every white
man who saw it would do a slow burn.[19]

The photograph could very well be one of the many that portray
Robeson as a Black Adonis, especially those of him as Shakespearian
actor or the nudes taken by Van Vechten that show him in the classic poses of the athlete. In fact, Bullock describes the photograph as a
work of art. The Link of this photograph is the construction of Jubine,
the artist. That the photograph is published in a New York tabloid is
a demonstration of art in the service of social justice. In "The Novel
as Social Criticism," Petry writes, "The novel like all other forms of
art, will always reflect the political, economic and social structure of
the period in which it was produced."[20] Jubine's photographs possess
both beauty and devastating honesty.

Although Petry stresses the artistic nature of Jubine's photographs, she has him publish them in fashion magazines and newspapers. For Petry, the press is an arena of conflict. As a former reporter
for the Black press, she understood the power of the media in shaping
public consciousness about race. In both *The Narrows* and *The Street*,
she demonstrates the way the mainstream press feeds racial hatred
and fear by exaggerating the size and potential danger of Black people, by painting portraits of Black neighborhoods as jungles. And yet,
through Jubine she also demonstrates the possibility of an alternative

use of the press. Jubine prefers that his photographs be printed as a series and not out of context so that they create a narrative. He uses photography as a means of indicting the wealthy while portraying the dignity of the poor without romanticizing their poverty. When Bullock does publish Jubine's photographs in the *Monmouth Chronicle*, they are part of an important series on housing and poverty. When he chooses to ignore him, he allows his paper to be used in the service of capital and racial violence. Jubine is a minor but important character, for as the narrative's artist, he is the vehicle through which Petry speaks. Interestingly, in both *Country Place* and *The Narrows*, Petry chooses to have the author's perspective articulated by white men, the pharmacist in *Country Place* and Jubine here. When Bullock accuses him of setting up his photographs, Jubine responds, "Jubine watches. Jubine waits. Jubine records but Jubine never, never interferes." Through Jubine and the novel's other white characters we gain even further insight into the novel's critique of American capitalism.

If Link is a Robesonesque character, his lover, the beautiful blonde Camilo is a forerunner to Sophia, Malcolm X's married white lover in *The Autobiography of Malcolm X*. Even as Camilo falls in love with Link, she continues to maintain a sense of entitlement, paternalism and condescension. She uses her wealth to pay off hotel staff, maître d's, and others in order to create a cocoon for herself and her Black lover. She often speaks to Link as if her were her servant. When he expresses his resentment and chooses to end their relationship, she accuses him of rape. She represents an elite class in the midst of transition. In the novel, this transition is "the passing of aristocrats"[21] to "millionaires" from people like Abbie Crunch, who possesses "an air of quiet elegance . . . attributed to aristocratic old colored women and a handful of aristocratic old white women"[22] and her late husband's former employer, "the Governer" to "common" people like Mamie Powther who "is Dumble Street." Throughout the novel there is a sense of flux about class matters, and it is characterized by a kind of vulgarity among both the wealthy and the poor. On the one hand, the houses of the Narrows are being torn down and replaced by high-rise projects. On the other, it is not a white mob that kidnaps and murders

Link, but instead educated, wealthy whites seeking to protect their name and their wealth.

Malcolm Powther, butler to the Treadways and husband of Mamie, is representative of an old-fashioned, loyal servant, proud of his proximity to wealth and whiteness. He makes note of the confusion created by differences and changes in class. He oversees Mrs. Treadway's annual midwinter tea for young women who work in her munitions plant. While he used to enjoy the tea because the young ladies wore their best dresses and were on their best behavior, he comes to despise them when they spread gossip about Camilo following her accusation of rape. He used to make distinctions between the young women and the rowdy workmen, for whom Mrs. Treadway holds a summer picnic on her mansion's grounds. He observes:

> These girls smelt of perfume, their hair curled, they were wearing their new Spring dresses, but they were exactly like the sweaty beer-drinking workers, who invaded the park in July. They too, resented the fact that the Madam belonged to the millionaire class. . . . The beer drinkers wrecked the grounds or tried to and the tea drinkers . . . were just as hostile.[23]

Yet Petry, like Jubine, recognizes the dignity of the poor Irish women who hold their families together, the honesty of the poor white farmer's wife who refuses to say a Black escaped convict raped her, the generosity of Miz Doris, F. K. Jackson's housekeeper, and Mamie Powther's lack of hypocrisy. The novel's worst characters are the status-hungry Bullock and Malcolm Powther. Each of them worship wealth and are easily bought and controlled by it. Furthermore, each is also fully aware of their complicity and wrestles with their cowardice. The cuckold Powther, who looks in his wife's closets and bureau drawers for evidence of her infidelity, identifies with Camilo's husband. Consequently, when Mrs. Treadway requests that he accompany them to Dumble Street and "point out" (name names) Link, he agrees to do so. While waiting in the car with Mrs. Treadway, Captain Sheffield, and two of Sheffield's college classmates, Powther hears a sermon broadcast from the loudspeaker of a local storefront church:

> And the Lord said unto Cain . . . Where is Abel thy brother? . . .
> What hast thou done? . . .
> The voice of thy brother's blood crieth unto me from the ground.[24]

Powther is counterpart to slaves who hid their mistresses' silver from the Union Army or those who informed their masters of planned rebellions. He represents the worst extreme of a politics of respectability. Hearing the sermon, he thinks: "He wasn't my brother. I have to prove he wasn't my brother. Prove to these people . . . that all Negroes are not criminal, some of them are good, some of them are first-class butlers named Powther."[25] With this conviction, he identifies Link and delivers him to his murderers.

Powther and Bullock are linked by their cowardice, their willingness to be pawns to wealth, their inability to confront their wives for fear the women will deny them access to their bodies. As with Powther, Bullock also "points out" Link by using his paper to paint the Black community as violent, depraved, and dangerous. It is through Bullock that Petry articulates the connection between anti-Red and anti-Black ideologies and practices. In a moment of self-reflection about his complicity, he thinks:

> Even the State Department was acting like a harried housewife, searching out the hiding place of mice and cockroaches and bedbugs, any vermin that from time to time invade a house, searching carefully under beds and bureau drawers, and on closet shelves, in cellars and in attics, peering inside ovens, and sugar bowls, looking in every likely and unlikely place for communists and socialists, for heretics and unbelievers. . . .
> So what difference does it make, he thought, whether

we here in Monmouth hunt down Negroes or whether
we hunt down Communists?... There is a difference,
though at the moment it escapes me.[26]

Black and white disapproved of Link and Camilo, not because they
were involved in an adulterous affair but because of race. What ought
to have been a private, personal relationship between lovers is the
object of great concern to people who follow, pursue, and observe
them. A society obsessed with weeding out communists nourishes an
anti-Black racism, nourishes those who police the color line. A society that tolerates surveillance and censorship is dangerous for anyone
considered marginal or capable of threatening the status quo.

In *The Narrows*, Petry realizes the aesthetic vision she forwards
in "The Novel as Social Criticism." She creates characters who are
challenged to wrestle with themselves, who must confront their own
demons and cowardice. This is especially true of Bullock and Powther, who make possible Link's murder, who name names by pointing him out and paint a climate of fear by telling dangerous lies
about entire groups of people. The novel closes on a note of hope,
when Abbie, following her own self-critical self-reflection acknowledges her complicity in the downfall of Link and Camilo. Concerned
that Bill Hod will seek revenge on Camilo, Abbie decides, at novel's
end, to try and prevent further violence. Hand in hand with Mamie
Powther's unkempt "urchin" J. C. Powther, she goes to the police to
request protection for Camilo. So Petry gives us a vision where the
Black bourgeoisie, along with a child of the urban poor (who is sure
to benefit from his association with her), together take the moral high
ground by seeking to ensure peace, security, and forgiveness.

In the past twenty years, historians have produced a body of work
documenting a history of Black radicalism. A number of cultural
and literary historians have also started to include African American thinkers in broader histories of the Left. However, literary critics
and theorists (of African American literature) have sacrificed attention to politics and literary history in favor of more formalist and
theoretical concerns. Following the lead of Ralph Ellison, the emer-

gence of contemporary African American literary criticism sought to ensure more "literary" and less "sociological" readings of Black fiction in order to acknowledge the sophistication and artistry of these works. Ann Petry's *The Narrows* has fallen between the cracks of all of these efforts. Petry's work does not sacrifice artistry for politics, and yet it cannot be properly read or appreciated without attention to the political. There is little evidence that Petry actively participated in the left-leaning literary circles of Harlem during the years she lived in Connecticut; consequently, she does not emerge as part of groups of writers such as those gathered around Robeson's publication *Freedom Ways* or organizations such as the Harlem Writers Guild. Given her intensely private nature, it is difficult to place her. However, a close reading of her fiction reveals a great deal about her understanding of the relationship between political and aesthetic concerns.

Attending to Petry's fiction of the 1950s (and that of other under-appreciated Black authors) gives us a fuller view of that period. It also provides a bridge from the fiction of the 1940s to the work of the Black arts Movement in the late 1960s and '70s. As such, most histories leap from Ellison and Baldwin to a group of young militants who rediscover Richard Wright during the Black power movement. This gives an appearance of a Black radicalism that has lain dormant for over twenty years. Ann Petry should be a central figure in a revisionist history of African American literature; her novel *The Narrows* helps to demonstrate the aesthetic and political complexity of African American literary culture during the Cold War years. Additionally, *The Narrows* should join Zora Neale Hurston's *Their Eyes Were Watching God*, with which it shares a great deal, as an important forerunner to the later emergence of Black women's literature. While critics and writers alike have claimed that Black male writers have been most concerned about relationships between Black men and white men while Black women writers have focused on intra-racial matters, *The Narrows* attempts to do both by attending mutually to intimate familial and communal issues while also turning its attention to issues of race and, most importantly, class.

"IT TAKES TWO PEOPLE TO CONFIRM THE TRUTH"

The Jazz Fiction of Sherley Anne Williams
and Toni Cade Bambara

PUBLISHED IN 1977, Valerie Wilmer's *As Serious as Your Life: John Coltrane and Beyond* (alternately called *As Serious as Your Life: The Story of the New Jazz*) continues to be one of the most important books about the lives, aesthetics, and politics of the Coltrane-influenced generation of "free jazz" musicians. Wilmer's book is one of the first and still rare instances to also call attention to the family lives of musicians, as well. She devotes two chapters to women in the New Music.[1] While one focuses on the difficulties faced by women musicians, the other, titled "It Takes Two People to Confirm the Truth," is primarily concerned with the women who are the musicians' partners, wives, and companions. In this way, *As Serious as Your Life* is an important precursor to contemporary scholarship on the music, which seeks to understand the musicians and the music they produce in the context of the communities that support and sustain them. In addition, in her attention to gender and the roles of women as musicians and domestic partners, Wilmer also anticipates developments in the field.

Contemporaneous to Wilmer, a number of Black women writers, including Sherley Anne Williams and Toni Cade Bambara, also began to develop works of fiction that turn our attention away from the bandstand to the women who attend performances, the women in the booth or at the tables in the club, and the women who share domestic space with the musicians. And yet, with the exception of Gayl Jones's *Corregidora* and Toni Morrison's *Jazz*, few of these writers appear on syllabi, as symposia topics, or in a myriad of recent anthologies devoted to jazz literature.[2]

My understanding of jazz literature is informed by Sascha Feinstein's definition of jazz poems: "A jazz poem is any poem that has been informed by jazz music. The influence can be in the subject of the poem or in the rhythms, but one should not necessarily exclude the other."[3] So, for our purposes, jazz literature includes poems, novels, short stories, and literary essays that reference the music and musicians as central to the work's form or content.

Significantly, women have received attention as writers of jazz poems, and a number of them appear in jazz poetry anthologies, including Jayne Cortez, Sonia Sanchez, Ntozake Shange, and Harryette Mullen.[4] It is therefore surprising that Williams and Bambara have not yet made it into this emerging canon. Rarely, if ever, are they included in listings or bibliographies of jazz and literature.[5] Bambara's short story "Medley" appears in only one of the anthologies devoted to jazz literature, Marcela Breton's *Hot and Cool: Jazz Short Stories* (1990).[6]

Nathaniel Mackey's series of epistolary novels features women as musicians, and Candace Allen's novel *Valaida*, inspired by Valaida Snow, is about a female instrumentalist. The protagonist plays violin as well as trumpet. Mackey's creative and critical writings are central to any discussion of jazz fiction, and in all probability, Allen's novel will begin to receive the attention of scholars as well.[7] Consequently, fictional female jazz musicians should begin to gain the attention of critics who study jazz fiction. However, to my knowledge, Sherrie Tucker's pioneering essay, "'Where the Blues and the Truth Lay Hiding:' Rememory of Jazz in Black Women's Fiction" (1992), which focuses on works by Bambara, Maya Angelou, and Xam Cartiér, is the only critical work to focus on jazz fiction by women specifically.

Quite possibly, stories by Bambara and Williams are not included in emerging canons of jazz fiction because they center the voices of women who are not instrumentalists but who share their lives with the musicians. Inspired by Wilmer's example, this essay will posit two such stories, "Tell Martha Not to Moan" by Sherley Anne Williams and "Medley" by Toni Cade Bambara, as jazz literature. Both authors use fiction as a vehicle that allows them to respond to discourses surrounding the music, be they other forms of fiction or stories and stereotypes that abound within the jazz community. Furthermore, each author sheds light on aspects of jazz communities often unseen in writings about the music.

Including these stories in the emerging canon of jazz literature or in interdisciplinary studies of the music will challenge or alter many of the major paradigms used to discuss that literature. In one of the best critical works on jazz fiction, *The Color of Jazz: Race and Representation in Postwar American Culture* (1997), Jon Panish compares representations of jazz and jazz musicians by Black and white writers during the 1950s and early 1960s. Panish argues that "Black and white Americans differ fundamentally in their use and understanding of jazz as an African American cultural resource . . . [and that] these differences are linked to racial developments in the social, economic, and political spheres during this era."[8] Focusing on representations of Greenwich Village, Charlie Parker, jazz performance, and improvisation in the works of writers as diverse as Jack Kerouac, Amiri Baraka, Ross Russell, and John A. Williams, Panish argues that "in most general terms, white texts tend to romanticize the jazz musician's experience, stereotype jazz heroes, dehistoricize and decontextualize the development of the music, and emphasize competitive individualism over any sense of community. Black texts, on the other hand, tend to present the jazz musician as an admirable but complicated figure; set the development of the music in a clear tradition that is continually repeated and revised; make connections between the music, the musician, and social experience; and inextricably link the accomplishments of the individual with the success of the community" (Panish 1997, xix).

In *Blowin' Hot and Cool: Jazz and Its Critics* (2006), John Gennari also posits important differences between Black and white critics and jazz writers, although he is more concerned with critics than with writers of fiction. Gennari's argument is more nuanced than that of Panish in that his distinctions are less Manichean. According to Gennari, "Across lines of color . . . a romanticism imbues every [white] jazz critic's engagement with the music." Nonetheless, "it has been crucial for . . . these critics to use their white privilege on behalf of the musicians" (8–9).

In "'Where the Blues and the Truth Lay Hiding:' Rememory of Jazz in Black Women's Fiction" (1992), Sherrie Tucker focuses on jazz fiction by Black women writers, whom she credits with creating an alternative historiography to that posited by jazz critics and historians of the music. Tucker's essay anticipates many of the arguments she makes in her important study of women jazz musicians, *Swing Shift: "All-Girl" Bands of the 1940s* (2000). According to Tucker, writers such as Maya Angelou, Toni Cade Bambara, and Xam Cartiér create "a site in which we find a record of meaning, as well as existence for Black women in the field of jazz." This project, Tucker argues, runs counter to conventional jazz criticism and histories, in that the women "depict jazz as being part of Black women's lives and Black women as part of jazz."[9]

In *The Color of Jazz*, Panish writes about texts of the 1940s and 1950s, and although he does cite a few women writers, he is primarily interested in men. The stories of Williams and Bambara are just as influenced by their times, the late 1960s and early 1970s. Neither woman romanticizes the musicians; however, in the case of Williams, the potential success of the individual musician is in direct opposition to the success of the community as it is represented by the woman and child he leaves behind. Neither woman focuses on the singular virtuosity of the musician. Tucker calls our attention to women as musicians and historians of the music, and, in so doing, she posits an alternative figure and history to those found in conventional works. This essay will focus on women as members of jazz communities and as partners who refuse to romanticize the musician and insist upon highlighting his relationship to others. "The Sister until very, very recently was unconcerned, unappreciative and deaf to jazz. She knew that a Black jazz musician would never make a dollar or get ahead or give her any concern or consideration, as she always demanded of a Black husband. She is a matriarch, but her values are the establishment values in this country: the fine home, the big car, and the front" (quoted in Valerie Wilmer, *As Serious as Your Life*, 191). Valerie Wilmer attributes the above quotation to a woman, "white herself, but married for years to one of the great Black bass players." According to Wilmer, the woman's view (not unlike that of the Moynihan Report) represents the traditional attitude toward Black women. (I am not sure where Naima or Alice Coltrane or Fontella Bass would fall in the above categorization.) Wilmer writes that this is an attitude that began to change because of the Black power movement:

> But this was in the 1970s, after Malcolm X, after Stokely Carmichael had informed women that their position in the movement should be 'prone,' and after the Black woman's consciousness had been stirred to realize the importance for the man's self-esteem of rejecting the privileged role she is alleged to have enjoyed in white society by virtue of her sex. Although the evidence that she is equally exploited and frequently more so than the Black man has been clearly expounded, the pressures on Black women to support the man, whether or not he is able to provide, are very strong" (191).

In the remainder of the chapter, Wilmer focuses on a number of Black and white women who are married to or live with musicians. Williams and Bambara write against both the image of Black women as materialistic and bourgeois and the pressure to accept Black male patriarchy. Bambara also challenges the notion of Black women as unappreciative or unconcerned about the music. Both writers give us characters that frequent jazz clubs. In spite of Abbey Lincoln's well-known angry assertion that "We are the women whose bars and recreation halls are invaded by flagrantly disrespectful, bigoted, simpering, amoral, emotionally unstable, outcast, maladjusted, nymphomaniacal, condescending white women," neither Bambara nor

Williams seems concerned with the presence of white women.[10] In fact, white men and women are all but absent in their social milieu. These writers were both self-proclaimed Black feminists/womanists and along with Alice Walker, Toni Morrison, and Ntozake Shange, they were among the primary architects of the renaissance of Black women's writings in the 1970s and 1980s. Like these other writers, they were primarily concerned with what Hortense Spillers calls the "intramural" relations between Black people, mothers and daughters, men and women, and women friends.

The Black Woman: An Anthology (1970), edited by Bambara, is a founding text of this literary movement, informed both by the Black freedom struggle and the feminist movement. The Black Woman is a showcase of a new generation of Black women poets, novelists, critics, and scholars. It included works by Walker, Audre Lorde, Nikki Giovanni, Abbey Lincoln, et al.; it also included Sherley Anne Williams's first published story, "Tell Martha Not to Moan." Originally published in the Massachusetts Review in 1968, "Tell Martha Not to Moan" exhibits many of the qualities that characterize Williams's later work. The central character, Martha, is a single welfare mother; her lover, Time, is a jazz musician. Ordinarily invisible to novelists, politicians, and the mainstream public, or else viewed only as a sexual being who is dependent on the tax dollars of the middle class, Martha is here the protagonist of the story. Although she is not the first working-class or working-poor woman to appear in Black fiction, she is unique. Unlike Ann Petry's working-class heroine, Lutie Johnson, Martha is not an ambitious, noble, and chaste member of the "deserving poor." She is not even working-class. Unlike Annie Allen of Gwendolyn Brooks's poetry collection of the same name or Maud Martha in Brooks's novel Maud Martha, Williams's Martha does not speak in the poetic language of the Western literary tradition. Martha is a sensual young woman who has a child out of wedlock and who chooses to live with her lover outside of marriage, as well. She is sensual and funny but lacking in self-confidence. Her language is the eloquent Black English that Williams grew up hearing. "My mamma a big woman, tall and stout and men like her cause she soft and fluffy looking. . . . Since I had Larry things ain't been too good between us. But—that's my mamma and I know she gon be there when I need her. . . . Her eyes looking all ove me and I know it coming" (47).[11] Without lapsing into stereotypical dialect, Williams presents Black speech in much the way that Zora Neale Hurston did with the Black Southern language of Janie in *Their Eyes Were Watching God.*

"Tell Martha Not to Moan" gives us a woman who ultimately wants the stability and security of a stable family and relationship. However, unlike the dismissive remark in the Wilmer text, it lends complexity to the character by charting her personal history and fear of abandonment. At the story's opening, Martha's mother confronts her with a series of questions about her second pregnancy: "When it due, Martha?" "Who the daddy?" After Martha responds, "Time," her mother asks, "That man what play piano at the Legion? . . . What he gon do about it? . . . Where he at now?" This series of questions by a woman whom some may consider a matriarch portrays a mother's concern for the well-being of her daughter and unborn grandchild. They immediately set up an authoritative voice that questions Martha's actions and Time's integrity. This interrogation ends with "Martha, you just a fool. I told you that man wasn't no good first time I seed him. A musician the worst kind of man you can get mixed up with" (48).

Mamma's voice is the voice of authority not only because of her age and experience but also because she sets the frame of the narrative. Consequently, her characterization of Time makes the reader suspicious of him even before he enters the narrative. Her voice haunts but does not dominate the remainder of the story. Martha's interior voice is the dominant one of the narrative.

Williams provides her readers with insight into Martha's inner self, her limitations as well as her aspirations. At eighteen years of age, she is the very young mother of a toddler, not yet fully mature and lacking a sense of direction. Her lover, the piano player Time, is the complex intellectual—a frustrated Black artist in a racist society. In her critical work, *Give Birth to Brightness*, Williams devotes an entire chapter to the figure of the Black musician in Black American literature, "The Black Musician: The Light Bearer." Published in 1972, *Give Birth to Brightness* explores works by Amiri Baraka, James Baldwin, and Ernest Gaines. Interestingly, the book focuses on male writers and very masculinist folk forms, figures, and themes. Her central argument is that Black male writers have created a brilliant literature that provides "a vision of Black life." In the brief time that Time is in Martha's life, he does bring light and enlightenment, as well as a vision of Black life. He possesses a politicized racial consciousness that Martha lacks.

Not only is Time a bearer of the tradition of Black music, his appearance and his appreciation of Martha have identified him as a "conscious" brother. Martha recalls the first time she sees him. She and her friend Orine are in a club called "the Legion" and Time is the new pianist. She remembers: "First time I ever seed a man wear his hair so long and nappy—he tell me once it an African Bush— but he look good anyway and he know it." At the end of the set, he approaches her saying, "You, . . you my Black queen." Martha takes "Black" as an insult. . . . "I ain't Black. . . . I just a dark woman." The Black consciousness movement seems not to have reached her small Southern town. Time tells her, "What's the matter, you shamed of being Black? Ain't nobody told you Black is pretty?" (30). In this exchange, Williams reveals a number of things about her characters. The musicians play for a Black audience and Time steps off the bandstand like a preacher from the pulpit. He is more politically and racially aware than Martha for whom Black is not yet beautiful. He both names and claims her: "Yeah, you gon be my Black queen." On the first night of their meeting, he informs her of his plans to go to New York: "Up in the City, they doing one maybe two things. In L.A. they doing another one, two things. But, man, in New York, they doing everything. Person couldn't never get stuck in one groove there. So many things going on, you got to be hip, real hip to keep up. You always growing there" (53). He is an ambitious and cosmopolitan man in possession of a clear vision of his desires and his future. Later that evening (or in the wee hours of the following morning) in a moment of postcoital bliss, he shares his dreams with Martha: "I up tight on the inside but I can't get it to show on the outside. I don't know how to make it come out. You ever hear Coltrane blow. . . . He showing on the outside what he got on the inside. When I can do that, then I be somewhere. But I can't go by myself. I need a woman. A Black woman. Them other women steal your soul and don't leave nothing. But a Black woman—" (55).

Time plans to fit Martha into the larger vision he has of his life; his political sensibility if not his emotions tell him that she is the woman to fill his slot because she is Black. He is the voice of a masculinist Black nationalism. Although his vision for his life and his music includes Martha, there is no place for her child, Larry, for whom he seems to hold resentment.

As their relationship develops, Time introduces Martha to the music, to aspects of Black history, and to a community of musicians who treat him as a kind of high priest. Time is consistently able to articulate his vision for his future. Martha is not; throughout the story, she is often rendered mute or inarticulate. He consistently paints a portrait of his vision, a vision inspired and informed by his nationalist politics. In contrast, she thinks, "It seem like all I got is lots little pitchers in my mind and can't tell nobody what they look like." She, too, has something inside, but as with Morrison's Sula, she lacks the means to express it.

If Time is resentful of Martha's devotion to her child, she is sometimes jealous of his music. It is a jealousy that comes to a head in the closing pages of the story. Listening to Time's conversation with other musicians, she realizes he is used to having a woman who provides for him while he pursues his music. Later, he asks her what she wants out of her life and then, "What you doing on the Welfare?" Having found her voice at his encouragement, she replies: "What else I gon do? Go out and scrub somebody else's toilets like my mamma did so Larry can run wild like I did? . . . If [my no good daddy] got out and worked, we woulda been better off" (62).

Martha has been abandoned by a father who did not provide and a mother who was forced to do so by being the primary breadwinner.

Time attempts to explain the role of "the man" in constructing the limited opportunities of both her and her father. Martha explodes: "You always talking bout music and New York City, New York City and the white man. Why don't you forget all that shit and get a job like other men? I hate that damn piano" (62). Like the "Sister" of the above quotation, Martha challenges, indeed assaults Time's dream and his music. But unlike the "Sister," she is not one-dimensional and materialistic. She is a woman already abandoned by her own father and the father of her child. She is a woman who relies on welfare, a woman not only deserving of affirmation and love but also deserving of a partner who is committed to building a life with her and sharing financial responsibilities, a partner who is able to accept her child and take care of his. Time is the devout musician, the politically conscious intellectual, but he is also a man who abandons his responsibility to his lover and their unborn child to fulfill his responsibility to the music. In the story's closing pages, Martha, pregnant with yet another child, sits awaiting his return. In "Tell Martha Not to Moan," music and mobility belong to the male musician, but language and storytelling ultimately belong to Martha. The first-person narrative puts control of the story in Martha's hands. Finally, the story, as it is rendered by Williams if not by Martha (for it is unclear how conscious Martha is of the implications of her telling), seems to anticipate Toni Morrison's quotation at the end of *Song of Solomon*. As the protagonist, Milkman, celebrates the ability of his ancestor to fly back to Africa, his lover Sweet asks, "Who'd he leave behind?"[12] Both Morrison and Williams remind us that Black male flight, be it literal or figurative, often results in abandoned wives, children, families, and communities.

Interestingly, in later works, Sherley Anne Williams's female characters possess both music and mobility. Dessa, of the novella *Meditations on History* and the novel *Dessa Rose*, is a fugitive slave who sings spirituals that communicate her plans for escape. In *Peacock Poems* (1975) and *Some One Sweet Angel Chile*, Williams creates a series of blues poems in the voice of Black women. In *Peacock Poems*, she begins her experiment with blues forms and presents poems of a woman's wandering the United States with her newly born son, John. *Some One Sweet Angel Chile* includes poems inspired by the life of Williams's muse and model, Bessie Smith.

It is not insignificant that although jazz does not provide Martha a means of mobility nor form, the spirituals (in a blues form) and the blues provide both for Williams's later characters, as well as for her own creative voice. In this way, she is not unlike Alice Walker, Gayl Jones, or others, for whom the classic blues singers serve as models for independent, creative, and mobile women.[13]

Toni Cade Bambara refuses to surrender jazz form. In her work, the music offers possibilities for women, as well. In "Medley," she does not give us a female instrumentalist, but she does give us a female musician. She also challenges certain conventions of jazz fiction, especially that of the heroic, mobile male musician, and she rewrites the scenes of virtuosic musical performance.

Much jazz fiction turns on the virtuosic performance of an individual musician. James Baldwin's "Sonny's Blues," Ann Petry's "Solo on the Drums," and Paule Marshall's *The Fisher King* are but a few examples of fiction that makes use of this trope. "Medley" was first published in Bambara's second collection of short stories *The Sea Birds Are Still Alive* (1974).[14] Also written in first person, "Medley" is the story of Sweet Pea (a nickname she shares with Billy Strayhorn), who has decided to leave her lover, Larry, a bass player. Sweet Pea has been on the road and returns to domestic chaos that helps to confirm her decision to leave. She enters, takes a look around the apartment, and decides to leave again: "I could tell the minute I got in the door and dropped my bag, I wasn't staying. . . . I definitely wasn't staying. Couldn't ever figure out why I'd come but picked my way to the hallway till the laundry-stuffed pillow cases stopped me. Larry's bass blocking the view of the bedroom" (103).[15]

When he calls from the bedroom, "That you, Sweet Pea?" she responds, "No, man, ain't me at all. . . . See ya around" and closes the door. We later find out that she informed him of her intentions before leaving. The bedroom that the two share is blocked by his bass. It

would seem to suggest that the music stands in the way of their intimacy . . . but this proves not to be the case, for much of their physical
and emotional intimacy takes place in the shower where they make
music together.

When she leaves the apartment, she meets friends at the jazz club
they often frequent. Once there, she shares the following with the
reader but not her friends:

> Larry Landers looked more like a bass player than old
> Mingus himself. Got these long arms that drape down
> over the bass like they were grown special for that pur-
> pose. Fine, strong hands with long fingers and muscu-
> lar knuckles, the dimples deep Black at the joints. His
> calluses so other colored and hard, looked like Larry
> had swiped his grandmother's tarnished thimbles to
> play with. He'd move in on that bass like he was going
> to hump it or somethin, slide up behind it as he lifted it
> from the rug, all slinky. He'd become one with the wood.
> Head dipped down sideways bobbing out the rhythm,
> feet tapping, legs jiggling, he'd look good. Thing about
> it, though, old Larry couldn't play for shit. Couldn't
> ever find the right placement for the notes. Never pluck-
> ing with enough strength, despite the perfectly capable
> hands. Either you didn't hear him at all or what you
> heard was off. The man couldn't play for nuthin is what
> I'm saying. (105)

As a musician, Larry Landers is all style and no substance. He never
gets called for gigs. He is, however, a good man and devoted partner;
he is not the kind of musician who won't share household expenses or
chores. Unlike Larry, Sweet Pea, a manicurist, is in constant demand.
In fact, one of her regulars, a gambler, hires her to keep his hands
well-groomed on a weeklong trip to Mobile, Birmingham, Sarasota
Springs, Jacksonville, and Puerto Rico. As with Martha, Sweet Pea is
also a single mother, of a daughter who is away at boarding school.

Her goal is to find a home for herself and her daughter. By week's end, she has earned the $2,000 she needs to do so.

Even before she leaves for her trip with the gambler, Sweet Pea informs Larry of her intention to leave him. On the eve of her departure, they engage in a musical conversation that serves as the story's only virtuosic performance. Throughout their relationship, Larry and Sweet Pea sing and pantomime tunes in the shower. Unlike other scenes of virtuosic performance that focus on gifted individuals whose voices soar above the ensemble even as they are supported by it, Bambara gives us virtuosity as dialogue, conversation between a man and woman. The music, the quotations, and the improvisations contain all of the couple's anxieties, fears, and desires.[16]

Throughout the duet, they negotiate the terms and the end of their romance. There is no speech, no quotation marks, and no verbal exchange. Instead, he provides the rhythm and the chord changes, and she sings the sometimes-wordless melody. She starts with "Maiden Voyage," and he joins her doing a "Jon Lucien combination on vocal and bass, alternating sections, eight bars of singing words, eight bars of singing bass." Larry insists on "More Today Than Yesterday" followed by a series of love songs. Inspired by Larry's laying "down the most intricate weaving, walking, bopping, strutting bottom," Sweet Pea takes the melody up and out, away from the love songs. "Took that melody right out of the room and out of doors and somewhere out this world." The music travels for her, clearing the way, and Larry continues to provide her the foundation and support she needs even as he pleads his case. She returns to sing "Deep Creek Blues" as a means of acknowledging his pain. Even so, she notes: "Found myself pulling lines out of songs I don't even like, but ransacked songs just for the meaningful lines or two cause I realize we were doing more than just making music together, and it had to be said just how it stood." Larry returns to "I Love You More Today Than Yesterday," but Sweet Pea refuses to join him. She is "elsewhere and likes it out there." Instead of joining him, she ends with "'Brown Baby' to sing to my little girl." "Brown Baby," written for Oscar Brown Jr.'s infant son, Oscar Brown III, was first recorded by Mahalia Jackson in 1960.

Nina Simone and Lena Horne recorded it as well. By inserting this song into her improvisatory narrative, Sweet Pea is linking herself with a number of Black women singers and articulating her dreams for her daughter. The story ends with her lullaby to her child, so as with Martha, Sweet Pea chooses her child over her lover, but unlike Martha, she possesses both music and mobility.[17]

Both Sherley Anne Williams and Toni Cade Bambara are writers strongly influenced by Black music. For Williams, the blues eventually came to dominate her aesthetic sensibilities. Bambara finds her inspiration in jazz, the music that often plays a significant role in her fiction. Furthermore, she is also inspired by the music's rhythm, as well, often referring to some of her stories as "pieces written in 6/8 time."[18] Both women, writing as Black feminists/womanists, challenge received notions of Black women and their relationship to jazz music. Although Martha seems to fit the role of the woman who cannot support her man's aspirations, Williams does not demonize her. Instead, she painstakingly allows us to see the conditions that make her desires for financial and emotional stability perfectly reasonable. Bambara gives us a woman who understands the music well enough to use it as a means of communicating difficult and complex emotions. Both stories expand our notion of gender and jazz by insisting on the significance of the women who make their lives with the musicians and the music.

LEARNING HOW TO LISTEN

Ntozake Shange's Work as Aesthetic Primer

WHAT FOLLOWS IS a purely subjective analysis. The primer of my title refers to several meanings of the word:

    a. A prayer book or devotional manual for the use of lay people.
    b. A book that covers the basic elements of a subject.

For over three decades, Ntozake Shange's writing has been a source of pleasure and insight, as well as the subject of theoretical, historical, and cultural musings. In all of these instances, it has also served as a kind of primer that introduces readers to contemporary music, art, dance, and culinary practices. It also provides a context and a set of aesthetic principals for appreciating them. Furthermore, if the content of her work engages these art forms, the form of her written work does so as well. Her words dance, sing, and construct visual design on the page. This essay will focus primarily on music because this has been the subject of much of my research of late, but what is said here holds true for Shange's literary relationship to dance and the visual and culinary arts as well. Her meditations on and representations of Black art and its production yield exciting and beautiful insights:

    1. That Black art is cosmopolitan. That *cosmopolitan* doesn't have to mean a denial of Black identity or a distancing from

it . . . but instead a broadening of our understanding of what constitutes Black art.

2. That art is necessary for personal and collective survival.

3. Art, especially Black art, is a source of historical, political, and spiritual sustenance.

I WILL PLAY OLIVER LAKE LOUD
FOR COLORED GIRLS

for colored girls probably introduced a number of readers and spectators to Oliver Lake: "i will play oliver lake loud," says the lady in blue in Shange's 1975 choreopoem, *for colored girls who have considered suicide/when the rainbow is enuf.* "I will play oliver lake loud" stands out as one of the poem's statements of defiance, second only to "I found god in myself and I loved her, I loved her fiercely." Many must have wondered, who is this Oliver Lake? What does his music sound like? Why does it make the lady in blue so assertive, so defiant? Other musical figures populate *for colored girls*: Willie Colon, Archie Shepp, Eddie Palmeri, Charles Mingus. The club Slugs' even makes an appearance—lady in blue, disappointed that Willie Colon is not performing, instead discovers Archie Shepp:

> & *if jesus cdnt play a horn like shepp*
> *waznt no need for colored folks to bear no cross at all.*[1]

Along with Jayne Cortez, Toni Cade Bambara, and others, Shange introduced Black women into literature who were creative, multilingual, bohemian, literate, hip to avant-garde jazz and Latin music, and political. These were women whose work emerged from the encounter of the Black arts movement with feminism. The new music—post-Coltrane free jazz—was central to the rhythms, sounds, and settings of the work they produced. References to music (especially jazz) appear throughout the poems; jazz musicians, literal and fictional, appear as characters. In Shange's work, music is everywhere. The lan-

guage of her poetry and prose is itself musical; she is always attentive
to sound.

As with Bambara, Alison Mills, and Sherley Anne Williams,
Shange creates women characters who are involved with jazz musicians.[2] In addition, throughout her career, Shange has frequently
performed with musicians: Oliver Lake is a frequent collaborator,
as is David Murray, with whom she recorded *Wild Flowers*. In this
collaboration, Murray, Shange's former husband, improvises on
tenor sax and bass clarinet to accompany her reading of her poetry.
Both Lake and Murray were founding members of the World Saxophone Quartet.

Though she is most often spoken of as part of a multicultural
group of artists and feminists from the Bay Area (where *for colored
girls* was first developed), Shange's experience on the New York scene
was especially influential. For a time, she lived with other artists on
the Lower East Side, and when she returned from the West Coast in
the 1970s, she became part of the loft scene. Producer, director, and
choreographer Aku Kadogo, who was part of the original cast of *for
colored girls*, recalled: "When I met Ntozake, it was Ntozake, Paula
[Moss], myself and a woman called Kirstin. And I was actually working as a dancer with Ntozake. So we did a lot of improvisation. We
would go to bars. Ntozake would read, and we would dance. And the
musicians would join in and play with us. So I've spent a lot of time
talking about the music scene and being in the music scene. The loft
scene was coming. The Art Ensemble of Chicago was there. David
Murray had just come to town. There was so much going on."[3]

Shange was part of a generation of avant-garde Black artists who
were pushing boundaries and creating new vocabularies and communities. This scene was a generative one, and it is both source and
setting for much of her work. Like Bambara and Williams, who are
both a bit older than she is, Shange addresses the peculiar bind some
Black women found themselves in during the Black power and Black
arts movements, particularly those who were part of artistic communities. They confronted images of Black women as materialistic,

bourgeois, and unwilling to support the artistic aspirations of Black men, while at the same time, they struggled against the pressure to accept Black male patriarchy. [4] In contrast, Shange and other artists gave us Black women characters who were appreciative of and concerned about music, women who frequented jazz clubs as supporters of the music, if not lovers of the musicians. They all seemed primarily concerned with what Hortense Spillers calls the "intramural" relations between Black people—mothers and daughters, men and women, and women friends.[5] While first readings reveal the gender conflict represented by the women writers of the '70s, interestingly, jazz is often (but not always) the common place, the meeting ground, the space of genuine communication between Black men and women. And while the male musician speaks in tongues, it is the woman writer who has the gift of interpretation.

In her first novel, *Sassafrass, Cypress and Indigo* (1982), Shange presents women who are not only the lovers or wives of jazz musicians, but who are also artists in their own right: Sassafrass, the weaver, live-in lover of Mitch, an avant-garde saxophonist and heroin addict; and her sister Cypress, a dancer who marries the very successful musician/composer Leroy McCullough, whose "horns" and "arms" had "offered her horizons where she was free to see what she chose, feel what she had to, be what she dreamed."[6] Here the musician/dancer, male/female artist relationship is not one of rivalry, jealousy, or insecurity. Instead, it is one that enables Cypress's own creative journey and risk-taking. But for our purposes, it is the baby sister, Indigo, who serves as the representative of Shange's understandings of music and its spiritual and political implications. Through Indigo, Shange posits a theory of Black music, indeed, of Black art—one that is clearly informed by the Black aesthetic, but as is the case with much of Shange's work, in Indigo, the Black aesthetic (cultural nationalism) meets feminism: her priestlike musician is female, not a woman, but a girl. If *for colored girls* opens with the plea that the poet "sing a black girl's song," Indigo plays her own song, and in doing so, she also plays the songs of her ancestors, while creating a pathway for the yet-to-be-born, who, as a midwife, she will later usher into this world.

SOUND FALLS ROUND ME LIKE RAIN ON OTHER FOLKS *I LIVE IN MUSIC*

The magic child Indigo—with the moon in her mouth—is a consort of the spirits; she learns to allow them to speak to and through her, especially through her music-making. She is a fiddler. When her uncle John makes Indigo a gift of a fiddle, he tells her: "When them slaves was ourselves & we couldn't talk free, or walk free, who ya think be doin' our talkin' for us?" His answer is a poem: words made music.

> Them whites what owned slaves took everythin' and was ourselves & didn't even keep it fo' they own selves. Just threw it on away, ya heah. Took them drums what they could, but they couldn't take our *feet*. Took them languages that *we speak*. Took off wit our spirits & left us wit they *Son*. But the fiddle was *the talking one*. The fiddle be callin' our gods what left us/be givin back some devilment & hope in our bodies worn down & lonely over these fields & kitchens. Why white folks so dumb they was thinkin' that is we didn't have nothing of our own, they could come controllin', meddlin', whippin' our sense on outta us. But the Colored smart, *ya see*. The Colored got some wits to em *you & me*, we ain't the onliest ones be talkin' with the unreal. What ya think music is, whatchu think the blues be, & them get happy church musics is about, but talkin' with the unreal what's mo' real than most folks ever gonna know. (Emphasis added)[7]

Internal rhyme links *feet* and *speak*, and in doing so demonstrates the relationship between the elimination of physical mobility and the elimination of linguistic and imaginative mobility of language. "Colored smart you see / The Colored got wits to em you & me" joins Uncle John and Indigo to the enslaved ancestors. The rhyme of *Son* and *one*: the divine in Christianity is the Son (Jesus), but the fiddle is the one. The instrument (like Archie Shepp's horn) provides access to the divine. The music speaks the unspoken, speaks what the enslaved could not say, expresses the reality of their existence and their longings and aspirations. Indigo first learns to let the fiddle speak her own concerns: "Whenever she wanted to pray, she let her fiddle talk. Whenever she was angry, here came the fiddle. All the different ways of handling a violin & bow came to Indigo as she needed."[8]

Eventually the community says, "Too much of the Holy Ghost came out of Indigo & that fiddle."[9] She is too involved in the spirit world and in the misery and weightiness of her people's history. Fearing that she "was dwelling dangerous on the misery of the slaves who were ourselves," Uncle John sends her "toward the beauty of this world & the joys of those who came before."[10] So, like Abbey Lincoln, Indigo learns to listen to the sparrows and the wrens, and she "mimick[s] the jays & peckers."[11] Music allows her to converse with nature, and nature takes her to the realms of the spirits. Shange tells us, "No creature that moved escaped Indigo's attention. If the fiddle talked, it also rumbled, cawed, rustled, screamed, sighed, sirened, giggled, stomped, and sneered." Before long, she can look at those around her, put her soul in theirs and pull out "the most lovely moment in [their lives]. & played that. You could tell from looking that as Indigo let notes fly from the fiddle, that man's scar wasn't quite so ugly. . . . The slaves who were ourselves aided Indigo's mission, connecting soul & song, experience & unremembered rhythms."[12]

Although she uses the fiddle to express her feelings, to commune with the ancestors, to play what she hears in the natural world, and, ultimately, to lend beauty and healing, though she "plays from the heart," her mother and the extended family of her community "let her be," even as they cringe at the sound of her playing. The teachers she needs find her. There is Pretty Man, who sends his woman Mabel to buy records for the magic girl/child—Bartók's Violin Concerto no. 2, Ray Nance, Stéphane Grappelli, and Bach. Pretty Man tells her to listen closely and then play what she hears. Through Indigo, Shange gives us a pedagogy for the gifted child:

1. Play free, consort with the spirits, play from the heart.
2. Converse with the birds, play what you hear in the natural world but also what you see.
3. Listen and learn to play by ear.

Eventually, "Pretty Man called everything from Bach to Ellington inside of one tune," and the girl fiddler rises to the occasion.

Through Indigo, Shange reminds us of the centrality of Black music to Black aspirations for freedom. Furthermore, she insists that the artist must commune with ancestral spirits but cannot remain among them. She must also engage the transcendent beauty of the natural world and the tradition of her instrument. Finally, Shange demonstrates the necessity of discipline of practice.

Through Indigo, Shange sends readers on a quest for the fiddle and for the fiddlers. Historically, we lost a sense of the centrality of this string instrument to African American culture. Certainly, fiddles were important in early jazz, but even before that many of the enslaved played the fiddle. In fact, Miles Davis came from a line of enslaved string musicians on his father's side. Advertisements for runaway slaves indicate that many of them were fiddlers. The WPA slave narratives of a runaway, fugitive, and fiddler mention that he lived in a cave near a plantation and would come out and play for his enslaved brothers and sisters at their dances. They, in turn, provided him with food. So, there is a relationship between these musicians—these fiddlers—and the love and quest for freedom that seem to have characterized many of them.

The curious reader on a quest might discover extraordinary finds: India, Cooke, Regina Carter, Akua Dixon, John Blake, the late Marlene Rice and Billy Bang, as well as the groups Quartet Indigo and the Uptown String Quartet. Here, dwell the freedom-loving, freedom-singing notes of Indigo and the fugitive fiddlers of long ago. In another context, Shange wrote of the late Billy Bang: "the energy he is able to generate in this instrument that has struggled so hard for its voice in the jazz arena is startling, unnerving and reassuring simultaneously."[13]

I STOPPED LOOKING FOR ROOTS AND HEROES AND HEROINES AND I FOUND MY PEERS.

—Ntozake Shange, *Lost in Language & Sound*

In Shange's work, music serves as the conduit for spiritual and political longings. The notes fly free; the music invokes the ancestors. Throughout her oeuvre, music, indeed, all of Black art, from Bearden's collages to Diane McIntyre's choreography, provides a map, a route to, a way OUT, but also a meditative way into the self. This is a notion of the arts that Shange inherits from the Black arts movement. This is also the power of Shange's literature: the sheer beauty, seriousness, playfulness, momentum, and mobility of her writing also honor the ancestors—first by acknowledging their suffering and their beauty, and then by daring to imagine freedom for her own and future generations.

But freedom and music are not only parts of the plot; not only do they provide some of the content, they provide the basis of the form as well. While much has been written about the jazz-like structure of novels like Morrison's *Jazz* or Ellison's *Invisible Man*, few have looked at the formal qualities of Shange's prose for structures and feelings most often associated with music. (Her poems, however, are read in this way.) In the space that remains, I want to turn to the formal qualities of Shange's writing.

> It was all interconnected.... I'd listen to the music and hear what they were saying at the same time, so I was always integrating the two things.... I'd do my homework, writing things, listening to Cuban rhythms and Brazilian rhythms. I think that accounts for some of my ability to work musically with language.[14]

There are three elements of Shange's writing worth considering in this regard: the look of the words on the page, spelling and syntax, and rhythm. The experience of reading Shange's work—whether poetry or prose—is always rhythmic, dancelike. Significantly, for a writer who became one of the faces of Black feminism in the late 1970s and early 1980s, Shange has always claimed Amiri Baraka and Ishmael Reed as among her greatest literary influences. Known for her lowercase letters and slashes, Shange attributes these devices to the influence of Baraka's *The Dead Lecturer* and *The System of Dante's Hell* and Ishmael Reed's *Yellow Back Radio Broke-Down*. (She was influenced by their syntax and structure, not by their content.) She says she selects lowercase letters because she likes "the ideas that letters dance, not just that words dance." The look on the page is also an effort to make her own reading of her work more interesting, while at the same time making it more challenging for those of us who read the work—we have to engage with it, move with it, even as we are moved along by it. Simply on a visual level—the way the words look on the page—Shange's writing dances. She is also known for "odd" spelling, so that *you* becomes *ya*, *with* becomes *wit*: She spells them as she hears them. As the characters speak to her, she hears the musicality of their speech, and she has to invent a notation system to represent them. Just as the sounds of Black music have not always fit within the Western musical system of notation, the English language, the King's English, the words available to her cannot always represent the sounds of the spoken word or their full meaning.

From the look that influences the way we read the line to the spelling and the phonetic, we might add the rhythm underneath. To read Shange's work is a rhythmic and lyrical experience. She has written about this element:

> I'll hear very peculiar rhythms underneath whatever I'm typing, and this rhythm affects the structure. For instance, if I'm hearing a rumba, you'll get a poem that looks like a rumba on the page.[15]

We probably have to hear Shange read her own work or listen to an actor who has been given the stage instruction "Rumba-like" in order to hear what she is describing here. Shange doesn't seem to privilege music-making over writing; instead, she sees them as part of the same process—a process of being grounded in rhythm, of attending to the notes of the spoken word. In one poem, she even includes time signatures and opens each stanza with a treble or bass clef. Throughout her work, she makes explicit the implied relationship between music and poetry, between musician and poet, between the shared artistry of sound and word.

Ntozake Shange's body of work offers an invitation to enter into the dynamic, multidimensional world of Black art. Her creative project is one that informs and teaches all who accept her invitation, and it guides us through a whirlwind of color, sound, movement, and meaning. To partake of her artistic generosity is to be initiated into a community that creates the world anew upon each reading.

REMAKING THE EVERYDAY

The Interior Worlds of Kathleen Collins's Fiction and Film

DOES THE DISCOVERY OF a lost writer change our understanding of the past, or does it shape our experience of the present? If the playwright, author, and filmmaker Kathleen Collins had received more recognition during her lifetime, would her work have changed the way we think about and create American—especially African American—film and fiction today?

These are the questions raised by the posthumous publication of two collections of Collins's writing: *Whatever Happened to Interracial Love?*, a collection of sixteen short stories, and *Notes from a Black Woman's Diary*, which includes short stories, plays, and screenplays, excerpts from an unpublished novel, and a selection of letters, as well as the titular notes. Both volumes have been edited by Collins's daughter, Nina Lorez Collins, who in the weeks following her mother's death from breast cancer in 1988 at the age of forty-six filled a steamer trunk full of her unpublished writings. Some twenty years later, the younger Collins went through the trunk's contents, and we're now the beneficiaries of some of the works she discovered there.

During her lifetime, Kathleen Collins saw one of her screenplays become a movie—*Losing Ground* (1982), which she also directed—and one story and one play published. But she never achieved critical acclaim, and with the exception of a small group of aficionados on the film-festival circuit, few people saw her movie. Had these newly published works been available in her lifetime, she would have joined an emerging group of Black women writers in the 1970s and '80s that included Alice Walker, Toni Cade Bambara, and Toni Morrison. As a filmmaker, Collins shared more with independent directors like Charles Burnett, whose films present a quiet but steady focus on quotidian Black life, than Spike Lee, but *Losing Ground* helped pave the way for the latter's work, too, as well as for films like Julie Dash's *Daughters of the Dust* (1991), which was the first feature film directed by an African American woman to be distributed in the United States.

The titles of the two volumes are compelling, if somewhat misleading. They call attention to an issue that Collins's work rarely centers on: race. Collins doesn't deny its existence or significance; her writing and films are not set in some post-racial utopia. In fact, in the brilliant title story of *Whatever Happened to Interracial Love?*, she reminisces about a moment when idealistic young activists tried to live beyond race, only to remind us how entrenched we are in a world in which inequalities are often shaped by it. Even though race is a subject in her writing, her work is not driven by its drama. The stories of *Interracial Love* are more likely to engage race than are those of *Notes*, but they do so in indirect and subtle ways. "I could have occupied myself with race all these years," Collins explains in one diary entry. "The climate was certainly ripe for me to have done so. I could have explored myself within the context of a young Black life groping its way into maturity across the rising tide of racial affirmation. I could have done that. After all, I'm a colored lady. . . . But I didn't do that. No, I turned far inside, where there was only me and love to deal with. . . . Instead of dealing with race I went in search of love." For the most part, Collins's characters are artists and bohemians, almost always Black or, if white, then involved in interracial relationships—romantic, erotic, platonic. Race informs their existence but does not define it. In the screenplay for the unproduced film *A Summer Diary*, Lilliane, the widow of a sculptor and former merchant marine named Giles, who recently killed himself, says of her husband's depression, "I used to think it just had to do with race, that he hated the humiliation, but now I think it went further than that, there was something in him that found life ridiculous, a joke of some kind." The humiliation of race is a given, but it cannot explain by itself our more existential struggle with the absurdity of life.

Here is the brilliance of Collins's work in all of its quietude: its turn within, its placement of the interior and subjective in the context of the social and political. Collins recognizes the power of those structures that remake everyday life, for better and worse, but she chooses instead to shine a light on the inner workings of complex souls. First person is her preferred mode of narration; there is little dialogue between her characters and little to no evidence of racial strife or economic struggle. Her stories are just as likely to be set in rented summer homes in small towns along the Hudson River as they are in Harlem or Greenwich Village. The difficulties of relationships, the longing for love and recognition, the experience of forthright sexual encounters and betrayals, and the compulsive drive toward creativity—these are the engines that drive both her fiction and nonfiction forward. Like her diary entries and essays, her stories are peopled by figures who write, paint, design, read. Sometimes they are in conversation with each other, but most often we find them alone with their own thoughts.

Writer Danielle Evans, who provides the foreword to *Notes*, is right to call Collins "a magician in her use of interiority." Across multiple genres, Collins makes it her project to explore the inner lives of her characters. As she writes in the diary entry cited earlier, instead of race, she turned "far inside." And in so doing, she accomplished something quite revolutionary: she gave us Black characters—particularly Black women—with rich, complicated interior lives. In this way, and even in her settings, she is more akin to Virginia Woolf than to many of her contemporaries, such as Walker and Morrison. Walker wrote fiction that is more explicitly feminist, with a clearer sense of politics, while Morrison's rich and complex novels are most often historical in nature.

The desire to explore and represent interiority may account for Collins's long-standing interest in film. Through the placement of the camera, the point of view, and the voice-over, film provides multidimensional access to a character's inner thoughts. Take Sara, the protagonist of *Losing Ground*, the screenplay for which is published in *Notes*. She is a Black woman, a philosophy professor. The film opens with her in a university classroom, lecturing to a group of young male students on the existentialists, war, chaos, and philosophy. Played by the luminous Seret Scott, Sara is married to Victor, a successful abstract painter whom she envies for his ability to reach states of personal satisfaction through the practice of his art.

Sara is in the midst of researching and writing a philosophical treatise on "ecstatic experience," and through it she hopes to discover her own private forms of pleasure and happiness. Seated in a library, Sara "is reading with such intensity that the words seem to spill forth," Collins tells us. A man who has been observing her approaches her and says, "I have rarely seen anyone read with such intense concentration." When he asks what she's researching, Sara replies that she's writing an essay and explains her thesis: "That the religious boundaries around ecstasy are too narrow, that if, as the Christians define it, ecstasy is an immediate apprehension of the divine, then the divine is energy . . . amorphous energy. Artists, for example, have frequent ecstatic experiences."

Sara is one of the rare representations of a Black woman intellectual, a thinker, in film and literature. At the center of the story is not her struggle with a racist coworker or sexist lover; instead, she struggles with her ideas and creative aspirations within the context of her marriage. Indeed, she is such an intellectual that though she longs to experience the ecstatic, she chooses instead to theorize about it. Much of the film concerns her journey away from her hypercritical mind and into a more creative expression of herself through acting. As such, Sara is a singular figure in American cinema, one that we have not seen before, or since, *Losing Ground*.

Reading Collins's diaries, we find that she often mined her own interiority for her fictional work. The section in *Notes from a Black Woman's Diary* taken directly from her journal includes a kind of metacommentary. "When I re-read parts of it, a feeling of solidity takes hold of me. If it is also well written and manages to go to the heart of the moment as I lived it, leaving me free, now, to recall it with all its contours intact, then I feel great satisfaction."

The excerpts give insight into her process, her longing, and the bits and pieces that reappear in the narrative context of her fiction. In the stories, plays, and screenplays, characters repeat lines from the diary verbatim; as Collins explains, "Writing had given the experience an autonomous existence . . . existing in a place that has a larger meaning." The privacy of the diary also allows her to write about the difference between her Black and white lovers: White men are less emotionally available, she says. With Black men, "while the behavior may be complex, contradictory, often inexplicable, the emotional core is extremely accessible." And then she confesses, "All the men I have cared deeply about seem to share one thing in common, regardless of race: A remarkable masculine self-possession before which I do nothing but yield."

Such honesty may not have been well received during the time she wrote these words, when we wanted unyielding feminist heroines. But in her diaries, Collins offers us a portrait of a self wrestling with its different impulses. She willingly surrenders before a form of confident masculinity, but at the same time, she laments that "men become themselves out of a refusal of certain kinds of limitations, women out of an acceptance of them. Women are bound. . . . We *are* in bondage to life. A woman's life is a terrible thing. . . . I believe in liberation, but I don't believe it is at all the thing we think it is." Her diaries are a place for questioning, for contradiction, for exploration. And herein lie the makings of her art.

Yet for all of Collins's attention to the interior, to the quiet moments of reflection, she is not apolitical. As a college student at Skidmore, against the wishes of her conservative, middle-class parents, she traveled south to join the Student Nonviolent Coordinating Committee and take part in a voter registration drive in Albany, Georgia. She documents this time in a set of letters collected in *Notes*, which provided the source material for a number of the stories in *Whatever Happened to Interracial Love?*, including the one that gives the collection its name.

In one of these letters, dated August 3, 1962, and written to her sister Francine, Collins asserts, "For one must move upon the things that one is committed to. . . . I wanted with all my soul to go south and I wanted to go to jail—because I wanted to pray that right would triumph. I wanted to pray on the steps of city hall in Albany. To confront all of those policemen and city officials with the moral issue— the fact that they have made us dogs—but I wanted to force them to see me and others as human beings who feel pain and frustration, who, too, can cry and be hurt."

When Collins returns to this period of her life to fictionalize it, she does so with the distance of time and the wisdom of hindsight. In the story "Whatever Happened to Interracial Love?," the protagonist recalls a brief time when she, a Black woman engaged to a white freedom fighter, and her elite white roommate, involved with a Black "Umbra poet," share an apartment on Manhattan's Upper West Side. They welcome a bevy of artists and activists and are committed to the vision of the world for which they're fighting: one beyond race, beyond color. But the story is narrated from a later date, when that dream has clearly faded, brought to its demise by the failure of the Democratic National Convention to seat the Mississippi Freedom Democratic Party in 1964, by the calls for Black power (an unnamed Stokely Carmichael and Bob Moses make cameos), and by the inadequate commitment of those who professed devotion to a post-racial future but did little to realize it. And the story is told through the lens of an interracial relationship that could not survive these harsh realities.

The stories of *Whatever Happened to Interracial Love?* reveal a gifted writer who excels at the form. Her subjects are smart, daring young women, the daughters of "prominent Black families," who escape the tight confines of the respectable futures planned for them in ways that only economically and educationally privileged daughters can. At times, Collins turns her eye to the society that produced these women, but more often than not, she focuses on their struggles to maintain a sense of dignity and self-worth in a still-segregated society.

Set in the decades between the Supreme Court's 1954 *Brown v.*

Board of Education decision and the early 1980s, the works fall into no established literary categories. They are akin neither to Ralph Ellison and James Baldwin nor to the Black arts movement writers. In many ways, these works take the mantle of one of Collins's literary idols, Lorraine Hansberry—not the Hansberry of *A Raisin in the Sun* but the Hansberry of *The Sign in Sidney Brustein's Window*, in which we encounter an interracial group of Greenwich Village bohemian intellectuals as they navigate relationships fraught with racial and sexual tension. How ironic that, like Hansberry, who died at the age of thirty-four, Collins also died far too young, leaving us to wonder what kind of work a longer life might have yielded.

It is not clear that the critics and readers of her time would have been ready for a Black woman author who wrote so explicitly about sex and sexuality or so unapologetically about the relationships (sexual and otherwise) between Black women and white men. However, had the work been available, it would certainly have expanded our sense of the possible for Black women as artists, thinkers, and subjects. In many ways, the times in which we live seem ripe for the stories that Collins tells and ready for a Black woman polymath. A moment that has produced a variety of Black literary voices, filmmakers, and playwrights seems ready, finally, for the gifts that Collins has to offer.

It is a testament to her writing that we leave these volumes wanting more: more writing by her and more information about the works we do have. The stories do not need explanation and analysis; they do, however, call for more contextualization, which will be the work of a new generation of scholars, critics, and artists who discover Collins as a result of these collections. This is truer of the selections in *Notes from a Black Woman's Diary*, and thus why Phyllis Rauch Klotman's introduction to *Losing Ground* and the occasional editorial commentary are welcome. But the commentaries are only a beginning. We still want and need more from and about this remarkable writer.

A PLACE OF FREEDOM

Gayl Jones's Brazilian Epic

U PON ITS PUBLICATION IN 1975, Gayl Jones's literary debut, *Corregidora*, was met with great acclaim. Jones's mentor and teacher, the poet Michael Harper, had introduced her work to his friend, the editor and novelist Toni Morrison, who published *Corregidora* and also Jones's second novel, *Eva's Man*, the following year. Still in her mid-twenties, Jones was immediately heralded for her genius by readers as diverse as James Baldwin and the *New York Times* critic Raymond Sokolov. Part of what drew them was what Sokolov referred to as her "nonchalance" and "ease" of style, which served as her fiction's "consummate deception." Writing with a clarity and matter-of-factness that quietly understated her work's difficulty, Jones often relayed moments of intense brutality with a kind of quotidian ordinariness.

This was evident in her first novel. Set in Kentucky and narrated by a blues singer named Ursa Corregidora, it was both an intimate history and a family one. Telling the story of several generations of Black women, two of whom—Ursa's great-grandmother and grandmother—have been raped repeatedly by their master, Old Man Corregidora, the novel also followed Ursa herself, who chooses to devote her life to her music, even though she cannot wholly escape her family's past of sexual violence and trauma.

In the fiction that followed, Jones's attention to the complicated, sometimes disturbing psyches of her characters intensified. *Eva's Man* and *White Rat* offered stories of psychological complexity, experiences of sexual violence and trauma, and explorations of her female characters' interiority and agency. In *Eva's Man*, for example, the protagonist first poisons and then castrates her lover after feeling trapped in his apartment, while in *White Rat* we get stories centered on a bevy of unique, if marginalized and often troubled, characters who are presented with unrelenting clarity.

With Jones having published three works of fiction in three swift years, many of her admirers expected a similar creative pace in the 1980s. But while Jones spoke of working on "another novel . . . *Palmares*" and released an exquisitely beautiful book-length poem, *Song for Anninho,* that was set after the destruction of the community that would be the subject of *Palmares,* she did not publish any new fiction until the late 1990s. When she did, it was not *Palmares* but *The Healing* and *Mosquito,* the former about a faith healer traveling through small-town America and the latter about a Black woman trucker who transports Mexican immigrants across the Texas border. In many ways, the two novels—full of humor and a sense of optimistic possibility—marked a departure for Jones. But her newfound momentum stopped abruptly after a sensational personal tragedy. A *Newsweek* profile accompanying the publication of *The Healing* led a SWAT team to the home she shared with her husband, Bob Higgins. The police had an outstanding warrant for his arrest on a fourteen-year-old weapons charge. After a standoff, Higgins committed suicide as the agents rushed the house. Fearing Jones would take her own life, the authorities placed her in a mental institution. It was an unthinkable occurrence under any circumstances, but especially so for a writer who avoided publicity and vehemently refused to share anything about her personal life. In an early interview with the literary critic Claudia Tate, Jones had observed:

> The writers whom I would most like to be like are those whose works have a certain kind of reputation, but the person, the writer, is more or less out of it. I would want to maintain some kind of anonymity. I think of J.D. Salinger. . . . I guess that's the kind of reputation that I'd

like . . . where you can go on with what you're doing, but
you have a sense that what you do is appreciated . . . that
there is quality to what you're doing.

Jones was denied this privacy, and the publicity surrounding her
writing did far worse. It was no surprise she soon disappeared from
public life.

Nonetheless, Jones continued to write through her tragedy, working with particular intensity on *Palmares*. Now published, the book
proves to be one of her most ambitious and, at times, extraordinary
works of fiction. *Corregidora* was one of the first examples of what
would become a genre of Black fiction dealing with the legacy, consequences, and what Saidiya Hartman calls the "afterlife of slavery," a
new body of literature that depicted the mundane sexual violence and
ongoing generational trauma that is the inherited legacy of slavery in
the United States and throughout the Americas. The life and afterlife
of slavery is also *Palmares*'s subject, but following so many formidable contributions to this new body of work—including Morrison's
Beloved, Hartman's *Scenes of Subjection* and *Lose Your Mother*, and
Marlon James's *The Book of Night Women*—Jones was faced with a
difficult question: How does someone write in the considerable wake
of a literary genre that she helped to create and define? Jones's answer
is a sweeping epic, set in seventeenth-century Brazil, that focuses
as much on the meaning of freedom as it does on the experience of
enslavement. In form and in content, *Palmares* aspires to do what
Jones's early works of fiction did, but much more, as well: to develop
a narrative form that embodies the complexity, mixtures, contradictions, and possibilities of the Americas with their multiracial population, multilingual heritage, and syncretic religious practices.

It is almost a cliché to call a work of art "epic," because the word
is now used to mean anything long and involved. Traditionally, the
term referred to a long poem, especially those ancient poetic texts
that drew on an oral tradition and told of the adventures of a questing
hero. These texts also sought to tell the history of a nation: Homer's
Iliad and *Odyssey*, Virgil's *Aeneid*, the Old English *Beowulf*, and the

Malian *Epic of Sundiata* are among the genre's defining works. But for contemporary readers and critics, the term has come to include a variety of creative works beyond poems, what Franco Moretti calls a "super-genre" that supersedes both novels and poems.

Palmares has all the elements we've come to expect of an epic. It is long. It follows a single figure on a quest to return home and reconcile with a beloved one. It features a series of episodic encounters with mythical, magical, or otherworldly figures. In this case, the questing figure is a formerly enslaved Black woman, Almeyda, who looks for her husband and longs for Palmares, a maroon society, better known in Brazil as a *quilombo*, a settlement of fugitive slaves and free Blacks. In the novel, Palmares becomes as much an idea as it is a place, an ever-shifting geographical location embodying a form of Black autonomy in the midst of a slave society. As place and idea, it provides the opportunity to contemplate the meaning of freedom.

Almeyda, who is called "Almeydita" for the first ninety pages, is a spiritually and intellectually gifted child who lives on a Brazilian plantation with her mother and grandmother. She is precocious and self-aware: "I was seven and I was a slave," she says emphatically. Having been chosen by a Jesuit priest, Father Tollinare, to receive a formal education, she becomes one of his "experiments" and is taught geography, the Bible, and how to read and write. Almeyda is also educated in matters of the spirit, healing, and history by her grandmother, who is alternately identified as a healer, a madwoman, and a consort of the spirits. If literacy will assist Almeyda's quest for freedom, knowledge of the spiritual realm will allow her to experience it.

Almeyda first hears of Palmares as a child. A white man and his Black wife visit her master and share tales of the legendary settlement of free Blacks and fugitive slaves. The stories, relayed to her by her mother, spark Almeyda's interest in the place "where Black men and women are free." When, in adolescence, she is sold to a cassava farmer, her curiosity and longing only increase. Without explanation, a group of "men from the Quilombo" arrive and ask, "Do you wish to come freely with us and be . . . a free woman?" Her answer is "Yes"— and, just like that, she is taken to her longed-for destination.

Now a beautiful woman, Almeyda is chosen by one of the settlement's leading figures, Anninho, to be his wife. His selection confers on her the status of free woman, but Almeyda soon learns that in Palmares there are also captives, prisoners, and slaves. Palmares is a free space for some Blacks, but it is also a place of hierarchy and social stratification. Often, we learn, freedom is a process, something to be fought for, something precarious. Palmares is merely a temporary physical space of freedom, a place always embattled, attacked, destroyed, and reconstituted elsewhere. There is always a new Palmares on the horizon.

Eventually, the Palmares that Almeyda settles in is raided and destroyed by the Portuguese. Jones chooses not to portray the destruction of the free African state; instead, for most of the rest of the novel, we follow Almeyda on her journey to find her husband in hopes of helping rebuild the space where Black people are free. Her search for Anninho constitutes this epic's *Odyssey*-like quest. Almeyda, often disguised as an old woman, encounters many figures, guides, and teachers along the way who help her shape her conceptions of freedom and discover her own spiritual gifts. Palmares, for Almeyda, is a state of mind, a state of being, even more than a physical location.

The truest freedom offered by Palmares is a spiritual consciousness that transcends time and space and challenges linear notions of temporality. Healers, diviners, and prophets exist both inside and outside of time, capable of traveling vast expanses of land and occupying multiple dimensions. The spiritually gifted, including Almeyda, can experience the past, present, and future as parallel contexts. For others, freedom exists in the realm of the imagination—and this is the case for Almeyda as well. Her grandmother tells her, "The imagination is broad. It ranges." Another character, an aspiring writer, states, "I believe in the force of the imagination."

Jones, too, clearly believes in the imagination and its force. It takes a fecund imagination, after all, to give us this sprawling novel, one that describes and contains multiple forms and genres. Chapters are devoted to a maker of dictionaries, a travel notebook left by a European woman, and a fictional narrative written by a mixed-race freeman. All of these are invoked to tell a New World story in a New World language, contained within the broader tale that Almeyda herself tells. In a very early interview with her mentor Michael Harper, Jones said, "I really think of myself as a storyteller. . . . 'Storytelling' is a dynamic word, a process word. 'Fiction' sounds static. 'Storytelling' for me suggests possibilities, many possibilities."

Almeyda fulfills this role in the novel. She is, as she explains to a woman she encounters, "an itinerant storyteller." Later, she crystallizes her wish to be "writing histories of the country . . . of this place, this Palmares." But Almeyda confronts a quandary that many novelists also experience: "How can one write such a history and live through it at the same time?" For Jones, and for Almeyda, the answer is found in storytelling itself. By telling a story about the pursuit of freedom, Jones and Almeyda also create a place where Black freedom, if not realized, can at least be imagined, and thus remains a possibility.

TREATING THE
SERPENT'S STING

In Toni Cade Bambara's *The Salt Eaters*, a healer, Minnie Ransom, advises the protagonist, Velma Henry, to
learn "the difference between eating salt as an antidote
to snakebite and turning into salt, which is succumbing
to the serpent." Black feminism aspires to be a politics
and mode of analysis that provides an antidote to the
violence of misogyny, racism, and poverty. While all of
my writing is informed by Black feminism, these essays
seek to advance specifically Black feminist critical and
theoretical interventions that address the relationship
between history, cultural production, representation, and
the legacies of white supremacy. They range from pieces
that elucidate the way a wide range of writing by Black
women activists and writers confront and attempt to
remedy the impact of the discursive and physical assault

Black women have experienced throughout history to
explorations and analyses of important African American
cultural and political figures, from Malcolm X to Michelle
Obama and Beyoncé.

TEXTUAL HEALING

Claiming Black Women's Bodies, the Erotic, and Resistance in Contemporary Novels of Slavery

On the next day, which was the 8th of the month of August, very early in the morning, by reason of the heat, the seamen began to make ready their boats, and to take out those captives, and carry them on the shore as they were commanded. And these, placed all together in that field, were a marvellous sight, for amongst them were some white enough, fair to look upon and well proportioned; others were less white like mulattoes; others again were as Black as Ethiops, and so ugly, both in features and in body, as almost to appear (to those who saw them) the images of a lower hemisphere.[1]

—DE AZURARA, *mid-fifteenth-century royal librarian, keeper of the archives in Portugal, chronicler of the discovery and conquest of Guinea*

Why increase the sons of Africa, by Planting them in America where we have so fair an Opportunity, by excluding all Blacks and Tawneys, of increasing the lovely White and Red?[2]

—BENJAMIN FRANKLIN, *"Observations Concerning the Increase of Mankind" (1751)*

The first difference which strikes me is that of colour. Whether the black of the negro resides in the reticular membrane between the skin and scarf-skin, or in the scarf-skin itself; whether it proceeds from the colour of the blood, the color of the bile, or from some other secretion, the difference is fixed in nature, and is as real as if its seat and cause were better known to us. And is this difference of no importance? Is it not the foundation of a greater or less share of beauty in the two races? Are not the fine mixtures of red and white, the expressions of every passion by greater or less suffusions of colour in the one, preferable to that eternal monotony which reigns in the countenances, that immovable veil of Black which covers all the emotions of the other race? Add to these, flowing hair, a more elegant symmetry of form, and their own judgment in favour of whites, declared by their preference for them, as uniformly as is the preference of the Oran-ootan for the Black woman over those of his own species. The circumstance of superior beauty, is thought worthy attention in the propagation of our horses, dogs, and other domestic animals; why not in that of man?

—THOMAS JEFFERSON, *Notes on the State of Virginia*

[The slave women were] clumsy, awkward, gross, elephantine in all their movements; pouting, grinning, and leering at us; sly, sensual, and shameless, in all their expressions and demeanor; I never before had witnessed, I thought, anything more revolting than the whole scene.

—FREDERICK LAW OLMSTEAD, *The Cotton Kingdom*

Note the remarkable development of the labia minoria . . . which is so general a characteristic of the Hottentot and Bushman race . . . [that they are] sufficiently well marked to distinguish these parts at once from those of any of the ordinary varieties of the human species.

—WILLIAM H. FLOWER DESCRIBED HIS DISSECTION OF AN AFRICAN WOMAN IN AN 1867 ARTICLE OF THE *Journal of Anatomy and Physiology*

THIS LITANY OF quotations is by now familiar to the student and scholar of Black history and cultures. The movement from visual difference (the color Black) to ugliness, from ugliness to inferiority strikes us immediately. Yet these observers did not stop at skin color;

they initiate a discourse of Black inferiority that stands on "evidence" derived from cranial measurements and genital mutilation. Through these discourses the Black body came to bear specific cultural meanings: These discourses constitute all Black people as unsightly, deformed, diseased. An entire body of literature served as ideological justification for the enslavement, torture, dismemberment, and domination that came to characterize New World slavery. The Black body is an ugly body and therefore a nonhuman one. This inhuman object is a beast of burden—but it is also an object of desire.

These discourses help to justify the litany of torture and dismemberment, also familiar by now: lynched bodies, broken necks, mutilated genitals, severed hands and feet. In addition to these historical acts of physical torture, Black peoples also have been subjected to ideals and standards of physical "beauty" that are created in opposition to them. Cornel West notes:

> White supremacist ideology is based first and foremost on the degradation of Black bodies in order to control them. One of the best ways to instill fear in people is to terrorize them. Yet this fear is best sustained by convincing them that their bodies are ugly, their intellect is inherently underdeveloped, their culture is less civilized and their future warrants less concern than that of other peoples.[3]

In this way, many Black people have been convinced that their bodies are, in fact, ugly—primarily because of their color, but also because of their size and shape, as well. As such, they are often complicit in maintaining standards that oppress them.

For my purposes, what is especially significant is the way in which difference is inscribed on the bodies of Black women. Black women come to represent extreme examples of otherness as is evidenced by their color, their hair, their facial features, their buttocks, and their genitals. In addition to the obsession with the Black penis (as is evident in the lynching and castration rituals of the late nineteenth and early twentieth centuries), those who sought to establish evidence of Black bestiality often turned to the "overdeveloped" genitals of Black women.

If white supremacist and patriarchal discourses construct Black women's bodies as abnormal, diseased, and ugly, Black women writers seek to reconstitute these bodies.[4] Some Black women have arduously documented the impact of artificial standards of beauty on Black women's lives. They have also explored the consequences of Black women's efforts to meet these standards. While these writers document the pain, domination, and exploitation of Black women's bodies, in the past decade many other Black women writers have started to explore female bodies as sites of healing, pleasure, and resistance. These writers also replace the dominant discourse's obsession with the visual Black body with a perspective that privileges touch and other senses. They are engaged in a project of reimagining the Black female body—a project done in the service of those readers who have inherited the older legacy of the Black body as despised, diseased, and ugly. I want to refer to this literary project as "textual healing."[5]

The manner in which Black women writers address this legacy of the ugly Black body begs for the attention of Black feminist critics. In addition to its literary merit and theoretical implications, part of the power of some writing by Black women is its transformative potential for the lives of all of us who continue to be haunted by the legacy of white supremacy and male patriarchy. Reading these novels may help to raise our consciousness about the degree to which historic discourses have constructed all of us.

Because both Black and white readers still tend to live with the repercussions of the white supremacist legacy, the texts serve to make the wounds of that legacy real for their non-Black and male readers as well. Furthermore, these texts force all readers to occupy the critical subject category of the Black woman. For many Black women readers in particular, the texts historicize notions that they have come to understand as indications of what is" wrong" with them—their hair is "too coarse," their behinds, hips, and thighs "too large" for cloth-

ing, their facial features "too broad," their color "too dark." By histo-
ricizing the social constructions of these standards, writings by Black
women begin to perform a textual healing for all readers.

||||||||||

> Progressive Black women artists have shown ongoing con-
> cern about healing our wounds. Much of the celebrated fic-
> tion by Black women writers is concerned with identifying
> our pain and imaginatively constructing maps for healing.
> —BELL HOOKS, *Sisters of the Yam*

This essay marks my attempt to locate the transformative possibilities and pedagogical potential of Black women's literature. I am
interested in the way that the literature guides readers towards a consciousness about the manner in which white supremacy and patriarchy have constructed notions of Black women's bodies as ugly and
despised. Furthermore, I believe this literature also provides a scheme
for resisting these constructions. Before turning to my readings of
Michelle Cliff's *Abeng* and Sherley Anne Williams's *Meditations on
History* and *Dessa Rose*, I want to place the works under consideration
within a larger body of writing by Black women. Secondly, I will pro-
pose a framework for reading these texts as acts of textual healing.[6]
Contemporary Black women writers of fiction, criticism, theory, and
popular self-help books, along with Black women theologians and a
burgeoning grassroots movement spearheaded by the National Black
Women's Health Project are all participating in this communal project of textual healing. The most popular pop-spiritual/-psychological
books by Black women are books that celebrate Black women's bodies in an effort to counter the destructive effects of racialized hierarchies of beauty. I am thinking here of best-selling books such as
bell hooks' *Sisters of the Yam*, Susan Taylor's *In the Spirit*, and Maya
Angelou's *Wouldn't Take Nothing for My Journey Now*, to name a few.
Many of these popular books emphasize the importance of touching.
Angelou writes of her days as a dancer when just before entering on

stage, she "would find [older] women's hands on my body. Three or four would stroke my back, pat my behind, caress my arms. Looking back, I realize that the women's strokings were sensual rather than sexual. Because they encouraged me, they participated with me in the dance" (96).

Similarly, Susan Taylor describes her own efforts to heal herself from the day-to-day traumas she faced as a Black woman:

> Suddenly I felt my arms wrapping around my own body. I began holding myself in my own embrace, kissing my shoulders, my arms, my knees—every part of my own body I could reach. It wasn't a sexual experience but a deeply sensuous and healing one. It was a laying on of hands. (36)

Both women emphasize the healing and affirming nature of sensual touch. They stress the difference between sexual and sensual because the latter embraces a greater range of physical contact. Taylor uses a religious metaphor of "laying on of hands," a ritual still practiced by Black women in Christian churches as well as Yoruba-influenced rituals of healing. It is not surprising that Taylor chooses a spiritual/religious metaphor to describe this moment, since for many Black people, the church is the site for challenging the impact of white supremacist discourse about Black beauty and ability. Consider the numerous sermons and addresses that begin with the phrases, "My, my what a beautiful group of people we are." Or "Don't we look fine this morning?" Black women writers have drawn liberally from this tradition in their literary efforts.

In addition to the Christian traditions cited above, other African-based spiritual practices encourage healing rituals as well. Yoruba priestesses Iyanla Vanzant and Luisah Teish offer directions for performing healing baths in their books. In *Jambalaya: The Natural Woman's Book of Personal Charms and Practical Rituals*, Teish recommends that rape survivors and battered women undergo cleansing baths given to them "by another woman who truly cares about

[them]."[7] These texts fall short of actually linking notions of healing with political action.

The text most specifically concerned with physical health and healing, *Body & Soul: The Black Women's Guide to Physical Health and Emotional Well-Being* (a publication of the National Black Women's Health Project), opens with a section titled "Our Bodies." The section includes a chapter titled "Our Skin, Hair, Eyes, and Teeth." Yet, this is not a beauty manual. Challenging racist constructions of Black women's bodies is fundamental to the text's goal of encouraging Black women toward physical, spiritual, and psychological health.

Angela Davis and June Jordan, two veteran political activists and writers, provide the foreword for *Body & Soul*. Their foreword signals the political nature of the text. They write:

> We cannot conceptualize healthy bodies, psyches, and communities without addressing problems that have always been taboo. This means we must go beyond the Civil Rights framework that privileges men over women and the public sphere over the private. (xi)

Note the movement from individual bodies to psyches to communities. The imagined Black woman reader posited in this foreword is one who sees herself as part of a community in struggle. Davis and Jordan encourage readers to challenge the sexism that causes them to believe that issues of emotional and physical well-being are "private" and therefore not political. According to Davis and Jordan, attention to the taboo, to the private, leads to radical redefinition of wellness and health:

> *Body & Soul* offers us much needed guidance as we try to put ourselves back together. This book leads Black women back to ourselves, to take our health needs seriously and to try and think about good health as being much more than the mere absence of disease. Body and soul challenges us to let go of the narrow definitions of health

imposed on us by people who don't care about us—who don't know how we live or die. This book maps the terrain of Black women's health consciousness. (xi)

Davis and Jordan see the book as integral to Black women's road to wellness. The terrain of Black women's health consciousness mapped by this text is a terrain of resistance against racism, sexism, xenophobia, and homophobia:

> Wellness also means that we take seriously our capacity to love. Learning to fearlessly love and respect our individual and collective bodies and souls, we can become warriors against cancer, AIDS, high blood pressure, and pervasive violence and stress that afflict our communities. We can also more forcefully demand social respect for our reproductive rights. *Body & Soul* urges us to take care of those bodies and souls we love and to act on the political implications of that love. (xii)

Here, Davis and Jordan assert that attention to individual healing lays a foundation for entering a community of resistance.

As with Angelou, Taylor, Davis, and Jordan, novelists and poets as diverse as Ntozake Shange, Gloria Naylor, Toni Cade Bambara, and Paule Marshall all devote some part of their texts to the healing and celebration of Black women's bodies as a means of healing their psychic wounds.[8] These novelists share the concerns of the pop self-help books but are much more complex than those texts because, as is the case with *Body & Soul*, their novels historicize and politicize their representation of the Black female body. Furthermore, they imagine new possibilities for Black women. In Ntozake Shange's poem "a layin on of hands" the suicidal persona turns within in order to "find god" in herself. This divine love allows her to turn out and share it with a community she names—a community of "colored girls who have considered suicide." All of the authors suggest that retreat to experience sensual touch precedes an opening out to others.

Healing does not presuppose notions of a coherent and whole subject. The body is not a "given concrete one can call on or return to in
order to recover a truer self."⁹ For the writers under consideration, the
healing is never permanent: it requires constant attention and effort.
I am using the term *healing* to suggest the way in which the body,
literally and discursively scarred, ripped, and mutilated, has to learn
to love itself, to function in the world with other bodies and often
in opposition to those persons and things that seek to destroy it. Of
course, the body never can return to a pre-scarred state. It is not a
matter of getting back to a "truer" self, but instead of claiming the
body, scars and all, in a narrative of love and care. As such, healing
does not deny the construction of bodies, but instead suggests that
they can be constructed differently, for different ends.

Black women writers create characters who along with Patricia
Williams might say of themselves:

> There are moments in my life when I feel as though a part
> of me is missing. There are days when I feel so invisible
> that I can't remember what day of the week it is, when
> I feel so manipulated that I can't remember my own
> name. . . . There are times when I catch sight of my reflec-
> tion in store windows and am surprised to see a whole
> person looking back. Those are times when my skin
> becomes gummy as clay and my nose slides around on
> my face and my eyes drip down to my chin. I have to close
> my eyes at such times and remember myself, draw an
> internal picture that is smooth and whole; when all else
> fails, I reach for a mirror and stare myself down until the
> features reassemble themselves like lost sheep. (229)

Of course, the whole subject that she sees in the mirror is a fictional
one, giving the illusion of coherence. Similarly, so is the one she constructs when she closes her eyes and "remembers" herself before looking into the mirror in search of the fictional coherent self. These are
necessary acts for those of us who are constantly bombarded with

very strong fictions that seek to define us as "invisible" or hypervisible and that seek to "manipulate" us.

It is here that a phenomenological vocabulary might help us to gain access to the significance of Black women writer's reimagination of Black female bodies. In her discussion of Maurice Merleau-Ponty, Judith Butler finds such a vocabulary useful for feminist thinkers who want to avoid the pitfalls of essentialism without giving up political possibilities. According to Butler:

> Merleau-Ponty maintains not only that the body is an historical idea but a set of possibilities to be continually realized. In claiming that the body is an historical idea, Merleau-Ponty means that it gains its meaning through concrete and historically mediated expression in the world. ("Performative" 272)

If the idea of the Black body as despised, diseased, and ugly is an historical idea, it is an idea that can be revised in ways that allow for alternative descriptions. If the Black body as a victimized body is one that has concerned Black thinkers, Black women writers, particularly Sherley Anne Williams and Cliff are currently in the process of reimagining it as a body engaged in acts of pleasure and political agency. This process of reimagining Black women's bodies moves from focusing on a body that is constructed in history and that carries that history within and on it, to a body capable of being remade.[10]

In "The Body in Its Sexual Being," Merleau-Ponty tells us that at any point, subjects are capable of retreating from their current bodily experience to access some past or imagined moment that sustains them. This is what Patricia Williams does when she closes her eyes to remember herself and when she faces herself in the mirror. Importantly, Merleau-Ponty notes,

> But precisely because my body can shut itself off from the world, it is also what opens me out upon the world and places me in a situation there. The momentum of exis-

tence towards others, towards the future, towards the world can be restored as a river unfreezes. (164–65)

Merleau-Ponty's words suggest that the very ability to retreat within, to listen to oneself, to shut off the world, is what allows for the possibility of reentering the world and existing within a community or at least contributing to the conditions for a community. We might carry these possibilities even further by asserting that these temporary retreats are absolutely necessary for the communal project of healing and resistance. For the Black characters created by Black women writers, these moments of retreat are sometimes individual, but usually they are enacted with another human being. They are almost always erotic moments of touching, as well.

The erotic is an important but problematic site of reclamation for Black women. In her pioneering article, "Uses of the Erotic: The Erotic as Power," Audre Lorde was among the first to encourage women, particularly women of color and lesbian women, to claim and celebrate the erotic as "a resource" the recognition of which will provide women with "the energy to pursue genuine change within our world." According to Lorde, "The erotic is a resource within each of us that lies in a deeply female and spiritual place, firmly rooted to the power of our unexpressed or unrecognized feeling" (53). She defines the erotic as an "assertion of the life-force of women." In Lorde's view, the erotic is intimately related to the spiritual and the political. To be effective, the spiritual and the political must be connected by a "bridge" of the erotic, the sensual. Because of this, women who are empowered by the erotic are "dangerous" to systems that oppress them. Though many would consider much of Lorde's essay essentialist, I think it is important to note that she precedes many feminist theorists in linking the erotic to power and resistance.

Yet the burden of a historical legacy that deems Black women "oversexed" makes the reclamation of the erotic Black female body difficult. Unless the way that body is constructed in history and the continued pain of that construction are confronted, analyzed, and challenged, it is almost impossible to construct an alternative that seeks to claim the erotic and its potential for resistance. Furthermore, the difficulty in claiming the erotic is evident in the fact that so few writers, unlike many Black women musical artists, link the erotic to notions of spirituality and resistance rather than sexual pleasure for the sake of pleasure.

To claim the erotic as a foundation for resistance is of fundamental importance to Williams and Cliff. By their attention to Black female sexuality, Williams and Cliff return to the site of the most formidable violence for Black women as slaves.[11] Each author documents the sexual violation of Black women slaves prior to exploring possibilities of the erotic for resistance.

As I will discuss in detail below, both Sherley Anne Williams and Michelle Cliff portray the reclamation of Black female bodies through various sexual, maternal, and spiritual acts. For Cliff and Williams these acts are a fundamental component of Black female resistance to their oppression. Each writer situates her character in the historical context of American slavery, for during slavery the most horrendous acts are committed against Black women and the most vitriolic myths and images of them emerge. In their focus on slavery, Williams and Cliff go back to the source of many of the discursive constructs that continue to circumscribe Black women's lives and their experiences of their own bodies: constructs that name them as promiscuous, unsightly semi-humans. Dessa of the novella *Meditations on History* and the novel *Dessa Rose*, and Inez of *Abeng* both participate in acts of sensual touch that prepare them for resistance.[12] Through acts of intimacy with other bodies, the women prepare to enter into a future that is different from the present they know. It is this preparation for the future that forces them to resist actively any efforts that would deny the realization of their own plans for that future. Acts of sensual touch are central to the novel's depiction of Black women's bodies and the relationship of those bodies to resistance. Mae Henderson explores Williams's portrayal of the abuse and scarring of Black women's bodies in her brilliant article, "Speaking in Tongues: Dialogics, Dialectics, and the Black Woman Writer's Literary Tradition." According to Henderson, Dessa's whip marks signify "the literal inscriptions of Dessa's body." They are evidence of "the white man's attempt to exercise discursive dominion over Dessa." For Henderson, Dessa is able to "seize discursive control of the story" (130–31). Because of my interest in the way that the novels confront the ongoing material legacy of white supremacy, my reading builds upon Henderson's but departs from it in that I want to keep our attention focused on the body. Where Henderson moves from the body to text, I want us to consider what these authors do with the body once they have chronicled it as a site of exploitation and domination. Here, I am concerned less with the construction of an alternate text than I am with specific acts of resistance recorded in each text and the relationship of those acts to the healing of women's bodies. As such, the texts narrate the healing and the resistance. In this way, the author's storytelling, like the character's remembering, acts as a means of confronting the legacy of slavery and reimagining a different future for their characters and for the readers, as well. They perform a textual healing.

|||||||||||

Dreams was one the reasons you got up the next day.
—DESSA ROSE

Sherley Anne Williams's novella *Meditations on History* and her novel *Dessa Rose* both tell the story of Dessa, a runaway slave who twice escapes slavery. Dessa attempts to murder her master in revenge for his killing of her beloved husband, Kaine. Dessa is punished for the attempted murder, but the nature of that punishment suggests that she receives it because she dared to enact sexual agency in a way that neither gives pleasure nor property to the slave master: Dessa Rose is eventually beaten in the very place on her body from which she enacts sexual agency. In the novel, the white woman Ruth observes that "Dessa's loins looked like a mutilated cat face. Scar tissue plowed through her pubic region so no hair would ever grow there again" (166). Mae Henderson notes: "The location of the inscriptions—in the area of the genitalia—moreover, signals an attempt to inscribe the sign *slave* in an area that marks her as woman. . . . The effect is to attempt to deprive the slave woman of her femininity" ("Speaking in Tongues" 126–27).

Following the beating, Dessa is sold to a slave driver, who is concerned that he will not be able to sell her because of the scars on her body. The scars give her away as a rebellious slave. However, before he can sell her, the pregnant Dessa helps to plan and enact an uprising on a slave coffle. She, along with her male comrades, is eventually caught. Dessa's captors hold her in a holding cell in anticipation of the birth of her child. She is to be executed following the birth. However, Dessa escapes again to join a community of runaways living on the dilapidated plantation of the delusional white woman Ruth.

The intimate moments between Dessa Rose and her husband Kaine and later, her lover, Harker, help to lay the foundation for Dessa's agency. In the opening pages of *Meditations on History*, Dessa—imprisoned in a holding cell—retreats to her memory of her husband Kaine, as a means of sustaining herself. In this memory, Dessa arrives home to her cabin after having worked all day in the fields. Feeling the coarse dirtiness of her clothing and her head rag, she tries to clean up before making love with Kaine.

> "Hmmmm mmmmm. But that ain't all I wants a touch of," he said holding her closer and pulling the dirty, sweaty rag from her head. . . . He stood with one leg pressed lightly between her thighs, his lips nibbling the curve of her neck.
>
> "I got to clean up a little." . . . He ran the tip of his tongue down the side of her neck . . . His fingers caught in her short kinky hair, his palms rested gently on her high cheekbones . . . He kissed her closed lids, his hands sliding down her neck to her shoulders and back, his fingers kneading the flesh under her tow sack dress and she wanted him to touch all of her . . . "Mmmmmmmmm mmmm." He pulled up her dress and his hands were

inside her long drawers. "I sho like this be-hind." His hands cupped her buttocks.

This was love talk that made her feel almost as beautiful as the way he touched her. . . .

It was gone as suddenly as it had come, the memory so strong, so clear it was like being with him all over again. Muscles contracted painfully deep inside her and she could feel the warm moistness oozing between her thighs. (208)

In narrating this scene, Williams narrates a seemingly private space and time. I say "seemingly" because the cabin belongs to the master, who at any time has the "right" to enter, for slaves have no "right" to privacy. In addition to the potential interruption of the master, the narrator enacts an interruption of Dessa's narrative as well. We as readers are put in the position of the master: we experience a moment of voyeurism as we interrupt the moment, the memory. In this context, distinctions between public and private collapse.

Sex stolen away from the gaze of the master is a dangerous pleasure—a vulnerable zone of safe space. Yet, although the privacy of this moment is tenuous, it does offer the possibility of a space outside the control of the master: that space is the space of the female orgasm. The orgasm is a site of agency in that it is a moment of self-immersion for the slave—a space beyond the control of the master. It is an instance of Merleau-Ponty's retreat within oneself. Significantly, orgasm is the space where the body loses control of itself. In a system in which the master's control of the slave body is so overdetermined, where every activity (particularly procreative sex between Black men and women) is within his control, the orgasm constitutes a site where the body moves beyond the control of itself and as such eschews control of any kind. The power of Dessa and Kaine's lovemaking to transcend the master's control takes on added significance when one notes that Kaine affirms and loves those very parts of Dessa that white standards of normalcy and beauty degrade. He does not reject her because she is sweaty or dirty from a day's work. His fingers caress the hair considered "bad" in contrast to Jefferson's preferred "long flowing hair" of those of European descent. He kisses her nose whose form J. J. Virey called "hideously flattened" in his *Dictionary of Medical Sciences* (1819). And he tenderly caresses her buttocks— whose shape was thought to have "hideous form" (Gilman 231–32) and became the object of "scientific" inquiry. As such, their lovemaking serves to resist dominant norms of white standards of beauty.

Even though this moment is a remembered one, it brings Dessa to orgasm in her present. Memories of the *sound* of Kaine's voice and the *feel* of his touch lead Dessa's muscles to "contract painfully deep inside . . . and [causes a] warm moistness [to begin] oozing between her thighs." Note the prepositions *inside* and *between*. These words connote interiority; the sensation takes place within Dessa's body, contained for her own pleasure, outside the reach of others. Williams narrates a scene that puts "Black agency center stage with no white presence at all" (West 125).

The memory of the moment provides a safe space for Dessa even more in the present of the narration than it did originally. It creates a space in her mind to which she can return to temporarily escape her material conditions and surroundings while also claiming her physical self. Throughout the text, such moments—as they appear in daydreams, nightdreams, and memories—are instances that allow her to recall affirmation, sensual touch (through sex or acts like hair-braiding) and advice from elders. These moments of remembered touching, pleasure, affirmation, playfulness, and laughter are not in and of themselves acts of resistance, but they are acts of nurturing and sustenance that become resources for resistance. As described by Merleau-Ponty, such moments of retreat help Dessa to navigate the world once she reenters it. They help her to situate herself within a community of people with common goals and visions—other fugitive slaves. By the end of the novella, Dessa—strengthened by her memories of Kaine and his love for her—escapes the holding cell with the assistance of several other slave characters.

In the above scene from *Meditations on History*, Dessa is self-conscious about her appearance because she knows it does not fit the standard of feminine beauty established by white men. In the novel *Dessa Rose*, Dessa escapes the holding cell to live with a group of fugitive slaves. Yet even in this novel, Dessa is haunted by images of her body as ugly and undesirable. This haunting is especially evident in three sections of the novel. Though she has escaped immediate harm, she nonetheless continues to have the scars from the first whipping. Second, she is forced to question her own desirability as a Black woman when she walks in on one of her comrades making love with the white woman Ruth. Third, she comes face to face with one Black man's internalization of the standards that deem her ugly and unfeminine. In order to overcome these obstacles so that she can once again participate in resistant acts, Dessa must once again engage in sensuous and erotic acts that affirm her.

Her knowledge of her scars fills her with fear and self-doubt. She thinks, "And I had the marks on my privates. It wasn't uncommon to see a Negro with scars and most of us carried far more than we ever showed, but I felt crippled, and I didn't want Harker nor no one else to see me" (207–8). Note the use of the word *crippled*. Not only does she feel unattractive, but she also feels disabled—"deprived of strength, efficiency, wholeness, or capability for service."[13] As such, she is prohibited from feeling desired. This is certainly not a condition from which to launch an act of resistance.

In addition to her self-consciousness about her scars, Dessa is further disabled when she catches the white woman Ruth engaged in sexual intercourse with one of her Black male comrades. Focusing on Ruth's white skin and long, wavy red locks, Dessa begins to question her own desirability. She constantly asks herself, "Is that what [Black men] want?" (199).

When she expresses her disappointment, pain, anger, and betrayal, another fugitive, Ned, tells her, "Yo all just jealous cause he not diddling you. Don't nobody want no old mule like you." Ned, a fellow fugitive, a Black man, confirms the "validity" of the white supremacist linkage between Black women and animals. One is here reminded of the words of Zora Neale Hurston's Nanny in *Their Eyes Were Watching God*: "De nigger woman is de mule uh de world so fur as Ah can see" (29). The angry Dessa asks herself, "Had [Kaine] really wanted me to be like Mistress . . . that doughy skin and slippery hair?" She begins to remember the bodies and features of herself and other slave women. "My heels was so rough they snagged a tear in them sheets up to the House. Janet had that kind of skin remind you of hickory-red-brown and tough: Flora's skin was smooth as a peach peel, hands big and hard. But Ned wasn't talking about no color, no feel." The violence of Ned's language reinforces paradigms that Dessa has tried to resist by retreating to memories of Kaine and his affirmation of her. But now she questions the power of her memories, as well. Believing that all Black men desire white women, and feeling rejected by them, Dessa at first chooses to not join the other runaways in an elaborate con game that will ultimately ensure their freedom. Dessa's inhibitions about her body contribute to the absence of the will to resistance.

Once again, an act of heterosexual intercourse makes Dessa consider herself desirable and worthy of love. As such, she is able to reenter the community of runaways and join them in their quest for freedom. Harker, her lover, tells her:

> "Dess? Dessa, you know I know how they whipped you."
> His head was right by my leg and he turned and lifted my dress, kissed my thigh. Where his lips touched was like fire on fire and I trembled. "It ain't impaired you none at all," he said and kissed my leg again. "It only increase your value." (208)

Sensual and erotic touch between a Black man and Black woman appears to serve as an act of healing and affirmation. Her scars are redefined as a site of desire. We might read his mention of the whipping and the inference of the scars that result from it as his recognition of the scars as marks of her resistance to slavery. As such, they add to her desirability. Following this moment, and the assurance of Harker's commitment to her, Dessa is able to further resist enslavement. She joins other former slaves and the white woman Ruth in a scheme to earn enough money to move West into free territory.

However, note the term "increase your value," with which the passage ends. "Increase your value" is very ambiguous. It might mean that the scars of your struggle increase your value as a human being. Yet it might also mean increase your value as a possession. This is an instance where the discourse of the novel collapses into the very discourse that it seeks to counter. This is but one instance where Williams's narration of an attempt to resist constructions of Dessa as undesirable also seems to sanction the way in which she is valued in a patriarchal culture. Her "fortune" is in her ability to evoke desire in a man. Herein lies the potential danger of seeking healing from the psychological wounds of patriarchal and white supremacist constructions of beauty only in Black male validation. Heterosexuality acts as a plot catalyst to action and as a narrative resolution throughout Williams's novel. *Dessa Rose* shares this sense of heterosexual resolution with Toni Morrison's *Beloved* and Gayl Jones's *Corrigedora*. Michelle Cliff avoids the "male validation" model posited in the work of Williams, Morrison, and Jones. She allows for such validation within the context of women's friendships and lesbian relationships. *Abeng* attempts to provide an even more politicized understanding of the construction of Black bodies as ugly bodies. In this novel, a young girl, Clare Savage, is growing up in Jamaica in the 1950s. Clare is the fair-skinned, mixed-blood, middle-class great-great granddaughter of white slave owners and Black slaves. She is the direct descendent of Judge Savage, an Englishman who burned his one hundred slaves on the eve of their emancipation. Her entire life is made up of a series of negotiations with the contradictions of class, color, and sexual orientation in her own lineage and her life. Clare knows that "She lived in a world where the worst thing to be—especially if you were a girl—was to be dark. The only thing worse than that was to be dead" (78).

On a visit to Judge Savage's dilapidated estate, the young Clare (who knows nothing about the savage history of her family) daydreams about its glory days: "Clare assumed the women who had lived in the great house had been as white as the women on the [wall] paper." Cliff goes on to tell us the story of at least one of the women who lived in Judge Savage's old house, the bronze woman, Inez. Judge Savage had kidnapped and forced Inez to become his concubine when she was eighteen. Unlike other "mixed-blood mistresses," Inez, whose parents were "a half-blood Miskito Indian and an Ashanti Maroon," is an important actor in the resistance activities of darker slaves. Unlike the biracial heroines of Frances Harper or William Wells Brown, Inez is not just the object of sexual harassment, but she is also the object of sexual abuse. Having been raped for six weeks by the white judge who enslaves her, "she had survived by planning her escape, waiting for emancipation, and devising a way to avenge herself" (34). To assist her with her plan, Inez visits a slave, Mma Alli, an obeah-woman. Mma Alli shares her magic with the slaves and counsels them on how and when to escape. Of Mma Alli, Cliff says,

> Mma Alli had never lain with a man. The other slaves said she loved only women in that way, but that she was a true sister to the men—the Black men: her brothers. They said that by being with her in bed, women learned all manner of the magic of passion. How to become wet again and again all through the night. How to soothe and excite at the same time. How to touch a woman in her deep-inside and make her womb move within her. She taught many of the women on the plantation about this passion and how to take strength from it. To keep their bodies as their own, even while they were made subject to the whimsical violence of the justice and his slave drivers. (35)

With Mma Alli a sexual act is a ritual that provides Black women with a spiritual center that helps sustain them through violence and abuse. Her wisdom echoes Audre Lorde's conviction that "In touch with the erotic, I become less willing to accept powerlessness." Such is the case with Inez, who goes to Mma Alli to have an abortion. After giving Inez a tea of roots and leaves to induce contractions in her womb, Mma Alli "began to gently stroke [Inez] with fingers dipped in coconut oil and to pull on her nipples with her mouth, and the thick liquid that had been a mixed-up baby came forth easily" (35). Cliff's description of this moment calls to mind Zora Neale Hurston's description of a Jamaican ritual performed on young brides-to-be by older women. In these rituals, the older women prepare the younger women for their sexual duties by lecturing, bathing, and stimulating them. Hurston reports:

> [The old woman] massages the girl from head to foot with this fragrant unction. The toes, the fingers, the thighs, and there is a special motional treatment for every part of the body when the body massage is over, she returns to the breasts. These are bathed several times in warm water in which something special had been steeped. After that they are massaged ever so lightly with the very tips of the fingers dipped in khus khus. This fingertip motion is circular and moves ever towards the nipple. Arriving there, it begins over and over again. Finally the breasts are cupped and the nipples flicked with a warm feather back and forth, back and forth until there was a reaction to stimulation. The breasts stiffened and pouted, while the rest of the body relaxed. But the old woman is not through. She carries this same light-fingered manipulation down the body and the girl swoons. (*Tell My Horse* 290)

Hurston's description is no less sexual, but it is a ritual performed in the service of heterosexual union. Following the ritual, the older woman tells the younger, "The whole duty of a woman is love and comfort. You were never intended for anything else" (292). In contrast, Mma Alli's erotic ritual is performed in the service of resistance. Furthermore, it is not an act that ensures heterosexual reproduction, but instead, because it is an act of abortion, it challenges heterosexuality and male control over female sexuality and reproduction. Because it is performed by a woman who is an avowed lesbian, it challenges heterosexuality even more.

Cliff's passage challenges several received notions, the most obvious of which is the notion that lesbianism is European. Furthermore, in this instance, abortion of the oppressor's baby from a Black woman's body is an act of healing that body as well as an act of resistance. To claim the erotic as a foundation for resistance is of fundamental importance to Williams and Cliff. Inez emerges from this moment of retreat ready to assist the Black slaves in preparing for their future as freedmen. Such preparation means that they must be prepared to survive. Thus, Inez situates herself in a community of other Blacks, in the woods, in possession of food, supplies, and weapons, in gaining their freedom.[14]

Significantly, Clare inherits the transgression of the lesbian moment and the resistance of the slaves as well as the legacy of the slave holder. She finds herself attracted to her best friend and playmate, the poor, dark-skinned Zoe. Her relationship with Zoe makes her intolerant of injustice and racial and ethnic prejudice. While the novel documents the legacy of white supremacy on the island of Jamaica and its impact upon an individual like Clare, it also narrates her resistance to that legacy, a resistance grounded in the erotic nature of her attraction to and love for her dark friend. In providing an alternative history of Jamaica, one that includes the experience of slaves and women like Inez, the novel itself stands as an act of discursive resistance.

Michelle Cliff exposes the social construction of standards that deem Black bodies ugly, undesirable, and lacking in intellectual ability. Furthermore, she documents the sexual terrorism suffered by Black women. However, the text goes on to document resistance to these constructions and resistance to the terrorism as well. Finally, Cliff imagines a Black female sexuality and resistance that is not dependent on male validation.

||||||||||

IT IS NOT insignificant that, in another contemporary novel of slavery, Toni Morrison's *Beloved*, the character for which the novel is named, Beloved, the ghost of those "Black and angry dead," remembers the Middle Passage as a place where "we are all trying to leave our bodies behind" (210). In contrast, Denver, the child of freedom, recalls Baby Suggs's advice to her:

> Slaves not supposed to have pleasurable feelings on their own; their bodies not supposed to be like that, but they have to have as many children as they can to please whoever owned them. Still, they were not supposed to have pleasure deep down. She said for me not to listen to all that. That I should always listen to my body and love it. (209)

Listening to one's body and loving it is an important step for all women who have been conditioned to hate their bodies. Affirmative sexual relations and rituals of spiritual renewal help to lead one to the stance of self-love and self-care. However, clearly the reclamation of the sexual body and affirmation of the spiritual self are not in and of themselves enough to constitute acts of resistance; in and of themselves they do not alter the conditions that oppress Black women. This is why neither of the writers I have discussed ever take the easy path of asserting that sexual love and spiritual healing lead immediately to the alleviation of oppression. However, each of these texts does serve to raise a level of consciousness about the manner in which Black women have come to know and feel about their bodies. Each provides a path out of this prison. Such work serves to let individual Black women understand the ideologies and conditions that have led them to feel the way that they do about themselves. In this way, it is no longer a case of individuals suffering from their individual dissatisfaction with themselves. By coming to terms with the ways they have been constructed by racist ideologies and historical acts of torture, they can begin to release the elements of those ideologies that they have internalized. This is most definitely an important step toward a political consciousness, which in turn is the most necessary step for active resistance.

All three of the texts discussed in this essay begin to perform the important cultural work of healing one of the most devastating legacies of the white supremacist venture. Williams and Cliff know that these issues are of primary importance in confronting and healing the distortions of white racism. Among those distortions are distortions of the Black body, particularly the bodies of Black women. The writers demonstrate that Black women's bodies are historical and not essential. As such, each of them is able to imagine and invent new possibilities of pleasure and political agency for Black women, their bodies, and the communities they inhabit.

"IRONIES OF THE SAINT"

Malcolm X, Black Women, and the Price of Protection

THIS ESSAY GROWS out of two concerns: First, the re-rise of what I want to call a "promise of protection" as a more progressive counter discourse to elements of misogyny in Black popular culture; second, my feeling that the emergence of Malcolm X as an icon of younger African Americans requires a serious and sustained examination and engagement of all aspects of his legacy. Malcolm X has not been the subject of a Black feminist critique in the way that Richard Wright or Miles Davis have been. When I looked to Black feminist thinkers who have written on Malcolm, few of them were as critical of his views on women as I had expected. Patricia Hill Collins, Barbara Ransby, and Tracye Matthews are among the few to call attention to Malcolm's gender politics.[1]

Black women are reluctant of being critical of Malcolm X: theirs is a reluctance born from the desire not to have such a critique co-opted by those who already hold him in contempt and disdain and a reluctance grounded in the genuine love, respect, and reverence that many Black women have for Malcolm. I must admit that even as I write this essay, I share this reluctance, for there are few Black male leaders whom I hold in as much esteem as I do Malcolm. Nonetheless, while I recognize Malcolm to be a man of his times and a man with tremendous capacity for growth, I am disturbed by any tendency to uncritically adopt his political and rhetorical stance, particularly around gender.

In this essay, I will articulate some of the reasons why so many Black women, even Black feminists, appreciate and revere Malcolm and his legacy. Then I hope to offer a reading of his position on women, not as a means of discrediting the esteem in which we hold him, but as a means to move us beyond the oppressive gender politics embedded in his rhetoric. Malcolm X offered Black women a promise of protection, an acknowledgment of the significance of white racist assaults on Black beauty, and an affirmation of Black features, particularly hair and color. In the remainder of this essay, I will examine these two important aspects of his legacy.

THE PROMISE OF PROTECTION

> Her head is more regularly beaten than any woman's and by her own man; she is the scapegoat for Mr. Charlie; she is forced to stark realism and chided if caught dreaming; her aspirations for her and hers are, for sanity's sake, stunted; her physical image has been criminally maligned, assaulted, and negated; she's the first to be called ugly, yet never beautiful, and as a consequence is forced to see her man . . . brainwashed and wallowing in self-loathing, pick for his own the physical antithesis of her. . . . Then to add insult to injury, she . . . stands accused as emasculator of the only thing she has ever cared for, her Black man. . . . Who will revere the Black woman? Who will keep our neighborhood safe for Black innocent womanhood? . . . Black womanhood cries for dignity and restitution and salvation. Black womanhood wants and needs protection and keeping and holding. Who will keep her precious and pure? Who will glorify and proclaim her beautiful image? To whom will she cry rape?
>
> —ABBEY LINCOLN[2]

Malcolm X's appeal to a broad range of Black women lay first in his courage and commitment to Black liberation and second in his attempt to address the call sent out by Abbey Lincoln and cited above; a call that had been voiced many times prior to Lincoln's articulation of it: "Who will revere the Black woman? Who will keep her precious and pure? Who will keep our neighborhoods safe for innocent Black womanhood? Who will glorify and proclaim her beautiful image?" The terms *precious, pure, innocent, beautiful,* and *revere* were (and in many instances, continue to be) particularly important to African American women. Each of these terms has been equated with white womanhood and thereby with femininity—both privileged spheres in our society; spheres where Black women have historically been denied access. Poor and working Black women, and dark-skinned Black women especially, have been excluded from the discourse of the precious, pure, and protected.

However, as appealing as the promise of protection and the guarantee of purity are, they are also intensely problematic: these are the very same terms used by white American men, particularly white Southern men, to repress white women and to systematically brutalize Black men—all in the name of protection and (race) purity.

My term "promise of protection" is influenced by Jacquelyn Dowd Hall's term "rhetoric of protection." Hall uses the phrase to describe the discourses of a pure and protected white womanhood in the American South. According to Hall, "the rhetoric of protection [was] reflective of a power struggle between men." She continues, "the right of the southern lady to protection presupposed her obligation to obey."[3] I have chosen not to use the word "rhetoric" because I want to avoid the implications of the word that suggest a discourse lacking in conviction or earnest feeling. Malcolm's desire to "protect" Black women grew out of a sincere concern for their emotional, psychic, and physical safety; it was also reflective of the power struggle between Black and white men and Black men and women. Furthermore, the pure and protected Black woman of his vision was also obligated to obey her protector—the Black man. The exchange is as follows: the woman gets protection; the man acquires a possession.

Nonetheless, many Black women were willing to accept the terms of this contract. Barbara Omolade explains, "The extremes of American patriarchy, particularly under slavery, pushed Black women outside traditional patriarchal protection." Consequently, the promise of patriarchal protection was certainly much better than the methodical abuse suffered by Black women throughout much of their history in the New World. As had been the case a century earlier with their recently freed foremothers, the assurance of their safety was a very appealing vision for many Black women: It stood in direct opposition to the degrading images that bombarded them on a daily basis and the harsh reality of many of their lives. Omolade notes, "Most Black women accepted traditional notions of patriarchy from Black men because they viewed the Afro-Christian tradition of woman as mother and wife as personally desirable and politically necessary for Black people's survival."[4]

Malcolm X's promise of protection comes from a long tradition in African American writing and organizing. The National Association of Colored Women was formed in 1896, in part to protect the name and image of Black women. Leaders like W. E. B. Du Bois and Alexander Crummell both called for the protection of Black women from rape, physical abuse, and economic poverty.[5] Large numbers of the urban women to whom Malcolm X spoke were the daughters of or were themselves women who fled the South in an attempt to escape the threat of rape from white males. Black women also found themselves the victims of economic exploitation, unfair employment practices, medical experimentation, and domestic violence. Who was deemed better to play the role of protector than Black men? This, of course, is a role that had been denied Black men throughout history.

Malcolm's promise of protection assumes a stance of victimization on the part of those who need to be protected, without allowing much room for their agency in other spheres. It places the woman in the hands of her protector—who may protect her, but who also may decide to further victimize her. In either case her well-being is entirely dependent on his will and authority. Note Malcolm's words upon hearing the dynamic Fannie Lou Hamer speak of her experiences in Mississippi:

> When I listen to Mrs. Hamer, a Black woman—could be my mother, my sister, my daughter—describe what they have done to her in Mississippi, I ask myself how in the world can we expect to be respected as men when we will

allow something like that to be done to our women, and
we do nothing about it? How can you and I be looked
upon as men with Black women being beaten and nothing being done about it? No, we don't deserve to be recognized and respected as men as long as our women can be
brutalized in the manner that this woman described, and
nothing being done about it, but we sit around singing
"We shall overcome."[6]

Later, when introducing her at the Audubon, Malcolm would refer to
her as "the country's number one freedom-fighting woman." However, the predominant tone of this passage refers to Hamer only as
victim in need of protection—not the protection afforded to citizens
by their governments (which the South and the nation at large did
not provide) but the protection of a Black man. Hamer's victimization makes Black men the subject of Malcolm's comment. When read
closely, the above statement is not a paragraph about Fannie Lou
Hamer but about the questionable masculinity of Black men, particularly those Black men of the southern civil rights movement, such
as Martin Luther King. If Black men protected "their" women, then
Ms. Hamer would not be a victim of such abuse. Nor would she be
a freedom fighter—that would be a position monopolized by Black
male protectors.

According to Malcolm in his *Autobiography*, "All women by their
nature are fragile and weak: they are attracted to the male in whom
they see strength."[7] This assertion of the nature of Black women
leaves little room for women like Fannie Lou Hamer, Ella Baker, Sep-
tima Clark, Harriet Tubman, Mary McLeod Bethune, Ida B. Wells, or
Angela Davis.

Malcolm's general understanding about the nature of women was
acquired in childhood through witnessing the abusive actions of his
father as well as from his days on the streets of Boston and New York.
While the discourse of protection emerges from the Nation of Islam,
it does not challenge Malcolm's earlier notions of women's nature.
Instead, the Nation provides him with a framework that still accepts

women's nature as fragile and weak, that also sees women as manip-
ulative, but that encourages men to protect and respect instead of
abuse them. Malcolm's mentor Elijah Muhammed shared his sense
that the protection of the Black woman guaranteed Black men their
manhood: "Until we learn to love and protect our woman, we will
never be a fit and recognized people on earth. The white people here
among you will never recognize you until you protect your woman."[8]

In all of the instances cited above, women are subordinate to men,
whether as the objects of abuse or protection. In the *Autobiography*,
Malcolm notes:

> Islam has very strict laws and teachings about women,
> the core of them being that the true nature of man is to
> be strong, and a woman's true nature is to be weak, and
> while a man must at all times respect his woman, at the
> same time he needs to understand that he must control
> her if he expects to get her respect.[9]

Protection is not in and of itself a bad thing. Patriarchal societies such
as ours foster misogyny from which all women need protection. A
racist patriarchal society is particularly dangerous for Black women.
However, protection need not be equated with possession. Of course,
until the day arrives when we no longer live in a patriarchal society,
women need to be protected from misogyny and paternalism; however, instead of fighting simply to protect women from misogyny, we
must all engage in the fight to eradicate patriarchy as well as racism.
This dedication is nowhere apparent in Malcolm's writing. Finally,
it is one thing to protect an individual so that she may actually live
with a greater degree of freedom, that is, make our streets safe so that
women may walk alone at night. It is another thing entirely to "protect" someone and in so doing to limit their freedom and mobility.
We must be careful to distinguish offers of protection that are made
in a context that places limitations on women's freedom.

In a brilliant Afrocentric feminist critique of African American
nationalism, "Africa on My Mind: Gender, Counter Discourse and

African-American Nationalism," E. Frances White argues that "Black nationalism is an oppositional strategy that both counters racism and constructs utopian and repressive gender relations."[10] Herein lies the paradox of Malcolm's promise of protection. When considered only in contrast to the external discourse of white supremacy, Malcolm's proposal of protection seems to offer a radical stance on Black womanhood. However, if we consider what his discourse shares with white sexist discourse, we see something altogether different. Again, White warns:

> In making appeals to conservative notions of appropriate gender behavior, African-American nationalists reveal their ideological ties to other nationalist movements, including European and Euro-American bourgeois nationalists over the past 200 years . . . European and Euro-American nationalists turned to the ideology of respectability to help them impose the bourgeoisie manners and morals that attempted to control sexual behavior and gender relations.[11]

Malcolm X's promise of protection falls under the rubric of the "ideology of respectability." The protected woman is the "respectable" woman. The man who protects her is the respected man.

THE AFFIRMATION OF BLACK BEAUTY

> I know he loved me for my clear brown skin—it was very smooth. He liked my clear eyes. He liked my gleaming dark hair. I was very thin then and he liked my Black beauty, my mind. He just liked me.
> —BETTY SHABAZZ[12]

In addition to the promise of protection, Malcolm X also offered all Black people, and Black women in particular, an affirmation of Black features and physical characteristics. In so doing, he followed the lead of Marcus Garvey and Elijah Muhammad. To many, this may seem unimportant or shallow, but when considered in light of constant white supremacist assaults on notions of Black beauty, it is of profound significance. From the minstrel caricatures to "serious scientific" studies, Black difference has always been predicated on Black bodies. Big Black lips, nappy Black hair, large Black thighs and derrieres, Black Black skin, "oversized" Black genitals.

Though African Americans always fought such assaults by establishing and maintaining their own sense of their humanity, dignity, capability, and beauty, perhaps in no realm have our oppressors been more successful than in convincing us of our own ugliness. Throughout our history on this continent, Black Americans have accepted and revised white standards of beauty. Yet for large numbers of Black women, these standards continue to be oppressive, particularly when they are upheld by other African Americans. In 1925, Walter White observed: "Even among intelligent Negroes there has come into being the fallacious belief that Black Negroes are less able to achieve success."[13] The color tension between Marcus Garvey and W. E. B. Du Bois is legendary. Garvey questioned Du Bois' credibility as a leader by accusing him of wanting to be "everything but Black" and Du Bois referred to Garvey as "fat, Black, and ugly."[14] Du Bois's comment is something of a floating trinity in Black America. Like the floating blues lyric that appears in diverse songs and contexts, so too does the phrase, "fat, Black and ugly"—readily available as an all-too-familiar taunt. Or, witness Colin Powell's statement in an interview with Henry Louis Gates—"I ain't that Black."[15]

If Black men have used color and features as weapons against each other, the impact of a color hierarchy on Black women has been especially devastating. In a heterosexist society, standards of beauty always impact upon women more harshly than upon men. Because Black women were always compared to "the white woman"—the standard bearer—in the eyes of mainstream society and in the eyes of far too many Black men, they fell short of this ideal.[16]

By the time Malcolm X began speaking to Black audiences, Black women had suffered centuries of "humiliating and detested images of [them]selves imposed by other people."[17] Pages of Black magazines were filled with advertisements for hair-straightening and skin-lightening products; most Black sex symbols were café au lait at best: Lena Horne, Dorothy Dandridge, Eartha Kitt. As Malcolm gained notoriety, Black audiences would see the emergence of darker beauties like Abbey Lincoln, Cicely Tyson, and Nina Simone, but these would still be rare. It is in this context that we must be aware of the appeal of Malcolm's affirmation of Black features and color. Also, we must remain cognizant of the class connotations of a color hierarchy in Black communities.

When Malcolm X spoke out against racist hierarchies of beauty, Black women heard an admired and respected leader who finally took seriously an issue that had affected them profoundly—an issue that is often not given serious attention by Black leaders and thinkers because it is not considered "political" and because it calls for a self-critique that few leaders have been willing to endure. This was not the case with Malcolm X: "Out in the world, later on, in Boston and New York, I was among the millions of Negroes who were insane enough to feel that it was some kind of status symbol to be light-complexioned—that one was actually fortunate to be born thus."[18]

Many Black people, particularly women, welcomed Malcolm's willingness to break the silence around "the color thing." The issue of colorism, of distinctions based on grade of hair and keenness of features, tears at the very fabric of who we are as a people. In the way that certain feminist critiques of the nuclear family uncovered the sexist aspects of that institution, so too do critiques of white standards of beauty and desirability reveal hidden dimensions in Black family life. Malcolm exposed this when he said, "I actually believe that as anti-white as my father was, he was subconsciously so afflicted with the white man's brainwashing of Negroes that he inclined to favor the light ones. . . . Most Negro parents . . . would almost instinctively treat any lighter children better than they did the darker ones."[19] With humor and pathos Malcolm taught Black people to see the way they came to hate their color, their hair, their features. He also connected this understanding with their political awakening.

> You know yourself that we have been a people who hated our African characteristics. We hated our heads, we hated the shape of our nose, we wanted one of those long dog-like noses, you know; we hated the color of our skin, hated the blood of Africa that was in our veins. And in hating our features and our skin and our blood, why we had to end up hating ourselves.[20]

While contemporary Black critics like Lisa Jones and Kobena Mercer[21] challenge the adequacy of the notion of self-hatred for understanding the personal aesthetics of African Americans, Malcolm still has much to teach us about the way we have often uncritically adopted white supremacist standards. Although the Black Church has also been a sight of affirming Black beauty, Malcolm went a step further and suggested that we rid ourselves of all remnants of the white supremacist legacy, including straightened hair. It is quite ironic that other members of the Nation would later charge the organization with its own brand of colorism. In a CBS documentary on Malcolm X, one member even claimed that Malcolm's ascendancy to a position of leadership was aided by his fair coloring.[22] In fact, Malcolm X is even somewhat oppositional from the official Nation of Islam stance on issues like hair and color in his celebration of unstraightened Black hair.[23]

For Black women in Malcolm's audience, greetings like "My beautiful Black brothers and sisters" with which he opened some of his talks, must have come as rare and welcome salutations.[24] In February 1992, *Essence* magazine ran a special issue on "Honoring Our Heroes." Malcolm was on the cover and one of the featured articles was an as-told-to narrative by his widow, Betty Shabazz. Audrey Edwards and Susan Taylor opened the narrative with the following: "He has come to embody the best in Black men: strong and uncompromising, clear—committed to securing power 'by any means necessary.'"[25] In that quotation, Malcolm's wife Betty Shabazz recalls her own feeling of affirmation in Malcolm's aesthetic appreciation of her Blackness.

Black women cherished Malcolm's willingness to affirm them as worthy of respect, love, and admiration. All hierarchies of beauty are ultimately oppressive. And yet, in a context where Black women have been constructed as ugly just because they are Black, it has been necessary to affirm them by acknowledging the beauty of Blackness in all of its various guises. Still, our challenge isn't to reverse this hierarchy but to redefine beauty while questioning it as the most important characteristic for a woman to possess. Finally, our goal ought to be to dismantle all such oppressive hierarchies altogether.

The appreciation of the variety and diversity of Black beauty is nowhere more evident than in Black nationalist movements. However, this affirmation of Black beauty rarely leads to a progressive gender politics. In fact, nationalist movements of all sorts have also been characterized by their patriarchal ambitions. At best Black women can expect to be called "Black queens," and we all know that where there are queens, there are kings: a pairing that is rarely an equal one (not to mention the class and antidemocratic implications of such titles).

During his time, Malcolm's promise of protection and affirmation of Black beauty were welcome and needed. However, even then they held evidence of a very problematic gender politics. Our task is to scrutinize this aspect of his legacy with a critical eye. Of course, we must hold on to and value that which sought to affirm Black women, but we must rid ourselves of and revise all elements of his philosophy that might be detrimental to them.

WOMANIST MALCOLM?!

> do not speak to me of martyrdom
> of men who die to be remembered
> on some parish day.
> i don't believe in dying
> though i too shall die

and violets like castanets will echo me.
　　　　　　—FROM "MALCOLM" BY SONIA SANCHEZ

It is quite significant that in spite of the profound sexism of some of his writing, Malcolm X continues to be a hero for many Black women, even many Black womanist critics, theorists, and artists, myself included. Most Black women who had the opportunity to hear Malcolm never flocked to cover their bodies and hair, walk two steps behind their men, and join the Nation of Islam. Nevertheless, many of them appeared to have voiced their admiration and respect for his vision and for his commitment to Black women and families. In my classes, it is most often white women who are the first to raise concerns about the sexist moments in the *Autobiography*, while many of my Black women students immediately jump to Malcolm's defense, claiming him as a hero.

Black women thinkers like Angela Davis, bell hooks, and Alice Walker have all acknowledged his impact on their intellectual development and politicization. Davis and Walker have sought to rescue his legacy from the misogyny of those Black leaders who followed him. hooks applauds his affirmation of Blackness in the midst of a society that despises all that is Black. Patricia Hill Collins is one of the few contemporary Black feminist thinkers to provide a sustained critique of Malcolm's gender politics in an effort to make Black nationalism more accountable to Black women.[26] Perhaps Collins is able to launch such a critique because she shares Malcolm's Black nationalist politics.

If Black women critical thinkers have been reluctant to forward a critique of the sexism inherent in much of Malcolm's legacy, Black women creative writers, particularly our poets, have praised him in terms that celebrate the very patriarchy of his masculinity and held that up as his value to us as a people. Sonia Sanchez, Lucille Clifton, Margaret Walker Alexander, Gwendolyn Brooks, and Alice Walker are all among the women who have written poems in honor of Malcolm X. In 1968, Brooks published "Malcolm X":

Original.
Ragged-round.
Rich-robust.

He had the hawk-man's eyes.
We gasped. We saw the maleness.
The maleness raking out and making guttural the air
and pushing us to walls.

and in a soft and fundamental hour
a sorcery devout and vertical
beguiled the world.
He opened us—
who was a key,
who was a man.

Brooks's Malcolm is the one who is loved and revered by many Black women: a Black man, male, Malcolm who could protect us and "open" us, as he was a key. The "us" of this poem is a feminized Black people who are in need of a very masculinized Black leader.

Some Black women have pinned their hopes on "What might have been the direction of Malcolm's thinking on questions of gender had he not been so cruelly assassinated?" For some sense of this, we all turn to one statement in particular that has come to represent a kind of beacon light for us:

> One thing that I became aware of in my traveling recently through Africa and the Middle East in every country you go to, usually the degree of progress can never be separated from the woman. If you're in a country that is progressive, then woman is progressive. If you're in a country that reflects the consciousness toward the importance of education, it's because the woman is aware of the importance of education. But in every backward country you'll find the women are backward, and in every country where

education is not stressed it's because the women don't have education. So one of the things I became thoroughly convinced of in my recent travels is the importance of giving freedom to the woman, giving her education, and giving her the incentive to get out there and put that same spirit and understanding in her children. And frankly I am proud of the contributions women have made in the struggle for freedom and I'm one person who's for giving them all the leeway possible because they've made a greater contribution than many of us men.[27]

This is the comment that leads some Black women to say that Malcolm began to reconsider his stance on women, their nature, and their role in the Black freedom struggle. It is seen as part of the overall growth and change he experienced following his travels through Africa and the Middle East. Patricia Hill Collins has pointed out that even here, women are not agents. They are given freedom and education so that they may better act upon their roles as mother.[28]

By the end of his life, it appears Malcolm not only changed his opinion about women's position in society, but he also began a much-needed self-critique. In the important essay "Black Popular Culture and the Transcendence of Patriarchal Illusions," Barbara Ransby and Trayce Matthews cite the following excerpt from a letter Malcolm wrote to his cousin-in-law in 1965:

I taught brothers not only to deal unintelligently with the devil or the white woman, but I also taught many brothers to spit acid at the sisters. They were kept in their places—you probably didn't notice this in action, but it is a fact. I taught these brothers to spit acid at the sisters. If the sisters decided a thing was wrong, they had to suffer it out. If the sister wanted to have her husband at home with her in the evening, I taught the brothers that the sisters were standing in their way; in the way of the Messenger,

in the way of progress, in the way of God himself. I did
these things, brother. I must undo them.[29]

If Malcolm himself came to be aware of the need to "undo" the work
of his teachings about women, certainly we must recognize this need
as well. Beyond wondering how Malcolm's view of women might have
changed, we are left with the task of critiquing and revising what he
left us. The reemergence of his popularity with young Black people,
the use of his discourse by present-day nationalist leaders requires
us to provide a systematic critique of those elements of his thought
that place limits on Black women. Angela Davis suggests we concern ourselves with "the continuing influence of both those who see
themselves as the political descendants of Malcolm and our historical
memory of this man as shaped by social and technological forces that
have frozen his memory, transforming it into a backward imprison-
ing memory rather than a forward looking impetus for creative political thinking and organizing."[30]

Just as there are some who want only to preserve the racial politics
of the pre-Mecca Malcolm, so too are there those persons who want
to freeze his pre-Mecca statements on women. We must move from
Abbey Lincoln's call for a Malcolm-like Black man who will revere
and protect us in the traditional sense of these words. And we must
imagine the possibility that Malcolm's legacy might lead to a celebration of the Malcolm X of Alice Walker's poem, "Malcolm":

> *Those who say they knew you*
> *offer as proof*
> *an image stunted*
> *by perfection.*
> *Alert for signs of the man*
> *to claim, one must believe*
> *they did not know you at all*
> *nor can remember the small, less popular*
> *ironies of the Saint:*

that you learned to prefer
all women free
and enjoyed a joke
and loved to laugh.

—Alice Walker[31]

Walker's Malcolm is a man who "learned to love all women free." A mythical Malcolm, yes (for perhaps the real ironies of the saint are that he loved Black women—yet could not imagine them as equal partners, and in this way he is no different than most men of his time), but no less mythical than the one who fuels contemporary images of him in popular culture and nationalist discourses.

Malcolm's tremendous capacity for self-reflection, growth, and revision can serve as an example for us. A serious and critical engagement with his words and thought leads us to the understanding that we must respect and acknowledge his continuing importance and significance while moving beyond the limitations of his vision.

CONFLICT AND CHORUS

Reconsidering Toni Cade's
The Black Woman: An Anthology

FIRST ENCOUNTERED *The Black Woman: An Anthology* in the early 1970s (certainly before March 24, 1972, the day my father died), when I was seven or eight years old. My father and I would alternate trips to the Free Library of Philadelphia with trips to our favorite bookstore—Robin's. In the early '70s, Robin's was a vibrant place where you could purchase books, especially those by radical writers and by writers of color, and a bevy of underground newspapers, among them the *Panther Newspaper* and *Rolling Stone*. Works by Thomas Jefferson and Thomas Paine sat next to those by Mao Tse-Tung and Frantz Fanon. There were displays of the latest offerings of Amiri Baraka, Jerry Rubin, Abbie Hoffman, and Eldridge Cleaver. In these days of Barnes and Noble and Borders, Robin's is fighting the good fight for its life. But back then, it was a place where you went not only to purchase books but also to find out where the meetings and rallies were going to be held, and where you were sure to find ongoing political debates and dialogues as well.

On one of these trips, I spotted *The Black Woman*. Staring from the cover directly at me was a beautiful brown woman with a large Afro that merged with the black background. I had to have that book. At home, huge pictures of Kathleen Cleaver—perfect Afro, light glistening eyes, beauty mark in the middle of her forehead—and of Angela Davis—huge Afro and round granny glasses—graced my bedroom wall. I loved these women, they were my idols, they populated my fantasy world; and my parents' stories of them helped me to learn the geography of northern Africa, the politics of race in the United States, facts about Vietnam and Cuba, definitions of communism and socialism. Because of Angela, I knew who Ronald Reagan was a decade before he became president of the United States. Those photographic images of Angela and Kathleen were my iconography for what it meant to be a revolutionary Black woman.

However, one crucial thing stood between me and the golden beauties who graced my wall. In the still-color-conscious Black world of McDaniel Elementary School in South Philadelphia, I was constantly reminded that I was "Black" (which always seemed to be qualified by phrases such as "and ugly," "and shiny," "and crispy"), not at all like Angela or Kathleen, who were light-skinned. So, you see, I was in desperate need of a browner, Afro-ed revolutionary image. I didn't mind if she wasn't as dark as me, just as long as she was brown. Nina Simone, Roberta Flack, and Abbey Lincoln did not meet my purposes because I could not and did not sing. Assata Shakur's autobiography with her own chocolate face gracing the cover had not yet appeared. I needed a rapping sister, a poet or journalist or writer. And this anonymous sister on the Cade anthology was going to be the one. Lacking name or voice, she could become what I was going to make of her, of us—revolutionary, writer, lawyer, and world traveler. By possessing the book, I could possess the woman, could become the woman—or so I reasoned.

Now, my father would buy me books on my asking, but I always had to tell him why I wanted a particular title. Because it had a pretty woman on the cover was not going to sit well with him.

I looked through the book. There were names I recognized—Nikki Giovanni and Abbey Lincoln. And a lot I did not recognize: for instance, who was this Toni Cade (was that her on the cover?) and what did it mean to "edit" something?

> ME: Daddy, daddy will you buy me this book?
> DADDY: Why do you want it?
> ME: There is poetry in it. Some by Nikki.

DADDY: Well, I will make a deal with you. I will buy it for
    you if you promise to remember one of the poems and
    recite it to me.

Now, that was almost too easy. I was always remembering poems and
reciting them. Hadn't I just remembered Nikki Giovanni's "Revolutionary Dreams" and recited it to him and all those friends of his on
the corner of the bar? I got lots of quarters and "That little sister sure
is something."

Within a week I had imagined myself as that woman on the
cover and created a whole life for us. There were two new poems by
Nikki in there, but I decided to add a new poet to my repertoire. I
loved the Audre Lorde poem ending "Nor give a damn whose wife
I am." But I was afraid that would count as cursing, and I wasn't
allowed to curse, so I picked "Poem" by Kay S. Lindsey. Then, much
to his delight, I recited both "Revolutionary Dreams" and "Poem"
for my father:

> Anyway I gave birth twice
> And my body deserves a medal for that
> But I never got one.
>
> Mainly because they thought
> I was just answering the call of nature.
>
> But now that the revolution needs numbers
> Motherhood got a new position
> Five steps behind manhood.
>
> And I thought sittin' in the back of the bus
> Went out with Martin Luther King.

After I finished my proud recitations—having actually understood
little about the last poem except the back of the bus stuff and women
walking behind men like the Muslims do sometimes—my father

applauded and kissed me and then asked, "Which one of those women are you going to be, baby girl?" And I, thinking he meant the poets and not the personas, said confidently, "Why both, Daddy, I am going to be both."

2

The tension implied in these two poems and in my father's question is one of the internal tensions of Toni Cade's anthology, and it is this which makes it such a unique and still-important document. The current political moment calls for a reconsideration of this founding text of contemporary Black women's thought. By "reconsideration" I mean we need to reconsider *The Black Woman* as a text, but also to reconsider the mission of Black feminist thought and its relationship to Black feminist politics, Black women's lives, and related struggles for Black liberation.

At its inception, Black feminist thought (including fiction, literary criticism and theory, the social sciences, and polemics) claimed a relationship to political struggle. As more Black women began to enter the academy, Black feminists sought legitimacy there—a seeking that led to a movement away from blatantly political commitments to Black freedom. Here, I am primarily concerned with the arena of Black women's writing which has received unprecedented recognition by the mainstream literary establishment in the three decades following the publication of Bambara's anthology. And while Black women still make up few of the American professoriate, Black women academics are among our most significant intellectuals.

Audre Lorde and Toni Cade Bambara are two Black women who did not abandon activism for their writing, nor did they separate the work of writing from their activism. And they both managed to create exquisitely beautiful works of art as they did so—works of art that articulated not only the conditions of Black women and Black people in general but also a vision of hope and possibility. In their very different ways, they each provided a guide for reimagining our reality. Both women were present in the important anthology to which I want to turn my attention now.

The Black Woman: An Anthology is one of the first major texts to lay out the terrain of Black women's thought that emerged from the civil rights, Black power, and women's liberation movements. *The Black Woman* was published in 1970, in the same era that produced Toni Morrison's *The Bluest Eye* (1970) and Alice Walker's *The Third Life of Grange Copeland* (1970).[1] In May of that year, the first issue of *Essence: The Magazine for Today's Black Woman* hit the newsstands. Finally, it was the year that a brilliant Marxist professor of philosophy, Angela Davis, was placed on the FBI's Ten Most Wanted list; and it was one year after Kathleen Cleaver joined Eldridge in exile in Algeria (1969).

In this anthology we find the vibrancy, excitement, politics, and rhetoric of the time, and we have the articulation of the dilemma confronting Black women activist intellectuals. In the preface, Cade notes the need for the anthology:

> The "experts" are still men, Black or white. And the images of the women are still derived from their needs, their fantasies, their secondhand knowledge, their agreement with the other "experts."... White woman have also produced the canon of literature fondly referred to as "feminist literature."... And the question for us arises: how relevant are the truths, the experiences, the findings of white women to Black women? Are women after all simply women? I don't know that our priorities are the same, that our concerns and methods are the same, or even similar enough so that we can afford to depend on this new field of experts white, female.[2]

Here Bambara situates the anthology at the nexus of two oppositional discourses—Black nationalism and feminism—both of which were profoundly limited by their failure to acknowledge sexism and racism respectively. She articulates the critique launched by Black women that challenged the normalization of women as white and middle-class and of Blacks as male. In so doing, she anticipates the title of another important anthology, *All the Women Are White, All the Blacks Are Men, But Some of Us Are Brave* (1982).[3] In fact, she sends out the call to which two decades of Black women's creative and critical writings would respond.

Ironically, the blindness that Bambara points to in her preface is reproduced in the *New York Times* review of the book. In February 1972, the *Times* published two book review sections, one specifically for paperback books. The editors explained: "Because so many important recent paperbacks address themselves to the overriding issues of the day, a large portion of this section is devoted to critical appraisals of leading works in these fields: Women's Lib, Blacks, Ecology, Law and Order, Vietnam, Youth and Cities." Alan Dershowitz wrote the "Law and Order" review essay. Martin Kilson wrote the essay on recent books by Blacks. There are no books by women in his essay. In the essay on books by women, Annie Gottlieb makes one mention of a book by a Black woman: "The Women's Liberation movement which emerged from the militant New Left . . . has produced . . . substantial anthologies: 'Sisterhood Is Powerful' . . . [and] 'Voices from Women's Liberation.' . . . To these, in militancy and beauty and selfhood must be added an excellent anthology of black women's writings: 'The Black Woman,' edited by Toni Cade." Gottlieb subordinates the Cade anthology to the other two and offers no real analysis of its contents.

The book was widely reviewed in contemporary Black publications, including *Black Scholar* and *Black World.* It seems to have immediately opened doors for the publication of other books by Black women, and it clearly met Black women's hunger for works of intelligence, beauty, and rigor. In the early '90s Ann duCille wrote that *The Black Woman* "stands as a pivotal text," a "founding text of contemporary Black feminist studies," and E. Frances White notes, "Toni Cade's *The Black Woman* reached out to early Black feminists as we emerged battle-scarred from our confrontation with cultural nationalists."[4]

The Black Woman is not a Black feminist text as we have come to understand that term. Nonetheless, it is a text that paved the way for an emerging Black feminism that came to flower in the late '70s and early '80s—a Black feminism that I want to suggest has found a greater life in the literary marketplace and the academy than it has in the lives of far too many African American women (a topic to which I will return).

Unlike so many of the anthologies on Black women that followed it, Bambara's text was not only concerned with articulating a Black feminist ideology; nor was it primarily concerned with the establishment of an academic field of Black women's studies. Clearly, she recognized that the establishment of the field was necessary for drawing attention to the lives and works of Black women and for providing analyses, critiques, and visions for a liberation movement that made Black women's freedom from racism, sexism, and poverty central to its goals.

In editing *The Black Woman*, Toni Cade Bambara also recognized that the book would identify a market to publishers. In an interview that appears in the posthumously published *Deep Sightings and Rescue Missions*, edited by Toni Morrison, Bambara notes:

> I put together this anthology that I felt would open the door and prove that there was a market. Sure enough, within the second month that the book came out, it went into a new edition. The book was everywhere. There were pyramids of *The Black Woman* in every bookstore. All I knew in the beginning was that it had to fit in your pocket and be under a dollar. I didn't know anything about publishing, but I stuck to that.[5]

Imagine that motivation: To open the door for others while making sure the people about whom you care the most can read, carry, and afford the book. In this day and time, that in and of itself is enough to give one the credentials of a "politically engaged" or "public" intellectual.

Nonetheless, the identification of a market and the establishment of an academic field were not Bambara's primary concern. Again, in the preface to *The Black Woman* she writes:

> The work grew out of impatience: ... an impatience with the halfhearted go-along attempts of Black women caught up in the white women's liberation groups around the country. Especially out of an impatience with all the "experts" zealously hustling us folks for their doctoral theses or government appointments. And out of an impatience with the fact that in the whole bibliography of feminist literature, literature immediately and directly relevant to us wouldn't fill a page.[6]

Most significantly, she notes of the contributors: "Many are professional writers. Some have never before put pen to paper with publication in mind. Some are mothers. Others are students. Some are both. All are alive, are Black, are women. And that, I should think, is credentials enough to address themselves to issues that seem to be relevant to the sisterhood."[7]

The anthology includes a diverse collection of writings that seek to address these questions. Among these are poems by Nikki Giovanni, Kay S. Lindsey, and Audre Lorde, fiction by Paule Marshall, Alice Walker, Sherley Anne Williams, essays by Abbey Lincoln, Jean Carey Bond, and three by Toni Cade herself among at least a dozen others. Most interestingly, the anthology also includes excerpts from the "Poor Black Women's Study Papers," a group working paper on Black women in cities, and the transcript of a rap session of women students from City University of New York. I find the latter especially fascinating because the dialogue shows the contest over the direction of young Black women's self-definition, their strategies for empowerment. One finds phrases like "Why do we have to wait for the man supposedly to do something before we make a move?" followed by "Men are our leaders, you know." Here is a true dialogue, debate between Black women, talking to each other.

3

The chorus of voices in *The Black Woman* shares a sense of political urgency, a sense of the importance of internal critique, a sense of the diversity of Black women and their ties to Black nationalism, feminism, and Black men. If the chorus of voices lends to its vibrancy, so too does the conflict inherent in its contents. A struggle is going on here, and it is an exciting and important one. One need only read the classic piece by Abbey Lincoln, composer, intellectual, actress, singer, poet, "Who Will Revere the Black Woman?" republished from *Black World*. Lincoln writes:

> Who will revere the Black woman? Who will keep our neighbor hoods safe for innocent Black womanhood? Black womanhood is outraged and humiliated. Black womanhood cries for dignity and salvation. Black womanhood wants and needs protection and keeping and holding. Who will keep her precious and pure? Who will glorify and proclaim her beautiful image? To whom will she cry rape?[8]

Similarly, Fran Saunders's essay, "Dear Black Man," is a plea for understanding and support from Black men. She asks, "Are we to be told what to do and how to do it, without benefit of being able to sit back and be lovely and feminine and delicate and to be taken care of in the bargain?"[9] This question implies Black women will accept Black men as the leaders of family and community in exchange for the benefits of femininity: protection and security. The dominant emotions of these two essays are disappointment, pain, and yearning. There is no critique of patriarchy or of femininity. Instead, they fit within a long-standing tradition of African American thought and politics of protection and respectability. The call for reverence and protection stems from a sincere concern for Black women's psychic and physical safety; however, the pure and protected Black woman of this vision will also be obligated to obey her protector—the Black man.[10]

Nonetheless, many Black women continue to be willing to accept the terms of this contract. The promise of patriarchal protection is certainly much better than the methodical abuse suffered by Black women throughout much of their history in the New World. It also seems to offer a solution to the problems faced by so many heterosexual Black women who find themselves struggling to raise families without the economic and emotional support of a male partner. Even many women who find themselves in abusive relationships would trade in physical and emotional violence for protection and reverence. This continues to be a reality for a great many Black women.

Lincoln and Saunders gave voice to these desires in a way that few Black women publicly articulate today; this is in spite of the fact that the large number of women who supported the Million Man March and who attend Rev. T. D. Jakes's sermons and purchase his books— such as *Woman, Thou Art Loosed! Healing the Wounds of the Past*— clearly seem to desire a form of Black patriarchy.[11]

Of course, as I've argued elsewhere, protection is not in and of itself a bad thing. Patriarchal societies such as ours foster misogyny from which all women need protection. A racist patriarchal society is particularly dangerous for Black women. Nonetheless, it is one thing to protect an individual so that she may actually live with a greater degree of freedom. It is another thing entirely to "protect" someone and in so doing to limit their freedom and mobility. We must be careful to distinguish offers of protection that are made in a context that limits women's freedom and mobility.

In contrast to the calls for protection articulated by Saunders and Lincoln, other contributors to *The Black Woman* clearly recognize the danger of such notions. Their essays begin to theorize a Black feminist politics and praxis. Most of these share the pain of the two essays discussed above, but the pain has turned to frustration and anger. As such, this change begins to lay the groundwork for the emergence of a Black feminist politics. Among the essays that fall into this category are those by Jean Carey Bond, Kay S. Lindsey, Toni Cade, and Frances Beal. Beal's essay, "Double Jeopardy: To Be Black and Female," is one of the first to articulate a theory of multiple oppression suffered by Black women.

In one of her own contributions to the volume, Toni Cade Bambara argues against the stance presented by Lincoln and Saunders:

> There is a dangerous trend observable in some quarters of the movement to program [Black women] out of their "evil" ways into a cover-up, shut-up, lay-back-and-be-cool obedience role. She is being encouraged—in the name of the revolution no less—to cultivate "virtues" that if listed would sound like the personality traits of slaves. We rap about being correct but ignore the danger of having one-half of our population regard the other with such condescension and perhaps fear that half finds it necessary to "reclaim his manhood" by denying her peoplehood. We have much, alas, to work against. [We must] face the task of creating a new identity, a self, perhaps an androgynous self, via commitment to the struggle.[12]

Here, Bambara not only offers a critique but also an alternative, a vision for moving forward. She may be one of the first Black women to suggest that an identity of androgyny might help further Black struggle, long before current critiques of Black "masculinity" by Black men, gay and straight, and Black feminists.[13] Indeed, many of the essays seem to ask, "What kind of women are we going to be? What kind of movement is ours going to be? What does our fiction, poetry, sociology, theory, look like? What does it mean to be a Black woman in the United States? What is our role in the continuing struggle for Black liberation?"

Bambara's anthology also demonstrates the kind of political and cultural work that publications can accomplish.[14] Its chorus of voices reminds us of the extra-academic origins of Black women's intellectual work and of its concern with something other than curriculum, canons, fields, careers, and academic publication. And while the academy is certainly an important site of struggle, it is not the only one where socially and politically engaged intellectuals ought to find themselves. In no way do I mean to belittle our academic and professional endeavors; I, for one, have greatly benefited intellectually, personally, and professionally from the presence of Black intellectuals in the academy. Here, I want to suggest the ways that social and political contexts shape the conception, publication, and reception of books. The social and political context out of which *The Black Woman* emerged—and out of which Toni Cade Bambara emerged as a public figure—was one which held intellectuals accountable for their writings and actions. Many people engaged in diverse political movements; an even larger group knew that something was at stake for oppressed peoples. This is not the case in the predominantly white academy. We must ask of intellectuals both inside and outside the academy, to whom are you accountable? Who is your constituency? In the absence of a social movement, this is a difficult question to answer.

4

In the years after the publication of *The Black Woman*, something crucial happened. First, the political climate of the country shifted to the right; with this change, any program to alleviate the conditions of poor people and Black people was swept off the national agenda. Black feminists tended to retreat from the hostility and homophobia they often encountered when they tried to raise feminist concerns in all-Black settings, be they Black churches or cultural nationalist venues. Black women academics and critics continued to talk to and argue with white feminist and Black male scholars, but they have not continued the dialogue among Black women who share different gender politics—a dialogue so evident in *The Black Woman*. One need only look at the anthologies that followed *The Black Woman*. *Homegirls: A Black Feminist Anthology* (1983), edited by Barbara Smith, provided a safe discursive space for Black feminists—heterosexual and lesbian—to present their ideas. *Women in Africa and the African Diaspora* (1996), edited by Rosalyn Terborg-Penn, Andrea Rushing, and Sharon Harley, attempted to forge a relationship between Black nationalism and Black women's struggles against sexism. Similarly, there is an emerging discourse of Africana womanism within Afrocentrist intellectual arenas and publications. Among these, Clenora Hudson-Weems's *Africana Womanism: Reclaiming Ourselves* (1995) is perhaps best known. Finally, Beverly Guy-Sheftall's *Words of Fire: An Anthology of African-American Feminist Thought* (1995) contains historical writings by "academics, activists, artists, community organizers, mothers . . . race women, socialists, communists, Christians, atheists, lesbian and straight, traditional and radical." However, today, we are hard-pressed to find written evidence that these groups of Black women intellectuals continue a contemporary dialogue in print.

Black nationalist women have accused leftist and left-liberal Black feminists of being too influenced by white feminism and thus remaining marginal to the concerns of most Black women. Black leftist and left-liberal feminists, too often wounded from encounters with certain Black nationalists, have had little desire to continue a dialogue with anyone articulating a nationalist perspective. In *The Black Woman* there was still a possibility for dialogue; a possibility that also existed in the person and work of Toni Cade Bambara. Not only did Bambara's anthology contain essays from various standpoints; it also presented the proceedings from actual dialogues and debates. Furthermore, the book became a catalyst for reading and discussion groups around the issues it raised.

I think many self-identified Black feminists have assumed that the notion of a nationalist feminist was oxymoronic. Black feminist historians Deborah Gray White and Paula Giddings have argued convincingly that Black nationalism and Black feminism have historically been "like oil and water."[15] In the course of all this, we all lost something very significant: the opportunity to really impact the lives of large numbers of Black women. I also think that the disconnection between Black women who are feminists and Black women who are nationalists is often based on class as much as it is on ideological differences.

While most Black women will never accept complete domination by Black men, many are far more open to the promises of protection and support offered by many forms of Black nationalism. Similarly, while the majority of Black women are not cultural nationalists—willing to live in polygamous households, cover their hair, and change their names—many are attracted to the affirmation of Blackness and the open confrontation with white supremacy offered by Black nationalist ideologies. Finally, many Black women recognize what so many Black feminist intellectuals fail to see: the diversity within Black nationalism itself. While certain forms of cultural nationalism, perhaps the most visible forms, are conservative on gender relations, other strains of nationalism range from the politically conservative to liberal to radical. Many Black women see room to negotiate gender roles within this continuity. Unfortunately, women and their rights are rarely more than symbolic in even the most radical strains; but we ought not conflate them all.

I cannot help but think that if Black feminist intellectuals, Black nationalist women intellectuals, and Black women who identified themselves as neither nationalist nor feminist had maintained an ongoing dialogue, Black feminists might not have been so caught off guard by such developments as the publication and popularity of Shahrazad Ali's *The Blackman's Guide to Understanding the Black-woman* or the tremendous support of Black women for Clarence Thomas, Mike Tyson, O. J. Simpson, and the Million Man March. Furthermore, had we continued to engage in dialogue with Black women who are not in the academy or in feminist organizations, we might have had a greater impact on the ways these events were viewed and analyzed by many Black women.

Had Black nationalist women been less hostile to Black feminists, including Black lesbian feminists, perhaps the platform of the historic Million Woman March held in Philadelphia in October 1997 would have reflected a more sustained engagement with Black feminism. This is a march that many Black feminists, including myself, did not attend because of the lack of an explicit feminist politics. (I think Toni Cade Bambara would have been there, because that is where so many Black people were.) While that platform does not appear to be a feminist one, it is especially representative of the concerns of many poor Black women. Among these issues were Black women in the penal system, Black families' access to quality health care, and Black women drug addicts and those in recovery. There is no reason why these issues should not be Black feminist issues. On the other hand, any event organized to give voice to the concerns of Black women ought to have included the issues of rape and domestic violence on the platform: both absent from that of the Million Woman March. These absences call into question the impact of the march, beyond that of symbolism and momentary euphoria, on the lives of Black women.

A rereading and reconsideration of *The Black Woman* by Black feminists would stress the importance of an ongoing dialogue and debate between Black women despite ideological differences. We have proved willing to continuously debate with white feminists in spite of the stubborn persistence of racism. The desire and need to speak with other Black women does not preclude the desire or need for an ongoing dialogue with white feminists and other women of color. Regardless of what many of our non-Black allies might argue, intra-racial solidarity is not racist.[16] A rereading and reconsideration of *The Black Woman* by Black nationalist women would expose the pitfalls of certain elements of Black nationalist ideology for women's freedom. For instance, women such as Abbey Lincoln no longer ask for protection and reverence in the same way, because they have learned that it comes at too high a cost.

As a Black feminist, I believe it is urgent that we acknowledge and attempt to come to terms with the continuing appeal of Black nationalism to large numbers of Black people, particularly Black women. Had the Million Woman March been organized by Black feminists, would we have had the same turnout? Unless we seek to come to terms with Black nationalism, it is highly unlikely that we will be successful in attempts to create a mass movement. The Black Women in the Academy Conference of January 1994 at MIT and the Million Woman March are evidence that, across class and ideological boundaries, Black women are seeking the terms and plans by which we will organize our lives and our struggles in the next century. Both events left us wanting for a program, a political or intellectual agenda, an organization that addresses the struggles of African American women. Only the Black Feminist Caucus of the Black Radical Congress seems to be attempting to address this void.

I am in agreement with Beverly Guy-Sheftall's astute observation:

> Black feminist discourse is inherently oppositional because it runs counter to mainstream points of view both within and without African American communities. Being oppositional, especially if you're Black and female, requires courage and tenacity. Being feminist exposes you to criticism, hostility, and even outright misogyny.[17]

However, at the end of the twentieth century, when the class divide in the Black community is wider than our ancestors ever could have anticipated, at a time when young Black women are the fastest growing segment of the prison population and of those contracting HIV, it is of utmost importance that we initiate the kind of dialogue evident in *The Black Woman*. Such a dialogue would allow for a Black feminism that E. Frances White describes:

> Because I value the contributions of nationalists . . . I want to engage them seriously. Yet, it is the kind of feminism that demands attention to internal community relations that leads me to interrogate this discourse even while acknowledging its ability to undermine racist paradigms. This kind of Black feminism recognizes the dangers of criticizing internal relations in the face of racist attacks but also argues that we will fail to transform ourselves into a liberated community if we do not engage in dialogue on the difficult issues that confront us.[18]

White's brilliant essay, "Africa on My Mind: Gender, Counter Discourse, and African American Nationalism," from which the above quotation is taken, is exemplary of the kind of dialogue about which I write.

5

By including essays representative of the diversity of Black women's thought, Toni Cade Bambara did not avoid contest, controversy, and debate. She did not avoid the messiness involved in laying the groundwork for social struggle. Instead, she seems to have seen it as essential to the integrity of the volume. One of Bambara's primary characteristics as a "political intellectual" is that she was willing to jump right into the mess and provide a space for its articulation, all the while maintaining her own stance as a feminist greatly influenced by Black nationalism, without compromise. She maintained a vision of Black people that took for granted their capacity for growth, change, and long-term struggle.

The sites of intellectual work are always shifting. There is nothing inherently wrong about the move that took place when the academy opened its doors ever so slightly. Bambara, however, chose not to enter completely into the academy. She taught college classes, but she also became an independent filmmaker, directing the documentary *The Bombing of Osage Avenue*. She nurtured the founding of the Image Weavers, a collective of young Black women independent filmmakers who carry on her mission of making interventions in Black women's lives through film. Most of the works to emerge from this collective have an explicit Black feminist agenda, but this work is not fearful of being labeled "Black nationalist" because its concerns are primarily with Black women—heterosexual as well as lesbian—and because its desire is to encourage and provide a ground for intra-racial dialogue.

Toni Cade Bambara and her groundbreaking anthology remind us to aspire toward the important tasks before us, regardless of the institutional settings we occupy. Among these tasks, three of the most important are: (1) Articulate the struggles of the underrepresented; (2) Raise the consciousness of and provide alternative visions for the communities to whom we are dedicated; (3) Continuously offer internal criticism and analysis.

Toni Cade Bambara's life and work insist that we write books and essays, edit anthologies, do archival work, maintain tradition, or, for that matter, even construct canons. However, she insists that we do this for something other than, or in addition to, degrees, tenure, and celebrity status. And she insists that we keep talking to and arguing with each other in order to clarify our goals and our visions. The stakes are too high for us to abandon this kind of commitment. In closing, I want to turn to Bambara's own words from her novel *The Salt Eaters*. Bambara's important but underread novel is the story of a Black woman activist, Velma Henry, defeated by the sexism of her Black male comrades and the decimation of the revolutionary fervor of the movement by infiltration. Bambara writes:

> She thought she knew that. At some point in her life she was sure Douglass, Tubman, the slave narratives, the songs, the fables, Delaney, Ida Wells, Blyden, Du Bois, Garvey, the singers, her parents, Malcolm, Coltrane, the poets, her comrades, her godmother, her neighbors, had taught her that. Thought she knew how to build immunity to the sting of the serpent that turned would-be cells, could-be cadres into cargo cults. Thought she knew how to build resistance, make the journey to the center of the circle, stay poised and centered in the work and not fly off, stay centered in the best of her people's traditions and not be available to madness, not become intoxicated by the heady brew of degrees and career and congratulations for nothing done, not become anesthetized by dazzling performances with somebody else's aesthetic, not go under. Thought the workers of the sixties had pulled the Family safely out of the range of the serpent's fangs so the workers of the seventies could drain the poisons, repair damaged tissues, retrain the heartworks, realign the spine.
>
> Thought the vaccine offered by all the theorists and activists and clear thinkers and doers of the warrior clan would take. But amnesia had set in anyhow. Something crucial had been missing from the political/economic/social/cultural/aesthetic/military/psychosocial/psycho-

sexual mix. And what could it be? And what should she do?

The Salt Eaters is a feminist text; it encourages coalitions between other women of color as well as with other progressive causes. And it never loses sight of the goal of freedom for all Black people. The protagonist is healed not in order to retreat, but in order to continue in struggle.

In the above paragraph, Bambara provides an alternative use of tradition and cultural canon building—one that is inseparable from political struggle. Note the various, sometimes conflicting voices of this chorus. The paragraph serves as a warning against allowing terms we did not set to define us for ourselves. We need to turn to the kind of intellectual practice described by cultural critic Herman Gray, who calls on other Black intellectuals to expand our horizons, to make connections between the global and the local, to resist the seductions of professional preoccupation and disciplinary stability, to continue to understand specifically just how culture matters in the lives of people, and ultimately to make interventions that matter [to] offer the intellectual substance, the visibility, and access to produce an effective and consequential discourse and intervention in the public sphere that transcends limited and limiting academic and professional preoccupations.[19]

Bambara's anthology continues to offer this kind of challenge for all of us. She continues to ask: What kind of women are we going to be? What are we going to do?

THAT THE MOTHERS MAY SOAR AND THE DAUGHTERS MAY KNOW THEIR NAMES

A Retrospective of Black Feminist Literary Criticism

> All segments of the literary world—whether establishment, progressive, Black, female, or lesbian—do not know, or at least act as if they do not know, that Black women writers and Black lesbian writers exist. . . .
>
> Black women's existence, experience, and culture and the brutally complex systems of oppression which shape these are in the "real world" of white and/or male consciousness beneath consideration, invisible, unknown.
>
> —BARBARA SMITH,
> *"Toward a Black Feminist Criticism"*

> Within and around the modern academy, racial and gender alterity has become a hot commodity that has claimed Black women as its principal signifier. . . . Why have we—Black women—become the subjected subjects of so much contemporary scholarly investigation, the peasants under glass of intellectual inquiry in the 1990s?
>
> —ANN DUCILLE, *"The Occult of True Black Womanhood:*
> *Critical Demeanor and Black Feminist Studies"*

THE SPAN OF time that separates these two statements by preeminent critics gave birth to a rich and varied body of literature that seeks to uncover, explore, analyze, and theorize the lives and works of (primarily North American) Black women. Consequently, Barbara Smith's (1977) lament that Black women were invisible as subjects of scholarly attention was certainly not true by the time Ann duCille (1994) published her essay in *Signs: Journal of Women and Culture in Society*. This was largely due to the efforts of a small but significant cadre of Black women writers and scholars. The ventures of these pioneering critics proved to be so successful that Black men and white women also began to study the works of Black women writers. Even so, given the continued existence of racial and gender hierarchies as well as the systems of power that undergird them, there was still cause for concern. As duCille saw it, although Black women's texts gained a great deal of popularity, the Black women scholars who pioneered the study of these texts were becoming less and less visible—not only as members of university faculties but also in the footnotes of a voluminous scholarship devoted to Black women's writing.

While it is impossible to provide a critical review of all the work that falls under the rubric of Black feminist theory or criticism, this essay will consider key moments in the development of the field and its institutionalization in the academy, as well as provide an assessment of its current state and modestly look toward its future.[1] First, a word about nomenclature: although much of the early writing by Black feminist critics focused on the works of US Black writers, I have chosen to use the term *Black feminist criticism* instead of *African American feminist criticism*. It is under the rubric of Black feminist criticism that scholars have challenged one another to develop a more expansive understanding of the term. While we have not always lived up to such an inclusive critical practice, I do believe it is worth striving for.

Indeed, by the mid-1990s Black feminist literary studies was one of the most intellectually exciting and fruitful developments in American literary criticism. Today, many scholars and critics continue to contribute to and expand the field. Nonetheless, Black feminist criticism (as well as women's studies and African American studies) has experienced a backlash from both the Left and the Right. The overall assault on multiculturalism and political correctness as well as those critiques that fault the field for being a bastion of identity politics and essentialism have targeted Black feminist criticism and challenged its adequacy as a mode of critical analysis. Interestingly, it is quite likely that the latter critique of essentialism was made possible by the very terms and successes of Black feminist literary critics, who were among the first to call attention to the constructed nature of racial and gender identity.

THAT THE MOTHERS MAY SOAR

The 1970s were a heady time for the development of African American women's literature. But this productivity did not emerge in a historical and political vacuum. Historian Darlene Clark Hine notes, "In the 1970s and 1980s Black women searched for their place in the politics of race and gender" (1998, 201). As has been remarked a number of times, the development of African American women's literature and the criticism it spawned were a direct response to the masculinist bias of the civil rights and especially the Black power and Black arts movements (see Dubey 1994). Just as important, it was also a response to the feminist movement's tendency to normalize the experiences of middle-class white women as equivalent for all women. In both instances, Black women found themselves lost in the cracks, as *Black people* were gendered male, and *women* most often meant white women. Although the gender politics of the civil rights, Black power, and Black arts movements have often been critiqued harshly, those movements actually contributed a number of voices to what would become Black feminism. Toni Cade, Alice Walker, Angela Davis, June Jordan, and Audre Lorde were all actively engaged in the struggles of the 1960s. Some, like Walker, were involved in the women's rights movement, as well.

What began as internal debates within the women's and Black power movements would provide the basis for the literature that followed. The foundational text of an emerging Black women's studies is *The Black Woman: An Anthology*, edited by Cade (1970). Although that volume does not contain literary criticism, it does contain poetry, short stories, essays, and critical analysis by an emerging generation of Black women thinkers. The text is not addressed to an academic audience but instead to a diverse variety of Black women readers. The editor of and contributors to the volume saw the book as a tool in the liberation of Black people; Cade also sought to give voice to a politicized and articulate generation of Black women writers. Consequently, the text itself is not necessarily a feminist document; instead it holds a myriad of opinions about the status and place of Black women in the Black freedom movement, in the women's rights movement, and in American society at large. As such, it is one of the first multigeneric texts to center the experiences, concerns, and, most important, voices of Black women. Finally, the anthology contains works by women who would become central to the literary renaissance that followed its publication: Cade (not yet Bambara), Walker, Lorde, and Paule Marshall, to name just a few.

The Black Woman opened a decade that witnessed an explosion in Black women's creative writing. The year 1970 presented readers with Maya Angelou's *I Know Why the Caged Bird Sings*, Mari Evans's *I Am a Black Woman*, Toni Morrison's *The Bluest Eye*, and Walker's *The Third Life of Grange Copeland*. These writers continued to produce throughout the decade, and Gayl Jones, Ntozake Shange, Michele Wallace, and Jordan joined them. Shange's play *for colored girls who have considered suicide/when the rainbow is enuf* (the second play by a Black woman to reach the Broadway stage, in 1976) and Wallace's *Black Macho and the Myth of the Superwoman* (1978) set off firestorms of controversy. These writers published in genres as diverse as the novel, drama, poetry, and autobiography; in so doing, they openly challenged any notion of the Black community as a monolith of like ideologies, politics, and standpoints. They produced powerful narratives that focused on Black women's lives and that dared to expose the conflicts between Black men and women. Some, such as Morrison, Walker, and Wallace, became important literary and cultural critics, as well. Certainly, this generation of Black women writers was not the first: Zora Neale Hurston, Ann Petry, Gwendolyn Brooks, Sarah Wright, and others preceded them. Yet the atmosphere created by the political and social movements of the 1960s produced a context in which these writers could find an interested, informed, and astute audience.

In the late 1970s, Black women critics both within and outside the academy began to construct a critical discourse and a body of work that attended to the specificities of this new renaissance. Just as the political and social contexts of the early 1970s gave rise to a movement of Black women writers, so too did this period witness the emergence of Black feminist criticism. As with the creative writers, many of the first Black feminist literary critics had been politically involved with the social movements of the 1960s and 1970s. As the creative works gained more visibility, popularity, and in some cases notoriety, Black feminist intellectuals began to formally study Black women's history and literature. As early as 1972, Mary Helen Washington published "The Black Woman's Search for Identity: Zora Neale Hurston's Work" in *Black World*. In fact, *Black World* published a number of essays by African American women critics on Black women's fiction, and an issue devoted to Hurston.[2] Significantly, as critics began to construct a tradition of Black women's writing, they turned to Hurston as an important literary foremother. Hurston was significant to these younger critics not only because her work focused on Black women but also because of the way that work had been treated by Richard Wright and the critical establishment that followed him. In search of her own literary ancestors, Walker discovered Hurston. At that time, most of Hurston's books, with the exception of *Mules and Men*, were out of print. The stories of a generation of young Black women intellectuals sharing photocopies of her novel *Their Eyes Were Watching God*, passing it around as if it were contraband, are by now legendary. *Their Eyes Were Watching God*, which had been out of print for thirty years, was republished and soon became a staple in college and university literature classes. But Walker's most significant critical intervention came in the form of her essays about Hurston. In March 1975, Walker published the essay "In Search of Zora Neale Hurston" in *Ms.* magazine. During this time, Robert Hemenway published *Zora Neale Hurston: A Lit-*

erary Biography (1977), and, as noted above, Washington published important critical essays on Hurston.[3]

However, it was Walker who emerged as Hurston's most influential champion. Walker wrote a number of important essays about Hurston, placed a marker on her grave, and edited a collection of her writing, *I Love Myself When I Am Laughing . . . and Then Again When I Am Looking Mean and Impressive* (Hurston 1979). By privileging Hurston's use of Black English, Black folk culture, and the Black South, Walker created a tradition that originated with Hurston and that led directly to her own work. Her important collection of essays *In Search of Our Mothers' Gardens* (Walker 1983a) contained another highly influential essay, "Zora Neale Hurston: A Cautionary Tale and a Partisan View" (Walker 1983b). In addition to turning our attention to Hurston and others, that collection also introduced the term *womanist*, which Walker famously defines as a Black feminist who loves women (sometimes sexually) and who is committed to the welfare of Black people. Furthermore, a womanist is not a separatist, "except periodically, for health" (1983a, xi). Walker derived the term from the African American folk term *womanish*, often used to describe a young girl who is bold, precocious, and curious. For a number of Black women activists, artists, and intellectuals who identified feminism and the feminist movement with the concerns and goals of white women, Walker's terms provided an adequate naming. Black women theologians concerned with race and gender also took up the term to describe their own practices: Black womanist theology. Interestingly, a number of Afrocentric Black women critics chose to call their practice "Africana womanism" (Hudson-Weems 1993), even though the Black nationalist politics of their intellectual project differed greatly from Walker's own.[4] *In Search of Our Mothers' Gardens* also contains a number of other essays that helped shape the direction of Black feminist criticism. Finally, the collection demonstrates the major intellectual tasks of early Black feminist critics. The first of these tasks was archaeological: In order to construct a tradition that led to contemporary writers, such as Morrison and Walker, critics charged themselves with locating, teaching, and writing about earlier "lost" works by African American women.[5] Second, they created a critical vocabulary and framework for discussing works by African American women. Third, they theorized that body of work as well as the critical practices of Black feminist critics. The boundaries between these tasks are porous and flexible. Much of the early theorizing about Black women's writings came in the form of introductions to reissued works. Washington's important anthologies *Black-Eyed Susans: Classic Stories by and about Black Women* (1975), *Midnight Birds: Stories by Contemporary Black Women Writers* (1980), and *Invented Lives: Narratives of Black Women, 1860–1960* (1987) not only reintroduced a number of Black women writers but also served to posit the themes, structures, and concerns that held them together—and began to theorize the contours of that tradition. Similarly, Deborah McDowell's (1986) introduction to Nella Larsen's Harlem Renaissance novels *Quicksand* and *Passing* reclaimed these novels from a critical history that dismissed them or that read them only through the lens of race. McDowell also provided an alternative feminist reading that made the works relevant to contemporary readers and students. Beacon Press's Black Women Writers series is but one example of where one might find prefaces and introductions by scholars such as Frances Smith Foster and Hazel Carby.

Just as scholars rediscovered Hurston, so too did they begin to uncover works by her contemporaries and her literary forebears. Following his discovery of Harriet Wilson's novel *Our Nig*, the influential literary critic Henry Louis Gates Jr. served as the general editor for the Schomburg Library of Nineteenth-Century Black Women Writers—a forty-volume set. Once *Our Nig* was republished, it shifted our notion of literary history; prior to its publication, most scholars had cited Frances Ellen Watkins Harper's *Iola Leroy* as the first novel written by an African American woman. Although Gates's efforts made a number of important texts available, it was the hard work of feminist critics that helped situate these texts historically and provide frameworks for reading them. Foster, in *Written by Herself: Literary Production by African American Women, 1746–1892* (1993), and Claudia Tate, in *Domestic Allegories of Political Desire: The*

Black Heroine's Text at the Turn of the Century (1992), both histori-
cized and theorized these works. Foster helped bring our attention to
the works of nineteenth-century African American women writers,
especially Harper. Tate's earlier collection of interviews with contemporary Black women writers, *Black Women Writers at Work* (1983),
joined Evans's *Black Women Writers (1950–1980): A Critical Evaluation* (1984) is an important document of the Black woman's literary
renaissance of the 1970s and 1980s. In her critical work, Tate reaches
back to locate earlier Black women writers, and in *Domestic Allegories of Political Desire,* she takes on the marriage plot in Black wom-
en's fiction and argues that it constitutes a domestic allegory about
the political ambitions of Black people following emancipation and
Reconstruction. Similarly, Carla Peterson's 1995 *"Doers of the Word":
African-American Women Speakers and Writers in the North (1830–
1880)* focuses on Northern Black women's intellectual and political culture.

It is important to note that even as these critics constructed
tradition they did so knowing that they were positing a construct.
Hortense Spillers writes: "Traditions are not born. They are made.
We would add that they are not, like objects of nature, here to stay,
but survive as *created social events* only to the extent that an audience
cares to intersect them" (1985, 250).

BUT WHAT DO WE THINK WE'RE DOING ANYWAY

At the same time that a new generation of Black women critics and
writers were discovering earlier writers and using their work to help
establish a tradition of Black women writing in the United States,
African American women activists also founded a number of Black
feminist political organizations. The most famous of these is the Combahee River Collective; its fame is less a result of its greater activism
than of the fact that the collective left an eloquent written document,
"A Black Feminist Statement" (1977). This political group of Boston-
based Black feminists, founded in 1974, issued its famous manifesto at
the same time that one of its founding members, Smith, published the

first explicit statement of Black feminist criticism, "Toward a Black Feminist Criticism" (1977). In both documents we find early efforts to define Black feminism. The writers of "A Black Feminist Statement" put forth the following:

> Above all else, our politics initially sprang from the shared belief that Black women are inherently valuable, that our liberation is a necessity not as an adjunct to somebody else's but because of our need as human persons for autonomy.
>
> We believe that sexual politics under patriarchy is as pervasive in Black women's lives as are the politics of class and race. We also often find it difficult to separate race from class from sex oppression because in our lives they are most often experienced simultaneously.
>
> Although we are feminists and lesbians, we feel solidarity with progressive Black men and do not advocate the factionalization that white women who are separatists demand. Our situation as Black people necessitates that we have solidarity around the fact of race.
>
> We struggle together with Black men against racism, while we also struggle with Black men about sexism. (Combahee River Collective 1977, 204)

There are a number of things worth noting here. From the beginning, Black feminists have been committed to the freedom of all people, especially Black people. Black feminists have always seen their struggle as part of, indeed a necessary component of, the larger Black freedom struggle. The Black feminist critical practice that emerged from this politics finds its articulation in Smith's essay. For Smith, Black feminist criticism plays an important role in making Black women's literature "recognizable" (1977, 26) in that it provides a "non-hostile and perceptive analysis of works written" (27) by Black women. Although a number of Black women were engaged in creating a critical discourse around African American women's writing,

Smith's essay established the notion of Black feminist literary criticism. Since its publication, the essay has been reprinted in a number of anthologies; it was also issued as one in a series of pamphlets published by Smith's Kitchen Table Press, one of the institutional formations of Black feminism. "Toward a Black Feminist Criticism" seeks to make explicit connections between "the politics of Black women's lives, what we write about and our situation as artists" (Smith 1977, 26). Smith's essay first outlines the stereotypical racist and misogynist representations of Black women and then demonstrates the need for Black feminist criticism. Finally, and most controversially, she posits a reading of Morrison's *Sula* as a lesbian text. Smith argues, "a Black feminist approach to literature that embodies the realization that the politics of sex as well as the politics of race and class are crucially interlocking factors in the works of Black women writers is an absolute necessity" (Smith 1977, 27–28). And she insists that because of shared political, social, and economic experience, Black women writers also share thematic, stylistic, and aesthetic conceptions and approaches.

One need only chart the reception of Smith's essay in the years since its publication to derive a sense of the development of and challenges to Black feminist criticism, for her essay spawned an intertextual debate and dialogue that became central to the field. In 1980, McDowell built on and challenged Smith's conception of Black feminist criticism. McDowell's essay "New Directions for Black Feminist Criticism" (1980) marked Black feminism's move into the academy. This move began to yield a body of academically sophisticated works; although much of this work was no longer directly grounded in overt political struggle, these critics never lost sight of the political implications of their work. This is evident in Washington's observation that "what we have to recognize is that the creation of the fiction of tradition is a matter of power, not justice, and that that power has always been in the hands of men—mostly white but some Black" (1994, 444). Implicit in this sentence is the understanding that the fights over canons and curricula were in fact struggles for power. The academy became yet another location, another site in the centuries-long battle against white supremacy and patriarchy. And the creation of a tradition of Black women's writing, though itself a construction, was but a necessary tool in this struggle. From the beginning, Black feminist critics knew that literary traditions were not organic but were constructed with a mindful understanding of cultural politics. Carby, Barbara Christian, Beverly Guy-Sheftall, bell hooks, Nellie McKay, Valerie Smith, Hortense Spillers, Eleanor Traylor, Gloria Wade-Gayles, Cheryl Wall, and Sherley Anne Williams are but a few of the architects of Black feminist criticism in the 1980s.[6] While Traylor, Wade-Gayles, and Guy-Sheftall labored in historically Black institutions, the others entered elite white institutions in unprecedented (though still small) numbers; they sought to assist in the widespread transformation of the humanities taking place at the time. Along with Black women historians and sociologists, they greatly influenced their disciplines even if they did so from the margins. The move into the academy sometimes marked a shift from a focus on the social and political to the more linguistic and literary.

In "New Directions for Black Feminist Criticism" McDowell writes: "Unfortunately, Black feminist scholarship has been decidedly more practical than theoretical, and the theories developed thus far have often lacked sophistication and have been marred by slogans, rhetoric, and idealism" (1980, 154). Here McDowell echoes the critique of African American literary criticism launched by her contemporaries, Gates and Robert Stepto. McDowell challenged Smith to provide greater specificity in defining a lesbian aesthetic as well as less reductive understandings of the tradition of Black women's writings. (Ironically, although McDowell accuses Smith of oversimplifying, obscuring, and stripping lesbianism of its explanatory power, one of McDowell's most insightful and original essays would read the lesbian subtexts in Larsen's novels.) "New Directions" also calls on Black feminist critics to consider "the specific language of Black women's literature, to describe the ways Black women writers employ literary devices in a distinct way, and to compare the way Black women writers create their own mythic structures" (McDowell 1980, 158). In other words, she challenges critics of African American women's writing to engage in more rigorous study of the literary nature of Black women's writing and in so doing to demonstrate the artistic sophistication of these texts. Interestingly, when McDowell republished this essay in her collection *"The Changing Same": Black Women, Literature, Criticism, and Theory* (1995), she added a response or postscript where she reiterates or reconsiders a number of points. Of her criticism of the ideological dimension of Smith's essay, she writes, "I was fairly harsh in my judgment. I faulted [Smith] for allowing ideology to inform critical analysis, but now I know there is no criticism without ideology" (McDowell 1995, 23).

By the time Carby published her influential *Reconstructing Womanhood: The Emergence of the Afro-American Woman Novelist* (1987a), Black feminist critics had succeeded in constructing a tradition of Black women's writing from throughout the nineteenth and twentieth centuries. (Barbara Christian's important *Black Women Novelists* was published in 1980.) Carby provides a materialist analysis of writings by nineteenth-century African American women in order to demonstrate how they engaged in a process of reconstructing notions of womanhood and in so doing laid the groundwork for the forms of Black feminism that emerged in the late twentieth century. However, Carby argues against the notion of tradition and encourages a move away from the focus on experience or bonds between critic and novelists as a basis for critical practice. She argues that a "reliance on a common or shared experience is essentialist and ahistorical" (1987b, 16).

In *Reconstructing Womanhood*, Carby addresses Smith and McDowell by asserting that Black feminist criticism should be "regarded critically as a problem, not a solution, as a sign that should be interrogated, a locus of contradictions" (1987a, 15). She argues that the turn toward formalism often ignored the ways that Black women writers saw themselves as engaging in and helping shape political discourse through their fiction. Furthermore, in the closing chapter of *Reconstructing Womanhood*, "The Quicksands of Representation," Carby argues that locating the tradition in the figure of Hurston privileges the South and the folk tradition of that region over and against texts that focus on the experiences of the urban, migrant, and working-class populations. In this way, Carby joined Gloria Naylor, who proclaimed Petry, a writer of urban fiction, as her own literary foremother.

Although Carby's critique greatly influenced the direction of Black feminist criticism, others still argued in favor of an identifiable Black women's literary tradition. Michael Awkward explains that his own project in *Inspiriting Influences: Tradition, Revision, and Afro-American Women's Novels* (1989) is "to demonstrate, with reference to a small segment of the Afro-American woman's literary corpus, the accuracy of Smith's claim that 'Black women writers constitute an identifiable literary tradition'" (Awkward 1989, 13).

A number of critics took up Carby's notion of Black feminist criticism as "a problem, not a solution, as a sign that should be interrogated, a locus of contradictions" (1987a, 15). As such, by the early 1990s, we began to witness challenges to the very notion of Black feminist criticism as it had been conceived by Smith and other early critics. These challenges took many forms (see Fuss 1989; Baker 1991). In 1993, Deborah G. Chay published an extensive critique of Smith's essay. In "Rereading Barbara Smith: Black Feminist Criticism and the Category of Experience," Chay criticizes Smith for a "debilitating reliance on experience" (1993, 639) as well as for her ability to rightly protest Black women's political positions while failing to "theorize their transformation" (639). Furthermore, Chay claims, those Black feminist critics who built on and critiqued Smith's essay articulate Black feminist critical practice "as a tradition" but fail to "theorize the positions taken within that tradition" (648). According to Chay, these critics have failed to account for how the field "is itself constituted and transformed" (648). (It seems that Carby's work does in fact seek to do this.) Ultimately, Chay urges Black feminist critics to point to the ways that their "differentiation cannot be maintained" (649), and in so doing to demonstrate the continuing importance of their critical project.

In *Black Women, Writing and Identity: Migrations of the Subject* (1994), Carole Boyce Davies offered another challenge even as she helped redefine the field. She writes, "Black feminist criticism began as a subversion and counterarticulation to the terms of both Black and feminist criticism. But its limitation, so far, is that it is almost wholly located in African-American women's experiences" (1994, 31). Davies argues that the variety of Black women's writing globally and the diversity of languages in which Black women write call for Black feminist criticism to have "a consciousness of tentativeness and incompletion" (32) at its center. For Davies, "Black women's writing . . . should be read as a series of boundary crossings and not as a fixed, geographical, ethnically or nationally bound category of writing. In cross-cultural, transnational, translocal, diasporic perspectives this reworking of the grounds of 'Black Women's Writing' redefines identity away from exclusion and marginality" (4).

The primary arguments in *Black Women, Writing and Identity* appear in the two-volume collection of essays *Moving Beyond Boundaries: International Dimensions of Black Women's Writings* (1995) and *Moving Beyond Boundaries: Black Women's Diasporas* (1995). Both volumes argue for a geographically broad conception of Black feminist criticism. It should also be noted that even before the publication of Davies's books, Karla Holloway used Black feminist analysis to read texts across national, indeed, continental boundaries. Her *Moorings and Metaphors: Figures of Culture and Gender in Black Women's Literature* (1992) focuses on works by African American and West African women writers.

By the end of the decade, inspired by the work of Black feminist and critical race theorist Kimberlé Crenshaw, Valerie Smith argued in *Not Just Race, Not Just Gender: Black Feminist Readings* (1998) that Black feminist criticism provided a mode of reading that took account of the "intersections of constructions of race, gender, class and sexuality" (xiii). Smith seeks to uncover the way that the dominance of one of these categories often masks the others and serves to hide the interconnections among them. Smith does not limit her attention to texts produced by Black women. She writes: "Black feminism is not a biologically grounded positionality. . . . Black feminism provides strategies of reading simultaneity. . . . Black feminist inquiry

is a site of critique that challenges monolithic notions of American-
ness, womanhood, Blackness, or for that matter, Black womanhood"
(xv). Here Smith begins to lead us out of the sometimes-debilitating
maze created by critiques of essentialism.

In *Black Women, Identity, and Cultural Theory: (Un)becoming the
Subject* (2004), Kevin Everod Quashie continues this line of argument and actually seeks to rescue Barbara Smith's "Toward a Black
Feminist Criticism." Quashie argues, "Whatever Smith's errors of
overstatement, whatever presumptuous integrity she ascribes to the
dalliance between one Black female subject and another, her statement's usefulness is not mutilated. Nor is the larger case I am making: that Black women's cultural expressions are encountering and
grappling with poststructuralist terms and, in doing so, are articulating their own poststructure, their own guiding principles of the subject's becoming and undoing" (5). In other words, Quashie articulates
what Black feminists have known—that race and gender identities
have always been socially constructed, that Black feminists' project is
one of developing an alternative subjectivity to the one that has been
imposed on them in order to challenge and dismantle the ideological
structures that undergird their oppression.

Many of the articles and essays cited above first appeared in
anthologies and volumes sparked by a number of conferences and
workshops where Black feminist critics gathered to debate, discuss,
and define the field of Black women's literature. While critics engaged
in the important work of defining the role of the Black feminist critic
and the parameters of her intellectual process, they also located texts,
constructed a tradition (and in some cases contested tradition), and
analyzed and theorized that body of work. Mae Gwendolyn Henderson and Hortense Spillers are among the most influential crit-
ics/theorists. Henderson's original "Speaking in Tongues: Dialogics,
Dialectics, and the Black Woman Writer's Literary Tradition" (1989)
combined the linguistic theory of Mikhail Bakhtin with the Black
vernacular practice of speaking in tongues (glossolalia) in her discussion of Black women's texts and the role of the Black feminist
critic. Although Houston Baker's theorizing of the blues (1984) and

Gates's use of "signifying" (1988) have gained much deserved attention for their efforts to use the Black vernacular to help theorize African American writings, Henderson's lesser-known essay joins them in this project, but unlike the work of her two colleagues, gender is central to her analysis.

As did Henderson, Spillers places gender in the center of her theories of Black literature. In a series of important essays, Spillers influenced not only the fields of Black women's literary studies but also the broader fields of African American studies, women's studies, and psychoanalytic criticism. Lindon Barrett, himself a brilliant theorist of African American literature, writes:

> Hortense Spillers stages a confrontation between race and psychoanalysis, noting that psychoanalytic approaches are oddly absent from the leading critical paradigms of African American literary studies. Defining psychoanalysis in terms of its interests in locating "interior intersubjectivity," Spillers begins to detail its diacritical relation to race by arguing that the primary template for psychoanalysis is sexuality in its apparently necessary relation to concealment, whereas the primary symbolics of race and racialization rest on visibility, in matters understood ideally to be so plain as to be beyond concealment. This diacriticism persists further, Spillers argues, since race is conceptualized as a collective enterprise, whereas psychoanalysis focuses on the individual. She contends that race insinuates itself within ethnicities as an evacuated psychic space, an aporia that, more fully considered, discloses the concept of race as a cultural construct. The analytic curiosity is the means by which this point of evacuation supplies, nonetheless, fundamental content for psychic organization.[7] (Barrett 2005)

As Spillers sees it, of course, the psychoanalytic opens up the possibility to speak on all these levels. For many of us, Spillers rescued the psychoanalytic from the depoliticized, ahistorical realm into which we had placed it. In "'All the Things You Could Be by Now if Sigmund Freud's Wife Was Your Mother': Psychoanalysis and Race" (1996) and elsewhere, Spillers has argued that the psychoanalytic leads to "greater self-consciousness, a self-critical capacity in your relationship to others" (Haslett 1998). It is not something that is private and personal but a distinction "between the 'one' and the 'individual'"— individual in relationship to property and early modern capital and one as having been "put in place . . . by language, by one's relationship to the social" (Haslett 1998). Spillers sees the psychoanalytic as a way of getting to a more complex Black subjectivity, not simply that which is created by oppression, domination, violence, and economic exploitation, powerful as these forces are, but subjectivity that is created by agency.

Spillers's work has greatly influenced an entire generation of critics and theorists, and it, along with the work of other Black feminist literary critics, has helped produce works that reread African American cultural history and literature from perspectives informed by Black feminism. Sharon Holland's *Raising the Dead: Readings of Death and (Black) Subjectivity* (2000), Elizabeth Alexander's *The Black Interior* (2004a), Saidiya Hartman's *Scenes of Subjection: Terror, Slavery, and Self-Making in Nineteenth-Century America* (1997), Barrett's *Blackness and Value: Seeing Double* (1999), and Fred Moten's *In the Break* (2003) all acknowledge their debt to Spiller's work.

It is not surprising that many of these texts are informed by what is perhaps Spillers's most famous essay, "Mama's Baby, Papa's Maybe: An American Grammar Book" (1987). Of them, Holland's is most obviously indebted to Spillers's work, and it is a debt she acknowledges not only in the footnotes of her book but also in her opening, framing chapter as well as in her original and provocative reading of Morrison's *Beloved*. One of the most compelling things about Holland's use of Spillers to build her analytical framework is something that ought not be all that unusual but is: the sheer rarity of using the work of a Black woman thinker, not only as a text to be analyzed but as a tool and lens through which to analyze culture and history. Spiller's essay "Interstices: A Small Drama of Words" (1992) contributes one of the building blocks for Holland's framework. In "Interstices" Spillers writes, "[The Black woman] became instead the principal point of passage between the human and the non-human world. Her issue became the focus of a cunning difference—visually, psychologically, ontologically—as the route by which the dominant male decided the distinction between humanity and 'other'" (76). Holland elaborates upon this by noting that "What Spillers accomplishes in these two examples is astonishing. Black female bodies serve as passage between humanity and non-humanity as well as the articulation of that passage. I would suggest that this border, which is no border at all but a passageway, also encompasses the terrain between the living and the dead, between the ancestral and the living community. . . . Elaborating on Spillers's central point in 'Interstices,' that 'Black is vestibular to culture,' I would like to add that this space is both material and linguistic—a chamber housing the flesh and its attending language" (2000, 43). From here, Holland is able to posit a reading of the dead in Morrison's *Beloved* and in Randall Kenan's *Visitations of the Spirit*. In bringing together Morrison and Spillers, Holland stages an encounter, a performance, and an engagement whose counterpart in the performing arts might be a stage shared by Jessye Norman and Aretha Franklin, different genres but powerful voices, born of a similar context, pushing each other, higher and higher. Holland's is a luminous work of criticism that establishes her not only as an important feminist voice but also as a critic who brings Black feminist criticism to queer theory in her readings of Kenan.

If Holland is empowered by Spillers to insist on recovering mutilated bodies, so too is Alexander in her well-known and often reprinted essay on Rodney King, "Can You Be BLACK and Look at This? Reading the Rodney King Video(s)" (2004b), and throughout her recently published collection, *The Black Interior* (2004a). The very title of the collection and the charge around which it builds are inspired by Spillers, for so much of Spillers's project is concerned with the "interior": both with the "intramural" relations within Black life, particularly as they are organized around lines of gender, and with the "interpersonal," with "interiority," and with "intersubjectivity" (Haslett 1998). Alexander writes:

> If Black people are the subconscious of the Western mind, where is "the Black subconscious," both individually and collectively articulated? My interest is not in psychotherapeutic culture and African American literature—though what a fascinating topic that is—but rather the marker such language offers for identifying complex unexplored interiority beyond the face of the social self. If Black people in the mainstream imaginary exist as fixed properties deemed "real," what is possible in the space we might call surreal? . . . "The Black interior" is not an inscrutable zone, nor colonial fantasy . . . [but] inner space in which Black artists have found selves that go far, far beyond the limited expectations and definitions of what Black is, isn't or should be. (2004a, 4–5)

Perhaps in an attempt to relocate, if not altogether recover, the flesh, Alexander looks for the spaces designated and created by Black folk, spaces where the self is visible, in literal "Black interiors" (2004a).

So, in many ways, *The Black Interior* itself is quietly involved with Spillers, even though she is not most obviously there. But she is quite explicitly present in the collection's most famous essay, "Can You Be BLACK and Look at This?" (Alexander 2004b). Spillers's presence is felt not simply in the use of "Mama's Baby, Papa's Maybe" but also in Alexander's essay's bold insistence in its first line: "At the heart of this essay is a desire to find a language to talk about 'my people'" (2004b, 175). Alexander acknowledges that this phrase is romantic but insists on the necessity of using it in certain instances, such as in reference to the tape of the Rodney King beating. Yes, Alexander argues, race is a complex fiction but is "perfectly real in at least some significant aspects of our day-to-day lives" (175). In the version of the essay that appears in *The Black Interior*, she adds "'Post-Black'? Post-Script." Alexander asks, "What do Black people say to each other to describe their relationship to their racial group, when that relationship is crucially forged by incidents of physical and psychic violence that boil down to the 'fact' of abject Blackness"? (2004b, 176). It is Spillers, as well as a multitude of other African American thinkers, who helps build the case, who has done the difficult theoretical work from which Alexander explores these intramural moments. However, convincing as her case might be, in her post-Black postscript, Alexander is careful to acknowledge the critics who might accuse her of racial essentialism and those who have, particularly the loudest and perhaps most influential, Paul Gilroy. Gilroy sees Alexander's metaphorical notion of "collective memory" as veering toward "a dangerous kind of myopic nationalism" (Alexander 2004b, 175). Once again, Alexander politely reminds him that this is neither her aim nor her ideology: "I am thinking instead of how this particular metaphor can help explain the persistent and positively consolidating (non-nationalistic) aspects of collective identification" (176) between a group of people who share a historical, political, and spatial condition. So, for Alexander, Spillers and others help provide a way out of the constriction. It is important to note that Alexander is not specifically concerned with questions of feminism in her text. However, I would argue that her focus on the interior grows out of a Black feminist project. Writers and critics as diverse as Morrison, Spillers, and Washington have all noted that, while Black male writers focus their attention on relationships and struggles between Black and white men, Black women most often turn their gaze to the relationships among Black people. This is the focus that animates Alexander's project, and as such, it demonstrates the way that a critical practice informed by and engaging with the work of Black feminist critics can yield insightful, original, and exciting readings and analyses.

Spillers's influence is also evident in Saidiya Hartman's discussion of the management of slave women's sexuality, especially in case law (Hartman 1997). For Hartman, understanding the mechanisms at work that allow sexual violence against Black women to pass as seduction is central to understanding the quotidian violence necessary for the maintenance of slave society. Again, a reading informed

by the insights of Black feminism yields new insight into the conditions of the enslaved, both male and female.

Although I have focused on the works of feminist scholars here,
it is important to note that male critics of this generation display
the influence of Spillers as well. I am speaking in particular about
the work of two scholars, Moten and Barrett, whose work I seek to
champion every opportunity I get, not only because of their insights
but also because they seriously engage and are in dialogue with the
work of Spillers and a number of other Black women intellectuals.
In other words, they do not make patronizing nods or meaningless
lists of names, but they are actually informed by and in conversation
with the work of both their senior colleagues and their peers. I have
focused here on Spillers because she is the theorist most consistently
cited by these writers. However, it is clear, and I am certain that all of
the younger writers cited above would acknowledge, that they stand
on the shoulders of many of her contemporaries as well. What I hope
these examples demonstrate is the way that Black feminist literary
theory and criticism laid the foundation for a new wave of important
scholarship in the field of African American, African diaspora, and
American literary and cultural studies.

Black feminist literary criticism and theory inform all these
works, and all use these insights in order to read cultural and literary texts produced across boundaries of race, ethnicity, and gender.
Similarly, scholars Jennifer DeVere Brody and Kim Hall are Black
feminist scholars of the Victorian and Renaissance eras, respectively.
In *Impossible Purities: Blackness, Femininity, and Victorian Culture*
(Brody 1998) and *Things of Darkness: Economies of Race and Gender
in Early Modern England* (Hall 1995), Brody and Hall render Black
feminist analysis of texts and eras thought to be far removed from
the project of Black feminist literary criticism. In this way, all of these
authors prove Valerie Smith's dictum that Black feminism is a strategy of reading literary and social texts and contexts. As such, Black
feminist criticism has informed the emergence of newer fields of literary criticism, and it has animated analyses of film, theater, music,
media, and politics as well.

From the beginning, brilliant Black lesbian feminists have been central participants in the articulation of Black feminism (see, e.g., Bethel and Smith 1979; Shockley 1979; Barbara Smith 1991). Black feminist criticism early offered insight into the relationship between sexuality, race, and gender. It is not insignificant that Barbara Smith in "Toward a Black Feminist Criticism" (1977) reads *Sula* as a lesbian text. Nor is it trivial that one of the most important voices in this body of work is Lorde, especially her collection of essays *Sister Outsider* (1984) and her biomythology *Zami* (1982). Even though these critics often engaged in arguments with other Black feminists about their failure to adequately address issues of sexuality in the early 1980s, such a conversation was not yet taking place in the broader field of African American studies. Consequently, Black feminist criticism provided a space that allowed for the emergence of Black queer studies, and Black masculinity studies, as well. Situated at the nexus of Black studies and queer studies but subordinated by both, scholars interested in Black gay, lesbian, and transgender people provide a critique of both fields and a reading practice that lays claim to both. This field has given rise to exciting voices, including but not limited to Phillip Brian Harper, Holland, Dwight McBride, and Robert Reid-Pharr.

In addition to informing Black queer studies and Black masculinity studies, Black feminist criticism has also been used to demonstrate ways that a Black feminist strategy of reading has relevance outside of purely literary study. Critics such as Valerie Smith (1989), hooks (1995, 1996), Jacqueline Bobo (1995), Jacqueline Najuma Stewart (2005), Daphne Brooks (2006), Wahneema Lubiano (1992), Angela Davis (1998), Lisa Gail Collins (2002), and Patricia Williams (1991) have used Black feminist reading strategies to analyze film, theater, the media, music, visual arts, and the law. In fact, hooks's oeuvre offers a testament to the growth and versatility of Black feminist literary and cultural criticism. One of the earliest figures who sought to define Black feminism, hooks has brought her sensibility to bear on literary texts, film, media, the visual arts, pedagogical practice, and studies of class and of Black masculinity.[8]

BUT SOME OF US ARE BRAVE

In the thirty years since the publication of Barbara Smith's "Toward a Black Feminist Criticism," the field has experienced a tremendous amount of growth and growing pains to accompany it. It helped institutionalize the study of works by Black women of all nationalities, and, along with the work of historians, it led the way for the development of Black women's studies as a distinct field within both African American studies and women's studies.[9] The project initially provided a discursive intervention that sought to address the invisibility and silence of Black women in dominant critical discourses, as well as those oppositional discourses that emerged from the Black power and feminist movements. Since that time, Black feminist critics have succeeded in calling attention to the works of contemporary Black women writers, unearthed the writings of earlier artists, constructed and dismantled literary traditions, and provided a method of reading that centers an analysis based on the intersection of race, class, and gender. Along the way, the field has encountered critiques from within and without. It has withstood accusations of essentialism, political correctness, and crude nationalism. Although it continues to be a discourse in opposition to right-wing ideologies, it has often incorporated as well as challenged critiques of biological essentialism and US national chauvinism. Finally, Black feminist criticism has helped create the conditions for the emergence of other critical stances, such as Black queer studies and Black masculinities studies.

Work informed by the tenets of Black feminist criticism continues to be important for a number of reasons: Readings that focus on the intersections of class, race, gender, sexuality, and nationality with an eye toward equality and justice are especially valuable today; a critique that emerges from those whose positionality has made them experience physical, psychic, and economic violence at the hands of the United States from within its borders provides a unique insight into the workings of this global, imperial power. Now, in the first decade of the twenty-first century, Black feminist criticism finds itself at an important juncture. Given the misogyny of some of today's contemporary Black popular culture, as well as the impact of US imperialism on the lives of women of color and poor women globally, the insights of Black feminist criticism offer a mode of analysis worth heeding, for Black feminist criticism provides a strategy of reading but also informs a politics that measures a society and its culture by the place that the poorest women and girls occupy within it.

AT LAST ... ?

Michelle Obama, Beyoncé, Race, and History

L ATE IN THE EVENING on January 20, 2009, newly sworn-in President Barack Obama and First Lady Michelle Obama made an appearance at the Neighborhood Ball. One of ten balls they would attend that night, the Neighborhood Ball was the first of its kind. Conceived as a "people's ball," a celebration for ordinary citizens and the residents of Washington, DC, it launched the administration's efforts to establish a relationship with the city and to make the White House itself more accessible to the broader public. The ball featured such popular music entertainers as Shakira, Alicia Keyes, will.i.am, Mary J. Blige, and Stevie Wonder.

In the most memorable part of the evening, superstar Beyoncé Knowles serenaded the first couple during the ceremonial "first" dance. Because the event was televised live on ABC, the staging was dramatic. The First Lady and president stood alone on a circular stage. Cued by the lush instrumental introduction to the R & B classic "At Last," the couple began to dance atop the presidential seal that had been painted on the stage floor. Across from them, on a stage in the middle of the audience, the elegantly clad Beyoncé began to sing Etta James's timeless song. Smiling sweetly at the couple like Lena Horne's gorgeous Good Witch Glenda in *The Wiz*, Beyoncé began her performance in a stately manner. Mid-song, she reached into the guttural depths of her range to pull from the deep traditions of Black American music and, in doing so, expressed a range of emotions, from celebration to defiance. By the song's end, she was lyrically soaring. The Obamas applauded her; she bowed to them, overcome with emotion, before leaving the stage.

The moment was memorable for a number of reasons. The romance of the president and First Lady, which had captivated many during the campaign, was now on full display. Mrs. Obama, dressed in a floating, feminine white gown that offset her brown complexion, was dancing to the same song the president had selected for the first dance at their wedding. Here, they seemed to re-create that moment, as if renewing their vows before a nation of witnesses. But even more significant, because this was the inauguration of America's first Black president, because "At Last" is an R & B song, and because Beyoncé sang it in a style most often associated with soul and gospel, the song signified the triumphant culmination of what had long been a rather one-sided romance between Black Americans and their nation. The fulfillment of our democratic principles? The achievement of a color-blind, post-racial America?

The performance of both the dance and the song struck a chord across race and generation. For the enthusiastic young people in the audience that night, it represented the promise of youth, of their own experience of race as something significant—important, even—though not limiting or constrictive. This was the hip-hop generation, after all. For old-timers, particularly Black old-timers, the performance may have represented a bittersweet sense of victory. As witnesses of the painful struggles that produced this moment, they watched it in memory of the many thousands gone—and with some continued trepidation and fear. They wondered, "Have we come this far? Really?" For my generation of middle-aged Black professionals, educated at elite institutions during the Reagan 1980s, we saw ourselves: our generation's response to the difficult struggle that had made our ascension possible. We saw ourselves and thought: *At last.*

All these perspectives represent a tension that has and will characterize the Obama years. Conflicting viewpoints are not evenly divided between generations. Instead, each generation has its share of those, on the one hand, who are eager to get over "race"—to put it behind us, to regard it as a relic of a past for which we have little use. On the other side are those who are often cast as so pessimistic about our nation, they believe it incapable of change; they are considered too invested, either in their identities or their livelihoods—in their "narratives of victimization"—to accept the reality of our post-racial present. Somewhere in between are the pragmatists, who believe "We've come a long way, baby, but we still got a long way to go."

We do not live in a post-racial time. In fact, to use that term is lazy. We *do* occupy a historical moment in which race and racism operate differently than they have in the past. Our society has removed all race-based legal barriers to equality. To claim things have not changed is wrongheaded; to claim that struggles for racial equality are behind us, or that they can be taken care of solely by attention to class, is equally so. We *are* witnessing the death of an epoch of white supremacy. All around us, we experience its dying gasp—a desperate, dangerous gasp. But white supremacy is an old man who will not go gently into that good night. He will continue to find breath in elements of the Far Right, in the thinking of many mainstream white Americans, in other racial and ethnic groups, and, unfortunately, in far too many Black people around the world. Nor are we at the "end of the African American narrative"; there has never been just one such narrative anyway. And, as with all narratives, those that deal with the Black experience in the United States have always been constructed to meet the contemporary needs, desires, and aspirations of Black people in a constantly shifting racial terrain.

A nation without racism is not an impossible achievement. Also, there are other forms of oppression and exploitation that act powerfully in the lives of Black people. However, it is indeed premature to claim that we need no longer be aware of the existence of white supremacy and racism. The baleful racism that has been unleashed since the election of our first Black president should be sufficient evidence of this reality. That large numbers of white Americans voted for a qualified, intelligent Black candidate certainly is evidence of progress. It is proof that large portions of white America are becoming less racist. But "less racist" does not mean "post-racial." (Civil rights activist and scholar Cornel West, among others, has also made this distinction.) Too often in public discourse the phrase "post-racial" is used to suggest that Black people and their allies should cease raising concerns about continued racial inequality.

Legal theorist Roy L. Brooks notes that "the problem of race in the Age of Obama is not racism but racial inequality." For Brooks, racial inequality can be found not only in differences in financial resources but also in "human (education and skills) and social (public respect, racial stigma, the ability to get things done in society)" resources, as well.[1]

The major problem with the stance of post-raciality *and* with refusals to admit substantive change is that both are ahistorical and shortsighted. Let us return to the Neighborhood Ball and the women who shared the spotlight: First Lady Michelle Obama and the multitalented Beyoncé Knowles. What might we learn about the relationship between history and the ongoing significance of race by attending to their images and their cultural impact? Both Knowles and Obama occupy a space unimagined by earlier generations. A singing, dancing, acting Black woman who is also an entertainment mogul, and an Ivy League–educated, Harvard-trained lawyer-cum-First Lady clearly herald something new (the latter even more so than the former). Yet these extraordinary women each represent something profoundly American, something deeply rooted in America's racial past, and something familiar but outwardly unrecognized by much of their public. Each has chosen to reveal and/or hide particular aspects of that history in order to move more easily into the American mainstream. By focusing on these women—their relationship to a particular aspect of America's racial history and how they mobilize it—we may reach a better understanding of the place of race in the contemporary historical moment.

> I am married to a Black American who carries within her the blood of slaves and slave owners.
> —BARACK OBAMA, *Philadelphia, 2008*

Our first glimpse of Michelle Obama was at the 2004 Democratic National Convention in Boston. Along with two small daughters, she joined her husband onstage following his triumphant and inspiring convention address, his historic introduction to the nation. Tall and trim, dressed elegantly in a white skirt suit with fashionable three-quarter-length sleeves, hair conservatively coiffed, she looked polished, poised, professional. She was very much like any number of Black women in any major American city, but there was something striking and unexpected about seeing her on that stage. Black communities were abuzz. They not only wanted to know more about *him*, but just as often they asked, "Did you see his wife?" Observing her in the role of political spouse struck a chord. And, because people almost immediately began to talk about *him* as a future president, many Black Americans began to imagine *her* as a First Lady.

It was difficult to imagine any Black woman in that role, but Mrs. Obama's unmistakable "Blackness" made it an especially amusing possibility. Once Senator Obama announced his candidacy, Michelle Obama authenticated his Blackness for many African Americans. He was not the descendant of enslaved ancestors; he had not grown up in a Black community. But she was, and she had. The phrase "He married her" was stated as proof that he made a conscious choice to identify with Black people and to raise his children as African Americans. While she legitimated his racial authenticity for many African Americans, for some whites she became the lightning rod, the persistent reminder of his race. His opponents sought to paint her as the "angry," unpatriotic Black woman. After all, she was the one who brought him into Pastor Jeremiah Wright's orbit. And then, in February 2008, she made the comment: "For the first time in my adult lifetime, I am really proud of my country." More precisely, she said:

> What we have learned over this year is that hope is making a comeback. It is making a comeback. And let me tell you something—for the first time in my adult lifetime, I am really proud of my country. And not just because Barack has done well, but because I think people are hungry for change. And I have been desperate to see our country moving in that direction and just not feeling so alone in my frustration and disappointment. I've seen

people who are hungry to be unified around some basic
common issues, and it's made me proud.

This was a simple statement of a feeling shared by many for whom
the Obama campaign gave a sense of hope, a sense of national belonging, a sense of purpose. To be proud of one's country should be seen
as something good. It is a step in a process. Mrs. Obama was suggesting that people like her gain a sense of pride through working to
make their nation better. In the words of James Baldwin via Richard
Rorty, this is the work of "achieving" our country. Rorty writes of a
national pride that induces us to act on a vision of our country and
the possibility that we may perfect it. This kind of pride encourages us
to think of our citizenship "as an opportunity for action." [2] The vision
Michelle Obama, the descendant of slaves, put forth is one in which
Americans of every race and ethnicity can take part in making our
country even better. In so doing, she seemed to build on the conten-
tion James Baldwin made at the end of *The Fire Next Time*:

> If we— and now I mean the relatively conscious whites
> and the relatively conscious blacks, who must, like lovers,
> insist on, or create, the consciousness of the others—do
> not falter in our duty now, we may be able, handful that
> we are, to end the racial nightmare and achieve our coun-
> try and change the world.[3]

Cindy McCain, wife of Barack Obama's opponent, said she was
genuinely offended by Michelle Obama's remarks. She began to pep-
per her own campaign speeches with, "I have *always* been proud of
my country." What she and the press failed to state is that the two
women claimed significantly different historical relationships to their
nation. Cindy McCain is a wealthy blonde heiress of a beer distrib-
utorship. Michelle Obama is the daughter of working-class African
Americans and the descendant of slaves. Barack Obama's political
opponents seized on Michelle Obama's statement as yet another
example of her husband's lack of patriotism—an opportunity to

question his relationship to America. Later, John McCain and Sarah Palin would pursue this path until it unleashed some of the most hateful and frightening instances of racism in recent memory. If Ivy League–educated, upper-middle-class professional Michelle Obama could ever have appeared militant or "threatening," then, indeed, we are far from a post-racial society.

It may not be surprising that many white people in the small towns and rural areas of so-called middle America had never encountered someone like Michelle Obama. What is stunning is how unfamiliar she appeared to mainstream media and to many of her peers. Michelle Obama and her white female counterparts had attended similar colleges, worked in similar environments, and shopped in the same stores. Perhaps this lack of familiarity is simply evidence of just how segregated our generation remains in spite of the proximity in which we live our lives. As was the case with Mrs. Obama, few of us continued to room with our freshman roommates after our first year of college. We chose instead to live with people of the same race. For the most part, we attended different parties and listened to different music. After graduation, we most likely attended different churches and continued to socialize in largely same-race groups.

Michelle Obama's story is more extreme than what most of us experienced. When Obama, then Michelle Robinson, arrived on Princeton's campus in fall 1981, she met one of her freshman roommates, Catherine Donnelly, a native of New Orleans who was shocked to learn that her roommate was Black. Donnelly's mother, Alice Brown, who had driven her daughter to campus, was "horrified." She went to the campus housing office and demanded that her daughter be moved to another room. "I told them we weren't used to living with black people," Brown recalled in 2008 to the *Atlanta Journal-Constitution*.[4] There is no evidence that Obama was aware of Brown's reaction; nonetheless, her college thesis focused on racial issues at Princeton. The thesis itself would become the subject of controversy in campaign press coverage. In it, Obama had written, "No matter how liberal and open-minded some of my White professors and classmates try to be toward me, I sometimes feel like a visitor on campus; as if I really don't belong.... Regardless of the circumstances under which I interact with Whites at Princeton, it often seems as if, to them, I will always be Black first and a student second." Right-wing pundits used the thesis as fodder to accuse Obama of lacking gratitude and engaging in identity politics. They suggested she was ungrateful for the opportunities America had afforded her.

As the press pursued stories about Michelle Obama's days as a college student, the campaign commissioned genealogical research as well. With the assistance of the Obama campaign, the *Washington Post* reported Mrs. Obama's paternal family tree, while the *New York Times* covered the history on her mother's side. Obama's lineage demonstrated a trajectory familiar to the descendants of US-born slaves: enslavement, Reconstruction, and the Great Migration. On both sides, researchers uncovered ancestors who had been enslaved as well as evidence of anonymous white ancestry. They found evidence of each generation's efforts to provide its children with education and opportunity. They found family members who escaped the strictures of the Jim Crow South by migrating to Chicago.

Two ancestors in particular stand out: the one-armed boy Fraser Robinson and the five-year-old slave girl Melvinia. Fraser Robinson, Michelle Obama's paternal great-grandfather, was born in 1884 to a former slave. When Fraser was ten years old his arm was amputated because it had been broken by a tree limb. Francis Nesmith, the white son of an overseer, became fond of the young boy and employed him as a live-in servant. The one-armed young man taught himself to read and write and became a shoemaker and a newspaper salesman. Less is known about Obama's maternal ancestor, Melvinia. She appears in the will of her master as a "6 year old Negro girl" who would be bequeathed to his daughter. By the time she turned fifteen she gave birth to a child, the son of an unknown white father. Melvinia and the anonymous white man are the maternal great-great-great-grandparents of Michelle Obama.

From its construction to the servants who worked there, the history of the White House has always been intertwined with that of slavery. For the first time, a descendant of the enslaved lives there as

First Lady. Michelle Obama sought to present her family tree as evidence of a painful period of our nation's past, a history with which we should be familiar so that we can move beyond it. She told the *Post*:

> It's good to be a part of playing out history in this way. . . .
> It could be anybody. But it's us, it's our family, it's that
> story, that's going to play a part in telling a bigger story. . . .
> [It is a process of] uncovering the shame, digging out the
> pride that is part of that story—so that other folks feel
> comfortable about embracing the beauty and the tangled
> nature of the history of this country.[5]

Significantly, the *Post* reported that some of Obama's relatives were reluctant to talk too much about or "delve too deep" into the family's past for fear "of stoking racial tensions and damaging" Barack Obama's chances of winning the election.[6] Their fears were not unwarranted.

Michelle Obama's ancestry may have been a cause for an honest discussion about our nation's painful but inspiring history. Instead, for much of the campaign, she was consistently criticized from a number of quarters. She was too aggressive, too angry; she was not sufficiently demure and adoring. Throughout the campaign she was caricatured as a Sapphire-like loud-mouth matriarch. The *National Review* published a cover story calling her "Mrs. Grievance." The opposition website TheObamaFile.com seemed dedicated to portraying her as a gun-wielding Black militant. It wasn't just right-wing bloggers who portrayed her this way. The liberal *New York Times* columnist Maureen Dowd launched a continuous diatribe against her that continues to the present. In fact, it was Dowd who unearthed the old problematic adjective *emasculating* in her description of Michelle Obama. Other outlets reported the existence of a mysterious recording of Obama using the epithet "whitey" in a talk she gave at Trinity United Church of Christ, in Chicago. When asked about these charges, she is reported to have denied ever using the phrase, remarking, "It's such a dated word. I'm much cooler than that."[7] When she and her husband celebrated a primary victory with a fist-bump, a Fox News anchor called the gesture "a terrorist fist jab."[8]

Focus groups run by the Obama campaign found that, among white Americans, Michelle Obama was perceived as "unpatriotic," "entitled," and "angry." In the weeks leading up to the 2008 Democratic National Convention in Denver, the campaign worked hard to transform her image. The culmination of these efforts was her speech before the convention on August 25, 2008. The speech was preceded by a video, *South Side Girl*, which documented her "American" story, followed by a loving introduction by her brother. During her speech, she was articulate and empathetic, patriotic and visionary. She stressed education without referring to her own elite educational pedigree. She acknowledged her debt to the civil rights and women's movements without lingering on these subjects for too long. She was neither threatening nor loud. She was soft and feminine. She said, "I love this country." By the end of her speech, when she was joined by her daughters, she had won over a large number of Americans. Her approval ratings soared.

As First Lady, she is the most popular member of the Obama administration. She is Mom-in-Chief, the fashion plate whose every sartorial choice is scrutinized, and she has chosen a meaningful and necessary cause: the fight against childhood obesity. The minute she steps out of this safe zone, however, charges of "entitlement" return. Thus, she suffers the fate of many of her forebearers, from Jacqueline Kennedy to Nancy Reagan. However, she has been very careful not to do anything that might portray her as the "Black" First Lady. Her predecessors did not have to be concerned with their racial identity in the same way.

||||||||||

BEYONCÉ GISELLE KNOWLES first emerged as the lead singer of the successful 1990s girl group Destiny's Child. From the beginning, it was evident that she had been groomed as the group's star and was poised to break out as a solo act. Her father, Matthew Knowles, was the group's manager; her mother, Tina Knowles, their designer and fashion and hair stylist. Beyoncé's first solo effort, *Dangerously in Love*, released in 2003, earned five Grammy Awards. Since Destiny's Child disbanded in 2005, Knowles has released two other solo albums, *B'Day* in 2006 and *I Am . . . Sasha Fierce* in 2008. Each album has been a commercial and critical success. In addition, she has starred in a number of films, most notably *Dream Girls*, in which she played Deena Jones, a character inspired by Diana Ross, and *Cadillac Records*, in which she played a young Etta James. Knowles has also launched her own clothing line, House of Déreon, as well as a fragrance line. She has endorsement deals with L'Oréal, Tommy Hilfiger, Pepsi, and Emporio Armani. In 2008, she earned more than $87 million. In the course of her career, she has sold more than four hundred million records.

Knowles's father is African American; her mother is Black Creole. Tina Knowles was born in Galveston, Texas, to Agnès DeRouen, originally of Delcambre, Louisiana, and Lumis Albert Beyincé of Abbeville, Louisiana. After marrying, the couple moved to Galveston. Both were mixed race, French-speaking Creoles claiming African, French, and Native American heritage. While Beyoncé identifies as African American, she has always claimed her Creole heritage, which has been central to how she markets herself and her music.

Beyoncé follows in a long line of talented and beautiful Black women entertainers, such as Josephine Baker, Lena Horne, and Dorothy Dandridge. Diana Ross and Tina Turner have also been inspirations. A powerful singer and equally dynamic dancer, Beyoncé has cultivated an image that alternates between the good Southern girl; the couture glamour of Baker, Horne, and Ross; and the highly sexualized, near-athletic dancing ability of Turner and, to a lesser degree, the young Josephine Baker. Though she played Etta James, she shares little with the more "tragic" heroines of the tradition: James or James's idol, Billie Holiday. Nor does she share their artistry.

Beyoncé occupies the status she does because these pioneers carved a place for her in American popular culture. Like them, she can sing, dance, and act, but she is also able to reap the full rewards of her labor and to control fully the direction of her career. She writes most of her own songs and has served as executive producer or coproducer for a number of her films. Unlike her predecessors, she has not been forced to choose between "respectable lady" and "bombshell." She comfortably occupies both spaces, having selected the alter ego Sasha Fierce to express the latter. However, that she has chosen two public personas to separately convey her respectable and sexual selves suggests that Black women have yet to be granted the full privilege of expressing their sexual agency without paying a price. On the other hand, Beyoncé's two personas signify an intelligent career choice; she may be able to age gracefully into the more elegant persona. The men behind Knowles—her father Matthew Knowles and her husband Jay-Z—are powerful, successful Black men, but the degree to which they manage her career is minimal; and she appears to have escaped the need for white-male sponsorship. Billie Holiday and Sarah Vaughan were both managed by Black husbands; Diana Ross is perhaps one of the first Black women whose involvement with a Black male entrepreneur, Berry Gordy, resulted in full-scale superstardom. Furthermore, Beyoncé's music is not relegated to urban radio. She can pack stadiums. She brings different kinds of audiences to the movie theaters. She is beloved, and imitated, across race, class, sexuality, generation, and national borders.

Beyoncé fits within the niche of the fair-skinned, possibly mixed-race, sexual beauty: a category that was born in the New World centuries ago. That she seems neither angry nor tragic, that she did not rise from material poverty, that she is never heard lamenting the lack of options available to her because of her race: all make her a pop diva of and for our times. She represents a new America. She is not of the Obama era; she helped usher it in.

And yet Beyoncé is also deeply rooted in aspects of American history. She calls on and mobilizes both a personal and collective racial past to market herself to contemporary audiences worldwide. Beyoncé's very specific mixed-race identity is entangled within the histories of New World racial slavery and the racial hierarchies that the institution bore. In short, Beyoncé builds on the fantasy of the mulatta temptress, which has origins in New World cultures from Brazil to Cuba to the American South, especially New Orleans. By highlighting her Louisiana Creole ancestry, her fair skin, blond weave, and hypersexualized performance style, she has parlayed a centuries-old stereotype into a lucrative and dynamic career. (She has done so without the highly public meltdowns of stars such as Whitney Houston and Britney Spears.) Thus, she has opened doors for other artists while reinforcing certain notions—sometimes destructive—of what is desirable and beautiful.

The mixed-race or ethnically ambiguous woman is considered at once beautiful because of her proximity to whiteness and sexual because of her Black "blood." Historically, she was portrayed as a temptress or a seductress in order to justify her sexual exploitation. Over time she has been the object of fantasy for both Black and white men, from the slave South to contemporary Brazil. She has even found her way into the pantheon of new world deities in the forms of Erzulie in Haiti and New Orleans, Oshun in Cuba, and Oxun in Brazil, all of whom manifest as La Mulatta, a deity of beauty, creativity, and all things sensual.

Either Beyoncé herself or those who have styled her visual image are fully aware of this legacy. In early campaigns for her clothing line, in photographs that accompany B'Day, and in the video for "Déjà Vu," the first single released from that album, Beyoncé is portrayed as a figure in two separate but related narratives that derive from specific aspects of the histories cited above: the "fancy girl" trade of antebellum New Orleans, which morphed into the Storyville Brothels featuring "quadroon" and "octoroon" women in the late nineteenth century; and free women of color in Louisiana involved with the institution of plaçage, a form of concubinage. New Orleans has long been known for its permissive interracial sexual culture. The city's slave market was among the nation's largest and was characterized by its fancy girl trade, which sold mixed-race women into various forms of sex slavery. Historian Alecia P. Long notes that following the Civil War, "the city ceased to be the nation's largest slave market and most permissive port. Instead, it became a tourist destination that encouraged and facilitated indulgence, especially in prostitution and sex across the color line."⁹

By 1897, the city had established two vice districts, the most famous of which was Storyville. The fancy girl slave trade and the brothels were only two aspects of what Long refers to as "the commercial sexual culture of New Orleans." The institution of plaçage was not a form of prostitution but represented "the formal and sometimes even contractual arrangements between white men and women of color . . . which spelled out the financial terms of the relationships." These relationships and the terms by which they were governed were often negotiated by the young women's mothers, who presented their daughters at the famous octoroon or quadroon balls.

Beyoncé has presented an image that signifies both the brothel and plaçage traditions. In 2005, she and her mother launched their clothing line, House of Déreon, inspired by her seamstress grandmother, Agnès DeRouen. In the advertising campaign, Beyoncé was featured, with her mother in a supporting role as either a seamstress providing alterations or a beloved mother who offers an admiring glance or affectionate touch. In a few ads, Tina Knowles appears literally to present her daughter for the viewer's admiration and consumption. In one, both women wear evening gowns. In another, Beyoncé stands in front of a full-length mirror in satin-and-lace lingerie, or in a slip or slip-dress, while her mother can be seen in the mirror's reflection. All photographs are set in a boudoir or a lushly designed seamstress studio, and each has a photograph of the Creole matriarch in gilded frame. The ad campaign for spring 2010 featured a portrait of Beyoncé, bare shouldered and with her head wrapped elaborately in blue-and-green silk. The head wrap was adorned with a huge broach made of green stones, an image that recalled the tignons worn by Creoles of color in New Orleans. The head wrap, which resembles a West African gele, was worn by free women of color in New Orleans during the Spanish colonial period and later. In 1785, tignon laws were passed to enforce a dress code for *gens de couleur*, especially women, as a means of distinguishing them from white women. The women of color rivaled white women in fashion, style, and beauty. Once the laws forced women of color and Black women to cover their heads, the Creoles created highly stylized head wraps, decorating their tignons with jewels, feathers, ribbons, and other embellishments in order to distinguish their class standing.

If the ads for House of Déreon suggest plaçage, then the photos that accompany B'Day and the video for "Déjà Vu" are more explicit in their association. In them, Beyoncé wears a series of costumes, almost all of which resemble sexual costumes—from dominatrix to French maid. The most obvious finds her walking down a railroad track clad in a ruffled white cotton romper: a combination of blues singer Robert Johnson at the crossroad and photographer E. J. Bellocq's Storyville whores. Bellocq was best known for his images of Storyville's octoroon prostitutes. His photos inspired the 1978 film about child prostitution in New Orleans, Pretty Baby, starring Brooke Shields, as well as Michael Ondaatje's 1976 novel about mythical New Orleans trumpeter Buddy Bolden, Coming through Slaughter. The "Déjà Vu" video features Beyoncé as a sex-crazed woman, dancing in the wilderness or alternately lying seductively across velvet couches. At one point, she appears poised to perform fellatio on her partner, Jay-Z.

What is important here is the way that Beyoncé's image is grounded at the nexus of race, sex, and commerce. Significantly, New Orleans history boasts a number of mixed-race women who parlayed both concubinage and prostitution into economic independence, property ownership, and entrepreneurship. A select few became highly successful madams, and an even greater number were successful seamstresses and hairdressers. The high degree of Black property ownership in New Orleans has been attributed to the estates left by mixed-race foremothers. Certainly, Beyoncé earned her wealth with hard work and virtuosic talent. Nonetheless, the marketing of that talent via a visual vocabulary that references commercial sexual culture has helped ensure her success. Most of Beyoncé's audience, consumers of her clothing and music, are unaware of the history behind the images. For her stylists, that particular history may be part of an endless source of cultural references that they can refer to for inspiration. What is significant is the way that this particular set of images resonates with an important part of our nation's past. While any number of young women performers may choose to market themselves in similarly sexualized roles, Beyoncé's lineage signifies a particular kind of relationship to the images of herself that she projects.

Beyoncé's enormous success heralds an America where race no longer necessarily bars achievement but where old mythologies continue to resonate and sell. Furthermore, if she signals the dawn of a new day in which mixed-race heritage is valorized, a notion of a postracial culture does not necessarily follow. The veneration of mixed-race identity may challenge white supremacist hierarchies, but it can also accommodate a continued degradation of Blackness. One need only study the history of mixed-race societies such as Brazil and the Dominican Republic, where Black people still sit at the bottom of the racial hierarchy. Within the boundaries of the United States, we continue to live in a culture that devalues Blackness, as is evident in a variety of contexts, from children's preference for white dolls, to the value placed on white and mixed-race adoptees versus that placed on Black children, to the profound racial disparities that continue to plague Black communities nationwide.

The emergence and acceptance of Michelle Obama and Beyoncé as embodiments of American womanhood indeed signal a new racial era for our nation. Beyoncé has been easier for the public to accept because she is an entertainer, a long-accepted role for Black women. As a sex symbol, moreover, she does not present a threat to established categories. However, Obama's acceptance is more tenuous. She occupies a thoroughly new role for Black women and thus walks a very fine line; she must exercise discretion lest she express too firm an opinion or appear too confident. The mainstream acceptance of talented Black individuals is not without significance. That Blackness is relegated to the superficial or the sexual suggests a continued devaluation of Black people, their history, and their experiences. Nevertheless, images of Michelle Obama and Beyoncé are available to all our nation's girls; that they may now aspire to the previously unimagined heights occupied by their idols is perhaps the greatest indication of our nation's progress. Unfettered access to these heights will be the true test of our post-racial future.

IV.

ON CRISIS AND POSSIBILITY

In crisis there is opportunity: opportunity to rethink and rebuild. Some of these essays are responses to the urgency of crises like the 9/11 terrorist attacks, Hurricane Katrina, the COVID-19 pandemic, and a dangerous rise of book banning in the United States. Others focus on the possibilities offered by the Obama administration, even when I disagreed with it, to rethink both American cultural politics and the role of government in addressing systemic inequities that plague Black boys AND girls.

Significantly, in 2015, the White House supported the Collaborative to Advance Equity through Research, which included fifty institutions across the nation and made a multiyear commitment to invest in research by, for, and about the lives of women and girls of color. Along with my colleague, the sociologist Alondra Nelson, I was happy to lead Columbia University's initiative. The trajectory from critical engagement and constructive dialogue with government to taking advantage of the platform it provided to create partnerships with higher education, philanthropy, and grassroots organizations, is one example of finding possibility in crisis. This section closes with an opening: an exploration of visual art by Allison Janae Hamilton, whose work offers meditations on historic social and political crises that lead to ecological disaster. Her work also points us toward new worlds and life forms that may emerge on the other side of catastrophe.

ON THE FOURTH ANNIVERSARY
OF SEPTEMBER 11

AFTER 9/11, I stopped riding the subway for a little while. It wasn't a conscious decision. I didn't even notice it until a couple of months later, perhaps around Christmas. In fact, I only realized I'd stopped riding it when I felt a bit of trepidation descending into a cavernous tunnel. That's the way 9/11 affected a lot of us: no big phobias, just little gnawing ones we didn't even know were related to that horrific event. We don't live in a state of panic. Instead, we conduct our lives with caution, an irritating expectation that something catastrophic might be just around the corner. We share the watchfulness of people around the world who live with the expectation of arbitrary violence.

When bombs exploded in the trains in Madrid and London, we in Manhattan worried. When uniformed armed guards filled the New York subway stations, some of us opted for the bus or long walks. When, following the bombing of the London tube stations, police mistakenly identified a frightened young Brazilian as a terrorist and killed him, some of us experienced yet another kind of fear and anger. I love New York. I especially love the subway. In a residentially segregated city, it's one place where New Yorkers of every type come together: the young boys selling huge candy bars competing with the soliloquies of homeless men and women; the beautiful African American and Dominican teenagers sitting quietly. Next to them, the tanned fashionistas with their big engagement rings and ridiculously gorgeous stilettos; and my favorites, the hard-working, world-weary riders of every race and ethnicity.

I didn't ride the subway on September 11, 2001. As I emerged from a morning walk in Riverside Park, I saw a swarm of jet-black cars with darkened windows and screaming sirens headed downtown. I went uptown; first back to my apartment, where concerned family members and friends were calling. I heard news of the plane that flew into the World Trade Center and watched on television as another one flew into the second tower. Wanting to be in the street with others, I left the confines of my building. Like Ellington's "Take the 'A' Train," I sought the quickest way to Harlem, only on foot. I guess I felt I would be safest in a place where the streets are filled with brown and Black faces.

Later that day, I joined a friend, and we sat stunned at one of our regular outdoor cafes with others from our neighborhood, eating french fries and watching as F-16s flew overhead. We talked, listened to the radio, spoke with those who'd walked the long trek from downtown because, by now, the subway had stopped running. The explosions had destroyed some of the downtown stations. I thought about all of the riders, the candy-selling boys and the teens, the fashionistas, the workers, and the homeless, how many of them would be counted among the missing and the dead.

This year on the anniversary of 9/11, I will attend services at Riverside Church, one of our city's grand cathedrals. There, where people of diverse ethnic, racial, and national backgrounds will gather to worship, and where the fearless pastor often speaks out against the senselessness of war, we'll commemorate all the lives lost on that day and every day since. Yes, I'll go to church and then I'll take my chances and head for the subway.

HUMAN RIGHTS AND THE
KATRINA EVACUEES

THE HISTORY OF Black people in the United States is an epic saga of dislocation, dispersal and dispossession: the Middle Passage, the Underground Railroad, the wanderings of freedmen in search of their families following the Civil War, the Great Migration to Northern cities, the devastation of urban renewal. Black Americans have long experienced the instability, insecurity and disruption that accompany displacement. The current crisis facing Black New Orleanians is the latest chapter in this story.

Hurricane Katrina was an act of nature that disrupted many lives, but Hurricane Katrina did not cause this large-scale dispossession. Our society's failure to recognize the basic human rights of poor people is a major cause. Before Katrina, historic and structural intersections of race and class forced thousands upon thousands of Black New Orleanians to live in poverty. They were subjected to inferior schools, inadequate health care and housing, and governmental neglect. They were already the weakest and the most vulnerable when the hurricane hit, and then, as with poor Black communities of the past, they were left in the chaotic whirlwind as others with more resources fled to safety, still left when the levee, neglected for decades, broke and flooded the city, left languishing for days in inhumane and violent conditions before the federal government, their government, responded.

Now a city rich in Black history, a city that gave us Louis Armstrong and Mahalia Jackson, is in ruins. The poverty, the conditions of the Superdome and the convention center, the obscene days-long wait for help to arrive, the loss of a cultural legacy, the unidentified dead: all of these constitute violations of basic human rights.

Unfortunately, the structural conditions that lay the foundation for the New Orleans catastrophe exists throughout the nation. The US Census Bureau recently reported that the number of Americans living in poverty has risen 17 percent under the Bush administration. This year's United Nations report on human development asserts that the infant mortality rate in this country has also risen under the current administration. Now it's the same as Malaysia's. This is the first time in forty-seven years that the US has experienced a rise in infant mortality rates. Black children in the United States are twice as likely as white children to die before their first birthdays. Indicators like this point to the pitiful state of human rights in the United States.

Throughout our history, visionary African Americans, including W. E. B. Du Bois, Malcolm X, and Martin Luther King Jr., have insisted that our struggle wasn't just for civil rights but for human rights. Perhaps now is the time for the concerned and enraged among us to take up this call again in honor of the dead, the despised, the dispersed, and the dispossessed.

DNC DAY 2

Will America Accept First Lady Michelle?

B Y THE TIME Michelle Obama—the woman who many hope will be America's next First Lady—took center stage, the Pepsi Stadium was electric with anticipation. We'd just watched a well-produced video, *South Side Girl*, documenting her "American" story.

It was followed by her brother's loving introduction. Watching her, resplendent in teal, perfectly made-up and coifed, I wondered, "What will it take for Americans to love this woman?" Surrounded by tall placards with her name in bold white print, I thought, "What will the pundits make of her performance?" I had no doubt she would be elegant, beautiful, intelligent, and graceful. She always is. I wasn't concerned that she might slip up and speak a basic truth about our deeply flawed nation. She has learned her lesson, and there are now handlers to assure that she makes no such slips.

It is Michelle's Blackness that has deeply disturbed many Americans and much of the press, and it is that same Blackness that has endeared her to many, but not all, Black Americans. For those of us who share her race, gender, and generation, the negative reaction she has inspired is stunning. As with Michelle, we are the daughters of hard-working, even struggling, parents. We are the daughters who were constantly told that we mustn't ever fit the stereotypes "they" have of us. We were raised to take advantage of the opportunities created for us by the civil rights movement (and, though rarely acknowledged, by the feminist movement as well). We grew up in Black communities that were proud of us.

And, when we went off to predominantly white, elite colleges and universities, it was with the reminder that we must do better than well, and that we dare not forget those we left behind. Why are Black women like Michelle Obama, Black women who have been educated alongside and worked with white Americans as equals, so unfamiliar to so many Americans?

Unlike Oprah, a billionaire media mogul who serves as a spiritual mother to millions of American women, Michelle is mother only to her own precious daughters. An accomplished professional, a devoted mother, sister, wife, daughter, and friend, Michelle Obama is like countless other American women, and yet many white Americans have found it impossible to see themselves or their aspirations in her.

Maybe it is because they cannot imagine her as First Lady. "Lady" is not a designation easily bestowed upon Black women. In fact, it is an identity that we have had to fiercely fight for. In an effort to leave behind a legacy of forced labor and forced sex, formerly enslaved women valued ladylike behavior and instilled it in their daughters as if that alone would save the race.

However, in both legal and popular discourses, the privileges of ladyhood were reserved for white females. Many white Americans are comfortable with fictions of welfare and quota queens. Unfortunately, a younger generation, encouraged by irresponsible artists and greedy corporate conglomerates, have also grown comfortable with "video hoes." But are Americans ready to bestow that designation—Lady, First Lady—on a Black woman? And at what price?

Last night, Michelle Obama was all that one would have expected of her. She was elegantly dressed, replete with portrait collar and flattering three-quarter-length sleeves. Her hair was "appropriately" straight. She acknowledged her debt to past struggles for social justice, both for racial equality and gender equality. She was magnanimous towards Hilary Clinton. She was not threatening or loud. She did not raise an eyebrow. She painted a vision of a glowing future led by her husband. And she gave Americans a picture of themselves as a people striving together toward a better tomorrow. She gave no specific policy points (Americans tend not to like that in their First

Ladies) nor did she acknowledge any ongoing racial tensions. She was soft and feminine.

By the end of her speech, when she was joined onstage by her daughters and the stadium erupted in thunderous applause, my heart was full, but my mind was still aflutter with questions: Did she successfully do what the campaign wanted her to do? Will working-class white Americans feel any closer to her and, by extension, to her husband? Will middle-class white professional women and stay-at-home moms see themselves in her? Will self-conscious (and a few self-hating) Black Americans think she represented the race well?

I can almost say with certainty that elderly Black women, the Church, and neighborhood mothers, were indeed proud. And the rest of us who have loved her from day one can only pray for her protection, her safety, and her sanity on this mad journey.

LOVING BILLIE HOLIDAY DOESN'T MEAN BLACK GIRLS AREN'T SUFFERING

A Response to Joshua DuBois and My Brother's Keeper

IN RESPONSE TO a letter of protest signed by more than one thousand women of color, Joshua DuBois penned a thoughtful defense at the *Daily Beast* of President Obama and My Brother's Keeper, the $200 million public-private initiative to improve life outcomes and address opportunity gaps for men and boys of color. Inspired by Audra McDonald's Tony Award–winning stage portrayal of jazz legend Billie Holiday, DuBois argues that the signatories of the letter failed to grasp the president's sensitivity, devotion, and dare I say, even love for Black women. We can recognize this love and devotion in part, DuBois tells us, in the president's special fondness for Lady Day, her music and the pain and resilience expressed by her artistry.

I too have been moved by the biography and the artistry of Billie Holiday. My father, my first teacher and a jazz lover who always sought to share his interest with his younger daughter, introduced me to Lady Day and her music. I went on to devote a book to exploring her personal significance to me and to larger questions about gender, race, and class. Like DuBois, I also sat awestruck at McDonald's performance: one great artist paying homage to another. And, although I am one of the many women who signed the letter pressing the administration to include women and girls in this program, that does not mean I, or any of us, question the president's respect for Black women.

DuBois mentions the president's love for his wife and his two beautiful daughters. As so many of us do, I find that heartwarming. And it was with a sense of gratitude and pride that I watched him honor the two literary lions, Maya Angelou and Toni Morrison with the Medal of Freedom, the nation's highest civilian honor. Nor do I doubt that Black women will benefit from major Obama administration achievements, such as the Affordable Care Act, and the other projects including the STEM initiatives, which will support women students and researchers in science, technology, engineering, and mathematics.

And like DuBois, my husband and I also left the theater following McDonald's performance in a pensive state. I thought about the way Holiday expressed herself with such beauty and dignity in the face of unspeakable insults to her person: a gifted Black woman born in a nation that did more to thwart her promise than it did to nurture it. But here, my ruminations on Lady Day depart from DuBois's. I couldn't help but focus on how many of the problems that plagued Holiday continue to confront young, poor women of color today. Her girlhood difficulties were largely invisible to those in power; all too often the same is true for contemporary girls left to struggle alone in violent communities, failing schools, and institutions that do more harm than good.

Holiday was born in poverty to teenage parents. As with far too many girls, she was a victim of childhood sexual abuse. Rather than being recognized as a victim, she was sent to a home for wayward girls. Faced with little opportunity for education and employment, she first turned to prostitution, for which she served time in prison. Fortunately, she was talented, and those who could present her with opportunities soon recognized her musical gifts. While many young Black women face the constraints that beset Holiday before she turned twenty-one, few can rely on musical talent or the opportunity to perform as a way out of poverty. As an adult, Holiday began to use heroin, and her drug addiction was criminalized rather than treated. Similarly, contemporary Black women who experience sexual abuse, domestic violence, and drug addiction make up the fastest-growing prison population. Perhaps the greatest irony of DuBois's discussion of Billie Holiday is that in the programs supported by My Brother's Keeper, her suffering would still be ignored.

As with the other signatories to the letter to President Obama, I understand the myriad of difficulties confronted by young men of color. As a beneficiary of a wonderful single-sex education, I do not deny the need for gender-specific remedies. But when both boys and girls are drowning, you don't just throw life vests to the boys and hope that by saving them, you save the girls as well. The challenges facing girls and boys may require different kinds of research, different kinds of mentoring, different kinds of efforts from the corporate sector, but boys and girls should benefit from the overall vision of creating a stronger and healthier Black community.

But truth be told, although I would like to see young women included in My Brother's Keeper, the initiative falls far short of doing anything to truly address the crisis it recognizes, let alone the one it doesn't. It simply helps to call attention to the plight facing poor Black men and to highlight the private sector and foundation initiatives that have been in place already. Including Black girls would mean something different: not only acknowledging that their lives matter and encouraging research on issues they face but putting new material support behind programs that seek to address them. For there are currently exceedingly few private-sector or philanthropic resources directed at girls of color in the United States.

In the absence of a broad-based policy initiative and governmental resources that specifically address the crisis facing the Black community in its entirety, we ask that the major race-specific initiative to emerge from President Obama's administration not exclude young women. And this seems to be the crux of Mr. DuBois's problem with the letter that we sent to our president. "We just have a little more than two years left with the only Black president we've known, and perhaps the only one we'll see in a while," he writes. "I pray that we—Black folks, and especially the African American academy—use that time wisely, focusing out on the issues that matter, instead of in, on each other." Issues that matter? Black girls do matter. We are not focusing in on each other, but requesting that our president, a man many of us helped to elect and whom some of us continue to support, include women and girls of color in this particular vision. We are not only members of the "Black academy," as DuBois calls it, we are citizens of this democracy and heirs to a long tradition of Black citizens who have expressed our criticism while working with those in power to help bring about a more inclusive nation.

I am very fortunate to serve on the board of an innovative organization that serves Black youth, male and female, in Harlem, the Brotherhood/Sister Sol. I was drawn to "BroSis" because of their pioneering and creative work with both boys and girls. Founded by Khary Lazarre-White and Jason Warwin in 1994, the organization initially focused on young men. They soon recognized the need for similar programming for girls, and, in 1998, Dr. Susan Wilcox joined the leadership team and helped to expand the organization to include programs for young women. It is now a comprehensive and holistic youth development organization serving Black and Latino youth ages eight to twenty-two.

"BroSis" is organized into gender-specific chapters where young men and women have a safe space to express their fears, their concerns, to learn what it means to be a brother, a leader, a man, as well as a sister, a leader, a woman, and how to be brothers and sisters to each other. Our young people are active participants in creating an anti-misogynistic community that recognizes, values, and respects the full humanity of their brothers and sisters. As such, they seek to mirror the society they are committed to building. They walk the walk and talk the talk, and in so doing, they provide a model for the kind of inclusive and expansive vision that we should all share. This is the kind of work we should be doing.

TEACHING AFRICAN AMERICAN LITERATURE DURING COVID-19

HAVE BEEN TEACHING African American literature to college students for almost three decades. This year, my students in Introduction to African American Literature started the semester in a lecture hall on the campus of Columbia University and ended it scattered to the four corners of the Earth. Some had to quarantine for two weeks after returning to their countries. Others remain in rooms and apartments in New York, an epicenter of the pandemic. Some have lost family members; others have themselves been sickened by the virus. Some turned out to be more comfortable talking on Zoom than in a physical classroom; others find it alienating and prefer instead to reach out through email or on WhatsApp. Yet and still, they keep reading, they keep thinking. They have shown up, continuously, week after week. Teaching them in this pandemic has shed new light on the power of learning, community, and this extraordinary literature.

I miss my students terribly. Nonetheless this moment has allowed us to work together in a different way. The crisis stopped us in our tracks, but it also provided an opportunity. I decided to slow things down for them. Rather than continuing to read a novel a week, we read an essay and a short story by James Baldwin, one of Toni Morrison's shorter novels, and we spent the last two weeks reading Octavia Butler's *Parable of the Sower* (1993), a work of speculative fiction that portrays community-building in the midst of economic, social, political, and ecological catastrophe. Ultimately, Butler's novel—in which change and adaptability are major themes—encourages readers to consider what kind of future might be built on the other side of pandemic. How fitting.

My course changed in other ways, as well. I cancelled the take-home exam, which would have required students to provide a synthesis of their learning and to place texts in conversation with each other. Instead, I decided to focus on imaginative skills and asked the students to create a work of art in response to any of the texts we read. I also gave them a second assignment, to be shared on the last day of class. The description began with a quotation from Arundhati Roy's essay "The Pandemic as Portal":

Historically, pandemics have forced humans to break with the past and imagine their world anew. This one is no different. It is a portal, a gateway between one world and the next. We can choose to walk through it, dragging the carcasses of our prejudice and hatred, our avarice, our data banks and dead ideas, our dead rivers and smoky skies behind us. Or we can walk through lightly, with little luggage, ready to imagine another world. And ready to fight for it.

The description of the assignment was as follows

> As we pass through this portal, let's think about what we might take to the other side, and what we want to leave behind. One or two sentences per question. No more.
>
> 1. What one book from class would you want to take with you?
> 2. What, if anything, from your old life do you want to leave behind?
> 3. What do you appreciate that you would like to take with you?
> 4. What change, if any, would you like to see, and commit to bring about, on the other side?

Together the two new assignments—the response to the Roy quotation and the creative project—asked students not only to think about what they had read but also to make, build, and imagine. Toni Morrison said that in moments of crisis, "artists go to work. . . . That is how civilizations heal." In addition to their analytical skills, which are on display in every class, I wanted my students to stretch their imaginative ones as well.

My students did not disappoint me. In this season of unimaginable death, especially Black and brown death, these young people rose to the occasion. With careful consideration of the books and for each other, with a strong desire to help heal the world in which we live, they went to work. They created poems, paintings, and book covers inspired by Zora Neale Hurston, Gwendolyn Brooks, and others. One student, Alexzundra, an especially talented writer who was inspired by a scene in Hurston's *Their Eyes Were Watching God*, read an exquisite original prose poem over a short, meditative film: "Have I been captured, seen my reflection without seeing my face?" Another, Douglas, submitted a pencil drawing based upon the end of *Parable of the Sower*, imagining a new world rising like a phoenix from the ashes of the old. Butler also sparked the creativity of two talented musicians. Nigel and James each composed, performed, and recorded original songs inspired by the novel. Nigel's lyrics and acoustic guitar sought "to capture the moral relativism of Lauren's [Butler's protagonist] travel sonically," while James explained that he used "the chord progression to emphasize the importance of the word *change*. A new chord is cued each time the word is said." He then recorded himself playing a jazz trumpet solo over the chord progression. A third musician, Esther, recorded her solo piano medley of songs, from Ray Charles to Frédéric Chopin, that capture the works we've read. Ralph Ellison's *Invisible Man* inspired Justin and Isaac to write first-person narratives that I hope are just the beginning of longer works.

In answering the last of the four questions prompted by Roy, most of the students expressed the desire to leave behind the drive to be busy for the sake of being busy, and to part with performances of self that feel inauthentic to them, given the current crisis. Instead, they want to cultivate community. Significantly, they committed to addressing inequality, injustice, and environmental disaster. They want to join and create organizations and institutions committed to bringing about significant social change.

Because I strongly believe in the power of art and creativity, I hoped these assignments would allow my students to slow down and dig deep inside of themselves. They did and emerged as visionaries, just the kind of people we need now: global citizens, gifted with creativity and imagination, and capable of imagining a more just future. I hope to live to see the world my students create. As their teacher, I will do all I can to make sure they are able to do so.

BANNING TONI MORRISON'S BOOKS DOESN'T PROTECT KIDS. IT JUST SANITIZES RACISM.

THE FINAL DAYS of the Virginia gubernatorial campaign have featured a cameo by Nobel laureate Toni Morrison's 1987 novel *Beloved*. Republican Glenn Youngkin is running an ad bashing Democrat Terry McAuliffe for vetoing legislation in 2017, when McAuliffe was governor, that would have given parents the right to opt their children out of reading sexually explicit material in school. The ad features a mother who says her son, as a high school senior, suffered from night terrors after reading the book.

This may be an unexpected turn for Virginia politics, but it's not so unusual for Morrison's work to be at the center of censorship battles. Since the publication of her first novel, *The Bluest Eye*, in 1970, Morrison's books have often come under fire. In 1997, Texas prisons considered *Paradise* too dangerous for their libraries because it might incite "strikes or riots." In its yearly reports, the American Library Association often lists Morrison's novels among the most frequently challenged or banned books. Last year, a Southern California school board announced the reversal of its decision to remove *The Bluest Eye* from its core reading list for AP English Literature classes.

But this latest iteration of the controversy surrounding *Beloved* occurs in the context of nationwide debates about race and history, and in the closing days of a close political campaign. This suggests that bringing the book back up now, nine years after the mother featured in Youngkin's ad first complained about it, is less about the comfort of teenage readers and more about parents trying to elide the harsh truths and realities of our nation's history.

Censorship does not result in education, the pursuit of knowledge, or intellectual growth. What Morrison said about Mark Twain's *Huckleberry Finn* might also be said of her own writing. Concerning parental attempts to have Twain's classic removed from classrooms because of its use of a racially pejorative term, Morrison wrote that such efforts are the "purist and yet elementary kind of censorship designed to appease adults rather than educate children."

Morrison found the great brilliance of *Huckleberry Finn* to be "the argument it raises" about the role of slavery in our nation's identity and the way it thwarted our professed commitment to freedom and liberty. Even as she was herself offended by some aspects of the text, she nonetheless defended Twain's work from accusations of racism. She valued the way he called attention to race and slavery, she appreciated his elevation of an American vernacular, itself built upon the contributions of American Blacks to the language, and she critically engaged his novel in her own work, *Beloved*.

As such, she modeled for us a way of teaching, engaging and debating works of art. Confronting the difficult truths of the past in this way has given rise to our most powerful literature and to political movements that have helped the nation move toward a more expansive sense of its democratic principles.

Morrison saw efforts to ban her work as proof of its power, and she devoted much of her life to protecting the rights and safety of writers who risked censorship and worse. She understood that attempts to silence writers—indeed, to silence all artists—are authoritarian in nature. These efforts endeavor to keep citizens ignorant, if comfortable.

Literary history is full of examples of complex, difficult books replete with scenes of sex and violence, often told in controversial, if beautiful, language. The most sophisticated of these works do not sensationalize violence, nor do they insist that readers put themselves in the place of the characters, but instead, they encourage us to bear witness to the suffering of others. For literature to bear witness, it must engage with violence, even as it condemns it. From the Old and New Testaments to Harriet Beecher Stowe's *Uncle Tom's Cabin* or Elie Wiesel's *Night*, readers are confronted with powerful narratives that not only tell the stories of oppressed people but also hold the mirror up to humanity, often showing us parts of ourselves we'd rather not see.

Nowhere is this more apparent than in *Beloved*, a novel that includes sex, some of it consensual, much of it brutal and abusive. Such abuse constituted the horrific conditions of slavery. Nonetheless, sex in *Beloved* is not overly explicit, as Youngkin's ad and the earlier campaign against it would have us believe, although it can make for difficult and painful reading. If her novel is "obscene," that is because the institution of slavery was obscene. The novel is about slavery—including, but not limited to, the sexual abuse that it encouraged and relied upon as a tool of power. Significantly, *Beloved* is also about a mother, Sethe, seeking to protect her child from the horrors of that institution, which includes protecting her from sexual assault. For Sethe, murdering her child is better than having the girl face the terror with which she herself has lived as an enslaved woman.

Ultimately, Morrison's work asks the question, what kind of people can be capable of such inhumane cruelty? The refusal to confront this question, let alone explore the answers it may yield, sits at the core of attempts to ban Morrison. Her writings, and other historical and creative works, expose the ugly parts of our history, including its crimes against humanity.

The resurgence of opposition to *Beloved* coincides with the right wing's assault on critical race theory and, more broadly, on any attempts to discuss structural racism in classrooms. The history of slavery and its aftermath, which inspired *Beloved*, is directly related to examining the forms of systemic racism that inform every aspect of our society. Public schools have emerged as contentious sites in this ongoing battle because they, along with the voting booth, have long been places where ideological battles over the myths and meanings of our nation have been fought. In this instance, those who criticize

Beloved and want to ban what they call "critical race theory" claim that any works addressing the country's history of racial inequality and violence pose a threat to impressionable young minds. At best, this resistance is as uninformed as it is passionate. At worst, it is a distraction mobilized by political campaigns seeking to exploit age-old racial fault lines—a distraction that takes our attention away from the true threat to democracy posed by those who would dismantle voting rights, advance economic inequality, and undermine the sustainability of our planet.

Yes, parents—like Sethe in the novel—do want and should have the right to protect their children, but it is just as important for young people to explore difficult ideas in the context of a classroom, under the careful guidance of well-trained teachers dedicated to free expression and critical thinking. Studying literature offers us the opportunity to do just that.

Efforts to ban works like *Beloved* undermine democracy, even if they aren't intended to. Encouraging students to encounter new and different contexts provides an opportunity for them to understand experiences beyond their own, forces them to confront the evil that human beings can do to each other, as well as the decency, mercy, and love we are capable of offering one another. Engaging such books also allows them to imagine other times, places, and sets of possibilities. At this moment in our nation's history, we are in desperate need of a generation that has been exposed to and guided through our history, both the difficult past and the extraordinary wisdom and beauty offered to us by our greatest artists. Only then will they be able, intellectually, politically, and morally, to move all of us into a more just and democratic future.

ANCIENT HISTORIES AND NEW WORLDS

Allison Janae Hamilton

A LLISON JANAE HAMILTON creates worlds. Her lush and lus-
cious landscapes invite you to wonder as you wander. It is a world
of sound and sight, a world of motion, of tall green pine, of water-
rooted cypress; a world where masked women walk, skip, dance,
or ride on horseback, where reptilian figures inhabit the swamp
and pheasant the forest, and we share it all with them. She at once
immerses you in both a prehistoric and postbellum past while pro-
jecting you into a postapocalyptic, Afrofuturistic future. Her work
is fully imaginative, ethereal, and beautiful, but also grounded in the
realities of race, history, land, economic exploitation, and the impact
of climate devastation.

The landscape and history that inspire much of Hamilton's work
is the dense pinewoods of northern Florida. As scholar/artist, she is a
daughter of this earth, and like her forebearer, Zora Neale Hurston,
she knows it well. In ethnography and fiction, Hurston was one of
the first to document and write about this part of the Black South, to
offer firsthand accounts of the turpentine workers who lived in and
traveled through the pine forests, tapping the trees for the pungent,
gummy substance. As one of them told her, "Turpentine woods is
kind of lonesome."[1]

Hamilton builds upon this history to explore the relationship
between the people and the land, between the natural world and generations of Black peoples, and between the exploitation of labor and
nature. One senses, if not the "lonesome," then the solitude, the sin-

gularity of inhabiting this space. While we often place Black work-ers, enslaved and "free" in the context of plantation slavery, or cotton sharecropping, Hamilton expands our sense of the Black South, of the types of labor that Black people engaged in, and of the myriad cultures they produced. Northern Florida is dense and swampy, pop-ulated by a variety of bird and plant species, and reptiles—snakes and alligators. In this way, it may remind viewers of Louisiana, but it is unique even from that better-known space. Hamilton brings this landscape into the realm of the aesthetic, allowing it to give birth to her imaginings and in so doing making it a mythopoetic space, much like Jean Toomer did for the red earth and pine forests of rural Geor-gia in *Cane*, his genre-bending novel of 1923.

Although she is in dialogue with these literary forms, Allison is primarily a visual artist, and in her work, she also engages and builds upon the work of others, like filmmakers Julie Dash's *Daughters of the Dust* and Kasi Lemmons's *Eve's Bayou*. Both filmmakers showed us the deep, magical beauty of very specific locations in the South (the Sea Islands and the Louisiana bayou), and especially of the Black women who inhabit it, while also showing the limits of realism and linear narratives. For Dash, Lemmons, and Hamilton, the land is as much a part of the culture as is the food, the music, the spiritual tra-ditions that it gives birth to. Hamilton goes even further than they. She gives us a story, a deeply immersive one, with characters and narrative threads, but one must work to find and follow them; one cannot be a passive viewer. The more engaged we become, the more the work yields to us over time. Here, she also notes the influence of the highly popular *Game of Thrones*. In this way, each exhibition is almost episodic, building upon the last, taking us deeper in the forest and in the psyches of those illusive, sometimes masked figures who dance, walk, canoe, or ride on horseback. We view a canopy of trees, but we also encounter their actual trunks, smell the scent, and make note of the groomed horse tails that hang on the wall like a series of carefully curated whips. She invites us to participate in the magic-making, to join her in the act of creating.

Walking through an installation, or accompanying her downriver on a kayak, as the films allow you to do, one engages in an act of surveying. We may not know what has come before, but we have happened upon a landscape after disaster. There is the quiet that is disquieted. There is the stillness that is haunted. A fallen tree suggests something traumatic has occurred: a storm, or worse. These are ancestral grounds; one feels their presence, evoked by the ethereal figures who appear and then disappear as we wander past a still photograph, or as a filmed figure gallops by. Sometimes, we stumble upon the unknown, that for which we have no name, like the pink creatures (2018), flowing and folded ochre blobs, with tufts of horses' hair and pearl-adorned crowns. They are new life forms that could have emerged from the ocean's bottom or grown from the earth like fungi. Or the creatures, animal heads that seem to emerge from (rather than mounted upon) walls, familiar yet like no animal we have ever seen. We bear witness to a new era of evolution.

In this work, Hamilton sets us in the day after the end of the world, reminding us that all new worlds sit atop the ruins of old ones. And she offers us an invitation to join her as she builds it anew, ever mindful of the history that precedes us, ever open to the possibility that awaits our making.

ACKNOWLEDGMENTS

My deepest gratitude:

To Daphne Brooks, Salamishah Tillet, and Barbara Savage for encouraging me to gather and publish a collection of my essays. Although I'd always wanted to do so, this book would not exist without your encouragement. I am forever grateful to you for believing in the value of my work. Even more, I am grateful to you for decades of friendship and sisterhood.

To Michael Eric Dyson for the example of your own collections of essays, and for your consistency, support, and love. Thank you for being such a generous brother to me for all these years.

To Tanya McKinnon for saying yes, and for making sure the collection would see the light of day.

To Alexis Johnson for tracking down, printing out, and gathering dozens of essays in a big, annotated binder. As my first research assistant on this project, you set the bar high. All along, you were also writing your own beautiful and brilliant poetry. That you took the time, in the midst of your creative pursuits, to attend to this work with such care and attention is especially meaningful to me.

To Elleza Kelley for working tirelessly to figure out a system for tracking down permissions.

To Narcisa Núñez for picking up where Elleza left off by diligently seeking, following up, and ultimately acquiring permissions for both this book and my previous one. You saved the day on more than one occasion. (Both of you are at the very start of extraordinary careers as writers and thinkers; it's been an honor to have your intelligence and joyful presence involved in this project.)

To three wonderful writers, Beverly Gologorsky, Jane Lazarre-White, and Jan Clausen for reading some of these pieces at various stages in their development and offering your wise advice at crucial stages of my writing and thinking.

To the team at W. W. Norton: My editor, Amy Cherry for your patience and invaluable suggestions along the way; Huneeya Siddiqui for keeping everything on track; Rebecca Munro for managing the process; and Ashley Patrick, who practices copyediting as an art—the writing is better for your skill, intelligence, and careful eye.

To Shawn Mendoza and Sharon Harris at Columbia University for supporting me in ways too numerous to count. You make it all possible.

To the Andrew W. Mellon Foundation and the John Simon Guggenheim Memorial Foundation for the support that provided me the time to revisit and revise many of these essays, and to write a number of new ones as well.

To my family, especially my mother Wilhelmena Griffin, and my cousins Leon Carson and Irvin Carson.

And, as always, to Obery for listening, reading, and helping me make a way in this crazy world with joy and purpose. My love and admiration for you know no bounds.

NOTES

LADIES SING MILES

1. Miles Davis with Quincy Troupe, *Miles: The Autobiography* (New York: Simon and Schuster, 1989), 29.
2. Quincy Troupe, *Miles and Me* (Berkeley: University of California Press, 2000), 3.
3. Pearl Cleage, "Mad at Miles," in *Deals with the Devil, and Other Reasons to Riot* (New York: Ballantine, 1993), 40–41.
4. Salim Washington, conversation with author, July 8, 2000.
5. Hazel Carby, *Race Men* (Cambridge, MA: Harvard University Press, 1998), 144, 155–56.
6. *Miles: The Autobiography*, 55.
7. Cassandra Wilson in Bob Spitz, "The Hottest Voice in Music," *Sky Magazine*, September 1998.

WHEN MALINDY SINGS

I am grateful to Brent Edwards, Michael Awkward, Daphne Brooks, Barbara Savage, W. S. Tkwcmc, Vijay Iyer, Krin Gabbard, and Salim Washington for reading and/or commenting upon earlier versions of this essay. I also wish to thank members of the Jazz Study Group of the Center for Jazz Studies, Columbia University.

1. This listing is iconic and not empirical. In other words, I have not done an empirical investigation of how many times Black women have sung at all moments of national crisis, but, instead, I am interested in moments that stand out in the national memory.
2. See Barrett, *Blackness and Value*, 76.
3. See Maultsby, "West African Influence and Retentions in U.S. Black Music" and "Africanisms in African-American Music"; Southern, *The Music of Black Americans*; Stuckey, *Slave Culture*.
4. In *Black Power*, Richard Wright writes of his disappointment in a Ghanaian church choir because they don't sound like African American singers. He cites Dunbar's poem to describe the kind of singing he prefers:

I'd much rather have heard the kind of singing that Paul Laurence Dunbar described in his poem: "When Malindy Sings": "She just opens her mouth and hollers, / 'Come to Jesus,' 'til you hear / Sinners' trembling steps and voices / Timidlike a-drawing near; / Then she turns to 'Rock of Ages,' / Simply to the Cross she clings, / And you find your tears a-dropping / When Malindy sings." But that Gold Coast hymn evoked in me merely a cough of embarrassment behind my cupped palms (148).

> Richard Wright, *Black Power: A Record of Reactions in a Land of Pathos* (New York: Harper Perennial, 1995).

5. Story, *And So I Sing*, 186. According to Story, "Black singers (but not all them) have been said to possess inordinate ranges and indescribably warm, dark sound." She notes, "In the high voices the lower end of the Black voice is deeper, richer, more voluptuously shaped than that of many white singers." Joan Sutherland feels that Black singers have "beautifully rich, mellifluous and warm sound . . . with great sympathy, a loving sound." Story interviewed Barbara Moore, chair of the voice department at Dallas Southern University, who explained that the Black singing voice is actually the result of speech patterns and culture. According to Moore, most of her Black "students grew up listening to and emulating the decidedly low-voiced inflection of gospel singing and rhythm and blues." For Moore the "dark quality may be an extension of the speaking voice." Consequently, she says her Black students are much less likely than the white ones to explore the top range of their voices. This may be the case, although it doesn't explain the clarity of coloratura soprano Kathleen Battle.

6. Roland Barthes, "The Grain of the Voice" in Barthes, *Responsibility of Forms.*

7. See Mackey, "Other"; LeRoi Jones, *Blues People: Negro Music in White America* (New York: Morrow, 1963); Zora Neale Hurston, *The Sanctified Church* (Berkeley, CA: Turtle Island, 1981); Brent Edwards, "The Seemingly Eclipsed Window of Form: James Weldon Johnson's Prefaces," in *The Jazz Cadence of American Culture*, ed. Robert G. O'Meally (New York: Columbia University Press, 1998); Robert O'Meally, *The Jazz Singers: A Smithsonian Collection of Jazz Vocals from 1919-1994*, booklet accompanying compact disc box set (Washington, DC: Smithsonian Institution, 1998).

8. Quoted in Mackey, "Other," 269.

9. Ibid. Mackey also quotes Henry Spaulding, who wrote in 1863, "The most striking of their barbaric airs would be impossible to write out." See also Stuckey, *Slave Culture*, 81–83.

10. Mackey, "Other," 269.

11. Nathaniel Mackey identifies Black singing as part of a larger universe of Black linguistic practices "that accent variance [and] variability." He calls these practices "othering practices" that "implicitly react against and reflect critically upon the different sort of othering to which their practitioners, denied agency in a society by which they are designated other, have been subjected." See Mackey, "Cante Moro."

12. See Story, *And So I Sing.* Story contends that "Blackness as a description of the voice is not necessarily racial . . . it is a quality of vocal darkness, found in the sound of the Russian Feodor Chaliapin and the Italian Ezio Pinza. But a case is made for the particularly identifiable sound of certain geographic regions. . . . The Italianate, the Welsh, and the Slavic sounds all are determined by what the individual culture, through language and ethnic tradition, determines is beautiful" (187).

13. Ellison, "As the Spirit Moves Mahalia," *Saturday Review,* September 27, 1958, 43.

14. Maultsby, "Africanisms in African-American Music," 92.

15. I am reminded here of the voices of Patti LaBelle, Nona Hendryx, and Sarah Dash on "You Turn Me On": three women's voices, overlapping, all-powerful, bursting outside of language. It recalls Michael Poizat's rendering of the opera diva's voice as one where "the body's libidinal drives emerge in sound unmediated by language, producing a sensation of radical loss, whereby castration, difference and subjectivity are annulled." Dunn and Jones, in *Embodied Voices,* write that this "experience of loss threatens the stability of the patriarchal order" (9).

16. Wilson, preface to *Three Plays.*

17. So, this is not about jazz per se except to the extent that there are some streams of jazz that are related to forms of artistic and intellectual production that find their inspiration in African American expressive culture. Let me say that while I do not have time to focus on them here, I might also include George Gershwin on the Sea Islands or Frederick Delius at the St. John's River in Florida, who is said to have heard Black plantation workers singing at night and described that moment as "a truly wonderful sense of musicianship and harmonic resource in the instinctive way in which they treated a melody and hearing their singing in such romantic surroundings it was then that I first felt the urge to express myself in music" (Jack Sullivan, 19).

18. Sam Floyd writes:

> The impetus, tone and emotional quality of the blues may have come from Senegambia. Michael Coolen (1991, 3) has shown, for example, that Senegambians suffered inordinately from the slave trade, due to their convenient proximity to the Senegal and Gambia rivers, on which "slave factories" were located and where ships arrived to pick up human cargo. The consequent large concentration of Senegambian slaves in America . . . is the reason for the structural and tonal similarities between the blues and the Senegambian fodet, which (1) uses cyclical form, with phrases played or sung to an "alternated use of tonic and secondary tonal centers," (2) commonly has AAB text structure, (3) makes use of a vocal practice in which the song begins on a high pitch and "gradually moves to lower pitches at the end," and (4) contains a low level of virtuosity with the option of a "hot" performance always available (16). This description, obviously, could be applied as accurately to the blues. (*The Power of Black Music,* 75)

See also "From Mali to Mamie: The History of the Blues," part 1, *Southern Cross the Dog* (Winter 2003): 13–16. "Because of its proximity to Spain and Portugal, the chief slave-trading countries, most of the first slaves necessarily came from this region on the West Coast of Africa. This is the locus of the griot tradition and the strongest strain in the American Blues Tradition, with an emphasis on solo vocals. . . . Stringed instruments—predecessors to the banjo and the guitar—dominate the instrumentation, as does a distinct middle Eastern influence (again a matter of geography) that results in long droning melody lines" (14).

19. Attali, *Noise*, 14.
20. Barrett convincingly argues that for Black Americans, the singing voice "provides a primary means by which African Americans may exchange an expended, valueless self in the New World for a productive recognized self. It provides one important means of formalizing and celebrating an existence otherwise proposed as negative and negligible." (*Blackness and Value*, 57)
21. Here, I am speaking metaphorically. I am not comparing the sound of White's voice to the "sound" of a butterfly.

Works Cited

Attali, Jacques. *Noise: The Political Economy of Music*. Minneapolis: University of Minnesota Press, 1985.

Barrett, Lindon. *Blackness and Value: Seeing Double*. Cambridge, MA: Cambridge University Press, 1999.

Barthes, Roland. *Responsibility of Forms: Critical Essays on Music, Art and Representation*. New York: Hill & Wang, 1984.

Crowther, Bruce, and Mike Pinfold. *The Jazz Singers: From Ragtime to New Wave*. New York: Blandford Press, 1986.

Davis, Miles, with Quincy Troupe. *Miles: The Autobiography*. New York: Simon and Schuster, 1990.

Dunn, Leslie C., and Nancy A. Jones, eds. *Embodied Voices: Representing Female Vocality in Western Culture*. Cambridge, MA: Cambridge University Press, 1994.

Ellison, Ralph. "As the Spirit Moves Mahalia." In *Shadow and Act*. New York: Random House, 1965.

Floyd, Samuel. *The Power of Black Music: Interpreting Its History from Africa to the United States*. New York: Oxford University Press, 1995.

Holloway, Karla F. C. "The Lyrical Dimensions of Spirituality: Music, Voice, and Language in the Novels of Toni Morrison." In *Embodied Voices: Representing Female Vocality in Western Culture*, edited by Leslie C. Dunn and Nancy A. Jones. Cambridge, MA: Cambridge University Press, 1994.

Kerman, Cynthia Earl. *The Lives of Jean Toomer: A Hunger for Wholeness*. Baton Rouge: Louisiana State University Press, 1987.

Mackey, Nathaniel. "Other: From Noun to Verb." *Discrepant Engagement: Dissonance, Cross-Culturality, and Experimental Writing*. Cambridge, MA: Cambridge University Press, 1993.

――――. "Cante Moro." In *Sound States: Innovative Poetics and Acoustical Technologies*, edited by Adalaide Morris, 194–212. Chapel Hill and London: University of North Carolina Press.

Maultsby, Portia K. "Africanisms in African-American Music." In *Africanisms in American Culture*, edited by Joseph E. Holloway. Bloomington: Indiana University Press, 1990.

――――. "West African Influence and Retentions in U.S. Black Music: A Sociocultural Study." In *More Than Dancing: Essays on Afro-American Music and Musicians*, edited by Irene V. Jackson. Westport, CT: Greenwood, 1985.

Morrison, Toni. *Beloved: A Novel*. New York: New American Library, 1988 [1987].

Reagon, Bernice Johnson, and Sweet Honey in the Rock. *We Who Believe in Freedom: Sweet Honey in the Rock . . . Still on the Journey*. New York: Anchor Books, 1993.

Southern, Eileen. *The Music of Black Americans: A History*. New York: W. W. Norton, 1971.

Story, Rosalyn M. *And So I Sing: African-American Divas of Opera and Concert*. New York: Amistad Press, 1990.

Stuckey, Sterling. *Slave Culture: Nationalist Theory and the Foundations of Black America*. New York: Oxford University Press, 1987.

Sullivan, Jack. *New World Symphonies: How American Culture Changed European Music*. New Haven, CT: Yale University Press, 1999.

Tolbert, Elizabeth. "The Voice of Lament: Female Vocality and Performative Efficacy in the Finnish-Karelian itkuvirsi." In *Embodied Voices: Representing Female Vocality in Western Culture*, edited by Leslie C. Dunn and Nancy A. Jones. Cambridge, MA: Cambridge University Press, 1994.

Toomer, Jean. *Cane*. New York: Liveright, 1975 [1923].

Troupe, Quincy. *Miles and Me*. Berkeley: University of California Press, 2000.

Wilson, August. Preface to *Three Plays*. In *The Jazz Cadence of American Culture*, edited by Robert G. O'Meally. New York: Columbia University Press, 1998.

Discography

Barnwell, Ysaye M. *Singing in the African American Tradition: Choral and Congregational Vocal Music*. Homespun Tapes LTD (Cassette), 1989.

Ellington, Duke, and Mahalia Jackson. *Black, Brown, and Beige*. Sony; ASIN: BO1AY192VC (CD), 1999 [1958].

LaBelle. *Nightbirds*. Sony BOOU100AS2 (CD), 1995 [1974].

Myers, Amina Claudine. *Amina Claudine Myers Salutes Bessie Smith*. Leo Records BOOOO281VN (CD), 1996.

Simone, Nina. *Nina Simone Sings Nina*. Polygram Records 314 529 867-2 (CD), 1996.

Wilson, Cassandra. *Traveling Miles*, Blue Note D128340 (CD), 1999.

SONGS OF EXPERIENCE

1. LaShonda Barnett, *I Got Thunder: Black Women Songwriters on Their Craft* (New York: Thunder's Mouth Press, 2007).

QUIET, STILLNESS, AND LONGING TO BE FREE

1. Guthrie P. Ramsey Jr., *Race Music: Black Popular Music from Bebop to Hip-Hop* (Berkeley: University of California Press, 2004), 217.

2. A Martínez, "Half a Century Ago, Stevie Wonder Defined What an 'Artist's Classic Run' Could Mean," NPR, March 20, 2022, npr.org/2022/03/02/1083730542.

3. The clavinet is an electrically amplified clavichord that was manufactured by the Hohner company of Trossingen, West Germany, from 1964 to the early 1980s. The clavichord is a European stringed keyboard instrument known from the late medieval through the Renaissance, baroque, and classical eras. Historically, it was mostly used as a practice instrument and as an aid to composition, not being loud enough for larger performances. The clavichord produces sound by striking brass or iron strings with small metal blades called *tangents*. Vibrations are transmitted through the bridge(s) to the soundboard. "Clavichord Technique and Performance Practice: An Annotated Bibliography," Robert Kelley, December 1998, http://www.robertkelleyphd.com/clavichd.htm.

4. I am grateful to Guthrie Ramsey for calling this to my attention.

5. Mark Anthony Neal, *Black Ephemera: The Crisis and Challenge of the Musical Archive* (New York: New York University Press, 2022), 59.

6. "Minnie Riperton: *Perfect Angel*," https://www.discogs.com/release/898314-Minnie-Riperton-Perfect-Angel?ev=item-vc.

7. *UnSung*, season 2, episode 1, "Minnie Riperton," TV One, aired June 7, 2009.

8. Heikki Suosalo, "Deniece Williams," *Soul Express Online,* n.d., https://www.soulexpress.net/deniecewilliams.htm.

9. "The highest voice is coloratura. Their tessitura (where they sing most easily and beautifully) is from B above middle C and up the scale to G above high C. Their working range goes from E above middle C to A above high C. Lyric soprano tessitura is from A above middle C to F above high C. Working range is from D above middle C to G above high C. Dramatic soprano, mezzo soprano, and contralto are the lowest of the treble voices." From *The Voice of Singing* by Esther Andreas and Robert M. Fowells, Carl Fisher, 1970, in http://www.wikihow.com/Characterize-Your-Vocal-Range.

10. My sense of ethereal soul is informed by but distinct from the ethereal soul of Daoism in that I am specifically referencing a Black popular music genre that builds upon gospel, R & B, and jazz.

11. Barbara Christian, "Contemporary Period," in *Norton Anthology of African American Literature*, ed. Henry Louis Gates Jr. (W. W. Norton, 1996), 2011.

12. Kevin Quashie, *The Sovereignty of Quiet: Beyond Resistance in Black Culture* (Rutgers University Press, 2012), 74.

13. Jason King, "Maurice White: The Audacity of Uplift," *The Record: Music News From NPR,* February 5, 2016, https://www.npr.org/sections/therecord/2016/02/05/465703176/maurice-white-the-audacity-of-uplift.

FOLLOWING GERI'S LEAD

1. "In Celebration of William Levi Dawson: An Exploration of American Music and Identity at the Dawn of the Twenty-First Century," conference at Emory University, Atlanta, Georgia, March 3–5, 2005.
2. Farah Griffin, *If You Can't Be Free, Be a Mystery: In Search of Billie Holiday* (New York: One World Books, 2001).
3. "Invocation," *Merriam-Webster* online, https://www.merriam-webster.com/dictionary/invocation.
4. Geri Allen, "Oh Freedom," *Timeless Portraits and Dreams*, liner notes, Telarc, 2006.
5. *Melchizedek: Melch = King; Saddiq = Righteousness.*
6. Imani Perry, *May We Forever Stand: A History of the Black National Anthem* (Chapel Hill: The University of North Carolina Press, 2018), xiv.
7. Angelika Beener, "Geri Allen on First Christmas Album & Embracing It All," *Alternate Takes: Broadening the Jazz Perspective*, November 22, 2011, https://alternate-takes.org/2011/11/22/geri-allen-on-first-christmas-album-embracing-it-all/.
8. Geri Allen, "Flying Toward the Sound," *Flying Toward the Sound*, Motéma Music, 2010.

WRESTLING TILL DAWN

1. Jean Toomer, *Cane* (New York: Harper & Row, 1923; repr., New York: W. W. Norton, 2011), 3. Citations refer to the 2011 edition.
2. Toni Morrison, *Sula* (New York: Knopf, 1973), 174.
3. Ntozake Shange, *for colored girls who have considered suicide/when the rainbow is enuf* (New York: Charles Scribner, 1977), 63.
4. Toni Morrison, *Beloved* (New York: Knopf, 1987), 80.
5. Morrison, *Sula*, 3.
6. Morrison, *Sula*, 3.
7. Morrison, *Sula*, 22.
8. Toni Morrison, *The Bluest Eye* (New York: Knopf, 1970 and 1994; repr. New York: Holt, Rinehart and Winston, 1993), 82.
9. Morrison, *Beloved*, 321.
10. Toni Morrison, *A Mercy* (New York: Vintage International, 2009), 4.
11. Morrison, *A Mercy*, 83.

MINNIE'S SACRIFICE

1. Frances Smith Foster, *Written by Herself: Literary Production by African American Women, 1746–1892* (Bloomington: Indiana University Press, 1993).
2. Claudia Tate, *Domestic Allegories of Political Desire: The Black Heroine's Text at the Turn of the Century* (New York and Oxford: Oxford University Press) 1993.
3. Elizabeth J. West, "Black Nationalism" in *Oxford Companion to African American Literature* (New York and Oxford: Oxford University Press, 1996) 76.
4. Frances Smith Foster, ed, *A Brighter Coming Day: A Frances Ellen Watkins Harper Reader* (New York: Feminist Press, 1990) 124.
5. Eric Foner, *A Short History of Reconstruction* (New York: Harper and Row, 1990) 95.

6. Carla Peterson, *Doers of the Word: African American Women Speakers and Writers in the North (1830–1880)* (New York: Oxford University Press, 1995) 212.
7. Foner, *Short History of Reconstruction*, 106–7.
8. Foner, *Short History of Reconstruction*, 108.
9. Foner, *Short History of Reconstruction*, 86.
10. Foner, *Short History of Reconstruction*, 86.
11. Foner, *Short History of Reconstruction*, 110.
12. Foner, *Short History of Reconstruction*, 112–13.
13. Foner, *Short History of Reconstruction*, 86.
14. Foster, *A Brighter Coming Day*, 123.
15. Frances Ellen Watkins Harper, *Minnie's Sacrifice, Sowing and Reaping, Trial and Triumph*, ed. Frances Foster (Boston, MA: Beacon Press, 1994) 87–88.
16. Harper, *Minnie's Sacrifice*, 90.
17. Harper, *Minnie's Sacrifice*, 91.
18. Peterson, *Doers of the Word*, 198.

Works Cited

Berlant, Lauren. "The Queen of America Goes to Washington City: Harriet Jacobs, Frances Harper, Anita Hill." *American Literature* 65, no. 3 (September 1993): 549–74.

Boyd, Melba Joyce. *Discarded Legacy: Politics and Poetics in the Life of Frances E. W. Harper.* Detroit: Wayne State University Press, 1994.

Carby, Hazel. *Reconstructing Womanhood: The Emergence of the Black Woman Novelist.* New York and Oxford: Oxford University Press, 1987.

Foner, Eric. *A Short History of Reconstruction.* New York: Harper and Row, 1990.

Forbes, Ella. *African-American Women during the Civil War.* New York: Garland, 1998.

Foster, Frances Smith. *Written by Herself: Literary Production by African American Women, 1746–1892.* Bloomington: Indiana University Press, 1993.

Foster, Frances Smith, ed. *A Brighter Coming Day: A Frances Ellen Watkins Harper Reader.* New York: Feminist Press, 1990.

Griffin, Farah Jasmine. "Frances Harper in the Reconstruction South." *SAGE: A Scholarly Journal on Black Women* (1988): 45–47.

Harper, Frances Ellen Watkins. *Minnie's Sacrifice, Sowing and Reaping, Trial and Triumph.* Edited by Frances Foster. Boston, MA: Beacon Press, 1994.

Peterson, Carla. *"Doers of the Word": African-American Speakers and Writers in the North (1830–1880).* New York: Oxford University Press, 1995.

Tate, Claudia. *Domestic Allegories of Political Desire: The Black Heroine's Text at the Turn of the Century.* New York and Oxford: Oxford University Press, 1993.

West, Elizabeth J. "Black Nationalism." *Oxford Companion to African American Literature.* New York and Oxford: Oxford University Press, 1996.

ZORA NEALE HURSTON'S RADICAL INDIVIDUALISM

1. Valerie Boyd, *Wrapped in Rainbows: The Life of Zora Neale Hurston* (New York: Scribner, 2003), 35.

2. John Carlos Rowe, *Literary Culture and U.S. Imperialism: From the Revolution to World War II* (New York: Oxford University Press, 2000), 283.

3. Zora Neale Hurston, "Characteristics of Negro Expression," in *Hurston: Folklore, Memoirs, and Other Writings* (New York: Library of America, 1995), 838. Originally published in *Negro: An Anthology*, ed. Nancy Cunard (1934; repr., Bloomsbury, 1996).

4. Zora Neale Hurston, "Spirituals and Neo-Spirituals," in *Hurston: Folklore, Memoirs, and Other Writings*, 870.

5. Removing whites from the center of the narrative does not have to eschew this reality. Toni Morrison's novels are a case in point. Whites do not figure prominently in the majority of Morrison's texts, yet in these novels, the power of racism to shape the lives of Black characters is quite clear.

6. Zora Neale Hurston, *Their Eyes Were Watching God* (New York: Harper Perennial, 2006), 140.

7. Hurston, *Their Eyes*, 140.

8. Hurston, *Their Eyes*, 141.

9. Hurston, *Their Eyes*, 145.

10. Hurston quoted in Boyd, *Wrapped in Rainbows*, 109.

11. *Zora Neale Hurston: A Life in Letters*, ed. Carla Kaplan (New York: Doubleday, 2002), 442.

12. *Zora Neale Hurston: A Life in Letters*, 374.

13. Eric Foner, "How Radical Change Occurs: An Interview with Historian Eric Foner," by Mike Konczal, *Nation*, February 3, 2015, www.thenation.com/article/how -radical-change-occurs-interview-historian-eric-foner/.

14. Zora Neale Hurston, *Moses, Man of the Mountain* (New York: Harper Perennial, 1990), 75, 268.

15. Hurston, *Moses, Man of the Mountain*, 282.

16. Ernest Julius Mitchell II, "Zora's Politics: A Brief Introduction," *Journal of Transnational American Studies* 5, no. 1 (September 2013): 2. Some of the areas (Hawaii, the Philippines, Samoa) listed in this quotation from Mitchell were indeed United States territories at the time Hurston's book was published. Although the United States government did not officially refer to the Philippines, Hawaii, Guam, Puerto Rico, the Virgin Islands, or Samoa as colonies, the relationship of these territories to the United States is indeed a colonial one. See Daniel Immerwahr, *How to Hide an Empire: A History of the Greater United States* (New York: Farrar, Straus and Giroux, 2019).

17. Zora Neale Hurston, *Tell My Horse: Voodoo and Life in Haiti and Jamaica* (New York: Harper & Row, 1990), 57.

18. Hurston, *Tell My Horse*, 6.

19. Hurston, *Tell My Horse*, 7.

20. Hurston, *Tell My Horse*, 7.

21. Hurston, *Tell My Horse*, 72.

22. Mitchell argues that Hurston "emphasizes her disdain for the occupation with total

silence." Furthermore, he takes the position that when she does speak or write about marines in her correspondence, she is overwhelmingly negative. This is an especially generous reading of Hurston's stance on the occupation.

23. All references to this chapter refer to the version in the Library of America volume: *Hurston: Folklore, Memoirs and Other Writings.*

24. *Hurston: Folklore, Memoirs and Other Writings,* 782.

25. *Hurston: Folklore, Memoirs and Other Writings,* 783.

26. *Hurston: Folklore, Memoirs and Other Writings,* 783.

27. *Hurston: Folklore, Memoirs and Other Writings,* 784.

28. *Hurston: Folklore, Memoirs and Other Writings,* 785.

29. *Hurston: Folklore, Memoirs and Other Writings,* 794.

30. *Hurston: Folklore, Memoirs and Other Writings,* 794.

31. *Hurston: Folklore, Memoirs and Other Writings,* 787.

32. *Hurston: Folklore, Memoirs and Other Writings,* 790.

33. *Hurston: Folklore, Memoirs and Other Writings,* 791.

34. *Hurston: Folklore, Memoirs and Other Writings,* 793.

35. *Hurston: Folklore, Memoirs and Other Writings,* 793–94.

36. Zora Neale Hurston, "Why the Negro Won't Buy Communism" (1951), repr. *Journal of American Studies* 5, no. 1 (2013).

37. References refer to Library of America volume version of this essay: *Hurston: Folklore, Memoirs and Other Writings.*

38. *Hurston: Folklore, Memoirs and Other Writings,* 946.

39. *Hurston: Folklore, Memoirs and Other Writings,* 947.

40. Zora Neale Hurston, "I Saw Negro Votes Peddled," *Journal of Transnational Studies* 5, no.1 (2013): 3.

41. Hurston, "I Saw Negro Votes Peddled," 5.

42. Hurston, "I Saw Negro Votes Peddled," 6.

43. Hurston, "Why the Negro Won't Buy Communism," 4.

44. Hurston, "Why the Negro Won't Buy Communism," 4.

45. Hurston, "Why the Negro Won't Buy Communism," 5.

46. Hurston, "Why the Negro Won't Buy Communism," 6.

47. Hurston, "Why the Negro Won't Buy Communism," 7.

48. Hurston, "Why the Negro Won't Buy Communism," 10.

49. Hurston to Katherine Tracy L'Engle, October 24, 1945, and Hurston to Langston Hughes, May 31, 1929, in *Zora Neale Hurston: A Life in Letters,* 17.

50. "Court Order Can't Make Races Mix," in *Hurston: Folklore, Memoirs, and Other Writings.*

51. "Court Order Can't Make Races Mix," 957.

52. "Court Order Can't Make Races Mix," 957.

HUNTING COMMUNISTS AND NEGROES IN ANN PETRY'S *THE NARROWS*

1. A few critics have long been devoted to Petry's corpus. These include Hazel Erving, whose tireless efforts have brought us comprehensive bibliographies, biographical

information, and collections of critical essays, as well as Diane Isaacs and Heather Hicks.

2. Hazel Carby argues that "In the search for a tradition of black women writers of fiction, a pattern has been established from Alice Walker back through Zora Neal Hurston, which represents the rural folk as bearers of Afro-American history and preservers of Afro-American culture. This construction of a tradition of black women's writing has effectively marginalized the fictional urban confrontation of race, class and sexuality that was to follow *Quicksand*. Ann Petry's *The Street* (1946); Dorothy West's *The Living Is Easy* (1948); Gwendolyn Brooks's *Maud Martha*." See, Carby, *Reconstructing Womanhood: The Emergence of the Afro-American Woman Novelist* (New York: Oxford University Press, 1987).

3. Mary Helen Washington, "Alice Childress, Lorraine Hansberry, and Claudia Jones: Black Women Write the Popular Front." In *Left of the Color Line: Race, Radicalism, and Twentieth-Century Literature of the United States*, edited by Bill V. Mullen and James Smethurst (Chapel Hill: University of North Carolina Press, 2003) 204.

4. Washington, "Alice Childress, Lorraine Hansberry, and Claudia Jones," 185.

5. Ann Petry, *The Narrows* (Boston: Houghton Mifflin, 1953) 202.

6. Petry, *The Narrows*, 142.

7. See Bill Mullen, *Popular Fronts: Chicago and African American Cultural Politics, 1935–1945* (University of Illinois Press); Washington, "Alice Childress, Lorraine Hansberry, and Claudia Jones," 183–205.

8. Ann Petry, "The Novel as Social Criticism." In *The Writers Book*, edited by Helen Hill (New York: Harper Brothers, 1960), 33.

9. Petry, "The Novel as Social Criticism," 33.

10. Petry, "The Novel as Social Criticism," 33.

11. Petry, "The Novel as Social Criticism," 36.

12. Petry, "The Novel as Social Criticism," 36.

13. Washington, "Alice Childress, Lorraine Hansberry, and Claudia Jones," 184.

14. Quoted in Gerald Horne, *Race Woman: The Lives of Shirley Graham Du Bois* (New York: New York University Press, 2002) 105. Ann Petry to Shirley Graham, July 15, 1946, Shirley Graham Du Bois Papers, Schlesinger Library, Harvard University.

15. Petry, *The Narrows*, 138.

16. Petry, *The Narrows*, 144.

17. Petry, *The Narrows*, 145.

18. Petry, *The Narrows*, 265–66.

19. Petry, *The Narrows*, 365.

20. Petry, "The Novel as Social Criticism," 33.

21. Petry, *The Narrows*, 49.

22. Petry, *The Narrows*, 378.

23. Petry, *The Narrows*, 352–53.

24. Petry, *The Narrows*, 385.

25. Petry, *The Narrows*, 386.

26. Petry, *The Narrows*, 378.

"IT TAKES TWO PEOPLE TO CONFIRM THE TRUTH"

1. The New Music, also called free jazz, avant-garde jazz, or the New Thing, refers to the music first produced by Coltrane, Ornette Coleman, Cecil Taylor, and Albert Ayler, in the 1960s.

2. Gayl Jones, *Corregidora* (New York: Random House, 1975); Toni Morrison, *Jazz* (New York: Knopf, 1992).

3. Sascha Feinstein, *Jazz Poetry: From the 1920s to the Present* (Westport, CT: Praeger, 1997), 2.

4. While Shange's poetry is included in studies or anthologies of jazz poetry, her novel *Sassafrass, Cypress & Indigo* (New York: Picador, 1996) also prominently features the music and musicians. The same is true of her play *for colored girls who have considered suicide/when the rainbow is enuf* (New York: Scribner, 1997).

5. While I have been able to find no reference to Sherley Anne Williams's "Tell Martha Not to Moan," Toni Cade Bambara's "Medley" appears in at least two bibliographies: Marcela Breton, "An Annotated Bibliography of Selected Jazz Short Stories," *African American Review* 26, no. 2 (summer 1992): 299–306; and Richard N. Albert, *An Annotated Bibliography of Jazz Fiction and Jazz Fiction Criticism* (Westport, CT: Greenwood, 1996).

6. Marcela Breton, *Hot and Cool: Jazz Short Stories* (New York: Plume, 1990). The story does not appear in Richard Albert's *From Blues to Bop: A Collection of Jazz Fiction* (New York: Anchor, 1992) or David Meltzer's *Reading Jazz* (San Francisco: Mercury House, 1993).

7. Nathaniel Mackey, *The Bedouin Hornbook* (College Park, MD: Sun and Moon Press, 2000); Allen 2005. Maya Angelou's "The Reunion" has received little critical attention. The story focuses on Philomena Jenkins, a pianist. Published in Amina Baraka and Amiri Baraka, *Confirmation: An Anthology of African American Women* (New York: Morrow, 1983).

8. Jon Panish, *The Color of Jazz: Race and Representation in Postwar American Culture* (Jackson, MS: University Press of Mississippi, 1997), ix.

9. Sherrie Tucker "'Where the Blues and the Truth Lay Hiding': Rememory of Jazz in Black Women's Fiction." *Frontiers: A Journal of Women Studies* 13, no. 2 (1992): 26–44.

10. Abbey Lincoln, "To Whom Will She Cry Rape?," in Toni Cade Bambara, ed., *The Black Woman: An Anthology* (New York: Washington Square, repr. 2005), 95. (Originally published as "Who Will Revere the Black Woman?" in the first edition of the anthology [1970]).

11. All citations for "Tell Martha Not to Moan" are from Bambara 2005.

12. Toni Morrison, *Song of Solomon* (New York: Knopf, 1977), 328.

13. In this list we might also include the critics Deborah McDowell (see her introduction to Nella Larsen's *Quicksand* and *Passing* [New Brunswick, NJ: Rutgers University Press, 1986]); Hazel Carby, "'It Jus Be's Dat Way Sometime': The Sexual Politics of Women's Blues" in *Unequal Sisters: A Multicultural Reader in U.S. Women's History*, 2nd ed., Vicki L. Ruiz and Ellen Carol DuBois, eds. (New York: Routledge,

1994), 330–41; and Angela Davis, *Blues Legacies and Black Feminism: Gertrude "Ma" Rainey, Bessie Smith, and Billie Holiday* (New York: Pantheon, 1998).

14. Toni Cade Bambara, *The Sea Birds Are Still Alive* (New York: Random House, 1977).

15. All quotes from "Medley" are from Toni Cade Bambara, *The Sea Birds Are Still Alive* (New York: Vintage, 1982).

16. Significantly, Tucker's reading of the shower duet focuses on Sweet Pea's musical choices as a jazz canon that "included Black women along with men in [the] history of jazz," 38.

17. "Brown Baby" also became part of Brown's repertoire, and he would sing it throughout his career:

> *"As years go by I want you to go with your head up high*
> *I want you to live by the justice code*
> *And I want you to walk down freedom's road*
> *You little brown baby"*

According to Brown, the DJ who first played "Brown Baby" on the radio was told to remove it from his rotation list; it was removed from the shelves of a number of record stores as well.

18. 4/4 dominates in jazz, but triple meter is in no way rare. Songs such as "All Blues," "Footprints," and "Afro Blue," all standard fare for musicians participating in jam sessions, are all in triple meter. In fact, with the exception of hip-hop, most genres of Black music make use of triple meter. I am grateful to conversations with the musicians/composers/scholars Guthrie Ramsey, George Lewis, and Salim Washington for helping me to clarify this point.

LEARNING HOW TO LISTEN

1. Ntozake Shange, *for colored girls who have considered suicide/when the rainbow is enuf* (New York: Scribner, 2010 [1975]), 27.

2. Shange married David Murray in 1977, the same year he cofounded the World Saxophone Quartet with Oliver Lake, Hamiet Bluiett, and Julius Hemphill.

3. Khary Kimani Turner, "Rainbows for the City," *San Francisco Chronicle*, January 23, 2002.

4. See Val Wilmer, *As Serious as Your Life: The Story of the New Jazz* (London: Allison and Busby, 1977).

5. See Hortense Spillers, *Black, White, and in Color: Essays on American Literature and Culture* (Chicago: University of Chicago Press, 2003), 377.

6. Ntozake Shange, *Sassafrass, Cypress & Indigo: A Novel* (New York: St. Martin's, 1982). Harryette Mullen suggests that Murray is the model for McCullough. See Harryette Romell Mullen, "'Artistic Expression was Flowing Everywhere': Alison Mills and Ntozake Shange, Black Bohemian Feminists in the 1970s," *Meridians: feminism, race, transnationalism* 4, no. 2 (2004): 205–35.

7. Shange, *Sassafrass*.

8. Shange, *Sassafrass*, 33.

9. Shange, *Sassafrass*, 35.

10. Shange, *Sassafrass*, 96.

11. Abbey Lincoln, "Learning How to Listen," *Wholly Earth*, Universal, 1999.

12. Shange *Sassafrass*, 45.

13. Ntozake Shange, "bang on!" *lost in language & sound: or how I found my way to the arts* (New York: St. Martin's, 2011) 75. Originally published as liner notes for Billy Bang, *Bang On*, Just in Time Records, 1997.

14. Jessie Hamlin, "Ntozake Shange Weaves Tapestries of Poetry, Music, Dance in Her Search for Love's Meaning," *San Francisco Chronicle*, February 17, 2006.

15. Maria V. Johnson, "Shange and Her Three Sisters 'Sing a Liberation Song': Variations on the Orphic Theme," in *Black Orpheus: Music in African American Fiction from the Harlem Renaissance to Toni Morrison*, ed. Saadi Simawe (New York: Garland Publishing, 2003) 197.

TEXTUAL HEALING

Numerous people provided comments, suggestions, and advice at various stages of this essay. I wish to thank Elizabeth Alexander, Stephen Best, Michelle Frank, Saidiya Hartman, Harryette Mullen, Paul Rogers, Ines Salazar, students and faculty who heard a much earlier version of this talk at Hampshire College in April 1994, members of the Race and Representations Reading Group at the University of Pennsylvania and the Race and Gender Seminar at the University of Chicago.

1. Elizabeth Donnan, ed, *Documents Illustrative of the History of the Slave Trade to America*, 4 vols. (Washington, DC: Carnegie Institution of Washington, Division of Historical Research, 1932) 28.

2. Benjamin Franklin, "Observations Concerning the Increase of Mankind, 1751," https://founders.archives.gov/documents/Franklin/01-04-02-0080.

3. Cornel West, *Race Matters* (Boston, MA: Beacon Press, 1993) 122.

4. Black artists, cultural critics, and political figures have addressed the impact of white supremacy on Black people's conception of their physical selves. Both Marcus Garvey and Malcolm X read acts like hair straightening and skin bleaching as acts of self-discipline which indicate a desire to "look white." Black nationalist efforts such as these often seek to replace white supremacist standards with an oppositional hierarchy of beauty and femininity that attempts to privilege an "unadulterated" Black beauty. As is the case with the standards they seek to replace, these are also constructed on a fiction that claims to go back to a pure racial past and that ignores the fact that even in Africa, notions of femininity were constructed and gender roles were performances, as well. For more on constructions and performances of femininity in West Africa, see Sylvia Ardyn Boone's *Radiance from the Waters* (New Haven, CT: Yale University Press, 1986). Furthermore, while such standards were often closer to the physical appearance of many African women, they were nonetheless standards that repressed women's sexuality, mobility, and independence. Recently, critics like Kobena Mercer, following Ralph Ellison's lead,

have begun to suggest that Black people are not simply imitating whites but that acts like hair straightening lead to a hybrid aesthetic that is neither "Black" nor "white" but something altogether different.

5. This term is inspired by Marvin Gaye's classic song, "Sexual Healing." I am struck by the popularity of Black women's literature for individual readers, book clubs, and self-help groups. Furthermore, I find it interesting that the literature is often cited and used in epigraphs in books devoted to Black women readers that have little or nothing to do with formal literary study. While these interests are not the focus of this particular essay, they are the driving force behind the theorizing and the readings that follow.

6. I am struck by the popularity of Black women's literature for individual readers, book clubs, and self-help groups. Furthermore, I find it interesting that the literature is often cited and used as epigraphs in books devoted to Black women readers that have little or nothing to do with the formal literary study. While these interests are not the focus of this particular essay, they are the driving force behind the theorizing and the readings that follow.

7. See also Vanzant's *Tapping the Power Within* (222).

8. See, for example, Maya Angelou's *Gather Together in My Name*, Toni Morrison's *Song of Solomon*, Toni Cade Bambara's *The Salt Eaters*, Ntozake Shange's *for colored girls who have considered suicide/when the rainbow is enuf*, and Paule Marshall's *Praisesong for the Widow*.

9. I take this phrase from correspondence with Laura Doyle, March 8, 1995.

10. Such a move parallels Michel Foucault's theoretical move from an exploration of "technologies of power" to "technologies of the self." According to Foucault, technologies of power "determine the conduct of individuals and submit them to certain ends or domination." Technologies of the self "permit individuals to effect by their own means or with the help of others a certain number of operations on their own bodies and souls, thoughts and conduct . . . so as to transform them- selves in order to attain a certain stage of happiness, purity, wisdom, perfection and immortality" (18).

11. They also confront the post-slavery counter-discourse of African Americans, which sought to constitute Black women as "pure" and asexual, for this discourse has also proven to be oppressive as well. It limits any experience of sexuality to that of rape or in the context of heterosexual marriage for the sake of reproduction, and not for the sake of pleasure.

12. The novel *Dessa Rose* is an expansion of the earlier novella *Meditations on History*.

13. This definition is taken from Webster's *New Collegiate Dictionary*, 9th ed. (1983).

14. In *Abeng*, the act of aborting a baby from one's body is an act of resistance that leads to the healing of the Black woman, which leads to further resistance. In contrast, for Dessa Rose, giving birth to a free child and nursing him are acts of agency. This is the case, because Dessa is pregnant with Kaine's child, a child of a loving and affirming sexual relationship.

Works Cited

Angelou, Maya. *Wouldn't Take Nothing for My Journey Now.* New York: Random House, 1993.

Butler, Judith. "Performative Acts and Gender Constitution: An Essay in Phenomenology and Feminist Theory." In *Performing Feminisms: Feminist Critical Theory and Theater,* edited by Sue-Ellen Case. Baltimore, MD: John Hopkins University Press, 1990.

Butler, Judith, and Joan Scott, eds. *Feminists Theorize the Political.* New York: Routledge, 1992.

Cliff, Michelle. *Abeng.* New York: Dutton, 1984.

Donnan, Elizabeth, ed. *Documents Illustrative of the History of the Slave Trade to America.* 4 vols. Washington, DC: Carnegie Institution of Washington. Division of Historical Research, 1932.

Doyle, Laura. *Bordering on the Body: The Racial Matrix of Modern Fiction and Culture.* New York: Oxford University Press, 1994.

Foucault, Michel. *Technologies of the Self: A Seminar with Michel Foucault.* Edited by Luther H. Martin, Huck Gutman, and Patrick H. Hutton. Amherst: University of Massachusetts Press, 1988.

Frederickson, George M. *The Black Image in the White Mind: The Debate on Afro-American Character and Destiny, 1817–1914.* New York: Harper and Row, 1971.

Gilman, Sander. "Black Bodies, White Bodies: Toward an Iconography of Female Sexuality in Late Nineteenth-Century Art, Medicine, and Literature." In *"Race," Writing, and Difference,* edited by Henry Louis Gates Jr. Chicago: The University of Chicago Press, 1985.

Henderson, Mae Gwendolyn. "Toni Morrison's *Beloved*: Re-Membering the Body as Historical Text." In *Comparative American Identities: Race, Sex, and Nationality in the Modern Text,* edited by Hortense Spillers. New York: Routledge, 1991.

hooks, bell. "Dreaming Ourselves Dark and Deep: Black Beauty." *Sisters of the Yam: Black Women and Self-Recovery.* Cambridge: South End Press, 1993.

Hurston, Zora. *Tell My Horse.* In *Zora Neale Hurston: Folklore, Memoirs and Other Writings.* New York: Library of America, 1995.

———. *Their Eyes Were Watching God.* Urbana: University of Illinois Press, 1978.

Jordan, Winthrop. *White Over Black: American Attitudes Toward the Negro, 1550–1812.* Chapel Hill: University of North Carolina Press, 1968.

Lorde, Audre. "Uses of the Erotic: The Erotic as Power." *Sister Outsider.* New York: Crossing Press, 1984.

Merleau-Ponty, Maurice. *The Phenomenology of Perception.* London: Routledge, 1962.

Spillers, Hortense. "Mama's Baby, Papa's Maybe: An American Grammar Book." *Diacritics* (Summer 1987): 65–80.

Taylor, Susan. *In the Spirit.* New York: Harper Perennial, 1993.

Teish, Luisah. *Jambalaya: The Natural Woman's Book of Personal Charms and Practical Rituals.* New York: Harper and Row, 1988.

Vanzant, Iyanla. *Tapping the Power Within: A Path to Self-Empowerment for Black Women.* New York: Harlem River Press, 1992.

Villarosa, Linda, ed. *Body & Soul: The Black Women's Guide to Physical Health and Emo-*

tional Well-Being. With a foreword by Angela Y. Davis and June Jordan. New York: Harper Perennial, 1994.

West, Cornel. *Race Matters*. Boston, MA: Beacon Press, 1993.

White, Deborah Gray. *Arn't I a Woman?: Female Slaves in the Plantation South*. New York: W. W. Norton, 1985.

Williams, Patricia. *The Alchemy of Race and Rights: Diary of a Law Professor*. New York: Harvard University Press, 1991.

Williams, Sherley Anne. *Dessa Rose*. New York: William Morrow, 1986.

———. *Meditations on History*. In *Midnight Birds: Stories of Contemporary Black Women Writers*, edited by Mary Helen Washington. New York: Anchor Books, 1980.

———. "Speaking in Tongues: Dialogics, Dialectics, and the Black Woman Writer's Literary Tradition." In *Changing Our Own Words: Essays on Criticism, Theory and Writing by Black Women*, edited by Cheryl A. Wall. New Brunswick: Rutgers University Press, 1991.

"IRONIES OF THE SAINT"

1. See Barbara Ransby and Tracye Matthews, "Black Popular Culture and the Transcendence of Patriarchal Illusions," in Beverly Guy-Sheftall, ed., *Words of Fire: An Anthology of African American Feminist Thought* (New York: New Press, 1995), 526–35; and Patricia Hill Collins, "Learning to Think for Ourselves: Malcolm X's Black Nationalism Reconsidered," in Joe Wood, ed., *Malcolm X: In Our Own Image* (New York: Anchor Books, 1992), 59–85.

2. Abbey Lincoln, "Who Will Revere the Black Woman?" *Negro Digest* (September 1966), reprinted in Toni Cade, ed., *The Black Woman: An Anthology* (New York: Signet, 1970), 82–84.

3. Jacquelyn Dowd Hall, "'The Mind That Burns in Each Body': Women, Rape, and Racial Violence," in Ann Snitow, Christine Stansell, and Sharon Thompson, eds., *Powers of Desire: The Politics of Sexuality* (New York: Monthly Review Press, 1983), 335.

4. Barbara Omolade, "Hearts of Darkness," in Snitow et al., *Powers of Desire*, 352.

5. See Alexander Crummell, *Destiny and Race: Selected Writing, 1840–1898*, edited by Wilson Jeremiah Wilson (Amherst: University of Massachusetts Press, 1992); and W. E. B. Du Bois, "The Damnation of Women," in *Darkwater: Voices from Within the Veil* (New York: Harcourt, Brace, 1920), 164–85.

6. George Breitman, ed., *Malcolm X Speaks: Selected Speeches and Statements* (New York: Grove Weidenfeld, 1965), 107.

7. Malcolm X and Alex Haley, *The Autobiography of Malcolm X* (New York: Ballantine Books, 1990).

8. Again, here as with Malcolm, protection is really about manhood. It is quite significant that the editorial from which this statement is taken is in an edition of *The Final Call* devoted to Black women. Reprinted in *The Final Call*, July 20, 1994, 18.

9. Malcolm X, *The Autobiography*, 226.

10. E. Frances White, "Africa on My Mind: Gender, Counter Discourse and African-American Nationalism," *Journal of Women's History* 2, no. 1 (Spring 1990), 76.

11. White, "Africa on My Mind," 76.

12. Betty Shabazz, "Loving and Losing Malcolm," *Essence* (February 1992): 107.
13. Walter White, "Color Lines" *Survey Graphic* VI (March 1925): 682.
14. For an exploration of the color debate between Garvey and Du Bois, see V. P. Franklin, *Living Our Stories, Telling Our Truths: Autobiography and the Making of the African American Intellectual Tradition* (New York: Oxford University Press, 1996), 122–25.
15. See Henry Louis Gates, "The Powell Perplex," in *Thirteen Ways of Looking at a Black Man* (New York: Random House, 1997), 84.
16. Even today, more than twenty years after the "Black is beautiful" '60s and the Afro-centric '90s, colorism continues to thrive among African Americans. As recently as 1994, psychologist Midge Wilson of DePaul University asserted, "Studies show that successful Black men are particularly likely to marry light-skinned women." Karen Grisby Bates, "The Color Thing," *Essence* (September 1994): 132. See also Kathy Russell, Midge Wilson, and Ronald Hall, *The Color Complex: The Politics of Skin Color Among African Americans* (New York: Anchor Books, 1992).
17. "Editor's Statement" from the first issue of *Essence*, April 1970.
18. Malcolm X, *The Autobiography*, 4.
19. Malcolm X, *The Autobiography*, 4.
20. *Malcolm X on Afro-American History* (New York: Pathfinder, 1967), 86.
21. See Kobena Mercer, *Welcome to the Jungle: New Positions on Black Cultural Studies* (New York: Routledge, 1994); Lisa Jones, *Bulletproof Diva: Tales of Race, Sex and Hair* (New York: Doubleday, 1994).
22. See "The Real Malcolm X: An Intimate Portrait of the Man," *CBS News* video, 1992. Executive producer Andrew Lack, producer, Brett Alexander.
23. See E. Frances White, "Listening to the Voices of Black Feminism," *Radical America* 18, no. 2–3 (1984): 7–25.
24. Malcolm X, *The Autobiography*, 201.
25. Betty Shabazz as told to Audrey Edwards and Susan Taylor, "Loving and Losing Malcolm," *Essence* 22, no. 10 (February 1992): 50.
26. See bell hooks, "Sitting at the Feet of the Messenger: Remembering Malcolm X," in *Yearning: Race, Gender, and Cultural Politics* (Boston, MA: South End Press, 1990), 87; Angela Y. Davis, "Meditations on the Legacy of Malcolm X," and Patricia Hill Collins, "Learning to Think for Ourselves: Malcolm X's Black Nationalism Reconsidered," in Joe Wood, ed., *Malcolm X: In Our Own Image* (New York: Anchor Books, 1992), 36–47, 59–85.
27. Malcom X, radio broadcast interview in Paris, November 1964. The transcript from this interview can be found at http://www.koranselskab.dk/profiler/malcolmx/interview.htm.
28. Collins, "Learning to Think for Ourselves," 79.
29. I am grateful to Tracye Matthews for calling my attention to this letter. Letter cited in Guy-Sheftall, ed., *Words of Fire*, 530. It originally appeared in an unpublished manuscript by Paul Lee, "Malcolm X's Evolved Views on the Role of Women in Society."
30. Davis, "Meditations on the Legacy of Malcolm X," 44–45.

31. Alice Walker, "Malcolm," in *Her Blue Body Everything We Know: Everything Poems 1965–1990 Complete* (New York: Harcourt Brace Jovanovich, 1991), 291.

CONFLICT AND CHORUS

1. This was the beginning of the contemporary renaissance of Black women's writing. Maya Angelou's *I Know Why the Caged Bird Sings* appeared in 1969, Toni Morrison's *Sula* in 1973, and Gayl Jones's *Corregidora* in 1975. Bambara's own collection of short stories, *Gorilla My Love*, was published in 1972.

2. Toni Cade, preface to *The Black Woman: An Anthology*, ed. Toni Cade (New York, 1970), 9.

3. See Gloria T. Hull, Patricia Bell Scott, and Barbara Smith, eds., *All the Women Are White, All the Blacks Are Men, But Some of Us Are Brave: Black Women's Studies* (Old Westbury, NY: Feminist Press, 1982).

4. E. Frances White, "Listening to the Voices of Black Feminism," *Radical America* (1984).

5. Toni Cade Bambara, *Deep Sightings and Rescue Missions*, ed. Toni Morrison (1996), 230.

6. Toni Cade, preface to *The Black Woman*, ed. Cade, 10–11.

7. Toni Cade, preface to *The Black Woman*, ed. Cade, 11–12.

8. Abbey Lincoln, "Who Will Revere the Black Woman?" in *The Black Woman*, ed. Cade, 84.

9. Fran Saunders, "Dear Black Man," in *The Black Woman*, ed. Cade, 73–79.

10. Twenty years after the publication of her essay, Abbey Lincoln discussed her opposition to this cost for protection. See *You Gotta Pay the Band* (video documentary, 1992).

11. The National Association of Colored Women was formed in 1896, in part to protect the name and image of Black women. Leaders like W. E. B. Du Bois and Alexander Crummell both called for the protection of Black women from rape, physical abuse, and economic poverty. Large numbers of the urban women to whom Malcolm X spoke were the daughters of or themselves women who fled the South in an attempt to escape the threat of rape from white males. Black women also found themselves the victims of economic exploitation, unfair employment practices, medical experimentation, and domestic violence. Who was deemed better to play the role of protector than the Black man? This, of course, is a role that had been denied Black men throughout history. I discuss the "promise of protection" at length in my essay "Ironies of the Saint: Malcolm X, Black Women, and the Price of Protection," in Bettye Collier Thomas and V. P. Franklin, eds., *Black Women in the Civil Rights Movement*.

12. Toni Cade, "On the Issue of Roles," in *The Black Woman*, ed. Cade, 102–3.

13. See, e.g., Don Belton, *Speak My Name: Black Men on Masculinity and the American Dream* (Boston, MA: Beacon Press, 1995); Hazel Carby, *Race Men* (Cambridge, MA: Cambridge University Press, 1998); and Marcellus Blount and George Cunningham, *Representing Black Men* (New York: Routledge, 1996).

14. Even those with no explicit political or cultural agenda perform cultural work.

15. Deborah Gray White, lecture at the Mid-Atlantic African American Studies Seminar, Princeton University, October 3, 1998.
16. See Lewis Gordon, "In a Black Antiblack Philosophy," in *Her Majesty's Other Children* (New York, 1997), 115–34.
17. Beverly Guy-Sheftall, *Word of Fire: An Anthology of African-American Feminist Thought* (l995), 487.
18. E. Frances White, "Africa on My Mind: Gender, Counter Discourse, and African American Nationalism," *Journal of Womens History* 2 (Spring 1990): 74.
19. Herman Gray, "Is Cultural Studies Inflated? The Cultural Economy of Cultural Studies in the United States," in *Disciplinarity and Dissent in Cultural Studies,* ed. Cary Nelson and Dilip Parameshar Gaonkar (New York: Routledge, 1996), 203–16.

THAT THE MOTHERS MAY SOAR AND THE DAUGHTERS MAY KNOW THEIR NAMES

1. For a comprehensive bibliography of Black feminism, see the extraordinary online project compiled by Sherri L. Barnes, "Black American Feminisms: A Multidisciplinary Bibliography," http://www.library.ucsb.edu/subjects/Blackfeminism/.
2. In fact, 1970 is an important year in the history of *Black World*. Prior to then, the journal had been known as *Negro Digest*. Though both were published by John H. Johnson, the later incarnation brought significant intellectual and editorial changes influenced by the Black power movement. For more on Black women writers who published in *Black World*, see duCille (2005).
3. Washington also wrote the foreword to *I Love Myself When I Am Laughing* (Hurston 1979).
4. See Hudson-Weems 1993, 2004. Clenora Hudson-Weems contends that, historically and culturally, most Black women are not feminists. She insists that dealing with gender issues does not automatically make one a feminist, thus the feminist has no monopoly on gender issues.
5. This archaeological endeavor also produced important biographical work, such as Thadious Davis's *Nella Larsen, Novelist of the Harlem Renaissance: A Woman's Life Unveiled* (1994) and Alexis De Veaux's *Warrior Poet: A Biography of Audrey Lorde* (2004).
6. See Bell, Parker, and Guy-Sheftall 1979; hooks 1981, 1984, 1989; Wade-Gayles 1984; Christian 1985, 1987, 1989; Spillers 1985, 1987; Carby 1986; Williams 1986; McKay 1987, 1990; Smith 1989; Wall 1989.
7. It should be noted that in *Psychoanalysis and Black Novels* (1998) Tate joins Spillers in the project of bringing psychoanalysis to bear upon the literature of Americans.
8. See hooks 1981, 1984, 1989, 1990, 1992, 1993, 1994, 1995, 1996.
9. Given this, it is somewhat ironic that the nation's only department of Africana women's studies, at Clark Atlanta University, seems to be primarily focused on the social sciences. The program defines itself as follows: "Founded in 1982, the Africana Women's Studies is the only degree-granting women's studies program located in an historically Black college in the United States, the only women's studies program in the United States which offers the doctoral degree in Africana Women's

Studies and the only Africana women's studies program in the world. AWS provides opportunities for the systematic analysis of the convergence of gender, class and racial bias. It also focuses on the comparative examination of the contributions, problems, strategies and concerns of Africana women. Analytical approaches that rigorously compare and contrast the lives of all women by class, age and color without regard to their geographic location are strongly encouraged. AWS is cross-cultural, national, international and interdisciplinary in its focus. Similar to many nontraditional, interdisciplinary programs and departments, AWS has a small, stable core faculty with faculty associates from traditional departments." See https://www.cau.edu/school-of-arts-and-sciences/aawh/awh-resources.html),

Works Cited

Alexander, Elizabeth. 2004a. *The Black Interior*. Saint Paul, MN: Graywolf.

———. 2004b. "Can You Be BLACK and Look at This? Reading the Rodney King Video(s)." In Alexander 2004a, 175–205.

Awkward, Michael. 1989. *Inspiriting Influences: Tradition, Revision, and Afro-American Women's Novels*. New York: Columbia University Press.

Baker, Houston A. 1984. *Blues, Ideology, and Afro-American Literature: A Vernacular Theory*. Chicago: University of Chicago Press.

———. 1991. *Workings of the Spirit: The Poetics of Afro-American Women's Writings*. Chicago: University of Chicago Press.

Barrett, Lindon. 1999. *Blackness and Value: Seeing Double*. Cambridge, MA: Cambridge University Press.

———. 2005. "African American Literary Criticism since 1990." *Johns Hopkins Guide to Literary Criticism and Theory*. http://litguide.press.jhu.edu.

Bell, Roseann P., Bettye J. Parker, and Beverly Guy-Sheftall. 1979. *Sturdy Black Bridges: Visions of Black Women in Literature*. Garden City, NY: Anchor/Doubleday.

Bethel, Lorraine, and Barbara Smith, eds. 1979. "Conditions: Five, the Black Women's Issue." Special issue of *Conditions* 2, no. 2

Bobo, Jacqueline. 1995. *Black Women as Cultural Readers*. New York: Columbia University Press.

Brody, Jennifer DeVere. 1998. *Impossible Purities: Blackness, Femininity, and Victorian Culture*. Durham, NC: Duke University Press.

Brooks, Daphne. 2006. *Bodies in Dissent: Spectacular Performances of Race and Freedom, 1850–1910*. Durham, NC: Duke University Press.

Cade, Toni. 1970. *The Black Woman: An Anthology*. New York: New American Library.

Carby, Hazel V. 1986. "It Jus Be's Dat Way Sometime: The Sexual Politics of Women's Blues." *Radical America* 20, no. 4: 8–22.

———. 1987a. *Reconstructing Womanhood: The Emergence of the Afro-American Woman Novelist*. New York: Oxford University Press.

———. 1987b. "'Woman's Era': Rethinking Black Feminist Theory." In Carby 1987a, 3–19.

Chay, Deborah G. 1993. "Rereading Barbara Smith: Black Feminist Criticism and the Category of Experience." *New Literary History: A Journal of Theory and Interpretation* 24, no. 3: 635–52.

Christian, Barbara. 1980. *Black Women Novelists: The Development of a Tradition, 1892–1976*. Westport, CT: Greenwood.

——. 1985. *Black Feminist Criticism: Perspectives on Black Women Writers*. New York: Pergamon Press.

——. 1987. "The Race for Theory." *Cultural Critique* 6, no. 1: 51–63.

——. 1989. "But What Do We Think We're Doing Anyway: The State of Black Feminist Criticism(s), or My Version of a Little Bit of History." In Wall 1989, 58–74.

Collins, Lisa Gail. 2002. *The Art of History: African American Women Artists Engage the Past*. New Brunswick, NJ: Rutgers University Press.

Combahee River Collective. 1977. "A Black Feminist Statement." In *Feminist Frameworks: Alternative Theoretical Accounts of the Relations between Women and Men*, edited by Alison M. Jaggar and Paula S. Rothenberg, 202–9. New York: McGraw-Hill, 1978.

Davies, Carole Boyce. 1994. *Black Women, Writing and Identity: Migration of the Subject*. London: Routledge.

——, ed. 1995. *Moving Beyond Boundaries*. Vol 1, *Black Women's Diasporas*. New York: New York University Press.

Davies, Carole Boyce, and Molara Ogundipe-Leslie, eds. 1995. *Moving Beyond Boundaries*. Vol. 2, *International Dimensions of Black Women's Writings*. New York: New York University Press.

Davis, Angela Y. 1998. *Blues Legacies and Black Feminism: Gertrude "Ma" Rainey, Bessie Smith, and Billie Holiday*. New York: Pantheon.

Davis, Thadious. 1994. *Nella Larsen, Novelist of the Harlem Renaissance: A Woman's Life Unveiled*. Baton Rouge: Louisiana State University Press.

De Veaux, Alexis. 2004. *Warrior Poet: A Biography of Audre Lorde*. New York: W. W. Norton.

Dubey, Madhu. 1994. *Black Women Novelists and the National Aesthetic*. Bloomington: Indiana University Press.

duCille, Ann. 1994. "The Occult of True Black Womanhood: Critical Demeanor and Black Feminist Studies." *Signs: Journal of Women in Culture and Society* 19, no. 3: 591–629.

——. 2005. "The Mark of Zora: Reading between the Lines of Legend and Legacy." *S&F Online* 3, no. 2 (Winter 2005). https://sfonline.barnard.edu/hurston/ducille_01.htm.

Evans, Mari, ed. 1984. *Black Women Writers (1950–1980): A Critical Evaluation*. Garden City, NY: Anchor.

Foster, Frances Smith. 1993. *Written by Herself: Literary Production by African American Women, 1746–1892*. Bloomington: Indiana University Press.

Fuss, Diana. 1989. *Essentially Speaking: Feminism, Nature, and Difference*. New York: Routledge.

Gates, Henry Louis, Jr. 1988. *The Signifying Monkey: A Theory of Afro-American Literary Criticism*. New York: Oxford University Press.

Hall, Kim F. 1995. *Things of Darkness: Economies of Race and Gender in Early Modern England*. Ithaca, NY: Cornell University Press.

Hartman, Saidiya V. 1997. *Scenes of Subjection: Terror, Slavery, and Self-Making in Nineteenth-Century America*. New York: Oxford University Press.

Hemenway, Robert E. 1977. *Zora Neale Hurston: A Literary Biography*. Urbana: University of Illinois Press.

Henderson, Mae Gwendolyn. 1989. "Speaking in Tongues: Dialogics, Dialectics, and the Black Woman Writer's Literary Tradition." In *Wall* 1989, 16–37.

Hine, Darlene Clark, with Kathleen Thompson. 1998. *A Shining Thread of Hope: The History of Black Women in America*. New York: Broadway Books.

Holland, Sharon Patricia. 2000. *Raising the Dead: Readings of Death and (Black) Subjectivity*. Durham, NC: Duke University Press.

Holloway, Karla F. C. 1992. *Moorings and Metaphors: Figures of Culture and Gender in Black Women's Literature*. New Brunswick, NJ: Rutgers University Press.

hooks, bell. 1981. *Ain't I a Woman: Black Women and Feminism*. Boston, MA: South End.

———. 1984. *Feminist Theory from Margin to Center*. Boston, MA: South End.

———. 1989. *Talking Back: Thinking Feminist, Thinking Black*. Boston, MA: South End.

———. 1990. *Yearning: Race, Gender, and Cultural Politics*. Boston, MA: South End.

———. 1992. *Black Looks: Race and Representation*. Boston, MA: South End.

———. 1993. *Sisters of the Yam: Black Women and Self-Recovery*. Boston, MA: South End.

———. 1994. *Outlaw Culture: Resisting Representations*. New York: Routledge.

———. 1995. *Art on My Mind: Visual Politics*. New York: New Press.

———. 1996. *Reel to Real: Race, Sex, and Class at the Movies*. New York: Routledge.

Hudson-Weems, Clenora. 1993. *Africana Womanism: Reclaiming Ourselves*. Troy, MI: Bedford Publishers.

———. 2004. *Africana Womanist Literary Theory*. Trenton, NJ: Africa World Press.

Hurston, Zora Neale. 1979. *I Love Myself When I Am Laughing . . . and Then Again When I Am Looking Mean and Impressive*, edited by Alice Walker. Old Westbury, NY: Feminist Press.

Lorde, Audre. 1982. *Zami: A New Spelling of My Name*. Trumansburg, NY: Crossing.

———. 1984. *Sister Outsider: Essays and Speeches*. Trumansburg, NY: Crossing.

Lubiano, Whaneema. 1992. "Black Ladies, Welfare Queens, and State Minstrels: Ideological War by Narrative Means." In *Race-ing Justice, En-gendering Power: Essays on Anita Hill, Clarence Thomas, and the Construction of Social Reality*, edited by Toni Morrison, 323–63. New York: Pantheon.

McDowell, Deborah. 1980. "New Directions for Black Feminist Criticism." *Black American Literature Forum* 14, no. 4: 153–59.

———. 1986. Introduction to *Quicksand* and *Passing* by Nella Larsen, edited by Deborah McDowell, ix–xxxvii. New Brunswick, NJ: Rutgers University Press.

———. 1995. *"The Changing Same": Black Women's Literature, Criticism, and Theory*. Bloomington: Indiana University Press.

McKay, Nellie Y. 1987. "Reflections on Black Women Writers: Revising the Literary Canon." In *The Impact of Feminist Research in the Academy*, edited by Christie Farnham, 174–89. Bloomington: Indiana University Press.

———. 1990. "Literature and Politics: Black Feminist Scholars Reshaping Literary Education in the White University, 1970–1986." In *Left Politics and the Literary Profession*, edited by Lennard J. Davis and M. Bella Mirabella, 84–102. New York: Columbia University Press.

Moten, Fred. 2003. *In the Break: The Aesthetics of the Black Radical Tradition*. Minneapolis: University of Minnesota Press.

Peterson, Carla L. 1995. *"Doers of the Word": African-American Women Speakers and Writers in the North (1830–1880)*. New York: Oxford University Press.

Quashie, Kevin Everod. 2004. *Black Women, Identity, and Cultural Theory: (Un)becoming the Subject*. New Brunswick, NJ: Rutgers University Press.

Shockley, Ann Allen. 1979. "The Black Lesbian in American Literature: An Overview." In Bethel and Smith 1979, 133–42.

Smith, Barbara. 1977. "Toward a Black Feminist Criticism." *Conditions* 1, no. 2: 25–44.

———. 1991. "The Truth that Never Hurts: Black Lesbians in Fiction in the 1980s." In *Third World Women and the Politics of Feminism*, edited by Chandra T. Mohanty, Anna Russo, and Lourdes Torres, 101–29. Bloomington: Indiana University Press.

Smith, Valerie. 1989. "Black Feminist Theory and the Representation of the 'Other.'" In Wall 1989, 38–57. New Brunswick, NJ: Rutgers University Press.

———. 1998. *Not Just Race, Not Just Gender: Black Feminist Readings*. New York: Routledge.

Spillers, Hortense J. 1985. "Afterword: Cross-Currents, Discontinuities: Black Women's Fiction." In *Conjuring: Black Women, Fiction, and Literary Tradition*, edited by Marjorie Lee Pryse and Hortense J. Spillers, 249–61. Bloomington: Indiana University Press.

———. 1987. "Mama's Baby, Papa's Maybe: An American Grammar Book." *Diacritics* 17, no. 2: 65–81.

———. 1992. "Interstices: A Small Drama of Words." In *Pleasure and Danger: Exploring Female Sexuality*, edited by Carol S. Vance, 73–100. London: Pandora.

———. 1996. "'All the Things You Could Be by Now, if Sigmund Freud's Wife Was Your Mother': Psychoanalysis and Race." *Critical Inquiry* 22, no. 4: 710–34.

———. 1998. Interviewed by Tim Haslett for the Black Cultural Studies Web Site Collective, Ithaca, NY, February 4, 1998. https://processedlives.tumblr.com/post/124440873050/hortense-spillers-interviewed-by-tim-haslett-for.

Stewart, Jacqueline Najuma. 2005. *Migrating to the Movies: Cinema and Black Urban Modernity*. Berkeley: University of California Press.

Tate, Claudia, ed. 1983. *Black Women Writers at Work*. New York: Continuum.

———. 1992. *Domestic Allegories of Political Desire: The Black Heroine's Text at the Turn of the Century*. New York: Oxford University Press.

———. 1998. *Psychoanalysis and Black Novels: Desire and the Protocols of Race*. New York: Oxford University Press.

Wade-Gayles, Gloria Jean. 1984. *No Crystal Stair: Visions of Race and Sex in Black Women's Fiction*. New York: Pilgrim Press.

Walker, Alice. 1975. "In Search of Zora Neale Hurston." *Ms.* 3, no. 9: 74–90.

———. 1983a. *In Search of Our Mothers' Gardens: Womanist Prose*. New York: Harcourt Brace Jovanovich.

———. 1983b. "Zora Neale Hurston: A Cautionary Tale and a Partisan View." In Walker 1983a, 3–92.

Wall, Cheryl A. 1989. *Changing Our Own Words: Essays on Criticism, Theory, and Writing by Black Women*. New Brunswick, NJ: Rutgers University Press.

Wallace, Michele. 1978. *Black Macho and the Myth of the Superwoman*. New York: Dial Press.

Washington, Mary Helen. 1972. "The Black Woman's Search for Identity: Zora Neale Hurston's Work." *Black World* 21 (August): 519–27.

———, ed. 1975. *Black-Eyed Susans: Classic Stories by and about Black Women*. Garden City, NY: Anchor.

———, ed. 1980. *Midnight Birds: Stories by Contemporary Black Women Writers*. Garden City, NY: Anchor.

———, ed. 1987. *Invented Lives: Narratives of Black Women, 1860–1960*. Garden City, NY: Anchor.

———. 1994. "'The Darkened Eye Restored': Notes toward a Literary History of Black Women." In *Within the Circle: An Anthology of African American Literary Criticism from the Harlem Renaissance to the Present*, edited by Angelyn Mitchell, 442–53. Durham, NC: Duke University Press.

Williams, Patricia. 1991. *Alchemy of Race and Rights: Diary of a Law Professor*. Cambridge, MA: Harvard University Press.

Williams, Sherley Anne. 1986. "Some Implications of Womanist Theory." *Callaloo: A Journal of African American Arts and Letters* 9, no. 2: 303–8.

AT LAST . . . ?

1. Roy L. Brooks, *Racial Justice in the Age of Obama* (Princeton, NJ: Princeton University Press, 2009), 12.

2. Richard Rorty, *Achieving Our Country: Leftist Thought in Twentieth Century America* (Cambridge, MA: Harvard University Press, 1999), 11.

3. James Baldwin, *The Fire Next Time* (New York: Vintage, 1993), 105.

4. Brian Feagans, "Georgian Recalls Rooming with Michelle Obama," *Atlanta Journal-Constitution*, April 13, 2008.

5. Shailagh Murray, "A Family Tree Rooted in American Soil: Michelle Obama Learns About Her Slave Ancestors, Herself and Her Country," *Washington Post*, October 2, 2008.

6. Murray, "A Family Tree."

7. John Heilemann and Mark Halperin, *Game Change: Obama and the Clintons, McCain and Palin, and the Race of a Lifetime* (New York: Harper, 2010), 253.

8. "Fox Anchor Calls Obama Fist Pound a 'Terrorist Fist Jab,'" *Huffington Post*, June 9, 2008, http://www.huffingtonpost.com/2008/06/09/fox-anchor-calls-obama-fi_n_106027.html.

9. Alecia P. Long, *The Great Southern Babylon: Sex, Race, and Respectability in New Orleans, 1865–1929* (Baton Rouge: Louisiana State University Press, 2004), 1.

ANCIENT HISTORIES AND NEW WORLDS

1. Zora Neale Hurston, "Turpentine Camp-Cross City," August 1939, Florida Folklife from the WPA Collections, 1937 to 1942, 16, reprinted in Florida Memory, State Library and Archives of Florida, https://www.floridamemory.com/onlineclassroom/zora_hurston/documents/essay.

CREDITS

INDEX

Abdurraqib, Hanif, 51
Abeng (Cliff), 217–20, 339n14
abolition/emancipation, 108, 109–10,
  129
academia, 243, 245, 250–52, 255, 257,
  258–59
addiction, 42–43
Africa, 235–36
"Africa on My Mind" (White),
  228–29
African American studies, 103. See
  also *Slave Religion*
"African Blues" (song), 37
Africana womanism, 263
Africana Women's Studies, 344–45n9
Afros, 46, 58, 232, 239
agnosticism, 104
Alexander, Elizabeth, 275–77
Alexzundra (student), 314
"'All the Things You Could Be by
  Now if Sigmund Freud's . . .'"
  (Spillers), 273–74
Allen, Candace, 160
Allen, Geri
  overview, 67–68, 69
  as central to jazz, 80
  A Conversation with Mary Lou,
    73–76
  conversations and, 73
  Flying Toward the Sound, 78–80
  Griffin collaboration, 73–76, 78
  Griffin meeting, 68
  inspiration, 78, 80
  on jazz scholarship, 71–72
  responsibility to music, 72–73
  residencies, 77

Timeless Portraits and Dreams, 69–71
  Williams cyber-symposium trib-
    ute, 69
Allen, William, 19
"America" (song), 22
Anderson, Benedict, 15
Anderson, Marian, 13, 14, 16
Andrews, Dwight, 67
androgyny, 249
Angelou, Maya, 203–4, 336n7
"Ann Petry and the American
  Dream" (Lattin), 144
Annie Allen (Brooks), 144
Apollo, 74–75, 77
art (general), 173–74
Ashes and Embers (Horn), 8
Atlanta Exposition, 110
Attali, Jacques, 38
avant-garde Black artists, 175. See
  also Shange, Ntozake
Awkward, Michael, 270

Badu, Erykah, 63
Baez, Joan, 48
Baker, Houston, 272–73
Bakhtin, Mikhail, 272
Baldwin, James, 28, 83–84, 102,
  143–44, 287
Bambara, Toni Cade, 159–61, 162,
  163–64, 172, 197, 242–46,
  255–56. See also "Medley"; *The
  Black Woman: An Anthology*
Bang, Billy, 179
banning books, 316–19
Baraka, Amiri, 181

Barrett, Lindon, 17, 20, 272–73, 278, 328n20
Barthes, Roland, 18
Baskett, Fritz, 62
Bass, Fontella, 55–58
B'Day (album), 292, 294, 296
"Be My Husband" (song), 23
bearing witness, 317–18
beauty, 105-6, 199–203, 229–31, 233, 338–39n4
Beck, Jeff, 53
Bellocq, E. J., 296
Beloved (Morrison), 23–24, 88–89, 91, 94–95, 221, 275, 316–19
Beyoncé. *See* Knowles, Beyoncé
Bible, 148. *See also* Christianity
Black, Brown, and Beige (Ellington), 39
Black Boy (Wright), 134
"A Black Feminist Statement" (Combahee River Collective), 265–66
Black feminist theory/criticism
  overview, 258–61, 280–81
  the academy and, 267–69
  Carby and, 269–70
  class and, 269–70
  constructing tradition, 263–65, 272–78
  creating vocabulary, 263–64
  criticism of Smith, 269–70, 272
  early theorizing, 264–65
  geography, 270–71
  Hurston and, 262–63
  intersectionality, 271–72
  LGBTQ+ people, 278–79
  political organizations and solidarity, 265–66
The Black Interior (Alexander), 275–77
"Black Maybe" (song), 66
Black nationalism, 111–13, 167, 228–29, 233, 251–55, 338n4. *See also* civil rights movement
"Black Popular Culture and the Transcendence of Patriarchal Illusions" (Ransby and Matthews), 236

Black power movement, 163, 175–76, 260. *See also* civil rights movement
Black Power (Wright), 325–26n4
The Black Woman: An Anthology (Bambara)
  overview, 164, 242–44, 260–62
  dialogue in, 251, 253, 255
  feminism and, 245
  Griffin finding, 239
  market for, 245–46
  masculinity/femininity, 247–49
The Black Woman. Homegirls (Smith), 250
Black Women, Identity, and Cultural Theory (Quashie), 272
Black Women, Writing and Identity (Davies), 270–71
Black World (journal), 262, 344n2
Blackness, as concept, 64–65, 276, 286, 297–98, 305, 326–17n12. *See also The Black Interior*
Blackness and Value: Seeing Double (Barrett), 17
Blowin' Hot and Cool (Gennari), 161–62
blues, 47, 64–65, 102, 327n18
Blues Everywhere I Go (Odetta), 47–48
blues poems, 168–69
The Bluest Eye (Morrison), 85–86, 93, 316
bodies as inhuman, 199–201
Body & Soul (National Black Women's Health Project), 205–7
"The Body in Its Sexual Being" (Merleau-Ponty), 208–9
bondage, 187
Brashear, Oscar, 62
Brody, Jennifer DeVere, 278
Brooks, Gwendolyn, 144, 234–35
Brooks, Roy L., 285
Brotherhood/Sister Sol (BroSis), 311
Brown, Alice, 288
Brown, Oscar, Jr., 172, 337n17
"Brown Baby" (song), 172, 337n17
Brown v. Board of Education, 141–42
Burnett, Charles, 184

Butler, Judith, 208
Butler, Octavia, 312–13, 314

Cade, Toni. *See* Bambara, Toni Cade
Cameron, G.C., 54
"Can You Be BLACK and Look at
    This? . . ." (Alexander), 275
Cane (Toomer), 32, 321
"Cante Moro" (Lorca), 22
Carby, Hazel, 4, 7, 269–70, 335n2
Carey, Mariah, 63
Carter, Regina, 11–12
Castile, Philando, 66
"Cause We've Ended as Lovers"
    (song), 53–54
Cecily, 63
censorship, 147, 316–19
"Characteristics of Negro Expression"
    (Hurston), 125
Charles, Ray, 22
Chay, Deborah G., 270
Chess Records, 55
Christian, Barbara, 63–64
Christianity, 100–101, 148, 177–78,
    204. *See also* Church; God;
    spirituals/spirituality
Church, 22–23, 60, 204. *See also*
    Christianity; God
citizenship, 112–13, 117, 121, 139
Civil Rights Act, 117
civil rights movement, 45, 260. *See
    also* Black nationalism; Black
    power movement
Clark, Darlene, 260
Clark Atlanta University, 344–45n9
class
    Black feminist theory/criticism
        and, 269–70
    funkiness and, 93–94
    Harper and, 112, 113–14, 120–21
    Hurston writings, 127, 128
    The Narrows, 154–56
    nationalism and feminism, 253–54
    stereotypes of Black women, 162–63
clavichord, 330n3
clavinet, 51, 330n3
Cleage, Pearl, 4–5
Cleaver, Eldridge, 243

Cleaver, Kathleen, 239–40, 243
Cliff, Michelle, 210, 217, 222. *See also*
    Abeng
Clinton, Bill, 13, 14, 15
Collaborative to Advance Equity
    through Research, 299–300
collective memory, 277
Collins, Kathleen, 183
Collins, Nina Lorez, 183
Collins, Patricia Hill, 234, 235–36
colonialism, 131, 333n16
The Color of Jazz (Panish), 161, 162
coloratura voice, 330n9
*for colored girls who have considered
    suicide* (Shange), 86, 174, 261,
    336n4
colorism, 127, 199–200, 217–18,
    230–31, 240, 297, 342n16
Coltrane, Alice, 5–6
Coltrane, John, 5–6
Combahee River Collective, 265–66
"Come Sunday" (song), 39
Come to My Garden (Riperton),
    55–56
Coming through Slaughter (Ondaatjc),
    296
communism, 139, 145. *See also* Marx-
    ism; McCarthyism
conservatism, 123. *See also* Hurston,
    Zora Neale
A Conversation with Mary Lou
    (Allen), 73–76
Coolen, Michael, 327n18
co-optation, 38
Corregidora (Jones), 190, 192–95
The Cotton Kingdom (Olmstead),
    200
Country Place (Petry), 154
"Court Order Can't Make Races Mix"
    (Hurston), 141–42
COVID-19 pandemic, 312–15
"Crazy for This Democracy" (Hurs-
    ton), 136–37
creativity, 313–15
"Creepin'" (song), 51, 56
crisis, 299, 314, 314–15
critical race theory, 318–19
Crummell, Alexander, 226

"Dancing Mystic Poets at Twilight" (song), 79–80
Dash, Julie, 184, 321
Dash, Sarah, 21, 327n15
Daughters of the American Revolution, 14
Daughters of the Dust (film), 184, 321
Davies, Carole Boyce, 270–71
Davis, Angela, 205–6, 234, 237, 239–40, 243
Davis, Miles, 4–12, 33–36, 179
Dawson, William, 67
De Azurara, 199
The Dead Lecturer (Baraka), 181
Declaration of Independence, 6–7
Deep Sightings and Rescue Missions (Morrison), 245
"Déjà Vu" (music video), 294, 296
Delius, Frederick, 327n17
despair, 103
Dessa Rose (Williams), 210–12, 215–17, 339n14
displacement, 91–92
"Doers of the Word" (Peterson), 265
Domestic Allegories of Political Desire (Tate), 111, 265
Donnelly, Catherine, 288
Douglas (student), 314
Douglass, Frederick, 23, 110, 119, 132
Dowd, Maureen, 290
Du Bois, W. E. B.
  on Black music, 30–31
  Black women protection, 226
  Garvey and, 230
  Hurston and, 122, 125–26, 128–29, 139, 140–41
  McCarthyism and, 150
DuBois, Joshua, 308–11
duCille, Ann, 244, 258
Dunbar, Paul Laurence, 20, 26–27, 29–30, 325–26n4
Dunn, Leslie C., 29, 327n15
Dunning School, 129
Dust Tracks on a Road (Hurston), 134–35
Dylan, Bob, 48

Earth Wind & Fire, 59, 60–61
Edwards, Audrey, 232–33
Ellington, Duke, 39–40
Ellison, Ralph, 22, 143–44, 314
Embodied Voices (Dunn and Jones), 327n15
Epic Records, 57
epics, 192–93, 194
eroticism, 209–10, 212–14, 216, 218–20. See also sex
essentialism, 259–60, 269
Esther (student), 314
ethereal soul, 63, 64, 330n10
Evans, Danielle, 185
Eva's Man (Jones), 190–91
"Every Time He Comes Around" (song), 59
Eve's Bayou (film), 321
experts, 243

Fair Employment Practice Committee (FEPC), 138
Faulkner, William, 91
fear, 201
Feinstein, Sascha, 160
femininity
  feminization, 235
  M. Davis and, 3, 12
  protection and, 247 (see also protection)
  Riperton and, 58
  sirens and, 29
  slavery and, 212
  whiteness and, 225, 338n4
feminism, 197, 223, 243, 244–45, 251–55, 344n4. See also Black feminist theory/criticism
fiddles, 177–78
A Fire in the Bones (Raboteau), 103
The Fire Next Time (Baldwin), 287
Florida, 320–22
Floyd, Sam, 327n18
Flying Toward the Sound (Allen), 78–80
folk music. See Odetta
Foner, Eric, 116, 129
formalism, 269

Foster, Frances, 112, 264–65
Foucault, Michel, 339n10
Fourteenth Amendment, 117
Fran, Saunders,, 248
Franklin, Aretha, 13, 15, 52
Franklin, Benjamin, 199
"Free" (song), 61–62
free jazz, 159, 162–63
Freedman's Bureau, 109–10
freedom, 130–31, 248. *See also* abolition/emancipation
Freedom Ways (Robeson), 158
Fulfillingness' First Finale (Wonder), 49, 51, 56
Fullilove, Mindy, 91–92

Garrison, Lucy McKim, 19
Garvey, Marcus, 230, 338n4
At the Gate of Horn (Odetta), 48
Gates, Henry Louis, Jr., 264
Gaye, Marvin, 339n5
Gems, 55
gender norms, 47
genitals, 200, 201–2
genius, 125
Gennari, John, 161–62
Giddings, Paula, 251
Gilroy, Paul, 277
Giovani, Nikki, 241
Give Birth to Brightness (Williams), 165
Glover, Savion, 106
Go Tell It on the Mountain (Baldwin), 28, 143–44
God, 54–55, 70. *See also* Church; spirituals/spirituality
"God's Ancient Sky" (song), 79
Gordy, Berry, 52, 293
gospel, 22–23
Gottlieb, Annie, 244
Gray, Herman, 257
Great Jazz Women of the Apollo, 77
Griffin, Farah Jasmine
    Allen and, 73–76, 78
    Beloved and, 88–89
    body of work, 95
    Collaborative to Advance Equity through Research, 299–300
    dissertation, 89–90
    early years of books, 83–86, 239–42
    at Harvard, 87–88
    history studies and, 98
    jazz and spirituality, 102
    meeting Morrison, 89
    Morrison and scholarship, 90, 91
    9/11 and, 301–2
    Slave Religion and, 99
    teaching during COVID-19, 312–15
    See also specific books
Guy-Sheftall, Beverly, 251, 254

hair, 46, 58, 232, 239
hair straightening, 338–39n4
Haiti, 123, 125, 131, 133
Hall, Jacquelyn Dowd, 225
Hall, Kim, 278
Hamer, Fannie Lou, 13, 14–15, 226–27
Hamilton, Allison Janae, 320–22
Hancock, Herbie, 79
Hansberry, Lorraine, 189
"Happiness" (song), 53
Harley, Sharon, 250
Harper, Frances Ellen Watkins
    overview, 108–9
    Black nationalism, 111–13
    class division and, 112, 113–14, 120–21
    as first African American novelist, 264
    Literacy, Land, and Liberation, 113, 116
    on lynchings, 118–20
    political vision, 115–19, 121
    Reconstruction and, 108–14, 121
    on white alliances, 113–14
    women characters, 110
    writing as experimental, 112
Harper, Michael, 190
Hartman, Saidiya, 192, 277
head wraps, 295–96
healing, 202–7, 209, 217, 221–22, 339n5. *See also* resistance
The Healing (Jones), 191

Heinsen, Geerd, 18
Henderson, Mae Gwendolyn, 210–12, 272–73
Hendryx, Nona, 21, 327n15
heterosexuality, 217, 219–20
Higgins, Bob, 191
Holiday, Billie
  as abuser, 8
  addiction and, 43
  B. Obama's love for, 308
  early years, 309
  Griffin's father and, 41
  M. Davis and, 8
  manager of, 293
  "No Regrets," 41–42
  vocality of, 23
Holland, Sharon, 274–75
hooks, bell, 203, 234, 279
Hoover, J. Edgar, 150
Horn, Shirley, 4, 8–10, 12
House of Déreon, 292, 295–96
House Un-American Activities Committee (HUAC), 149–50. See also McCarthyism
Houston, Whitney, 13, 14
"How Shall We Sing the Lord's Song in a Strange Land?" (Bible), 17–18
"How'd I Know that Love Would Slip Away" (song), 61
Huckleberry Finn (Twain), 317
human rights, 303–4
humility and Raboteau, 106
Hurricane Katrina, 303–4
Hurston, Zora Neale
  overview, 122–23, 124–25, 142
  on aesthetic excellence, 125
  anthropological studies, 124
  on Black women's bodies and slavery, 215–16
  Carby's ideas, 269
  on class, 127, 128
  on colorism, 127
  on communism, 139–40
  on democracy, 136–39
  on desegregation, 141–42
  Du Bois and, 122, 125–26, 128–29, 139, 140–41
  early years, 123–24

  on freedom, 130–31
  on government overreach, 141–42
  Griffin discovering, 87
  Griffin's students and, 314
  growing conservatism, 133
  on Haiti, 133
  history and, 135
  on imperialism, 133, 135–37
  individualism, 123, 134–35
  as inspiration, 262
  on Jamaica, 132–33, 219
  libertarianism, 123
  on protest, 136
  on race relations, 140, 141, 142
  race relations in novels, 126–27
  on Reconstruction, 129–30, 135, 138
  romanticizing America, 131–32, 133, 140
  on spirituals, 125–26
  turpentine workers, 320
  on Washington, 128–29
  on white supremacy, 127–28

I Remember Miles (Horn), 9–10
"I Wanna Be by Your Side" (song), 54
If You Can't Be Free, Be a Mystery (Griffin), 41, 68, 76, 102
"If You Don't Believe" (song), 62
"If You Really Love Me" (song), 52
"I'm Glad There is You" (song), 75
Impossible Purities (Brody), 278
individualism, 134–35, 161
Inspiriting Influences (Awkward), 270
interiority, 275–77
Internal Security Act, 149
interracial relationships, 183, 184, 189
intersectionality, 271
"Interstices: A Small Drama of Words" (Spillers), 274–75
intraracial solidarity, 253
Invisible Man (Ellison), 143–44, 314
Iola Leroy (Harper), 109, 110, 111–12, 115, 264
Isaac (student), 314
Islam, 228, 232

"Isn't It a Shame" (song), 21
"It's a Shame" (song), 52

Jackson, Mahalia, 13, 14–15, 39
Jackson, Santita, 13, 15
Jamaica, 131, 132–33
Jambalaya (Teish), 204–5
James (student), 314
James, Etta, 282
"James Baldwin: His Voice Remembered; Life in His Language" (Morrison), 83
Jay-Z, 293, 296
jazz
    African American inspiration, 327n17
    Black women and, 162–63, 172, 176 (*see also* "Medley"; "Tell Martha Not to Moan")
    in Cold War, 38
    New Music, 159, 162–63, 336n1
    Shange and, 173–74
    spirituality and, 102
    triple meter, 337n17
    white women and, 6, 162–63
    See also Allen, Geri
Jazz (Morrison), 81, 89
jazz literature, 160–62. See also *As Serious as Your Life*; "Medley"; "Tell Martha Not to Moan"
jazz poems, 160, 336n4
Jefferson, Thomas, 6, 200
Jewish people, 17–18
Jim Crow, 46, 110, 129, 134, 137. See *also* segregation
Johnson, Andrew, 113, 114, 117
Jones, Gayl, 190–96
Jones, Lisa, 232
Jones, Nancy A., 29, 327n15
Jordan, June, 205–6
"Joshua Fit the Battle of Jericho" (song), 44–45
Journey into the Secret Life of Plants (Wonder), 53
Justin (student), 314

Kadogo, Aku, 175
Katrina storm, 303–4

Kay, Lindsey S., 241
Kelley, Robin D. G., 67, 72
Khan, Chaka, 13, 15
Kidjo, Angélique, 11
Kind of Blue (Miles), 7, 11
King, Jason, 64–65
King, Martin Luther, Jr., 116–17
Knowles, Beyoncé, 282, 285, 291–98
Knowles, Matthew, 291–92, 293
Knowles, Solange, 66
Knowles, Tina, 292, 295
Ku Klux Klan, 110, 117

LaBelle, Patti, 21, 327n15
Lake, Oliver, 174
Larsen, Nella, 264
"At Last" (song), 282
Lattin, Vernon E., 144
"a layin on of hands" (Shange), 206
laying on of hands, 204
Lemmons, Kasi, 321
"Les Fleurs" (song), 55–56
Lewis, David Levering, 31
LGBTQ+, 218, 220, 267, 278–79
libertarianism, 123
"Lift Every Voice and Sing" (song), 71
Lincoln, Abbey, 15, 20, 29, 46, 163, 224, 253
listeners
    Cleage and Davis, 4–5
    experience outside themselves, 4–5, 26
    gifted children, 178–79
    Holiday and interior voices, 42
    to oneself, 209, 221
Literacy, Land, and Liberation, 113, 116
Long, Alecia P., 294–95
Lorca, García, 22
Lorde, Audre, 241
Losing Ground (film), 184, 185–86, 189
love and Raboteau, 107
"Loving You" (song), 57, 58
lynchings, 110, 112, 118–19
Lynne, Gloria, 75

Mackey, Nathaniel, 20, 22, 160, 326n11
"Mad at Miles" (Cleage), 4–5
"Malcolm" (Sanchez), 233–34
"Malcolm" (Walker), 237–38
Malcolm X, 116–17, 154, 223–24, 226–31, 338n4
"Malcolm X" (Brooks), 234–35
male-only environments, 7
"From Mali to Mamie" (Winter), 328n18
"Mama's Baby, Papa's Maybe" (Spillers), 274
mammies, 16, 38
Marsalis, Wynton, 10–11
Marxism, 148
masculinity
    Black movements, 49, 260
    feminized Black people and, 235
    K. Collins on, 187
    of M. Davis, 3
    male-only environments and, 7
    protection and (see protection)
    "Tell Martha Not to Moan," 165–67
    vocal gender, 29
Matthews, Trayce, 236
Maud Martha (Brooks), 144
Maultsby, Portia, 22–23
May We Forever Stand (Perry), 71
"Maybe I Needed Heroin to Live" (Holiday/Dufty), 43
McAuliffe, Terry, 316
McCain, Cindy, 287–88
McCarthyism, 144–45, 149–50, 156–57
McDonald, Audra, 308
McDonald, Clarence, 62
McDowell, Deborah, 264, 267–69
McKay, Nellie, 144
Meditations on History (Williams), 210–15
"Medley" (Bambara), 169–72
"Melchizedek" (song), 70
Melvinia (M. Obama ancestor), 289
Mercer, Kobena, 338–39n4
A Mercy (Morrison), 96–97

Merkerson, S. Epatha, 73–74
Merleau-Ponty, Maurice, 208–9
Middle East, 235–36
migration, 89–90, 93–94
Miles and Me (Troupe), 34–35
Miles: The Autobiography (Davis and Troupe), 33–34
Million Woman March, 252, 253
Mingus, Charles, 5, 6
Minnie's Sacrifice (Harper), 109, 110, 111–12, 115–18, 119–21
misogyny, 228, 236–37. See also patriarchy/sexism; violence against women
Mitchell, Ernest Julius, III, 131
Mitchell, Joni, 42
mixed-race people, 132–33, 293–95, 296, 297. See also Knowles, Beyoncé
Moore, Barbara, 326n5
Moretti, Franco, 193
Morrison, Toni
    on Baldwin, 83
    banning of books, 316–17, 318–19
    Beloved, 23–24, 88–89, 91, 94–95, 221, 275, 316–19
    The Bluest Eye, 85–86, 93, 316
    classics and, 85
    complex portraits, 94
    on crisis, 314
    Deep Sightings and Rescue Missions, 245
    Griffin and, 87–88, 89, 95
    hauntings, 94
    as historical, 185
    on Huckleberry Finn, 317
    Jazz, 81, 89
    Jones and, 190
    A Mercy, 96–97
    Paradise, 91, 316
    racism despite white removal, 333n5
    scholarship and, 90, 91
    Song of Solomon, 90, 91, 168
    on sound, 27
    Sula, 83–84, 86, 91–93, 94
    understanding censorship, 317

"Unspeakable Things Unspoken,"
89
vocality in *Beloved*, 23–24
Moses, Man of the Mountain (Hurston), 124–25, 129–31
"mother of the nation," 15–16, 31, 38–40
Moton, Fred, 87, 278
Motown, 50, 52
Muhammed, Elijah, 227
mulattoes, 132–33, 293–94. *See also* mixed-race people
Murray, David, 173–74
My Brother's Keeper, 308, 310–11
Myers, Amina Claudine, 37
myths of vocality
overview, 26, 27–28
"mother of the nation," 15–16, 31, 38–40
myths about the hearer, 33–36
myths of vocal gender, 29
spirituals as dying, 32
voice of exile, 30–31, 37
voice of the divine, 30
"When Malindy Sings," 26–27, 29–30

The Narrows (Petry)
overview, 143–44, 145–46, 157–58
alternative families, 146–47
class, 154–56
critiquing McCarthyism, 144 45
Du Bois influencing, 150
mainstream press, 153–54
pride, 150–51
Robeson influencing, 151–52
sexuality in, 146–47
Nation of Islam, 228, 232
National Association of Colored Women, 226, 343n11
National Black Political Assembly, 63–64
National Organization for Decent Literature (NODL), 147
natural hair, 46, 58, 232, 239
Naylor, Gloria, 144
Neighborhood Ball, 282, 285
Nelson, Alondra, 299–300

New Deal, 142
"New Directions for Black Feminist Criticism" (McDowell), 267–69
New Orleans, 294–96, 303–4
Nigel (student), 314
Night (Wiesel), 318
9/11 anxiety, 301–2
9/11 memorial, 39
"No Regrets" (song), 41–42
"Nor give a damn whose wife I am" (Lorde), 241
Norman, Jessye, 13, 14
Not Just Race, Not Just Gender (Smith), 271
Notes from a Black Woman's Diary (Collins), 183, 184, 185, 186–87, 189
Notes on the State of Virginia (Jefferson), 200
"The Novel as Social Criticism" (Petry), 147–49, 153

Obama, Barack, 282, 285–86, 308–9
Obama, Michelle, 282, 285–91, 297, 305–7
"Observations Concerning the Increase of Mankind" (Franklin), 199
"The Occult of True Black Womanhood" (DuCille), 258
Odetta, 44–49
"Oh Freedom" (song), 69–70
Olmstead, Frederick Law, 200
Omolade, Barbara, 225, 226
Ondaatje, Michael, 296
opportunity, 299
oral tradition, 112
orgasms, 213
otherness, 201–2
Our Nig (Wilson), 264

Palmares (Jones), 191, 192
"The Pandemic as Portal" (Roy), 313–15
Panish, Jon, 161, 162
Parable of the Sower (Butler), 312–13, 314
Paradise (Morrison), 91, 316

Passing (Larsen), 264
patriarchy/sexism
  the academy and, 267
  as accepted, 226
  Black women's bodies and, 202–3,
    217 (*see also* ugliness)
  jazz and, 163, 175–76
  Malcolm X and, 234, 236–37 (*see
    also* protection)
  nationalism and, 233 (*see also*
    Black nationalism)
  protection (*see* protection)
  revolution and, 249
  voice/vocality and, 29, 327n15
  See also misogyny; violence against
    women
patriotism, 286, 287–88, 291
Peacock Poems (Williams), 168–69
Perfect Angel (Riperton), 56–58
Perry, Imani, 71
Peterson, Carla, 115, 121, 265
Petry, Ann, 144, 145, 147–49, 150,
  153–54, 158. See also *The Nar-
  rows*
Plessy v. Ferguson, 110
"Poem" (Lindsey, Kay), 241
Poems on Miscellaneous Subjects
  (Harper), 108
Poizat, Michael, 327n15
"Poor Black Women's Study Papers"
  (working paper), 246
possession, 225
post-Black, 276–77
post-raciality, 283–85, 297
poverty, 304, 308, 310
Powell, Colin, 230
power, 130
Preston, Billy, 54
Pretty Baby (film), 296
primers, 173
Primus, Rebecca, 20
Princeton University, 288–89
protection, 223–28, 247–48, 251, 253,
  343n11
psychoanalysis, 273–74, 344n7
Psychoanalysis and Black Novels
  (Tate), 344n7
purity, 224–25, 339n11

Quashie, Kevin Everod, 64–65, 272
Quicksand (Larsen), 264

Raboteau, Albert, 98–107
race, 283–84, 293, 297
Race Men (Carby), 7
race pride, 134
racial inequality, 285
racial uplift, 120
racism
  color and, 127, 199–200, 217–18,
    230–31, 240, 297, 342n16
  discussion of, 318–19
  founding fathers and, 199–200
  Hoover, J. Edgar, 14–15
  "less racist," 284
  in modern times, 284
  pseudo-science and, 199–201
  systemic, 318–19
  vocality and, 16, 19–20
  white people in narratives and,
    333n5
  See also slavery; white supremacy
Ramsey, Guthrie, 50, 68
rape, 226. *See also* slavery
Read Until You Understand (Griffin), 65
Reagon, Bernice Johnson, 15, 44–45,
  48
"Reasons" (song), 56–57
rebellion, 102–3
Reconstructing Womanhood (Carby),
  269
Reconstruction
  Du Bois's views, 129
  Harper and, 108–14, 121
  Hurston's views, 129–30, 135, 138
Reconstruction Radicalism, 116,
  117–18
Reed, Ishmael, 181
"Refractions" (song), 79
religion. *See* Bible; Christianity;
  Church; Islam; *Slave Religion*;
  spirituals/spirituality
"Rereading Barbara Smith" (Chay),
  270
"Rescue Me" (song), 55
resistance
  abortion as, 339n14

eroticism as, 210, 211, 213, 216–17, 219–20, 221–22
nurturing as, 214
political consciousness and, 221–22
respectability, 229, 249. *See also* purity
retreats, 209, 213–14
"The Reunion" (Angelou), 336n7
"Revolutionary Dreams" (Griffin), 241
rhythm, 180–82
Riperton, Minnie, 49, 51, 55–58, 64–65
Robert Normal and Industrial School, 124
Robeson, Paul, 150, 151–53, 158
Robin's bookstore, 239
Robinson, Fraser, 289
romanticism, 161–62
Roosevelt, Franklin Delano, 137, 138
root shock, 91–92
Rorty, Richard, 287
Ross, Diana, 52, 293
Rotary Connection, 55
Rowe, John Carlos, 125
Roy, Arundhati, 313–14, 314–15
Rudolph, Richard, 55, 56, 57
rural people, 335n2
Rushing, Andrea, 250

safe spaces, 4–5, 6
The Salt Eaters (Bambara), 197, 256
Sanchez, Sonia, 233–34
Sassafrass, Cypress and Indigo (Shange), 177–78, 336n4
Saunders, Fran, 247
Scott, Jill, 63
In Search of Our Mothers' Gardens (Walker), 87, 263
"In Search of Zora Neale Hurston" (Walker), 262
Seat at the Table (Knowles), 66
segregation, 46, 110, 134, 137, 141–42, 288
self-defense, 116–17
self-hatred, 231. *See also* colorism
Senegambia, 327n18

sensuality, 203–4, 209, 216. *See also* eroticism
As Serious as Your Life (Wilmer), 159, 162–63
sex
  Beyoncé, 292, 293–95, 296–97
  Dessa Rose, 212–14, 218
  The Narrows, 146–47
  purity and asexuality, 339n11
  Whatever Happened to Interracial Love? 189
  See also eroticism
sexism. *See* misogyny; patriarchy/sexism
"Sexual Healing" (song), 339n5
Shabazz, Betty, 229, 233
Shange, Ntozake, 86, 173–83, 180, 206, 336n4
Shepp, Archie, 174
"She's Leaving Home" (song), 53
"Signed, Sealed, Delivered I'm Yours" (song), 50, 51–53
Simone, Nina, 15, 23
singing Black women. *See* voice/vocality
sirens, 29
Sisters of the Yam (hooks), 203
Sketches of Southern Life (Harper), 110, 115
Slave Religion (Raboteau), 98, 99–101, 102–4, 105
Slave Songs in the United States (Garrison, Allen and Ware), 19
slavery
  abolition/emancipation, 108, 109–10, 129
  Black women's bodies and, 210–12, 213, 215–18, 221, 277
  blues music and, 327–28n18
  as dismemberment, 24
  free people and hierarchy, 194
  fugitives in Philadelphia, 108
  Harper's novels, 109
  Huckleberry Finn, 317
  humanity of enslaved, 100–101
  Hurston's views, 125, 135
  in New Orleans, 294
  as obscene, 318

slavery (*continued*)
  rebellion, 102–3
  resistance (*see* resistance)
  Sassafrass, Cypress and Indigo, 178, 179
  slave factories, 327n18
  slave trade, 199
  trauma, 190, 192
  vocality and, 23–25, 30–31, 46
  White House and, 289–90
  See also *Dessa Rose*; *Meditations on History*; Reconstruction
Slutzah, Steve, 56
Smith, Barbara, 250, 258–59, 265–67, 269, 270, 272
Smith, Bessie, 28
Smith, Valerie, 271, 278
Smithsonian Folkways, 46
And So I Sing (Story), 326n5, 326–17n12
Sokolov, Raymond, 190
Some One Sweet Angel Chile (Williams), 168–69
Song of Solomon (Morrison), 90, 91, 168
Sonny's Blues (Baldwin), 102
sopranos, 63, 330n9
Souls of Black Folk (Du Bois), 30–31, 126
South Side Girl (video), 291
Southern, Eileen, 19, 21
Spain, Amy, 118–19
"Speaking in Tongues" (Henderson), 210–11, 272–73
spelling, 181
spells, 21
Spillers, Hortense, 176, 265, 273–75, 277–78
"As the Spirit Moves Mahalia" (Ellison), 22
spirit possession, 100
"Spirituals and Neo-Spirituals" (Hurston), 125–26
spirituals/spirituality
  Allen and, 69–70, 76, 79
  in *Cane*, 32
  Du Bois on, 30–31, 125–26
  eroticism and, 209

healing rituals, 204
  Hurston on, 125–26
  jazz and, 102
  sex and, 218
  voice/vocality (general), 18, 21, 22, 23, 33, 38–39
  Wright and Wonder, 52
  See also Christianity; Church; God; *Slave Religion*
Stepney, Charles, 55, 56, 59
stereotypes, 162–63
Sterling, Alton, 66
Stevie Wonder Presents: Syreeta (Syreeta), 53
Story, Rosalyn M., 326n5, 326–17n12
Stowe, Harriet Beecher, 318
The Street (Petry), 144, 153
subconscious, 276
subways, 301–2
suffering, 106
Sula (Morrison), 83–84, 86, 91–93, 94
A Summer Diary (screenplay), 184–85
Supremes, 52
Sutherland, Joan, 326n5
Sweet Honey in the Rock, 48
"Sweetest Kisses" (song), 54
Swing Shift: "All-Girl" Bands of the 1940s (Tucker), 162
syntax, 181
Syreeta (Syreeta), 53
The System of Dante's Hell (Baraka), 181

Talented Tenth, 109
Tate, Claudia, 111, 264–65, 344n7
Taylor, Cecil, 79, 80
Taylor, Susan, 204, 232–33
technologies of power/of self, 339n10
Teish, Luisah, 204
"Tell Martha Not to Moan" (Williams), 164–69
"Tell Me Something Good" (song), 52
Tell My Horse (Hurston), 125, 131, 219
Terborg-Penn, Rosalyn, 250
terrorism. See 9/11 anxiety; 9/11 memorial

textual healing, 202–3, 211, 339n5. *See also* healing

Their Eyes Were Watching God (Hurston), 124–25, 126–28, 215–16, 262, 314

Things of Darkness (Hall), 278

This Is Niecy (Williams), 49, 59, 60–62

Thomas, Mickalene, 62

Timeless Portraits and Dreams (Allen), 69–71

Toomer, Jean, 3, 31, 321

torture, 201

touch, 203–4, 206, 209, 210, 214, 218–19

"Toward a Black Feminist Criticism" (Smith), 258–59, 265–67, 269, 272

traditions, 265

trauma, 92, 204–5. *See also* slavery

"Traveling Miles" (Wilson), 36

Traveling Miles (Wilson), 10–11, 36–37

Troupe, Quincy, 33–34

Tucker, Sherrie, 160, 162

Twain, Mark, 317

20 Feet from Stardom (film), 51

Tyner, McCoy, 79

"U, Black Maybe" (song), 63

ugliness, 199–203, 208, 214–15, 224, 230

Uncle Tom's Cabin (Stowe), 318

"Universal Sound of the World" (song), 54–55

university, 288–89

"Unspeakable Things Unspoken" (Morrison), 89

"Until You Come Back to Me" (song), 52

urban renewal, 91–92

"Uses of the Erotic: The Erotic as Power" (Lorde), 209

Valaida (Allen), 160

validation, 217

Vanzant, Iyanla, 204

Vaughan, Sarah, 75, 293

victimization, 226–27, 284

violence against women, 4, 5, 6, 8, 309. *See also* misogyny; patriarchy/sexism; slavery

voice/vocality
background vocalists, 51
birds and, 19–20, 57
Blackness and, 326–17n12
crisis and, 15–16, 39–40
as cultural style, 18, 20, 326n5
describing with verbs, 18–19
as epiphany, 27–28
exchanging self, 328n20
gospel style, 22–23
"mother of the nation," 15–16
myths and, 17 (*see also* myths of vocality)
othering practices, 326n11
patriotism, 14
racism and, 19–20
social struggle, 14–15, 16, 23–25, 45–47
sopranos, 63, 330n9
spells and, 21
tessitura, 330n9
as varied, 16–17
vocal darkness, 22
See also specific singers

voting, 138–39

Walker, Alice, 87, 185, 234, 237–38, 262–63

Washington, Booker T., 110, 111, 116, 122, 124, 128–29

Washington, Mary Helen, 145, 150

Weems, Carrie Mae, 78

wellness. *See* healing

Wells, Ida B., 116

West, Cornel, 89, 201, 284

West, Elizabeth J., 111

Wharton, Edith, 87

Whatever Happened to Interracial Love? (Collins), 183, 184, 187–88

"When Malindy Sings" (Dunbar), 26–27, 29–30, 325–26n4

Where I'm Coming From (Wonder), 52

"'Where the Blues and the Truth Lay Hiding'" (Tucker), 160, 162

White, Deborah Gray, 251
White, E. Frances, 228–29, 244, 254
White, Lillias, 39, 40
White, Maurice, 59, 60
White, Walter, 230
White Rat (Jones), 190–91
white supremacy
    the academy and, 267
    alliances and, 113–14
    beauty standards, 338n4 (*see also*
        ugliness)
    Black nationalism and, 229
    Church and, 204
    degradation and, 201–2
    as dismemberment, 24
    dying gasp of, 284
    fashion and, 295–96
    feminism and, 243, 246, 251, 260,
        266
    Hurston on, 127–28
    mixed-race and, 294, 297
    murder and, 114
    The Narrows, 154–55
    pseudo-science and, 199–201
    See also racism; slavery
white women
    Black preachers and, 101
    Communist Party and, 140
    Davis's album covers and, 6
    fashion distinguishing, 295–96
    feminism and, 243, 246, 251, 260,
        266
    fetishization of, 6, 216
    jazz musicians and, 6, 162–63
    purity and, 225
    sexism and Malcolm X, 234
    See also ugliness
"Why the Negro Won't Buy Commu-
    nism" (Hurston), 136, 139
Wiesel, Elie, 318
Wild Flowers (Shange and Murray),
    175
Williams, Deniece, 49, 56, 59–63,
    64–65
Williams, Patricia, 207, 208

Williams, Sherley Anne
    overview, 159–61, 222
    Black women and white women,
        163–64
    blues and, 172
    female music and mobility, 168–69
    Give Birth to Brightness, 165–66
    resistance and, 210
    on success, 162
    See also *Dessa Rose*; *Meditations
        on History*; "Tell Martha Not to
        Moan"
Wilmer, Valerie, 163. See also *As Seri-
    ous as Your Life*
Wilson, August, 28
Wilson, Cassandra, 3, 4, 10–12, 36
Wilson, Harriet, 264
Wilson, Midge, 342n16
womanists, 251, 263
*Women in Africa and the African
    Diaspora* (Terborg-Penn, Rush-
    ing, Harley), 250
Wonder, Stevie, 49–54, 56–61
Words of Fire (Guy-Sheftall), 251
*Wouldn't Take Nothing for My Journey
    Now* (Angelou), 203–4
Wright, Richard, 83–84, 134, 145,
    325–26n4
Wright, Syreeta ("Rita"), 49, 50,
    52–55, 64–65

Yale University, 98–99
Yellow Back Radio Broke-Down
    (Reed), 181
Yoruba people, 204
"With You I'm Born Again" (Pres-
    ton), 54
"You Turn Me On" (song), 327n15
You Won't Forget Me (Horn), 9
Youngkin, Glenn, 316, 318
"You're My Thrill" (song), 42

Zinn, Howard, 48
"Zora's Politics: A Brief Introduction"
    (Mitchell), 131